Charles W. Watkins

HEINEMANN BOOKS ON SOCIOLOGY

General editor: Donald Gunn MacRae

SURVEY METHODS IN SOCIAL INVESTIGATION

C. A. MOSER

Professor of Social Statistics
University of London

SURVEY METHODS

IN SOCIAL INVESTIGATION

HEINEMANN

LONDON

Heinemann Educational Books Ltd
LONDON EDINBURGH MELBOURNE TORONTO
SINGAPORE JOHANNESBURG AUCKLAND
HONG KONG NAIROBI IBADAN

SBN 435 82600 X (cased edition)
SBN 435 82601 8 (paperback edition)

23690

309

Published by
Heinemann Educational Books Ltd
48 Charles Street, London WIX 8AH
Printed in Great Britain by
Robert MacLehose and Co. Ltd
The University Press, Glasgow

CONTENTS

PREFACE

THIS book has grown out of a course of lectures given at the London School of Economics during the last few years. It is intended primarily as an introduction to the methodology of surveys for students in the social sciences but I hope that it may also be useful to the many whose work requires an understanding of the methods of surveys, including those who commission them and have to evaluate their results. The book is concerned primarily with what one thinks of as "large scale" surveys rather than with case studies of individuals, small groups or institutions.

Another type of reader whose needs have been particularly in my mind is the research worker in the social sciences who wishes to conduct an *ad hoc* survey but has little idea of the principles of sampling or questionnaire design or how to go about the processing and analysing of the results. He, unlike the professional surveyor with an established organisation of specialists, field workers and routine staff at his call, has to start from scratch, probably doing a good deal of the work himself and usually with very limited resources. My hope is that this book will provide research workers so placed with a groundwork of knowledge about general ideas; for instruction on practical details they can then turn to a survey manual or to a specialist for advice.

With such a potential readership in mind, I have tried not to overload the book with detail and technicalities, for the study of these without a sound understanding of general methodology can all too easily lead to the application of methods to situations for which they are ill-suited. I have tried, also, to stress the limitations of the survey approach and to caution potential users against an uncritical faith in its power. Not every research programme needs a survey, and indeed many questions can be dealt with as satisfactorily by "desk research" as by fact-collecting. With the social survey, as with any scientific method, part of the skill lies in knowing when to use it at all.

A good deal of space is given to the subject of sampling, for this, I have found, is the aspect of surveys which is the most difficult for the non-specialist to grasp.

The discussion is in the main confined to work carried out in Great Britain and some of the examples derive from surveys with which I have been connected either at the London School of Economics or as a consultant to market research agencies. Many of the references on methodological advances, on the other hand, come from the American literature.

As the total literature on the subject now runs into thousands of items, some guidance on reading is essential. I have given, at the end of each chapter, the references that seem to me most useful on its contents. References to general textbooks are given at the end of Chapter 1.

ACKNOWLEDGEMENTS

My thanks are due to the Director of the Gallup Poll for permission to reproduce the questionnaire attached to page 211; to the Controller of H.M. Stationery Office for permission to reproduce on page 210 the questionnaire used in the Family Census of 1946 and published on page 24 of "The Trend and Pattern of Fertility in Great Britain" (93); to the Editors of the *Journal of the Royal Statistical Society* for permission to reproduce from a paper by Moser and Stuart (194) the questionnaire that appears on pages 215–17 below as well as some other material, and also to quote from papers by Durbin and Stuart (66 and 68) and Gray and Corlett (102); to John Wiley and Sons for permission to reproduce (in slightly changed form) from W. E. Deming's *Some Theory of Sampling* (50) the diagram that appears on page 63; to the Cambridge University Press for permission to print in Chapter 7 an extract from *Tables of Random Sampling Numbers* by Kendall and Babington Smith (140); to the University of Oxford Institute of Statistics for permission to reproduce in Chapters 7 and 8 two tables from H. F. Lydall's *British Incomes and Savings* (165); to the Director of the Social Survey for permission to quote several extracts from *A Handbook for Interviewers* (239); to the Director of the Institute for Social Research, University of Michigan, for permission to give in Chapter 11 extracts from a conference report published by the Institute (257); to the American Marketing Association for permission to quote extensively in Chapter 14 from an article by Durbin and Stuart (67) which appeared in the July issue of the *Journal of Marketing*; to the British Tabulating Company for permission to reproduce in Chapter 14 a Hollerith 80-column dual-purpose punched card and for arranging the reproduction; to the McGraw-Hill Book Company to quote in Chapter 15 a paragraph from *Methods of Social Research* by Goode and Hatt (97); to the Social Science Research Council for permission to quote in Chapter 15 two paragraphs from Appendix A of *Pre-Election Polls of 1948* (196); to the Director of the United Nations Statistical Office for permission to give in Chapter 15 extensive extracts from *Recommendations concerning the Preparation of Reports of Sampling Surveys* (272); and to the Editor of *The Times* for permission to quote in Chapter 16 from the fourth leader that appeared on August 3rd 1955.

I have cause to be grateful to a number of people who have helped me in one way or another in the writing of this book. I owe a great deal to the advice and encouragement I have received throughout from Professor R. G. D. Allen, Professor D. V. Glass and Professor M. G. Kendall, all of the London School of Economics, and I must also, more formally, thank Professor Kendall for permitting me to draw for examples on the research projects carried out under his direction within the Research Techniques Unit at the School. These are described in references (12), (66), (67), (68), (192) and (194).

I am deeply indebted to three other colleagues of mine, H. S. Booker, J. Durbin and A. Stuart, who were each good enough to read through a draft of the book and from whose many penetrating criticisms and constructive suggestions I have benefited more than I can say.

Several survey practitioners have kindly given me assistance. I am grateful to Dr. H. Durant (Director of the British Institute of Public Opinion), Mr. L. Moss (Director of the Government Social Survey) and Mr. R. J. Silvey (Head of B.B.C. Audience Research), who read various sections of the book and made a number of valuable suggestions. Above all, I want to thank Mr. T. Cauter (Director of the British Market Research Bureau) and Mr. J. Downham (a senior research officer of the same organisation) who both gave much precious time to the reading of a draft of the book and who offered many constructive suggestions of the utmost value. The book in its final form is of course entirely my own responsibility and, in expressing my sincere thanks to all these gentlemen, I must emphasise that none of them necessarily agree with its final form or content.

I gratefully acknowledge a grant from the Social Research Division at the London School of Economics which covered some of the typing cost and the help of Mrs. D. W. Cleather and Miss J. A. Mathews (of the Typing Department) in this part of the work. Other parts of the typing were carried out by Miss J. A. Castle and Miss F. H. Johnson (of the Statistics Department) and I am grateful to them for their assistance. By far the major share of all the typing, however, has been done—and done superbly well—by Mrs. E. M. Strudwick, Secretary of the Statistics Department, and I wish to express to her my sincere gratitude for the enormous amount of help she has given me.

Mr. Alan Hill, of William Heinemann Ltd., has throughout been most considerate and helpful and I have much cause to be grateful to him, as also to Mr. A. R. Beal of the Education Department. Mr. C. R. Howe undertook the technical editing of the book and I should like to express my admiration for his skill and my thanks for the many improvements in literary presentation which he suggested.

My greatest debt of all is to my wife who, besides assisting me in many of the more tedious tasks of producing the book, helped me more than I can say by her unfailing encouragement and patience.

C. A. MOSER

LONDON SCHOOL OF ECONOMICS
September, 1957

CHAPTER 1

THE NATURE OF SOCIAL SURVEYS

1.1. Introduction

IT WOULD be pleasant to be able to open this chapter with a straight-forward definition of what is meant by a "social survey". In fact such a definition would have to be so general as to defeat its purpose, since the term and the methods associated with it are applied to an extraordinarily wide variety of investigations, ranging from the classical poverty surveys of fifty years ago to Gallup Polls, town-planning surveys, market research, the work of Mass Observation, as well as the innumerable investigations sponsored by research institutes.

As regards purpose, the range is equally wide. A survey may be occasioned simply by a need for administrative facts on some aspect of public life; or be designed to investigate some cause-effect relationship or to throw fresh light on some aspect of sociological theory. When it comes to subject-matter the only factor common to surveys is that they are concerned with the demographic characteristics, the social environment, the activities or opinions and attitudes of some group of people.

We can thus see that a satisfactory definition would have to be couched in much more general terms than that introduced by Wells when he defined a social survey as a "fact-finding study dealing chiefly with working-class poverty and with the nature and problems of the community" [282]. This might have covered the classical community and poverty studies but would hardly be adequate, the first part at any rate, to the modern forms of survey mentioned above.

But although I shall use the term "social survey" in a wider sense than that of Wells' definition, I am not attempting to cover all types of social investigation. The methods described in this book are most relevant to the type of approach one associates with official surveys, market and opinion research, and, to a considerable extent, with

1

sociological research. This does not necessarily mean the use of standardised, formal methods and the coverage of large representative samples. A researcher wishing to investigate certain aspects of family life may choose to confine himself to a handful of families, studying them intensively, rather than to make a more superficial examination of a large-scale sample.

These two approaches usually serve different ends and use markedly different methods: the intensive study of a few cases will tend to dig deeper, but may lose something in generality; it will probably use less formal interviewing techniques than the other, and in the analysis of results will give more prominence to non-quantified material. This is an important difference, but the methodology used for such "field studies" or "field experiments" is in many respects so similar to that of the social survey proper that I shall refer to them from time to time.

I hope, in fact, that the distinction between different kinds of surveys will be made clear by the context and I shall now discuss briefly the four major respects in which surveys differ from each other. These are purpose, subject matter, coverage, and source of information.

1.2. The Purposes of Surveys

The purpose of many surveys is simply to provide someone with information. That someone may be a government department wanting to know how much people spend on food; a business concern interested in finding out what detergents people are using; a research institute studying the housing of old-age pensioners. Whether the "client" in each case is well-advised to want these facts, or to seek them through a survey, need not worry us here. We are only concerned with noting that to him, as well as to the surveyor, the survey has a clear *descriptive* purpose.

To a social scientist, a survey may equally have a purely descriptive purpose, as a way of studying social conditions, relationships and behaviour. The sort of information needed may be how families of different size, composition and social status spend their incomes; how people are reacting to the latest productivity drive; what relation there appears to be between education and the possibility of moving up the social ladder. In this early, fact-finding, stage of the social sciences there is virtually no limit to the range of topics covered by surveys.

It must not be thought, however, that the purpose of surveys, whether in social research or elsewhere, is always so straightforward. Many enquiries are aimed to *explain* rather than to describe. Their function may be theoretical—to test some hypothesis suggested by sociological theory—or severely practical—to assess the influence of various factors, which can be manipulated by public action, upon some phenomenon—but, whichever be the case, the purpose is to explain the relationships between a number of variables. This may lead to extreme complexities in interpretation.

The usefulness of surveys (descriptive or explanatory) in social research is often debated and one does sometimes suspect social scientists of being excessively eager to use them—to leap into the field as soon as they have a problem, collect data, tabulate answers, write a report and regard the research as finished. It is the ill-considered launching of surveys, leading to the waste of much time and money and the accumulation (often) of unwanted data, that has given rise to the scepticism with which some sociologists regard "door-knocking" research.

It must be stressed that fact-collecting is no substitute for thought and desk research, and that the comparative ease with which survey techniques can be mastered is all the more reason why their limitations as well as their capabilities should be understood. Sound judgement in their use depends on this. It is no good, for instance, blindly to apply the formal standardised methods generally used in official or market research enquiries, to many of the more complex problems in which sociologists are interested.

Sometimes good judgement requires the deliberate sacrifice of quantitative precision for the greater depth attainable by more intensive methods of attack. An example will make this clear. There has recently been much discussion of the problem of "early leaving" from grammar schools—pupils leaving before the end of the grammar school course. To get the facts about this the Central Advisory Council for Education conducted a national sample survey, collecting a wealth of information about the problem: its dimensions, its association with social background and so forth [33]. One of the vital questions arising from this survey was *why* children from "working-class" backgrounds do so much less well at grammar schools than others. The official report put forward several possible explanations, among them the subtle influence of the parents' own attitude to education, the tradition and facilities of the home and the character of the neighbourhood.

Now to assess the influence of these factors on a child's achievement at his grammar school calls, not for another national sample survey, but for intensive study, preferably over a number of years, of a few carefully-selected schools. There would have to be interviews, possibly along informal lines, with children, parents, teachers and employment officers; and the interviewers would have to be chosen as much for their understanding of education as for their more routine professional skill.

Whether one could rightly call such further enquiry a social survey (rather than, for example, a field study) is a matter of terminology. What I want to emphasise is simply that there are types of field research that do not call for the apparatus of the large-scale sample survey.

To say this is not to underrate the usefulness of such surveys for many research programmes. In fact I believe that, in the majority of such programmes, they are invaluable *at some stage*. One occasionally hears a survey criticised on the grounds that it did not test a hypothesis or relate to any underlying theory. While there is often substance in this, the criticism is irrelevant to many surveys such as, for instance, the examples of straightforward factual enquiries mentioned before. Even these should always be preceded by carefully thought-out decisions about what is, and what is not, worth asking. But only in a trivial sense could it be said that this amounts to a set of hypotheses; in the narrower sense, implying the testing of a postulated relationship between two or more variables, the formulation of hypotheses is irrelevant to—and impossible for—many fact-collecting enquiries.

We must, after all, remember that the social sciences are still at an early stage of knowledge regarding human behaviour and social environment. To insist that a sociologist must not collect facts until he has a hypothesis would merely encourage the use of arbitrary hypotheses, which can be as bad as indiscriminate fact-collecting. The sociologist should look upon surveys as a way, and a supremely useful one, of exploring the field, of collecting data *around* as well as directly *on* the subject of study, so that the problem is brought into focus and the points worth pursuing are suggested. With such pilot information as a guide, a series of hypotheses can be formulated and tested by further empirical investigation.

Surveys thus have their usefulness both in leading to the formulation of hypotheses and, at a more advanced stage, in putting them to the test. Their function in a given research depends on how much is already known about the subject and on the purpose for which the information is required.

1.3. The Subject-matter of Surveys

The next chapter traces the evolution of surveys over the last seventy years or so, and it will be seen that there are few aspects of human behaviour that have not at some time attracted the social surveyor's attention. A catalogue of them is out of the question here[1]

[1] The *Register of Economic and Social Research*, published annually by the National Institute of Social and Economic Research, includes most surveys sponsored by the universities and research bodies and many of those under official auspices.

but it will be helpful to distinguish four broad types of subject-matter :[1]

the demographic characteristics of a set of people;
their social environment;
their activities;
their opinions and attitudes.

By demographic characteristics I mean matters such as family or household composition, marital status, fertility, age and so on. Some surveys (e.g. *The Family Census* conducted for the Royal Commission on Population [93]), are entirely on the demographic aspects of life but almost all surveys include some questions from this field.

Social environment is taken to cover all the social and economic factors to which people are subject, including occupation and income as well as housing conditions and social amenities. These are subjects which cover, in the widest sense, the question "How do people live?" The classical poverty surveys addressed themselves almost exclusively to answering this, just as our present-day regional planning surveys do.

Data on demographic factors and social environment are factual and their collection presents relatively few problems. They are less open to error (if definitions have been clear) than information on behaviour and opinions, because they are more objective. Furthermore their accuracy can more often be checked.

We turn now to the type of survey primarily concerned with "what people do"—their behaviour and activities. By this is not meant occupation (which forms part of social environment) but, for instance, use of leisure, travelling habits, expenditure patterns, radio listening and newspaper reading. Much of the work of the Government Social Survey lies in this field, and so does a good deal of market research.

Finally there is the type of survey concerned with people's opinions and attitudes. Opinion polls, as the name suggests, deal exclusively with these; in many other surveys they are of marginal importance. Opinion questions have their own peculiar problems and these are examined in a subsequent chapter.

1.4. Coverage of Surveys and Sources of Data

Surveys differ markedly in the way they cover a given population— the term being used in the statistical sense to mean the aggregate of persons or objects under investigation. Thus one can speak of the population of people over 20 years of age in England and Wales; the

---

[1] I should make it clear that this book is concerned with social rather than economic surveys and, although this distinction is not always easy to make, little will be said regarding surveys of shops, business firms or similar economic units.

population of miners in South Wales; the population of people travelling to work on the London Underground; the population of desks in a building.

The coverage of a survey can range from a few case-studies to a complete enumeration, from carefully-selected samples to arbitrary collections of volunteers; so it is clear that in considering coverage a surveyor must settle first the extent to which he wishes to generalise from his findings. There are surveys in which representativeness is of minor importance, but in most the intention is to draw population inferences. This intention, when it exists, must be recognised explicitly and the survey designed accordingly.

In social surveys as here interpreted the main methods of data collection are observation, mail questionnaires and personal interview. Surveys also generally make some use of documentary information, but studies based predominantly on statistical data, documents and historical records are not dealt with here.

1.5. Surveys and Experiments

It is regarded by many as a truism that the social scientist is rarely able to conduct strictly controlled experiments and, consequently, to establish the causative connections which are held to be the essence of scientific progress. There is no denying that strictly controlled experimentation is rarely feasible with human populations and that this does account for the tentativeness of many social research results. But I do not believe that this constitutes the fundamental weakness implied in the criticism.

In the first place, it is altogether false to imagine that research divides neatly into two categories—experiments and others—and that only the former can lead to valid causative inferences. Rather should one view researches as being ranged along a scale, with the most completely controlled experiment at one end and uncontrolled observation at the other. The closer one can approximate to the former the more confidently can causal inferences be drawn from the research and experience shows that the social scientist can often get reasonably close to this end of the scale.

In the second place, in both the social and the natural sciences progress depends as much on the accumulation of many pieces of evidence from different sources as on "proof" provided by experiments.

And thirdly, the examples of astronomy and meteorology—two sciences that do not lend themselves to direct experimentation—show that substantial progress can be made without direct experiment in the sense of manipulating the experimental material.

This brings us to the core of the matter: the meaning to be attached to the term "experiment". Jahoda *et al.* define it as "a way of organising the collection of evidence that a hypothesis may be tested" [129]; Greenwood suggests that "an experiment is the proof of an hypothesis which seeks to hook up two factors into a causal relationship through the study of contrasting situations which have been controlled on all factors except the one of interest, the latter being either the hypothetical cause or the hypothetical effect" [105].

Many alternative definitions could be cited but these two bring out the essential point, that the distinguishing feature of an experiment is the way the collection of the data is controlled, this in turn influencing the confidence with which causative inferences from the research may be drawn. These definitions leave open the method and type of control and a stricter definition is that of Festinger, who suggests that the essence of *laboratory* experimentation lies in ". . . observing the effect on a dependent variable of the manipulation of an independent variable under controlled conditions" [78].[1] This, of course, constitutes the social scientist's difficulty but the point insufficiently realised by the sceptics is that active manipulation is not the only form of experimental control. To illustrate, let us consider the much discussed issue of the connection between smoking and cancer of the lung.

The background to the various studies on this question is the enormous increase in the incidence of the disease in the past half century. In England and Wales, for example, the crude death rate from it jumped from 8 per million in 1900 to 321 per million in 1952 and, when all allowance is made for changes in the age and sex composition of the population, there remains no doubt that the increase is real. Nor can improved diagnosis, which certainly accounts for *some* of the increase, explain all of it. The relatively much greater increase among men than among women, among the old than among the young, and the continuance of the overall increase in very recent years, all argue against improved diagnosis being the entire explanation.

There are many environmental causes that might be responsible for the dramatic increase. Smoking[2] is certainly one, but exhaust fumes from the ever-increasing number of road vehicles, factory smoke, and increased exposure to cancer-producing substances in various occupations are among others to be considered. In order to examine these and other possible causes of the disease, various experi-

[1] This terminology will be followed here—the various "causes" an experimenter is investigating are called *independent variables*, the effect he is studying (or trying to produce) is called the *dependent variable*.
[2] The fact that the trends over time of smoking and of lung-cancer incidence have moved parallel has been merely suggestive—it is not in any sense evidence of a connection between them, nor has it of course been used as such by the investigators.

ments—some might prefer to say observational studies—have been made in a number of countries and Cutler discusses their combined evidence in an interesting paper [46]. All have shown a positive association between smoking and lung-cancer, although its extent has varied. The recent Medical Research Council studies in England and Wales, by Doll and Hill [54–57], have been models of research design and interpretation, and the present discussion will be confined to them. There is no space to go into details of methodology or results and for these readers are urged to refer to the original papers.

The purpose of the studies was "to determine whether patients with carcinoma of the lung differed materially from other persons either in their smoking habits or in some way which might be related to the theory that atmospheric pollution is responsible for the development of the disease" [55, p. 1271]. The basis of the research was a comparison, based on interviews conducted between 1948 and 1952, of 1,465 lung-cancer patients in a number of hospitals in England and Wales with a control group of 1,465 patients who were suffering from other diseases[1] and who were individually matched with the lung-cancer patients by sex (the great majority of both groups were men), by five-year age grouping and, in most cases, by being in the same hospital at the same time. The two samples were also closely alike in terms of social class composition.

A detailed study was made of the past smoking histories of the members of both groups and, after discussing possible biases, Doll and Hill concluded that the data were "reliable enough to indicate general trends and to substantiate material differences between groups" [55, p. 1273].

The differences did indeed prove to be very substantial. Among men, for example, only 0·5 per cent of the lung-cancer group were non-smokers ("persons who had never consistently smoked as much as one cigarette a day for as long as one year") as against 4·5 per cent in the control group. And whereas in the lung-cancer group 25 per cent had smoked (either just before their illness or, if they had previously stopped smoking, before they last gave it up) more than 25 cigarettes a day, or the equivalent in pipe tobacco, the corresponding figure in the control group was only 13·4 per cent. For women similar differences were found.

The many other striking results of these researches are recorded in the original papers, but what interests us here is the design. We note that the two groups were first matched on several important variables, the choice of these being governed by common sense, knowledge of the subject-matter and availability of data; and that the independent

---

[1] Patients suffering from certain diseases—e.g. cancer of the mouth—were not admitted to the control group.

variable of prime interest, i.e. the smoking habits of the patients, was studied retrospectively by questioning. These habits obviously could not be manipulated—made the subject of experiment. As to the accuracy of peoples' answers, Doll and Hill used what safeguards they could to eliminate bias, and it is unlikely that incorrect answers due to bad memory were the cause of the substantial association observed between smoking and lung-cancer.

The authors, in concluding that "smoking is a factor and an important factor in the production of carcinoma of the lung" [55, p. 1283], stressed that this did not mean that heavy smoking always leads to lung-cancer or that it is the sole cause of the observed increase in the disease. But apart from some evidence that people living in urban areas are more prone to it than those in rural areas, tobacco smoke is the only factor for which a strong association with cancer has yet been demonstrated. This alone makes the research findings worthy of attention.

We might now ask in what respects these studies fell short of strictly controlled experiments, as the natural scientist understands the term, and how important a difference this makes when the results are interpreted and evaluated. Doll and Hill were careful to emphasise that, *taken by themselves*, the studies demonstrated only an association, not a causative connection, between smoking and lung-cancer. Statistically, this observed association could just as well mean that lung-cancer causes people to smoke as that smoking causes the disease; equally it is compatible with the possibility that both have a common cause. On the first point, Doll and Hill state that medical opinion refutes the idea that the disease might be the cause and smoking the effect; and they rightly stress that such "subject-matter knowledge must be allowed to play its part in the interpretation of results".

The second problem is more troublesome and is indeed the crucial difference between a fully controlled experiment and even the best designed observational study. Since the groups of patients being compared could only be matched on a few factors, and since it was not possible to decide the membership of the two groups at random, one cannot be certain that the groups did not differ with regard to some crucial uncontrolled factor, *this* factor being responsible for the observed association.

To reduce this uncertainty, Doll and Hill compared the two groups on several relevant variables—occupational exposure, social class, place of residence, residence near gas works, exposure to different kinds of heating, previous respiratory disease—and on none of these factors were there significant differences between the two groups. It was therefore reasonable to dismiss them as possible causes.

But of course this kind of "control through measurement" could not conceivably be done with *all* the variables that might be affecting the issue. Let us suppose, for instance, that the observed association between lung-cancer and smoking was due, not to a direct causal relationship, but to an uncontrolled variable, say nervousness; i.e. that nervous people tend both to smoke more and also to be more liable to develop lung-cancer than others. Smoking and lung-cancer would still—correctly—be shown to be statistically associated although they are not causally related.

Now if we had data on "nervousness" for each respondent we could determine whether this third variable did or did not "explain" the association. If we had no such data, on the other hand, then with the above kind of design we could not (on statistical grounds) rule out the possibility that the association between smoking and lung-cancer was due to this common factor, nervousness. As the allocation of sample members to each group depended on whether they did or did not have lung-cancer and as their smoking histories were taken as given, it is feasible that the heavy smoking (and lung-cancer) group might have recruited itself largely from the nervous sections of the population, and *vice versa*. We can sum this up by saying that, when the membership of the experimental and control groups is, so to speak, determined by nature, one can never be *certain* that an observed statistical association between two variables is not due to one of these uncontrolled (and perhaps even unsuspected) variables. Hence the tentativeness with which causal inferences are made in social research work.

It will be helpful here to see how this difficulty could be overcome in theory. Let us imagine that the people comprising the experimental material could be manipulated at will. Having defined the population to be studied and recognised its heterogeneity, one would divide it into a number of more homogeneous sub-groups (this being equivalent to stratification in sample design)—perhaps town and country, several age and sex groups, occupations, and so on. From each layer of this multiple stratification a number of sample units would then be selected and *randomly* divided into two halves. One half would be told to smoke (a given amount) and the other half forbidden to smoke. After a certain time[1] the difference in lung-cancer incidence between the two groups would be compared.

It is, of course, the last step of this design—experimenting in a controlled way on a randomly selected group of people—that one cannot take in real life. Yet this is the vital step, for it is only by randomisation (leaving it to chance who shall be the smokers and non-smokers

---

[1] The time taken in the working out of effects in social experiments is often a complication. Apart from anything else, it may mean the loss of sample cases, which would affect the analysis.

in each sex, age, social class . . .) that one could neutralise the disturbing influence of all the uncontrolled variables, such as nervousness. Randomisation would ensure that nervous people are no more likely to be found in the experimental than in the control group.

Let us now summarise the ways by which an experimenter can control his independent variables:

(a) *Manipulation.* We have seen that in the smoking/lung-cancer study the experimenter could not manipulate the independent variable of main interest (smoking), i.e. he could not make randomly selected parts of the sample smoke stated amounts. The alternative is to select groups with different smoking-frequency histories and analyse their respective lung-cancer rates (or conversely group the sample according to whether or not they have the disease and then study their past smoking, as was done in the study described). For reasons explained such methods, if not accompanied by matching and, ideally, by randomisation, leave much to be desired.

(b) *Matching and measurement.* It is desirable to match the experimental and control groups on as many of the relevant independent variables as possible. In practice it can only be done on a limited number and the next best thing is to use a technique often called "control through measurement". Suppose that a possible explanation for the increase in lung-cancer is that more people are using gas fires, but that it was not possible, for some reason, to use this variable (whether or not a patient used a gas fire) for matching. One can still ascertain from the respondents whether they do or do not use gas fires and in the analysis distinguish between them. In other words, the relation between smoking and lung-cancer can be tested *within* each of the two groups. If the association persists, we shall know that the gas-fire variable is not the explanatory variable and vice versa.

(c) *Randomisation.* After the techniques of manipulation and matching/measurement have coped with whatever variables they are able to, there may still be some left uncontrolled, perhaps uncontrollable, by either means. It is here that the strictly controlled experiment and even the best-designed survey part company. For while the former can now dispose of the possible disturbing influence of all uncontrolled variables by the simple device of randomisation, the latter, in the nature of things, cannot.

A fully controlled experiment is an ideal to which a survey or partially controlled experiment can only approximate. But the approximation can come very close to the ideal if the study is designed carefully. In the above studies, several important independent variables were controlled by matching, many others of possible relevance were controlled by measurement, and all possible steps were taken to get accurate and unbiased data; so one can accept the results with a good deal of confidence. This is reinforced by the fact that comparable studies in other countries have shown similar associations. And various attempts to nail down the cancer-producing substance by animal experiments have added still further to the weight of evidence.[1]

Thus, although strictly controlled experiments on the subject were not feasible, it can be seen that a scrupulously designed study can significantly add to our knowledge of it. All scientific progress stems from the gradual building up of evidence, whether from strictly controlled experiments or otherwise. Cornfield [42] has stated how much medical science is indebted to evidence of statistical associations (as opposed to direct causative evidence). About vaccination and smallpox he says:

"If we believe that vaccination protects against the development of smallpox it is not because there has been a direct experimental demonstration but rather (a) there is a good deal of evidence that is consistent with this hypothesis, and (b) over the course of many years no evidence has been produced to support any alternative hypothesis. The truth of the matter appears to be that medical knowledge (and, one suspects, many other kinds as well) has always advanced by a combination of many different kinds of observation, some controlled, and some uncontrolled, some directly and some only tangentially relevant to the problems at hand . . ." [42].

Our discussion of the smoking/cancer research has focused attention on one particular problem of social science experimentation, that of subjecting people randomly chosen to experimental treatments (often the ethical aspect of this is uppermost: is it right to use human beings as guinea-pigs for experimenting on with new medical treatments?).[2] Whenever randomisation has to be ruled out on practical grounds, the possibility of "self-selection" is present and must reduce the confidence with which causal inferences can be drawn from the research.

Another sort of problem arises from what might be called the "indivisibility" of the experimental material. Suppose that an economist is asked to advise a government on whether it should raise the

[1] Before leaving this subject, I must mention an important current study, again directed by Doll and Hill, which follows an approach very different from their earlier ones. While these were retrospective, the current one is "prospective", in the sense that it seeks "to determine the frequency with which the disease appeared, in the future, among groups of persons whose smoking habits were already known" [56, p. 1452]. The persons concerned are members of the medical profession in the U.K., the great majority of whom have given information about their smoking and for whom information about cause of death is obtained from the Registrars-General when they subsequently die. The preliminary results [57] confirm those obtained from the retrospective studies.

[2] I cannot discuss this here and refer the reader to an excellent treatment in A. B. Hill [119].

Bank Rate. On what basis can he advise? He can use his theoretical knowledge, or be guided by what effect former increases have had here or in other countries, but the thing he cannot do is experiment. As the unit of experiment is the country, which is for this purpose indivisible, the economist can only compare what happens as a result of an increase with what he expected to happen or with what happened in the past or elsewhere; not with what would have happened if the Rate had been left unchanged. An experimental comparison is impossible.

This example illustrates another difficulty. An agriculturist trying out several soil treatments on selected experimental fields is not particularly worried by the possibility that the very application of the treatments may have a lasting effect; the fields are but a small sample from all the land available and the only risk is that, as a result of this experiment, they may be less suitable for future ones. The social experimenter is often in a much more difficult position. For many of his experiments it is not possible to partition off a part of society, try his treatments and then let things go back to what they were before. Even if a satisfactory Bank Rate experiment could be designed, once the Rate is altered, numerous changes are set in motion which cannot be reversed. The economist cannot make the experimental results the *basis* of policy, for in order to make the experiment he has already had to change policy. Any future experiment or policy-changes will start from different conditions.

It is characteristic of much of the social scientist's subject-matter that experiment and policy change are thus inseparable, so that the experiment becomes a way of doing things and not just a way of testing hypotheses.

With a less extreme type of experimental unit than in the Bank Rate example, experimentation at once becomes more practicable. An advertiser wishing to test the effect of, say, a new poster can try it out in one town or district and compare the public's subsequent buying behaviour with that of another town or district not subjected to it. If the two towns were comparable before the new poster appeared (and this can be assessed) a worthwhile test can be made with the experiment. To ensure a valid comparison, however, the towns or districts chosen should be sufficiently far apart to obviate the risk of the poster being seen by people from both; it is often difficult in social science experimentation to arrange for an effective insulation of experimental and control groups.

A good example of this type of experiment comes from the United States where, as in Britain, there is interest in the possibility of reducing dental decay by the fluoridation of water supplies. Various areas have from time to time increased the fluoride content of their water, and "before and after" comparisons have been encouraging. But, unsupported by comparisons with control areas, they could not lead to confident conclusions.

Now, however, have come the results of a more scientifically designed research experiment. This was based on two towns—Newburgh and Kingston—35 miles apart in the Hudson River valley, each with a population of about 30,000 and each with fluoride-deficient water supplies. In 1945 one (only) of the towns—Newburgh—had its water supply treated with sodium fluoride. After ten years it was found that the Newburgh children aged 6–9, who had lived with this fluoridated water all their lives, had 58 per cent less tooth decay than Kingston children of the same age group. For older children (who had lived in Newburgh continuously since 1945) the differences were only a little less marked; for 10–12-year-olds it was 52 per cent, and for 16-year-olds 41 per cent.

These results appear conclusive, but one is entitled to ask whether the two towns were really comparable. To check this and find if there were any factors that might have favoured the Newburgh children, many comparisons were made between the children of the two towns, including growth, bone structure, urine, vision and hearing. Nothing to suggest an unfair comparison was found, so the research seems to have provided a sound test of the hypothesis at issue.

Our concern so far has been to make clear the distinction between controlled experiments and surveys. The discussion has consequently centred upon what in American sociological literature are known as *ex post facto* (after the event) experiments. Such designs are of two types, neither of them involving actual manipulation of the experimental material: in the first a comparison is made of two or more groups matched in all relevant respects[1] except that one, and only one, of them has at some past time been exposed to the main independent variable. The hypothesis of interest is tested by comparing the incidence of the dependent variable in the two (or more) groups. This research looks from the past to the present, and is usually termed a *cause-to-effect* design.

In the second type, two (or more) groups differing in the dependent variable but matched in other respects are compared; and the researcher then looks back for possible explanations of the difference. This is the *effect-to-cause* design, and was illustrated by the lung-cancer study.

In both forms of the *ex post facto* design the element of randomisa-

[1] Matching, especially between individuals and not just sub-groups, is often no easy matter and may involve a heavy reduction of the original numbers. If one knows the extent of differences between the groups before the introduction of the experimental variable, it is possible to eliminate these in the analysis. The analysis of covariance (see 211) is the main technique for this purpose.

tion is absent, opening the door to possibilities of self-selection. Some would prefer indeed not to dignify this type of design by the term "experiment", but this seems to me to be carrying scientific purity too far; all one need acknowledge is that it is not a fully controlled experiment.

The emphasis in the present discussion on *ex post facto* experiments must not be taken to mean that manipulation of variables is impossible or even rare in social science. The fluoridation research illustrates a type of manipulation often used, and French and Festinger (in two chapters of Festinger and Katz [78]) refer to many experiments in natural settings, as well as social science laboratory experiments, in which various degrees of control and manipulation were exercised.

The designs employed may be grouped according to when the measurement of the dependent variable (y) takes place. Here the terminology of Jahoda *et al.* [129] is useful:

(*a*) *After-only design.* The effect on y is assessed by measuring its incidence in both the experimental group (E) and the control group (C) after the former has been exposed to the main independent—let us call it the experimental—variable (x). However much time has elapsed since this exposure, it may be assumed to have affected both groups equally and the main difficulty is to ensure their equivalence before the onset of the experiment. This is done by matching techniques, combined where possible with randomisation.

(*b*) *Before-after design.* An alternative is to use the same individuals for E and C, measuring y before and after the group has been exposed to x. The trouble with this design is that, since no control group is available for comparison, one cannot be sure how much of the observed change in y is due to x, and how much to other causes. Nor is this difficulty overcome by the type of design that uses different groups for the "before" and "after" measurements, the two samples being supposedly equivalent. The only advantage of this is that it avoids the problem of having to make repeat measurements on the same individuals.

(*c*) *Before-after design with control groups.* A better plan, and one that combines the advantages of (*a*) and (*b*) above, is to measure both the experimental (E) and the control (C) groups before and after exposure to x. The effect of x is then measured by comparing the changes in y in the two groups. There remains the possibility that the "before" measurement may stimulate interest (or boredom), thus making the experimental group unduly susceptible to x. A possible solution is to have a second control group, which is measured only after E has been subjected to x.

For simplicity I have supposed that only two groups are being compared—the experimental and the control; but actually one often wishes to compare several groups according to various levels of x. This is easily done with modern techniques of experimental design, and these also enable one to study in the same experiment the operation of many different independent variables, noting not only their separate effects (on the dependent variable) but also their "interaction" with each other: that is, the extent to which the effect of one variable depends on the value of another.

There is no end to the ingenuity and complexity of experimental designs, and the reader is given some references below. For an example of a complex design used for an experiment in survey methodology, see Durbin and Stuart [66].

Although I have in this section used the term "experimental" in a wider sense than would be acceptable to many natural scientists, I have not used it in the loose sense of meaning "new" or "of uncertain outcome". A university course, for instance, might be described as experimental if only because the intention is to abandon it if it proves unsuccessful; but to be strictly correct the word should be used only if the new course were tried on a random sample of students, the old one being continued with an equivalent random sample (hardly practical!), and if the success of the two courses, somehow measured, were then compared. In fact, whether the term "experimental" is justified depends wholly on the method by which the hypothesis is tested.

In a sense most social changes engineered by policy-makers (including new laws) provide an opportunity for testing some hypothesis; but generally too much is left uncontrolled for a strictly experimental pattern to be followed.

NOTES ON READING

1. This is an appropriate point for commenting upon the book literature on surveys. There are a number of good text-books on methods of social research in general, covering survey techniques. Perhaps the best of the modern texts are the symposia edited by JAHODA, DEUTSCH and COOK [129] and by FESTINGER and KATZ [78] respectively. An excellent book on survey analysis and design is by HYMAN [123]; this is concerned with fundamental principles rather than with techniques and makes more "advanced" reading than most. Students are recommended to consult also the works of GOODE and HATT [97], MADGE [168], and MOSTELLER [196]. The last is the authoritative post-mortem on the 1948 failure of the American pollsters and is an important critical account of polling methods. An earlier book on opinion polls was that by CANTRIL [28]; and an extremely detailed account of practical survey procedures is given by PARTEN [202]. A good text for those especially interested in market research is that by BROWN [24]. A volume edited by EDWARDS [73] brings together a number

of important British papers on market research. ABRAMS [1] gives a good general description of the role of surveys. YATES [291], apart from the technical matter of sampling to which I shall refer later, deals extensively with practical survey problems.

2. The papers by MARSHALL [179] and HARRISSON [114], and the book by WOOTTON [290] discuss provocatively the role of surveys and of quantitative methods in social research. KENDALL [138] discusses, with examples taken from many fields, the nature of the statistical approach.

3. The most extensive discussion of experimental sociology is the book with that title by GREENWOOD [105]. A well-known earlier book on the subject is by CHAPIN [34]. STOUFFER deals with experimentation in an article [250] and, at various points, in the volumes on the *American Soldier* [251, 252]. The discussion of various types of experimentation in MADGE [168] is also well worth consulting. A stimulating book on the methods of scientific investigation generally is that by BEVERIDGE [8]. The chapters on experiments in FESTINGER and KATZ [78], mentioned above, are very valuable. Among statistical texts on experimental design, that by COCHRAN and COX [37] is especially recommended.

CHAPTER 2

THE EVOLUTION OF SOCIAL SURVEYS IN GREAT BRITAIN

2.1. Introduction

THE HISTORIAN of social surveys in Great Britain has a relatively easy task. His main subject-matter is encompassed within about the last 70 years and there is no lack of records and documentary sources to guide him. He could, it is true, go further back and open his story with Cobbett or Defoe or even the Domesday Book, but it would be more sensible to begin with Eden, Mayhew and Booth. Of these Mayhew's fascinating book *London Life and the London Poor* [182], published in 1851, makes particularly entertaining reading and has been enjoying a considerable literary vogue in recent years; but it is Booth who should be considered the father of scientific social surveys.

In the 70 odd years since he commenced his enquiry into *The Life and Labour of the People of London* [13] great changes have occurred, alike in the amount and character of survey activity and in the public interest shown in it. At the turn of the century, two pioneers—Booth and Rowntree—were conducting large-scale surveys, stimulated by their personal concern about the living conditions of a large section of the population. During the next 20 years one or two others, notably Bowley, followed their example. By the late 'twenties and early 'thirties social surveys were being conducted in London, Tyneside, Sheffield, Southampton, Merseyside and many other cities. These, while differing in details of scope and method, all followed the broad pattern established by the pioneers. Subsequently, surveys began to be used in conjunction with town planning and other government activities, and the techniques were adapted to the needs of market and public opinion research. Today a government organisation is wholly occupied undertaking social surveys, market research has itself become a large-scale industry, social scientists regard the social survey as one of their most useful techniques, and courses on survey methodology are given in some universities.

A rapid historical account of these developments will be a useful preliminary to the description of present-day methods, which is the main purpose of this book. I should stress, however, that surveys will be mentioned for their methodological interest rather than for the importance of their results.

2.2. The Classical Poverty Surveys

Charles Booth's monumental survey was begun in 1886 and published, in a seventeen-volume edition, in 1902. Booth, a rich Liverpool shipowner, had been deeply disturbed by the poverty and living conditions of the working-class and set out to obtain "two series of facts —first, the relative destitution, poverty or comfort of the home and, secondly, the character of the work from which the various bread-winners in the family derived their livelihood" [13, i, p. 13]. His main problem was how to collect the information about the huge working-class population of London. "The root idea with which I began to work", he says, "was that every fact I needed was known to someone, and that the information had simply to be collected and put together." He consequently applied what Beatrice Webb later termed the "method of wholesale interviewing", collecting the information from School Attendance Officers—the people who possessed the most detailed knowledge of the parents of school children and their living conditions. Booth's approach is best illustrated by the following quotation:

"Of the wealth of my material I have no doubt. I am indeed embarrassed by its mass and by my resolution to make use of no fact to which I cannot give a quantitative value. The materials for sensational stories lie plentifully in every book of our notes; but, even if I had the skill to use my material in this way—that gift of the imagination which is called 'realistic'—I should not wish to use it here. There is struggling poverty, there is destitution, there is hunger, drunkenness, brutality and crime; no one doubts that it is so. My object has been to show the numerical relation which poverty, misery and depravity bear to regular earnings and comparative comfort, and to describe the general conditions under which each class lives" [13, i, p. 5].

On the basis of his data Booth put each family into one of eight classes, of which four were below and four above the poverty line. His definitions of the various classes were vague: "My 'poor' may be described as living under a struggle to obtain the necessaries of life and make both ends meet, while the 'very poor' live in a state of chronic want" [13, i, p. 33]. It was to be left to Rowntree to give these

B

concepts greater precision. The study, as a whole, was largely descriptive and sacrificed some generality through its exclusion of families without schoolchildren. Nevertheless, its startling results drew attention to the extent and severity of poverty and, as Beatrice Webb has shown, its political results were considerable. It was a pioneering contribution to the science of social study.

A decade after the start of Booth's investigation, Rowntree set out on his first survey of York, published in 1901 under the title *Poverty: A Study of Town Life* [219]. His approach varied in three important methodological aspects from that of Booth.

First, he set out to obtain information about the housing, occupation and earnings of *every* wage-earning family in York.

Secondly, he obtained his information *directly* from the families by using interviewers.

Thirdly, and most important, Rowntree gave far greater precision to the concept of poverty, originating the distinction between "primary" and "secondary" poverty. If a family had "total earnings insufficient to obtain the minimum necessaries for the maintenance of merely physical efficiency", it was regarded as living in "primary" poverty [219, p. 86]. If its "earnings would be sufficient for the maintenance of merely physical efficiency were it not that some portion of it then is absorbed by other expenditure, either useful or wasteful", then it was deemed as living in "secondary" poverty [219, p. 87]. The cost of minimum requirements of food and clothing etc. was ascertained, it being assumed that the food would be purchased as cheaply as possible and selected with a careful consideration for nutritive values. This was called the poverty-line standard. It excluded any clothing not deemed essential, and did not allow for "expenditure needful for the development of the mental, moral and social sides of human nature" [219, p. 87]. Rowntree purposely made his poverty-line standards precise and very stringent, so that they might be generally acceptable as a minimum.

The method of defining "secondary" poverty was more debatable. The number of households in which poverty was evidenced by obvious want and squalor, the appearance of the children and by talks with the neighbours was noted; and from this total the number deemed to be living in primary poverty was subtracted. Those remaining were regarded as being in "secondary" poverty. This calculation contained a crucial subjective element, but some distinction between the two types of poverty was undoubtedly valuable.[1]

[1] I cannot here discuss the concept of the poverty line *per se*, but must refer to the difficulty of relating this line to *actual* living conditions. Many commodities not allowed for in the classical poverty line calculations are in effect felt, by consumers, to be as necessary as food and rent. A recent discussion of the problem was given by Townsend [264].

More than a decade elapsed before the next important survey was begun. In 1912, Bowley made a study of working-class conditions in Reading, the first of the Five-Towns surveys which also covered Northampton, Stanley, Warrington and Bolton and was published as *Livelihood and Poverty* (15). Bowley's great methodological contribution was his use of sampling, which came to act as a decisive stimulus to social surveys. Nearly all the later poverty surveys followed this example (and his personal influence is discernible in the fact that many leading survey practitioners of today were his pupils at the London School of Economics). Both in this early survey and its follow-up study ten years later—*Has Poverty Diminished?* [16]—Bowley took care with the selection of the sample and the possible introduction of bias through refusals and non-contacts. Bowley confined himself to "primary" poverty but used a more realistic standard —based on actual spending habits—than Rowntree. He also took into account, as his predecessors had not, the varying food needs of children of different ages.

In the early thirties survey activity increased. Ford's investigation in Southampton, begun in 1928 and published under the title *Work and Wealth in a Modern Port* [84] largely followed the methods of Bowley, keeping the two types of poverty separate, and indeed introducing a third type—"potential" poverty. This denied the usual assumption that all family income was pooled, and was based on the income of the head of the household.

The year 1928 also saw the beginning of the monumental *New Survey of London Life and Labour*, published in a series of volumes between 1930 and 1935 [237]. This was planned as a sequel to Booth's survey of 40 years earlier and one part of it—the street survey—was aimed to provide a direct comparison with Booth's results. The other part was an enquiry among a sample of 1 in 50 of all persons living in private houses or as families.

In 1934 a survey of Merseyside was published, with D. Caradog Jones as its editor, under the title *The Social Survey of Merseyside* [131]. An interesting feature was the special study of subnormal groups. A social survey of Sheffield, published as *A Survey of the Standard of Living in Sheffield* [232], edited by Owen, set out to give a historical and contemporary picture of social life in Sheffield. Different pamphlets dealt with subjects such as milk supply, housing, licensing, unemployment, adult education, juvenile employment, public health, transport, and the standard of living.

Of the many other investigations of working-class poverty only two need be referred to, both initiated by Rowntree. In 1935 he directed a second survey of York, which was published as *Poverty and Progress* six years later [221]. In this he abandoned his previous poverty standard as being too stringent and unrealistic, and replaced it by his well-known "Human Needs Standard" developed in 1918 and brought up to date in 1937 [220]. He further did not repeat his attempt to measure "secondary" poverty. The survey report contained an illuminating analysis of the causes of poverty and the periods of life at which it was most acute, and also had sections on housing, health, education and leisure time activities. In an interesting supplementary chapter Rowntree attempted to measure the accuracy of sampling; all the survey schedules were arranged in street order and the results of different sizes of samples—1 in 10, 1 in 20, 1 in 30, 1 in 40 and 1 in 50—were compared. Practical sampling difficulties arising from non-response were of course by-passed in this analysis.

In 1950 Rowntree, this time in collaboration with G. R. Lavers, conducted yet another follow-up survey of York, *Poverty and the Welfare State* [223]. The book received a good deal of public attention, both because it was the first post-war survey wholly concerned with working-class poverty, and also because its findings suggested that the magnitude of the problem—which had been so startling in 1900 and even in 1935—had been reduced almost to vanishing point.

One or two comments on the methodology of the survey should be made. First, there is the question of how representative York is of urban Britain. Rowntree and Lavers affirm their belief in the views expressed in *Poverty and Progress*. "On the whole, we may safely assume that from the standpoint of the earnings of the workers, York holds a position not far from the median, among the towns of Great Britain. If on the one hand there is no important industry employing a large number of highly skilled and highly paid workers, on the other hand there are no large industries (though unfortunately there are isolated small businesses) where wages are exceptionally low" [223, p. 6]. The crucial part of this statement is the last; it implies that there is a small spread around the average earnings, with few very high and few very low earnings. In this case, one would expect less poverty here than in towns where there are substantial numbers of low-wage workers. This does not affect the validity of the comparison of the results for the three York surveys, but cautions against the tendency, evident in public discussion of this latest survey, to regard the problem of poverty as having disappeared.

Secondly, it is fair to point out that the poverty line, as adapted for this survey, is open to some criticism. The determination of the non-food amounts was arbitrary and there has been some suggestion that the line was unduly low and the amount of poverty consequently understated (see, for instance, the P.E.P. Broadsheet *Poverty: Ten Years after Beveridge* [206]).

As a final comment, it is regrettable that the authors did not avail themselves of the improvements in survey methods, and particularly in sampling techniques, which had taken place since the previous York survey.

2.3. Regional Planning Surveys

By the middle of the 'thirties, surveys were beginning to assume importance in the field of town planning and reconstruction. Housing development had formerly been carried out in an unplanned and chaotic manner, resulting in ugly and sprawling cities. This was the background and stimulus to surveys such as that initiated in Birmingham in 1935 by the Bournville Village Trust and published under the title *When We Build Again* [14]. The aim of the survey was to study the housing situation in and around Birmingham; the location of work and the workers' journey to it; the number of open spaces and parks, and other amenities of the city and its surroundings.

Surveys prior to 1939 in this field had had a different emphasis. That of *Becontree and Dagenham* carried out by Young in 1931–33 was inspired by the hope that "people, after studying the facts, will be better able to consider what should be done in the development of an estate such as Becontree, and that a report such as this should help in the formulation of policies to deal with the housing of working-class people in general" [293, p. 18]. The centre of interest of *Watling—A Survey of Social Life on a New Housing Estate* [63], conducted by Ruth Glass (then Ruth Durant) in 1932, was again different. Her enquiry was focused on two questions. Had the new estate of Watling grown into a community, in the sense of "a territorial group of people with a common mode of living, striving for common objectives"? And secondly, what part was the community centre playing in local life?

Social surveys in town planning did not, however, come into their own until after the Second World War when the need for widespread planned reconstruction gave them crucial importance. One of the most interesting of these was *Report on Luton* [106] by Grundy and Titmuss, a report on the town's population and housing, and on the social aspects of its public services.

Also interesting was the *Middlesborough Survey and Plan* [163], which gave especial weight to sociological factors. The feature of greatest methodological interest here was the use of a more precise concept of neighbourhoods. These were defined, demarcated and graded in terms of a multiple index of living conditions, based on six factors: net population density, number of houses per acre, percentage of houses with a rateable value less than £11, percentage of non-owner occupiers, percentage of chief wage earners with incomes of less than £5 per week, and number of retail shops per 1,000 people. A book on the *Social Background of the Plan* [94] relating to this survey, was published by Ruth Glass. The Midlands have also been the scene of a useful group of surveys in recent years: the planning survey of Herefordshire, *English County* [283], the survey of Birmingham and the Black Country entitled *Conurbation* [284] and that of Wolverhampton entitled *Midland City* [18] are among those now available.

Methodologically, most of these surveys follow the techniques for large-scale surveys discussed in the course of this book. Where they deviate from these it is usually in relation to specialised concepts— such as that of neighbourhoods in the Middlesborough Survey— rather than in general approach.

It is open to question whether the results of these surveys have been allowed to exert their due influence on town planning. It may be that some of them have not been as sociologically illuminating as one might wish, but a more decisive factor is probably the attitude toward social surveys of some planning authorities, who seem to view the demographic and social data provided with lukewarm interest.

2.4. The Government Social Survey

One of the most important developments in the survey field in Great Britain has been the establishment of the Government Social Survey. Founded in 1941, it has gradually become the leading organisation of its type and exerted an unquestionable influence in raising the standard of survey methods.

The Survey is part of the Central Office of Information and operates only at the request of Government departments and other official bodies, such as Royal Commissions. It does not initiate surveys. The commissioning department states its requirements and a scheme is then worked out by the Survey and submitted to the Treasury for approval. The Survey employs a headquarters staff of about 55, some 200 part-time interviewers spread over the country, and five regional organisers.

As may be imagined, the range of subject-matter covered by the Survey is extremely wide. The Central Statistical Office, the Board of Trade, the General Register Office and the Ministry of Health have been some of the Survey's main clients but many other departments have also commissioned enquiries. Detailed lists are given by Gray and Corlett [102] and Moss [195] and include: for the Board of Trade a pilot census of distribution, work connected with the retail trading statistics, and surveys on the demand for holidays and on clothing expenditures; for the Medical Research Council surveys on pneumoconiosis and on deafness; for the Ministry of Transport on road safety campaigns; for the Home Office on children and the cinema, and on shopping hours; for the Treasury on recruitment to the Civil

Service and on the demand for medals; for the Ministry of Fuel on recruitment to mining, on domestic fuel and on the demand for house fuel; for the Ministry of Works on space utilisation and on water heating; for the Royal Commission on Taxation on taxation and incentives; for the Ministry of Health on blood transfusion, on nutrition of housewives and on aspects of the National Health Service, such as general practice and nursing duties in hospitals; for the Ministry of Labour on women in industry, on men and mining, and on education and employment; for the General Post Office on the use of telephone directories; for the Colonial Office on public opinion on colonial affairs; for the Department of Scientific and Industrial Research on noise, light and heating in domestic dwellings, on road traffic problems and on the use of scientific and technical information in industry.

Among recent studies of methodological interest is the attempt to predict the success of training at Borstal institutions and in approved schools (see Mannheim and Wilkins [173]).

Three important *series* of enquiries should be mentioned. One was the Survey of Sickness (for the General Register Office) which for 6 years provided useful data on the nation's health until, in 1951, it became a casualty of a Government economy campaign. Another series still continuing is that on consumer expenditure. This has included reports on expenditure on gambling, laundry, holidays, household textiles, house repairs and domestic service, meals in restaurants, hairdressing and cosmetics. The importance of these enquiries lies in the use of their results for the Central Statistical Office's estimates of national income and expenditure. A third continuing enquiry is the National Food Survey carried out for the Ministry of Food. This major project provides valuable information on the adequacy of the diet available to families of different size and composition, in different parts of the country and in various social groups (see [267]).

Social Survey questionnaires cover both opinions and facts but political surveys are excluded: the Survey exists to collect data required for administration, not for party politics.

I should here note and welcome the increasing extent to which the Government Social Survey is participating in social and economic research. It has been linked with the social mobility enquiry at the London School of Economics, with the Savings Survey conducted by the Oxford Institute of Statistics and with the work of the Department of Applied Economics at Cambridge (in this case to give technical advice).

As the populations covered in the Survey's enquiries range very widely, so do their sample designs. Gray and Corlett [102], writing in 1950, reported that 46 per cent of their samples had been of the general adult population, 7 per cent of particular age and sex groups, 16 per cent of populations of households or housewives, and 31 per cent of other populations. About a fifth of the samples had contained 500 cases or less, about a third 3,000 or more. An average size of sample was about 2,000.

The Social Survey employs in highly organised form all the methods described in this book, and references to its work will frequently be made.

2.5. Market, Audience and Opinion Research

Market Research[1]

Market research in its widest sense has been a feature of commerce for decades. Whether through its executives, salesmen, or professional advisors, every firm tries to study its market and its marketing methods. But since the 1930's the approach has become much more scientific. The market research survey, using substantially the methods described in this book, has in turn given much of the stimulus to their development.

Market research in its modern form is enjoying an unprecedented vogue in Great Britain, and, no doubt, with modern mass-production of consumer goods and the increasing competition between brands, the importance of consumer surveys will grow rather than decrease. Already, many firms have small market research departments and a few employ their own field staff. But this latter scale of operation is beyond all but the largest firms and most consumer surveys are still done by specialist research agencies such as the British Market Research Bureau Ltd., Research Services Ltd., Market Information Services Ltd., Sales Research Services Ltd., Attwood Statistics Ltd., Social Surveys Ltd. (the market research side of the British Institute of Public Opinion), and A. C. Nielsens Co.

Such agencies are usually engaged simultaneously on surveys commissioned by a number of clients, covering different populations, products and types of question. Their association with clients is of varying degrees of closeness and is perhaps at its most useful when the agency is able to go beyond merely submitting survey reports, and can advise the management on the meaning of the results, their implications for the firm's marketing and distribution policy and so forth. Market research surveys proper find their greatest scope and usefulness in the study of the public's buying habits and views on

---

[1] This very brief sketch of the range of market research should be supplemented by reading the (introductory) chapter by Downham, Shankleman and Treasure in *Readings in British Market Research* [73]. These authors estimate, incidentally, that some 1,500 to 2,000 persons are now employed full-time on market research surveys in Britain, and that the total annual expenditure on this kind of work is about £3 to £3½ million.

specific brands of consumer goods. In this they fill important gaps in the manufacturer's knowledge, supplementing information contained in sales statistics, reports of sales representatives and so on.

The manufacturer naturally knows his total sales and usually how this is split up between wholesalers and retailers. But if, for instance, his marketing is mainly through wholesalers he will know little or nothing about the purchases and views of individual retailers, let alone the eventual consumers. And without market research he will know nothing about retailers' stocks. Hence the importance of the so-called "retail audit technique", by which details of stock levels, of counter sales and so on are obtained at regular intervals from a panel of retailers.[1] The technique is discussed by Treasure [265] and by Melhuish [184].

Manufacturers also often wish to know more about what *types* of people are buying or not buying their products, what they think of its quality, its presentation, its price; and how their attitudes are changing. Such knowledge is invaluable for guiding advertising policy, and it is no accident that many of the research organisations are linked to advertising agencies.

Special problems arise with new products. A manufacturer may wish to test out a proposed product in various forms, colours, flavours and so on and can avail himself of techniques of experimental design to assess the likely popularity of various alternatives. When the final choice is reduced to a few possibilities, the market researcher often tests their comparative sales appeal by placing them on the market, perhaps at varying prices, in different test areas.

Where the problem is to find the best form of an advertisement, market research methods can be used to throw light on the relative effectiveness of several alternatives. Equally important is the question of *where* advertising space is to be bought, for, clearly, the more people who read a particular publication, and the better-off they are, the more valuable is the advertising space. Readership surveys are used for this purpose, the best known being those conducted by the Hulton Press and by the Institute of Practitioners in Advertising.[2] The parallel field in commercial television is only just being opened up in Great Britain.

A certain amount of secretiveness regarding their work is to be expected of market research bodies but this is decreasing, as is evidenced by the fact that one is now able—as would not have been the case three or four years ago—to refer to a number of papers on market research activities in this country. (On organisation of market re-

[1] The use of panels—which have considerable importance in market research—is discussed in section 6.9 below.
[2] The Market Research Society has published an account of the development, application and problems of readership surveys [174].

search Cauter [31] has given an account of the set-up of one of the largest agencies.) The methods used in market research surveys are largely those explained in this book. The general pattern is personal interviewing of a sample of people, with occasional use of mail questionnaires and observation. There is still much use of quota (as opposed to random) sampling; both methods are discussed in Chapter 6. The usefulness and possible future development of market research are considered in the final chapter.

B.B.C. Audience Research

In 1936 the British Broadcasting Corporation set up a Listener Research Department to collect information about the listening habits and tastes of the British public, an attempt to establish some kind of substitute in the world of radio for the box-office of the theatre. When television came in, the Department changed its name to Audience Research.

To ascertain the amount of listening and viewing, a national quota sample (see Chapter 6) of 3,100 men and women is asked each day which of the programmes broadcast the previous day they had listened to (or viewed); *opinions* on these programmes are not sought. Interviewers use the "aided-recall" method, i.e. they remind respondents of the programmes in question. This enables the B.B.C. to estimate what percentage of the civilian adult population listens to (or views) their various programmes of the previous day's broadcasts. Apart from the usefulness to the producers of knowing trends in audience size these surveys produce much information of interest about the factors affecting listening numbers: time of broadcast, season, competing broadcasts, nature of broadcast preceding and following it, regularity of broadcast, content, general quality, publicity and so on.

Even ignoring the fundamental difficulty of radio-research, that of distinguishing between "listening to" a programme and merely "hearing" it as a sort of background noise,[1] sheer size of audience is not the best, certainly not the only, criterion of a programme's quality. The B.B.C. accordingly has volunteer panels of some 6,000 listeners and viewers whose opinions on programmes in their field of interest are regularly sought and analysed.

One can never of course be confident that volunteer panels are representative of the particular population one is interested in and the only safeguards—both used by the B.B.C.—are to ensure that different age, sex and social class groups are correctly represented and

---

[1] Audience Research does not regard a person as having "listened" to a programme if he heard less than half of it (news bulletins apart). "Background listening" is accepted unless the respondent has not even a vague memory of the programme.

that checks of representativeness (e.g. comparing results with those from *ad hoc* surveys) are made whenever possible. A description of the Department's work is given by Silvey [235].

Public Opinion Polls

Opinion questions figure in the Government Social Survey's work, in market research, in audience research, indeed in surveys of practically every kind; but in this section we will concentrate on two survey bodies whose work is almost exclusively the study of opinions.

The first is the British Institute of Public Opinion, founded in 1936 and one of the international chain of Gallup Institutes (see Durant [62] for a discussion of its methods). Opinion polls here do not enjoy anything like the publicity accorded to them in the United States, where nearly a hundred newspapers publish the Gallup results. However, the B.I.P.O. regularly publishes in the *News Chronicle* its survey findings on questions of the day and its forecasts of general and by-election results.

Election forecasts, although the most publicised of all polling activities, are probably the least valuable; there is, after all, little point in knowing approximately today what will be known accurately tomorrow—apart from the fact that forecasts of any kind appeal to our sporting instincts and that it is of some value to the parties to know the *trends* in opinion. To the pollster, the value of election forecasts is that they offer one of the few opportunities of demonstrating that their methods are sound. No wonder, then, that a failure like that of the 1948 U.S. election forecasts is taken so seriously (see Mosteller [196]).

What happened in 1948 was that the figures from the polls showed such close running as not to justify a prediction one way or another. But past prediction successes and the general mood of the day beguiled the pollsters into making an over-confident, and undoubtedly unwarranted, prediction. Unfortunately, this failure then made them over-cautious in forecasting the 1952 election when, looked at after the event, their poll results showed convincing evidence of the impending Eisenhower victory. But success in predicting elections is in many ways an unfair criterion of the value of survey methods generally, for this sort of forecasting faces special problems, notably the uncertainty of the voting turnout and of what the "undecided voter" will do. British general elections are somewhat easier to predict than the American, both because a larger proportion of the electorate turns out to vote and because there are fewer undecided voters; the B.I.P.O.'s prediction record is very good.

The aim of everyday opinion surveys is modest and unobjectionable. All political policies directly or indirectly affect the public, who in turn have views on them. Whether these views are well- or ill-informed, strong or mild, emotional or rational, nothing but good can come from the law maker and the administrator knowing what they are, and opinion surveys endeavour to inform them.

An organisation studying public opinion in a rather different manner is Mass Observation. Founded in 1937, its initial aims were to study modern society by using techniques akin to those more customary in anthropology. It has had an active career, without altogether keeping to its initial hopes and promises. Most of its reports are based on field surveys, but with more stress on general impressions, verbatim comment and "overheards" and less on formal interviewing and quantitative findings than in other opinion surveys. However, it is tending to make increasing use of standard survey procedures, such as sampling and interviewing. Apart from its *ad hoc* field surveys, Mass Observation retains a panel of volunteer informants, whose views on issues of the day are regularly published in broadsheets.

The informal techniques employed by Mass Observation, especially in its earlier days, cannot be dismissed out of hand as unscientific; but they do give rise to special difficulties and responsibilities, to be discussed later. An early critical review of Mass Observation was given by Firth [80].

2.6. Some Other Surveys

There remain to be considered the miscellaneous surveys, past and present, which do not fit into any of the classifications of the previous five sections. They range from Government-commissioned national enquiries to the individual sociologist, anthropologist or psychologist studying a handful of cases. They cover all types of subject-matter and use in varying form all the techniques available to the surveyor.

It is difficult to do justice to such a range in a book primarily devoted to methods without appearing to give undue space to examples and applications. My course, then, will be a compromise. I will mention a few selected surveys on each of a few selected subjects, hoping merely to demonstrate the wide range of application of survey methods.

(*a*) *Population.* Pride of place in this field must go to the biggest survey of all, the Decennial Population Census. In the 1951 Census, the latest of the series, the main feature of methodological interest was the use of sampling in the analysis (see [91]).

Another large-scale demographic enquiry was the Family Census conducted for the Royal Commission on Population in 1946, and published under the title *The Trend and Pattern of Fertility in Great*

Britain [93]. Its purpose was to fill the main gaps in our knowledge of fertility and family-building habits and to this end a sample of over a million married women were questioned. The report sets a high standard in its detailed discussion of all aspects of the survey's methods, including the sampling. The same Royal Commission sponsored an enquiry on *Family Limitation* [158], in which information on habits of birth control and attitudes to it was obtained from a sample of married women patients in the general wards of hospitals; the interviewing was done by doctors.

For further information in this field, readers should consult the demographic journals, the *ad hoc* publications of the General Register Office, the research reports of the Population Investigation Committee and so forth.

(*b*) *Urban life.* Although much material of sociological interest has been gained from the many English studies of urban life, there has been nothing here comparable to the Lynds' studies of "Middletown" in the United States (see Chapter 9). English investigators have usually been concerned to examine a particular section of a community or a special aspect of its activities, rather than to paint a picture of its whole life; however some of the current surveys—e.g. the study of social structure in a market town organised from Birmingham University, the social survey of Southampton, or the research on the social organisation of a city organised from Edinburgh University—may be more of the Middletown type. The work of the Institute of Community Studies, newly established in East London, will also be watched with interest.

A recent volume by Kuper and others entitled *Living in Towns* [151] contains a series of studies of life in urban communities in the Midlands, which made some use of survey methods; readers may also like to refer to the sociological survey of South-West Wales by Brennan [19].

(*c*) *Rural life.* Studies of rural life do not use formal survey methods to the same extent as those covering large population units like cities. Sampling problems barely arise and, in collecting the information, there is usually more scope for the skill and insight of the individual sociologist than for interviewers and questionnaires. In *Village Surveyed* [248], Stewart reported a study of a Kent village done in 1948, part of which was a social survey, in which three interviewers gathered information about all the families by questionnaires and observation. Rees, in his *Life in a Welsh Countryside* [212], produced information of genuine sociological interest. He made repeated visits to the village over a period of several years, gathering information by interviewing, general conversation and observation.

Other studies of rural community life in progress include anthropological-type researches into *Interaction Norms in a Shetland Community* and *A Study of Kinship and Community in the Western Isles of Scotland*, both organised from Edinburgh University.

(*d*) *Travelling*. Most people spend a good deal of their lives travelling to and from work, and the subject is clearly of sociological interest. A social and economic analysis, fortified in parts by survey data, was Liepman's *Journey to Work* [159]. Straightforward statistical surveys on travel habits have been sponsored by the London Transport Executive in London [164] and the British Transport Commission in Bristol [21].

(*e*) *Family expenditure*. Family expenditure has been one of the most fertile fields for the use of traditional survey methods. At the official level such studies are generally occasioned by the need to revise the weighting basis of retail price indices. Such was the Ministry of Labour's 1937/8 survey of the *Weekly Expenditure of Working-Class Households in the U.K.* [269] and the *Household Expenditure Survey* of 1953 by the same Ministry in consultation with the Central Statistical Office. This enquiry interestingly combined two methods of data-collection, interviewing and record keeping, each of which has certain merits. Questions relating to the household as a whole (on household composition; on details of the dwelling and expenditures related to it, etc.) were dealt with by the interviewer, while personal expenditure data were provided by the individuals. The survey covered the entire non-institutional population of the country, although some classes of households will be excluded when computing the weights for the new index.[1]

A pre-1939 investigation of the cost of living of middle-class families was carried out by Massey [180]. This was based on a sample of some 3,000 civil servants, government officials and teachers, and was arranged to be broadly comparable with the official 1937/8 enquiry.

Many other institutes and researchers have worked in this field. The Oxford Institute of Statistics has been carrying out surveys on the expenditure and nutrition of small samples of households for over a decade. These are based on households known, and willing to give information, to the investigators; a summary of the first decade of these surveys was given by Schulz [226]. Recently Lydall [165], at the same Institute, has been conducting a number of sample-interview surveys on the difficult subject of saving; his surveys have thrown a good deal of new light on income distribution, asset structure and so forth.

---

[1] At the time of writing, no report on it has been issued. See Utting [275] for a comparison of its methods with those of the Cambridge enquiries, mentioned below.

At Cambridge, the Department of Applied Economics has used household-budget surveys as part of its project on the social accounts of the county. This work has been described by Utting and Cole [276, 277]. From the same department has come a volume by Prais and Houthakker devoted to the problems of family expenditure surveys [210].

A less statistical study in this field is Miss Rowntree's research on *The Finances of Founding a Family*, a detailed examination of a small number of families in Aberdeen [224]. Other researchers are studying the distribution of income and expenditure *within* the family—see Young [292] for an expository article on this.

(*f*) *Nutrition*. A noteworthy nutritional survey was Boyd Orr's *Food, Health and Income* [200] of 1936. Unlike most previous and later investigators, Orr concerned himself with optimum, not minimum, dietary requirements. He asked what proportion of the population had a diet adequate for perfect health. To this end he divided the population into 6 income groups and studied family budget and diet records from 12 regional surveys. Other data on pre-war nutrition are reviewed in a report by the Carnegie Trust [218]. The *British Journal of Nutrition* is a useful source for those seeking other nutrition survey references.

(*g*) *Education*. Probably the most publicised educational researches have been those concerned with intelligence tests. There have been many small-scale surveys into the relation between intelligence-test performance and social background, family size and composition; and to these a paper by Burt [25] and a report to the Royal Commission on Population [260] may serve as a guide. A large-scale survey on *The Trend of Intelligence* [209] was carried out by the Population Investigation Committee and the Scottish Council for Education. Based on a sample of Scottish schoolchildren of a particular age-group this was designed to throw light on the thorny question of whether national intelligence was falling. A follow-up volume [227] discusses, among other things, the relationship of measured intelligence to height, weight and social background. Information on the careers of a sub-sample of the original sample continues to be collected to demonstrate what use is made of persons of varying intelligence in the life of Scotland.

A matter of considerable interest to sociologists is the relation between education and social mobility and this is the subject of a monograph by Floud, Martin and Halsey [83]. This is based largely on field surveys carried out as part of the research into social mobility at the London School of Economics (see below). It includes analyses of the social structure and secondary education in different areas and of the relationship between ability, opportunity, achievement and social class. A survey of the social and educational background of applicants for places in universities in 1955 and 1956 has been conducted under the sponsorship of the Vice-Chancellors' Committee. And P.E.P., in conjunction with the Government Social Survey, is investigating what jobs 1950 graduates are in at present, and to what extent arts and science graduates are entering industry. An enquiry into the social origins and structure of the school teaching profession was started in 1954 at the Institute of Education of London University, with the support of the Nuffield Foundation.

A survey by the Ministry of Education designed "to obtain an estimate of the mean score on a certain reading test of pupils aged 15 in grant-aided schools in England" is worth mentioning because of the sampling problems involved. These were described by Peaker [204]. The National Foundation for Educational Research, together with the Population Investigation Committee, has started a national survey of standards of attainment in reading and arithmetic at various ages.

(h) *Health.* In this country, as in most others, we know far more about mortality than about morbidity. On the latter, notifiable diseases apart, the information is unsystematised, especially since the discontinuation of the Government Social Survey's *Survey of Sickness.*

A current enquiry of impressive methodological achievement is being sponsored by the Population Investigation Committee [130]. To obtain data on the social and economic aspects of childbearing, expenditure on childbirth and the use made of maternity services, an enquiry was addressed to all women who were delivered of children in England, Wales and Scotland in a particular week in March 1946. Successful interviews were made with 90 per cent of them. The enquiry has since grown into a National Survey of the Health and Development of Children: a large number of the original children are still included in the investigation and records of their physical development, progress in school, reading ability and intelligence are being kept. This is a long-term study probably unique in social research.

The National Health Service and the standard of general medical practice have also been the subject of surveys. The British Medical Association sponsored an enquiry into General Practice [20], one part of which was a field study of a sample of 158 general practices, the other a postal enquiry directed to the remaining 17,616 general-practitioner Principals in the National Health Service. Some 70 per cent of these co-operated. A fuller qualitative appraisal of a number of "good" general practices was recently carried out by Taylor [258] under the sponsorship of the Nuffield Foundation. The Medical

Research Council and the London School of Hygiene and Tropical Medicine are two of many bodies engaged on social medical surveys.

(*i*) *Social mobility*. Virtually every survey of human populations is directly or indirectly interested in differences in environment, behaviour and attitudes between various social strata. One major aspect, namely mobility between different social strata, has been investigated over the last few years by research workers at the London School of Economics, under a grant made by the Nuffield Foundation. A first symposium on this entitled *Social Mobility in Britain*, edited by Glass [92], gives data about the social origin, education and occupational achievement of a national sample of some 10,000 adults. Ancillary investigations included enquiries into the social prestige of occupations, the relationship between education and social mobility, child upbringing and social class, social mobility and marriage, recruitment in a number of professions and the structure of voluntary organisations. A volume on the recruitment and social background of the Higher Civil Service has been published by Kelsall [136]: other products of the research, which is still continuing, are in preparation.

(*j*) *Leisure*. There have been many surveys concerned with special leisure activities such as cinema-going, reading, radio-listening, gambling. Some have concentrated on particular sections of the community such as students or children; others have covered the community as a whole. A study of the effects of television on children, sponsored by the Nuffield Foundation is in progress now; and a parallel enquiry concerning adults is being carried out by the B.B.C.

Two attempts to assess the amount of leisure available to people may be mentioned. One, by Moser [190], was concerned with the leisure patterns of housewives on three L.C.C. estates; the other, by Rich, a more extensive research into the leisure of a number of families, appeared in the volume by Kuper [151].

Rowntree and Lavers' book *English Life and Leisure* [222], which appeared in 1951 and was much publicised, took its material from a large number of informal interviews and some 1,000 case histories, about a fifth of which are recorded. Another recent book which gave an interesting view of leisure habits and urban life generally was Cauter and Downham's *Communication of Ideas* [32]. The bulk of the material came from a sample survey in Derby, which investigated elements of modern life connected with the communication and spread of ideas—education, reading, radio and television, the cinema, religion, travelling and so forth.

A vivid picture of the leisure pursuits of working-class people was drawn in Zweig's *Labour, Life and Poverty* [295]. Zweig has developed with remarkable success a mode of social study that owes little to the

formal techniques of surveys, such as sampling, standardised interviewing and questionnaires, and a great deal to his personality, his
ability to get people talking, and his skill in knitting their remarks
and his observations into a coherent picture. A skilled investigator
using this informal approach (which was, in a sense, originated by
Mayhew) can provide a fuller, more lively picture than the complex
apparatus of the representative sample survey. However, the two approaches achieve different ends and can rarely be considered as
alternatives.

(k) *Political behaviour.* Opinion polls aside, survey techniques have
not been as fully exploited in studying political behaviour as they
might have been; among the most informative election surveys so far
was that by Milne and Mackenzie [188], relating to the general election
of 1951.

Three other studies in this field can be mentioned. Birch and Campbell used survey techniques in an analysis of *Voting Behaviour in
a Lancashire Constituency* [9], which they conducted immediately
after the general election of 1950. Another study by Benney, Gray and
Pear, called *How People Vote* [6], reports on an enquiry into voting
behaviour in Greenwich before and up to the 1950 general election.
A book by Bonham [11] seeks, through the analysis of opinion poll
and other data, to study the voting behaviour of the "middle classes".

Readers interested in this field should refer to a critical bibliography on *Electoral Behaviour* published by U.N.E.S.C.O. [60] and
to an expository article by Butler [26].

(l) *Old age.* It is not surprising that the problems of old age have attracted the attention of social researchers. The physical, social and
mental problems of old people reflect some of the acutest hardships
remaining in our society. Much of the research has been sponsored
by the Nuffield Foundation, and two reports, in particular, should be
mentioned. One, entitled *Old People* [199], appeared in 1947 and was
in part based upon surveys designed to show how old people lived.
A follow-up enquiry by Sheldon studied *The Social Medicine of Old
Age* [233].

The National Council of Social Service has recently published *Over
Seventy* [197], an enquiry into the social and economic circumstances
of 100 people over 70, which paid special attention to their expenditure patterns.

The Ministry of National Insurance has issued the results of a survey designed to find out why people retire or continue at work [270], a
subject of great importance for economic and social policy.

(m) *Juvenile delinquency.* In 1942 Carr-Saunders, Rhodes and
Mannheim published *Young Offenders* [30], a study, largely statistical
of juvenile delinquents. The material dated from 1938, when the

first 1,000 juveniles brought to court after a particular date were studied and their social and environmental characteristics compared with those of controls coming from the same age-groups and schools as the delinquents. The second example is Fergusson's *The Young Delinquent* [77], a study of a large number of boys in Glasgow.

The current "Bristol Social Project" financed by the Carnegie United Kingdom Trust aims "to investigate and take part in the life of a developing community in Bristol in an attempt to establish practical means of tackling those stresses and strains which arise in such a community in the form of delinquency and other disturbance" [29]. This five-year project will be a "practical experiment" in social work based on a preliminary study. Local facilities and services may be amended and new ones tried out to encourage self-help activities.

(*n*) *Industrial relations and morale.* Survey methods are increasingly being utilised in the study of human relations in industry and appropriately a good deal of this work relies on informal methods of interviewing and on observational techniques. The reader interested in this field might refer to *Human Relations*, the journal of the Tavistock Institute of Human Relations, to the annual reports of the National Institute of Industrial Psychology, to the journal *Occupational Psychology* and to the reports on industrial morale and relations published by Liverpool University (the volume on dock workers [162] is a good example).

(*o*) *Special groups or problems.* There have been a number of studies of professions and occupational groups. Surveys of Higher Civil Servants and Teachers were mentioned earlier. A very different occupation, mining, is the subject of Zweig's *Men in the Pits* [296].

Graduate Wives was the title of a privately-sponsored survey published by P.E.P. [207]. Questionnaires were sent to a sample of married women graduates with the object of tracing the pattern of their lives and work since they left university.

A research making only marginal use of formal survey methods was Little's *Negroes in Britain* [161], which employed anthropological techniques in a study of the coloured community in Liverpool.

A well-known pre-1939 survey was *Working-Class Wives* by Marjorie Spring-Rice [241]. She studied the health and living condition of over 1,000 married working-class women, and her report made impressive reading as an example of an individual (though co-operatively sponsored) research relying little on formal methods. Still another example was Bakke's study of *The Unemployed Man* [4].

The many new social problems thrown up by the Second World War (evacuation for instance) made a fertile field for the social investigator. Good examples of researches done are *Our Towns* [289], published by the National Council of Social Service; and the report edited by Susan Isaacs [128] on a study of a group of London school children evacuated to Cambridge.

A recent study of anti-semitism by Robb [214] is of interest not only for its results but also for the range of observational, interviewing and analytical techniques used.

Conclusion

I again emphasise that this chapter is not to be taken as an exhaustive or critical survey of surveys, but only as the presentation of a number of examples to illustrate the evolution of social surveys in Great Britain and the wide variety of subject-matter to which the techniques have been applied.

NOTES ON READING

1. Short and readable accounts of the development of surveys are given by JONES [132] and ABRAMS [1] and by RUTH and DAVID GLASS [96]. MADGE [168] critically discusses a number of enquiries. POLITICAL AND ECONOMIC PLANNING published in 1950 two broadsheets [205] on the use of sample surveys in various fields. A much earlier book on social surveys, in the classical community-study sense, was that by WELLS [282].

2. The best bibliographical source on surveys is the *N.I.E.S.R.* Register [198] mentioned in the text. An up-to-date bibliography on urban surveys can be found in a booklet by RUTH GLASS [95].

3. The student is recommended to read some of the original reports on the early surveys which have become classics in their field, combining factual usefulness with a wealth of material and a vividness of description absent from many of their modern successors.

CHAPTER 3

THE PLANNING OF SOCIAL SURVEYS

3.1. Preliminary Study

THE PLANNING of a social survey is a combination of technical and organisational decisions. At some point all the methodological questions dealt with in this book have to be answered: what population coverage to aim at; what information to seek; how to go about collecting this information; how to process and interpret the results and so forth. None of these questions, however, can be answered on a purely technical level. The sample design is decided upon in the light of what is practically feasible as well as of what is theoretically desirable. Once decided, it in turn gives rise to numerous practical decisions of selection and organisation. In considering these matters, due regard must be paid to the purposes of the survey, the accuracy required in the results, the cost, time and labour involved and other practical considerations. Funds being invariably limited, the aim throughout is to utilise them to best advantage.

The nature of the planning problems will depend on whether the survey is being carried out by one of the existing permanent survey bodies or whether a special organisation has to be set up. If the former, matters like interviewer selection and training, field supervision and so on are already settled routine; and even considerations such as the *type* of sampling, *type* of data-collection and methods of tabulation are likely to follow well-established lines. The would-be surveyor who has not the facilities of a running survey machine at his disposal has obviously a much bigger and more difficult task and it is rarely possible for him to attain the efficiency of a professional organisation. Nevertheless there are many in his position and this chapter considers survey planning in the context of an *ad hoc* rather than an existing organisation.

In the preparatory stages, various lines of approach should be explored. Much can be gained from talks with experts, both with those familiar with the subject-matter of the survey and (informally) with survey practitioners. In my experience these latter are most generous in giving advice to research workers carrying out *ad hoc* surveys, even in helping with coding plans and the tabulation. Then, of course, a study of the available literature is a necessity in any good research. A wealth of information on most aspects of our national life issues from all directions: in the official sphere, statistical data, reports, white papers and blue books appear in immense numbers and on an increasingly wide range of topics. Publications such as the *Guides to Official Statistics* [127] and *The Sources and Nature of the Statistics of the U.K.*, edited by Kendall [139], are invaluable sign-posts but it is still a formidable job to find out even what official information is available on any given subject.

In the non-official sphere the output is equally voluminous and still more difficult to keep track of. *The Register of Social and Economic Research* [198], mentioned earlier, is the most useful indicator of the range of subject-matter being covered and of the research bodies working in this field.

With all this activity, care clearly needs to be taken to avoid duplicating work being done, or in plan, elsewhere. It is a well-known feature of scientific history that the same invention, the same theoretical advance, is often made more or less simultaneously by several workers. This kind of "coincidence", which is only a reflection of the current state of scientific knowledge and interest, frequently occurs also in the social sciences. Perhaps it is even more common here than in the natural sciences. Social research depends a good deal on what sources and data are available for study, and there is a consequent tendency for some parts of the field to be ploughed over and over again, while others remain virtually untouched. Or a certain problem—say the conditions of old people—may be in the public eye, thus stimulating a spate of investigations of it. Replication in different parts of the country or under different circumstances can, of course, be most valuable, but, if all research workers knew of each other's projects and were willing to collaborate more, a good deal of effort and money could be saved and channelled into the more unexplored fields. Often re-analysis, from a different standpoint, of the findings in someone else's research or a few additions to the questionnaire of a contemplated one could obviate the need for a separate project.

3.2. The Main Planning Problems

I now turn to discuss, in general terms, planning with special reference to social surveys. The problems noted will be dealt with in detail in later chapters.

(*a*) *Objectives and resources.* The first task of planning is of course precisely to lay down the survey's objectives—and this means more than a statement of broad aims. It is not enough to say that the survey is intended to find out about "the living conditions of old people". One should define precisely what, for the purpose of the survey, is meant by an old person; whether the enquiry is to serve as a basis for inferences to some population of old people and, if so, what this population is. One should make clear whether "living conditions" simply means a description of type of house, number of rooms, furniture and so forth, or whether income and expenditure data are wanted in order to gauge hardship. The initial statement should explain why the survey is being done, exactly what questions it seeks to cover, and what kinds of results are expected. Most important, especially if the survey is being done for a client, the statement needs to discuss how the information is expected to be used and what degree of accuracy is required.

Not the least important purpose of such a statement is that it will clarify the surveyor's own mind and thus probably lead to a more efficient enquiry (and one which will be the more easily explained to respondents). Failure to think out the objectives of a survey fully and precisely must inevitably undermine its ultimate value; no amount of manipulation of the final data can overcome the resultant defects.

Once the objectives are settled, the plan of the survey is directed to achieving them with the required accuracy and within the given resources. Any widening of the scope, whether by the inclusion of further questions or the extension to population groups of marginal importance, should be permitted only if it is certain that the resources will not thereby become spread too thinly for the survey to achieve its main purposes.

The statement of objectives must specify the methods to be used and be as explicit in what is practicable as in what is desirable. At so early a stage only the roughest budget is possible; yet some estimates of cost, time and labour have to be attempted.

(*b*) *Coverage.* The first steps are to define the population to be studied—its geographical, demographic and other boundaries—and to decide whether it should be fully or only partially covered. In the latter, and far more usual, case the method of selecting the respondents has to be determined and this normally means a sample in the statistical sense. A whole host of questions then arise: what type of sample is to be used; what is the appropriate sampling unit (administrative district or constituency; ward or polling district; household, family or individual etc.); what sampling frame—i.e. list, register, map—is available for the population in question and what difficulties there are in employing it for this particular sample design and unit; how big a sample is desirable to give the required accuracy and how big a sample is feasible on the available resources; if some economy is necessary, can the sample design be modified or the population restricted, say by cutting out marginal areas.

Provisions should be made in advance for dealing with non-response. Some non-response, both through refusals and non-contacts, is unavoidable but there are ways of reducing its magnitude and of estimating the effect of the non-response that remains upon the accuracy of the results. Follow-up approaches are necessary to increase response and the planner must decide how much time, labour and money it is worth spending on these.

(c) *Collection of data.* The choice of method for collecting the data is governed by the subject-matter, the unit of enquiry and the scale of the survey.[1] A study of crowd behaviour would call for observational techniques. For a survey among an educated section of the population—say a professional group—and concerned with a subject of close interest to its members, a mail questionnaire might be adequate. An enquiry among the general population, especially if it entails many complicated questions, would almost certainly call for personal interviewing, which might vary from the standardised, formal technique common in large-scale surveys down to informal conversations. Each method has its advantages and disadvantages.

(d) *Questionnaires.* Nine out of ten social surveys use a questionnaire of some kind and the framing and arrangement of questions is perhaps the most substantial planning task. Practitioners have their experience, common sense and certain general principles to aid them but they cannot rely on theoretical guidance in the same sense as they can in sampling decisions. Yet decisions on the scope of the questionnaire, its layout and printing, the definitions and instructions to go with it and on the wording and order of the questions have to be taken, however non-theoretical the basis.

(e) *Errors.* Every stage of the survey process is a potential source of error. Quite apart from sampling errors—which are the easiest to keep under control and to estimate—inaccuracies may enter through the interviewing, the questions, the editing, the coding, the tabulating and the analysis. Every practitioner is, for instance, aware of the risk of memory errors whenever questions about the past are asked (as they often are) and this is only one of many kinds of "response errors". In planning a survey one must try to anticipate the likely sources of error and take what precautions are possible to minimise them.

(f) *Fieldwork.* The quality of interviewers is of obvious importance

[1] The "unit of enquiry" is the unit, e.g. individual or household, about which information is required. It may or may not be the same as the sampling unit. One may pick a sample of individuals and ask them about the composition of the household—the sampling unit is the individual, the unit of enquiry the household.

in field surveys, and there is still a good deal of discussion on the merits of different types of interviewers and methods of selecting and training them. Every survey organisation must establish its policy on these questions, on the basis of its experience or internal research. The solitary research worker may have to use whatever field staff he can get.

Many organisational problems are bound up with fieldwork, more especially in recruiting field staff. There are the alternatives of employing full-time or part-time interviewers; of paying time-rates or piece-rates; of paying all interviewers equally or giving more to the more experienced workers, for difficult assignments or for especially good work; of briefing centrally or locally. The extent and method of field supervision has to be decided, and the checks to be made on the honesty and efficiency of interviewers.

(g) *Processing and analysis.* Although the fieldwork is the central stage of a survey, an enormous amount of work remains to be done after it. When the questionnaires come in, they must be scrutinised for errors, omissions and ambiguous classifications, before they are ready for coding and tabulation. Finally comes the analysis (usually involving statistical calculations), the interpretation of results and the preparation of the report.

This phase, like the fieldwork itself, must be considered in the planning if smooth running of a survey is to be ensured. An editing scheme should be devised, together with code lists and some tentative ideas for tabulation plans. It pays to write down in advance a list of the tabulations that are likely to be required—though it is foolish to suggest that tabulation plans can be drawn up in their entirety in the planning stages of a survey. More often than not, and certainly if the subject is of any complexity, many of the tabulations and analyses cannot be decided upon until one begins to handle the results.

(h) *Documents.* Once the above issues are settled the time is ripe for the final drafting and printing of documents. These include questionnaires, questionnaire instructions, interview record sheets, interviewer manuals and instructions, authorisation cards, time and expense sheets.

(i) *Timing, cost and staffing.* Problems of timing and organisation are so special to each survey that a general discussion serves little purpose. Decisions on the timing of the enquiry—in so far as there is room for choice—are governed by seasonal factors, the time at which the results are needed and so on. To chose an "unrepresentative" time for a survey may be as serious a defect as to study an unrepresentative sample. Once the date is fixed, it remains to set up a schedule for the completion of the various stages, and an estimate of their costs. These will include printing, sample selection, fieldwork (including travelling and subsistence) or mailing, processing and tabulating, preparation of the report, and overheads, in so far as they apply.

As regards the personnel to be used in social research surveys, there is much to be said for calling in several specialists. Various skills go to the making of a survey, and typically the sociologist, the psychologist and the statistician all have something to contribute. I am not necessarily arguing that team is always better than individual research; the former can involve hours of fruitless discussion and lead to disjointed research. But if the modern survey apparatus, as described in this book, is to be brought into action, it is well to make use of expert advice, especially regarding sampling problems and statistical analysis. And it is important that the statistician should be called in at the beginning of the survey, not at the end. Most statisticians are familiar with the request to look at a quantity of completed questionnaires "to see what he can make of the data". Too often the reply must be that, because of insufficiency of numbers, flaws in the design, faults in the questions or other avoidable mistakes, very little can be made of them.[1]

3.3. Pre-tests and Pilot Surveys

This brief catalogue of planning problems makes one thing plain: it is exceedingly difficult to plan a survey without a good deal of knowledge of its subject-matter, the population it is to cover, the way people will react to questions and, paradoxical though it sounds, even the answers they are likely to give. How is one to estimate how long the survey will take, how many interviewers will be needed, how much money it will cost, if one has not *done* some part of it? How, without trial interviews, can one be sure that the questions will be as meaningful to the average respondent as to the survey expert? How is one to decide which questions are worth asking at all?

Common sense suggests the necessity of doing a few test interviews or sending out trial forms by way of preparing for the main survey, and such informal trial and error is as much part of the preliminary study as are talks with experts and study of the literature. But it is necessary to go further, and to try out systematically all the various features of the main enquiry. This may take the form, first, of a series of small "pre-tests" on isolated problems of the design; and then, when the broad plan of the enquiry is established, of a pilot survey, a small-scale replica of the main survey.

The pilot survey is the dress rehearsal and, like a theatrical dress rehearsal, it will have been preceded by a series of preliminary tests

---

[1] A paper by Finney on "The Statistician and the Planning of Field Experiments" [79] contains much of relevance to the statistician's role in social surveys.

and trials. Pre-tests and pilot surveys are standard practice with professional survey bodies and are widely used in research surveys. Specifically,[1] they provide guidance on:

(i) The adequacy of the sampling frame from which it is proposed to select the sample. The features of some much-used frames—e.g. the register of electors—are well known but, if a less familiar one is to be used, its completeness, accuracy, adequacy, up-to-dateness and convenience should be tested.

One might be planning to use the pay roll of workers in a factory as the basis for drawing a sample. It is just as well then to give it a try beforehand—it may not be in convenient order or it may exclude some workers (e.g. those temporarily on leave) whom the survey is to include or cards may be temporarily removed from it when required for some other purpose. Whether or not such defects can be overcome is another matter; what is vital is to be aware of them before starting on the survey.

(ii) The variability (with regard to the subject under investigation) within the population to be surveyed. This is of vital importance in determining the sample design and we shall see later that the very decision on sample size requires some knowledge of the variability of the population. Suppose that a survey were being designed to find out the average weekly rent paid by the workers in a factory. The size of the sample needed to achieve the required precision would depend on how much variation there was in rent expenditure. Putting the point in extreme simplicity: if all the workers spent exactly 45s. a week (i.e. variability between them were zero) a sample of 1 would suffice to give all the required precision; if, on the other hand, the variability of expenditures were high (i.e. rents ranging from, say, 20s. to 60s. per week) a relatively large sample would be required to provide a sufficiently precise estimate. Thus it is clear that in order to decide on the sampling plan it is helpful, to say the least, to possess some prior knowledge of the population to be sampled; if this is lacking a pilot survey or informal enquiries may be used to provide it.

(iii) The non-response rate to be expected. The probable numbers of refusals and non-contacts can be roughly estimated from the pilot survey (and, partially, from pre-tests) and the effectiveness of various ways of reducing non-response can be compared. As a result, one data-collecting method may be chosen in preference to another, some questions may be excluded, the timing of interviews may be altered and so on.

One may, for example, be debating whether to collect data from a

[1] I shall not attempt to state definitively which functions belong to the pre-test and which to the pilot survey, since much will depend on the circumstances of the enquiry.

widely dispersed population by mail or by interview. The former is cheaper, but will it achieve an adequate response? Prior experimentation can provide the answer. Or one may be wondering what effect payment of respondents would have on the response rate; again preliminary study can help one to find out.

(iv) The suitability of the method of collecting the data. Alternative methods—observation, mail questionnaires, interviewers—are available and one needs data on their relative cost, accuracy and likely response-rates to make a sensible choice. The pre-tests and the pilot survey can also show whether the interviewers are doing an efficient job, whether too great a strain is placed on them or on the respondents and whether the interviews should be subjected to more checks.

(v) The adequacy of the questionnaire. This is probably the most valuable function of the pilot survey. The questionnaire will previously have been tested informally on colleagues and friends, but the pre-tests and the pilot survey offer a way of trying it with the kind of interviewers and respondents to be used in the main survey. Several points will have to be watched—the ease of handling the questionnaire in the field, the efficiency of its layout, the clarity of the definitions and, of course, the adequacy of the questions themselves. Is the wording simple, clear, direct, unambiguous, free from technical terms? Are there signs that some people are misunderstanding them or are insufficiently informed to give sensible answers, or that, perhaps for prestige reasons, they are answering inaccurately? Do the answers suggest that too much strain is being put on people's memories?

It is not easy to give rules for recognising questions containing such weaknesses. Sometimes the true distribution of answers is known, in which case major deviations from it are a warning that something is wrong with either sample or question. Too great a bunching of answers at one extreme *may* be indicative of a leading question, or it may mean that people are giving stereotyped answers. A substantial number of "Don't know" replies is often (though not necessarily) a bad sign—suggesting a vague question, one using uncommon words or going outside the respondent's experience. Such defects would lead also to a large number of "Don't understand" comments which, together with other reactions in the field, should be reported by interviewers. If people surround their answers with many qualifications, it may be that the questions could be improved. If many refuse to answer a particular question, possibly the order of questions should be altered so that the offending one is introduced more delicately, possibly it should be cut out altogether. Almost the most useful evidence of all on the adequacy of a questionnaire is the individual fieldworker's report on how the interviews went, what difficulties were encountered, what alterations should be made, and so forth.

(vi) The efficiency of the instructions and general briefing of interviewers. A scrutiny of the completed trial questionnaires may show that interviewers did not put a ring round the "not applicable" code when a question did not apply; that they omitted their own identity number from the questionnaire; that they did not comment on the course and success of each interview. Instructions were then clearly inadequate or the interviewers were doing a poor job. The pre-tests and pilot survey are of course themselves part of the interviewer training.

(vii) The codes chosen for pre-coded questions (see Chapter 12). Without the pilot survey it is often hard to decide on the alternative answers to be allowed for in the coding. One may wish to ask "What labour-saving appliances do you have in your home?" and to print all —or as many as one can think of—the possible answers on the questionnaire. In the pilot survey, this can be asked as an "open" question, all the replies being recorded verbatim; these may call to mind some appliances one might have overlooked.

(viii) The probable cost and duration of the main survey and of its various stages. If it appears that the survey will take too long or be too expensive, the pilot survey can be valuable in suggesting where economies can be made. The cost data will also have a bearing on the sample design.

(ix) The efficiency of the organisation in the field, in the office, and in the communication between the two.

The pilot survey will certainly help to clarify many of the problems left unsolved by previous tests, but it will not necessarily throw up *all* the troubles of the main survey; the much bigger scale of this is almost a guarantee of snags and headaches of which the pilot survey gave no warning.[1] However, a pilot survey nearly always results in major alterations to the questionnaire and a general increase in efficiency of the enquiry. It also has another use. Once the pilot survey is over, the research worker should ask himself whether, in the light of its results, the main survey is still worth carrying out as planned. There are cases in which an intelligent reading of the pilot survey evidence would lead him to take a more modest view of the main survey's potentialities; to see that some of the objectives are not worth pursuing because people are unwilling or unable to give accurate in-

---

[1] The surveyor unfortunately cannot foresee everything. The pilot survey for a recent national enquiry experienced a response rate of over 80 per cent; the main survey unluckily coincided with a widespread railway strike and with some adverse publicity for another survey and, whether for these or other reasons, achieved a response rate of less than 70 per cent.

formation; to realise that he cannot cover as wide a field of enquiry or population as planned. The pilot survey is thus the researcher's last safeguard against the possibility that the main survey may be ineffective.

The size and design of the pilot survey is a matter of convenience, time and money. It should be large enough to fulfil the above functions and the sample should ideally be of a comparable structure to that of the main survey; in practice it is rarely feasible for it to be as widespread as the main sample.

The design will be influenced by another factor. We have seen that the pilot survey helps to guide the choice between alternative methods of collecting the data, ordering the questions, wording and so forth. It should be designed, therefore, so as to ensure a strict testing of these alternatives. If two forms of a question are to be compared, each should be tried out on an equivalent (random) sample of respondents; otherwise the difference in answers between the two samples would be mixed up with differences between the samples themselves. If many types of comparisons are to be made simultaneously—between interviewers, questions, non-response methods, instructions and so on—this calls for strict methods of experimental design, such as were mentioned in section 1.5. These remarks apply equally to pre-tests.

NOTES ON READING

Readers may find useful a concise statement on the planning of surveys prepared by the U.S. BUREAU OF THE BUDGET [273]. Most of the books mentioned at the end of Chapter 1 have relevant chapters and I recommend PARTEN [202] for its concentration on practical details barely touched upon here.

CHAPTER 4

THE COVERAGE OF SURVEYS

4.1. Definition of the Population

T HE METHODOLOGICAL problems of surveys fall into three broad
groups: from whom to collect the information, what methods
to use for collecting it, and how to process, analyse and interpret it. In this chapter, and the four following it, I shall concern
myself with the first of these, namely the coverage of surveys.

The first step always is to define the population[1] to be covered, a
task that is never as easy as it sounds. The geographical delimitation
is often the simplest, although to decide that the survey is to be
limited to, say, England and Wales is still only the beginning. One
has then to decide whether to cover (by sample or otherwise) all parts
of England and Wales or to exclude areas which are thinly populated,
awkward to reach or for any other reason expensive from a fieldwork
point of view. Marginal areas like the Highlands of Scotland, Central
Wales, the Isle of Man can often reasonably be excluded; what
matters is that such exclusions are deliberate and explicit so that the
surveyor does not delude himself—or his client—that his coverage is
wider than in fact it is.

The definition of the population also involves the fixing of limits
other than merely geographical. If the survey is concerned with the
adult population of, say, Birmingham, where is the lower age-limit
to be drawn? Are persons in the Forces to be included? And what
about people living in institutions like hotels, prisons, mental homes
and hospitals? Every survey has its own problems of population definition, and these must be solved explicitly and precisely, with due
regard to what is practical. The surveyor, for instance, may wish to
include the institutional population, but if he finds that all the avail-

[1] I remind the reader that this term is used in its statistical sense, i.e. to denote
the aggregate of units to which the survey results are to apply. It need not,
though of course it often does, refer to a population of human beings. An
alternative term is "universe".

49

able sampling frames exclude it, he has either to compromise by adapting his coverage to that of the frame or to sample the institutional population by other means.

4.2. Complete, Incomplete and Sample Surveys

A population consists of a number of units of enquiry (see p. 42) and the surveyor must decide whether information is to be sought from all or only from some of these units, i.e. whether he should take a census or be satisfied with a sample. Before discussing this choice, I must digress for a moment and define the terms to be used.

The older text-books traditionally kept to this simple dichotomy of sample versus census, the latter term being taken to imply a complete coverage. This usage is actually without etymological justification (the word census derives from the Latin *censere*—to rate) and owes its acceptance to the historical association of the word with population counts, which have generally been complete enumerations. An important deviation from this terminology occurred in 1946, when the Royal Commission on Population conducted its sample enquiry into fertility [93], calling it the *Family Census*. Further emphasis that the term "census" should not be regarded as the antithesis of "sample" was supplied by the title Yates chose for his book on sampling, *Sampling Methods for Censuses and Surveys* [291]. I will broadly follow his terminology here. The distinction between a census and a survey is taken to lie in the *nature of the information* collected. The former term is generally confined to enquiries which are more or less straightforward statistical counts like censuses of population, distribution and production; the term "survey" applies to enquiries which go beyond simple enumerations. The distinction is by no means a hard and fast one, but, fortunately, it need not detain us here, since this book is mainly concerned with the kinds of investigations which one unhesitatingly calls surveys rather than censuses.

What matters much more is the description of the coverage of an enquiry. A survey (or census) should be called *complete* if virtually all the units in the population under study are covered and *incomplete* if a substantial number are arbitrarily excluded; the term *sample survey* (or census) should ideally be used only if the part of the population studied is selected by accepted statistical methods.[1] The words "sample" and "part" of the population are not and should not be treated as synonymous.

The use of the word "incomplete" to describe the coverage of a

[1] Taken strictly, this terminology would mean that one should withhold the word "sampling" from methods such as quota and purposive sampling, which lack the rigour demanded by theory. But this is contrary to common usage and the distinction between theoretically sound and other common sampling methods is better made by the terms suggested on p. 74 below.

survey also needs care. It should be reserved for cases where coverage or representation of a population is intended or implied, but where a part of this population is for some reason not covered. If a sociologist studies a group of 20 arbitrarily selected families the term would be appropriate only if he then claimed that his findings applied to a wider population of families.

So much for termimology. As for the factors that decide the choice between a complete and a partial coverage, in ninety-nine out of a hundred surveys the question does not arise, the populations being so large or dispersed that complete coverage is ruled out by shortage of money, time (especially if the results are required for administrative or policy purposes) or trained manpower. In a research survey into the work and leisure of housewives on three L.C.C. estates, for instance, the number of housewives included was determined solely by the number of interviewers available to do the fieldwork.

Where the research is concerned with a small or compact population—the children in a school, the inhabitants of a village or a housing estate, the workers in a small factory—it may be easy to cover all the members, so again the choice between complete and partial coverage barely arises. But suppose it does. Suppose that one wanted to study the leisure interests of the 3,000 families on a housing estate and that one *had* the resources to interview all the families. Would it be worth while to do so? The answer is almost certainly: "No."

Modern sampling methods make it possible to calculate how many families should be included in order to give results of the required precision—whatever that is—with a given chance of error (see next chapter for a discussion of this point). If this calculation shows that somewhere near 3,000 families are required, then of course a complete coverage *would* be desirable. But this is most unlikely—one would have to require unusually detailed analysis and high precision to need such numbers. More likely, a few hundred families would be sufficient and, if these were selected at random (see Chapter 6), the results obtained would apply to the 3,000 families with a calculable margin of error. There would be no point in going to the expense and trouble of a complete coverage.

But if the survey results are to be generalised in this way, then the part of the population chosen for study should be selected according to the rules of statistical theory. If it is not, inferences from sample to population cannot and must not be made rigorously. It is entirely wrong to make an arbitrary selection of cases, to rely on volunteers or on people who happen to be at hand, and then to claim that they are a proper sample of some particular population. I stress this because some social researchers still generalise uncritically from collec-

c

tions of cases to populations from which they were not properly chosen.

This is not intended to imply that a social survey, in order to be of any value, need be based on sampling methods. A sociologist may prefer to study half-a-dozen arbitrarily selected problem families very intensively, rather than to make a formal and more superficial enquiry among a larger, strictly selected sample of families. The two approaches, as has been said before, accomplish different ends and at their best are complementary. An extensive sample survey provides the quantitative material regarding the population—number of problem families, their size and composition, their main troubles and so on; the emphasis being on the aggregate, not the individual case. Then a small number of families can be picked out and studied intensively as so many case-studies.

Zweig's approach [295] is typical of another kind of investigation which proceeds without rigorous sampling methods. A large number of casual and informal interviews are conducted and their results combined into a report with manifold personal observations of behaviour and habits. Though no claim to strict representativeness is possible, the method, skilfully employed, produces a picture of undoubted sociological interest. It would be impracticable applied to a randomly selected sample.

It is clear that if a survey aims at a complete coverage, no problems of selection arise, while if it is to be confined to a few case-studies, their choice is dictated by availability and willingness of the persons to co-operate rather than by principles of selection. If the approach is akin to that of Zweig, though an effort is indeed made to interview a widely varying set of people, again there are no formal problems of selection. We are left with the large group of surveys in which the research worker wishes to select a part of the population in such a way that he will be able to draw inferences of calculable precision from it to the population. This necessitates the use of sampling and makes this a subject central to survey methodology.

4.3. The Idea and the Advantages of Sampling

The idea of sampling is neither new nor unfamiliar in everyday life. The tea-taster trying different brands of tea, the merchant examining a handful of flour from the sack, the physician making a blood-test—all these are employing the method of sampling. They do so with extreme confidence, because they have good reason to believe that the material they are sampling is so homogeneous and "well mixed" that the sample will adequately represent the whole.

These are somewhat trivial examples of sampling. The roots of modern sampling procedures are found—as Stephan has shown in an extensive historical account [247]—in many diverse fields: demography, agriculture, commerce, economic statistics, social surveys and so forth. Isolated instances of attempts to make representative selections occur a century or more ago, but modern sampling methods have been developed chiefly in the last 30 to 40 years.

The advantages of sampling, as against complete coverage, have become obvious in recent years and need be stated only briefly. In the first place, sampling saves money. It is obviously cheaper to collect answers from 400 families than from 3,000, although the cost *per unit* of study may be higher with a sample than with a complete coverage (partly because more skilled personnel is used, partly because new costs—e.g. sample selection—have to be added, and partly because overhead costs are spread over a smaller number of units).

In the second place, sampling saves labour. A smaller staff is required both for fieldwork and for tabulating and processing the data.

Thirdly, sampling saves time. Its use in the analysis of the 1951 Census of Population shows this. The scale of these censuses is so enormous that formerly it had taken many years to bring out the results, by which time they had inevitably lost some of their interest. In 1951, one per cent of the schedules were extracted for preliminary analysis and summary findings were available in 12 to 18 months.

Added to these practical advantages, a sample coverage often permits a higher overall level of accuracy than a full enumeration. The smaller numbers allow the quality of the fieldstaff to be at a higher level; more checks and tests for accuracy can be afforded at all stages; more care can be given to editing and the analysis. Finally, fewer cases make it possible to collect and deal with more elaborate information from each.

These are all advantages that flow from having to deal with smaller numbers than would be involved in a complete coverage. What gives statistical sampling an advantage over any other way of choosing a part of the population is that, when the estimates of the population characteristics are made from the sample results, the precision of these estimates can also be gauged from the sample results themselves. This crucial point will be explained in the next chapter, while in Chapter 6 different ways of designing samples will be discussed. It will become evident that sample design is often a complicated task. Human populations are nothing if not heterogeneous, far different from the kind of material the tea-taster or doctor are sampling in our simple examples. And not only are human populations very heterogeneous, but they also tend not to be "well mixed", similar types of persons being found in clusters; this tendency must be taken into account in designing samples. The other big difference between the sampler of human populations and the tea-taster—or even the agriculturist—is that the former has little effective control over his sampling units. He has to contend with people who refuse to be drawn into the sample, with others who are not available at the time of drawing and so forth; in other words his best design can be spoilt by non-response. This problem is discussed in Chapter 7.

4.4. The Use of Sampling in Great Britain

The first rigorous application of modern sampling methods to social surveys in Britain occurred in 1912 when, as already noted, Bowley undertook the survey of Reading. His pioneering use of sampling proved a great stimulus to social surveys, which had formerly been based on non-random selection (as with Booth) or on complete surveys (as with Rowntree). The combination of economy and accuracy, characteristic of sampling, appealed to social investigators, and practically all the major surveys of the inter-war years followed Bowley's example.

The first official use of sampling in England—a sample of documents—was in Hilton's 1923 enquiry into *The Personal Circumstances and Industrial History of 10,000 Claimants to Unemployment Benefit* [120]. Care was taken to ensure a representative sample and to avoid possible sources of bias. The sampling procedure was fully described by Hilton and, as Stephan has pointed out [247], it is strange that his methods were not sooner adopted by other Government Departments. It was not until 1937, in fact, that sampling was used in a large-scale official field investigation, the well-known Ministry of Labour enquiry into working-class expenditure [269], mentioned in Chapter 2. The thirties also saw the beginning of B.B.C. Listener Research and of many opinion and market research bodies, developments largely attributable to the possibilities of sampling. It was, however, the war which gave the decisive stimulus, both here and in America, to the use of sampling techniques, especially in government administration; and since then more and more surveys in all fields have utilised them.

There are many examples of official sampling other than those mentioned in Chapter 2. Sampling has been used recently in the census of production—a census concerned with establishments not individuals and, in future, sample surveys of production are to be taken in between the four-yearly censuses. A census of distribution is to be taken every 10 years, and sample surveys two or three times in the interval. The Ministry of Works' surveys of the building industry labour force, the Board of Trade's capital expenditure surveys and the Ministry of Agriculture's earning enquiries are three more examples. Among official enquiries involving the sampling of documents are the Commissioners of Inland Revenue's special income censuses, the Ministry of Labour's age-analysis of employed persons, the population estimates of the Ministry of National Insurance and, of course, the 1951 Census of Population.

With such extensive official use of sampling, one may ask whether there is ever a case for a complete census or survey? The population census is often cited as one requiring complete coverage and, while there is indeed a case to be made for this, it is not the one usually argued: namely that it is useful periodically to know population numbers and so forth with complete accuracy. The fact is that "complete coverage" and "complete accuracy" are illusory concepts, never attained in practice because of the many types of error that enter into any enquiry: errors of interviewing, response, coding, recording and tabulating among others.

The main justification for a complete coverage in the population census is the need for adequate numbers for analysis in the individual regions, conurbations, towns and rural districts for which results are required. In other words, a complete coverage may be desirable to ensure that the numbers in the small areas are sufficient for their purpose, not because of any particular merit in the idea of completeness itself.

This argument applies most forcibly to the estimates of population size and the other major demographic data. For some of the other figures collected—e.g. number of households having fixed baths—less accuracy might, however, suffice; if so, *these* questions might be addressed to a sample of the population, even though others are asked of everybody. This is an example of multi-phase sampling (see Section 6.6), as used in the United States Population Census. It should be seriously considered for the 1961 census in Great Britain.

NOTES ON READING

1. The book by YATES [291] is recommended as the best general book on sampling. The first five chapters are not technically difficult.

2. Among the text-books recommended at the end of Chapter 1, JAHODA, DEUTSCH and COOK [129], GOODE and HATT [97] and FESTINGER and KATZ [78] have particularly useful discussions of survey coverage.

3. Accounts of the history of modern sampling methods are given by SENG [228] and by STEPHAN [247].

4. Accounts of the use of sampling in Great Britain are given by MOSER [189, 193]. The UNITED NATIONS STATISTICAL OFFICE periodically publishes summaries of sample surveys carried out all over the world [271].

5. Many of the developments in sample design and practice have taken place in the United States and the book in two volumes by HANSEN, HURWITZ and MADOW [112] contains most of the important material and references. The second of the two volumes deals with the theory and therefore requires of the reader fairly advanced mathematical facility.

CHAPTER 5

BASIC IDEAS OF SAMPLING

5.1. Introduction

M Y AIM in this chapter is to explain in fairly general terms the principles underlying sampling theory. I do not attempt to present the theory itself in rigorous terms, to derive formulae or to bring in all the refinements of which the sample designer should be aware.[1] In fact, I have in mind less the needs of the sample designer than those of the student or research worker who wants to know something about basic principles.

Only a few technical expressions need be used. One much-used pair of terms distinguishes between "attributes" and "variables".[2] If one simply notes for each individual whether he possesses or does not possess a certain characteristic—blue eyes, a T.V. set, a given opinion on equal pay—this characteristic may be called an attribute. Quantification then lies in *counting* how many possess this attribute and how many do not. Alternatively, one may be interested in the actual magnitude of some variable characteristic for each sample member—his age, height and income, for example; then quantification involves *measuring* the magnitude of the characteristic in each case.

The distinction between attributes and variables is not as fundamental as is sometimes suggested. A variable can always be transformed into an attribute by a broad grouping: the variable "age", taking values, say, from 21 upwards can be turned into an attribute by dividing into, say, "21 to 45" and "46 and over". Conversely, any attribute can be changed into a variable by allocating the score "1" to all who possess the attribute and "0" to those who do not. Suppose that 40 out of 100 people have blue eyes; the proportion with this attribute would then be 0·4. One could treat this as a variable,

---

[1] I also confine myself for simplicity to "large" samples—see p. 71 below.

[2] Other terms for this dichotomy are qualitative and quantitative or enumeration and measurement data. Attributes are also, for reasons implied in the following paragraph, called 0–1 variables.

scoring 0 for those who do not have blue eyes, and 1 for those who do. The average of this variable for the 100 people is

$$\frac{(60 \times 0) + (40 \times 1)}{100} = \cdot 4$$

The distinction is thus not basic, nor does the *logic* of sampling theory differ in the two cases. In this chapter the ideas of sampling will be explained mainly with reference to variables, but this is only a matter of convenience.

One other pair of terms must be explained—"statistic" and "parameter". The former refers to the value of a variable (or attribute) calculated *from a sample*, the latter to the value of the variable (or attribute) *in the population*, which one is trying to estimate. Thus, if a sample of households is selected in order to estimate average expenditure on rent in a district, the sample average is a "statistic", and the (unknown) population average a "parameter".

5.2. Estimation and Testing of Hypotheses

It is helpful to distinguish two objectives of sample surveys:

(*a*) The main purpose is generally to *estimate* certain population parameters—the average[1] age of students in a college, the proportion of workers in a factory working overtime and so on. A sample is selected and the relevant statistic (average or proportion) calculated and an estimate of the corresponding population parameter is then made on the basis of this statistic. But, anticipating a later point, since all sample results are subject to sampling errors, it is necessary to accompany this estimate with a statement about its own precision. As we shall see, this statement is made in terms of what is called a "standard error".

(*b*) A second possible purpose may be to *test a statistical hypothesis* about a population—e.g. the hypothesis that at least 25 per cent of the households in a town have T.V. sets. A sample of households is selected and the proportion possessing sets calculated; it emerges that 19 per cent have T.V. sets. The question now is whether the sample result is such as to discredit the hypothesis or whether it lends support to it. To answer this, one needs a criterion by which the deviation of the sample result from the hypothetical value can be judged; this criterion again is found in the measure of precision mentioned in the previous paragraph.

[1] Throughout this book, the terms "average" and "mean" refer to the arithmetic mean of a number of observations, i.e. $\bar{x} = \frac{1}{n} \sum_{i=1}^{n} x_1$ is the sum of the values of x divided by the number of items. $\sum_{i=1}^{n}$ denotes summation over the n items.

These two objectives, estimation and testing hypotheses, though they lead to distinct parts of statistical theory, are far from unconnected, and the link which concerns us here is the mechanism by which both are accomplished: the standard error. Since the first purpose—estimation—is far the more common in social surveys, most of the ensuing discussion will be illustrated in terms of it.

But two points of fundamental importance must first be emphasised. For one thing, statements based on sample results are always probability statements. A decision to cover only a sample, rather than every member, of a population means leaving the field of description and certainty and entering that of inference and probability. An extreme illustration will make this point clear. Suppose a survey in a factory employing 3,000 workers is conducted to estimate the proportion of workers who smoke cigarettes. If coverage is complete, i.e. if *every* worker is interviewed, and 1,500 are found to be cigarette smokers, one can state as a fact that the proportion of smokers in the population is 50 per cent. But if we had interviewed only 2,998 of the workers and found 1,499, that is 50 per cent, to be cigarette smokers, the proportion in the whole population, i.e. the 3,000 workers, would still be taken as 50 per cent, but this would be an estimate and not a statement of fact. Knowledge regarding some of the population members would be lacking; any conclusion about the population must be given in terms of probability.

Secondly, it must be emphasised that the principles outlined in this chapter rest on the assumption that a random method of selection (or, in American terminology, probability sampling—see Chapter 6) is employed. A random method is one with which each member of the population has a known chance of being selected into the sample. To a sample selected by non-random methods the theory and its convenient consequences cannot be applied.

5.3. Accuracy, Bias and Precision

The basic ideas of sampling are best made clear by considering a small model population and confining ourselves to what is called *simple random sampling*—a method of selection whereby each possible sample of n units from a population of N units has an *equal* chance of being selected. Let us assume that the population consists of four members aged 15, 17, 18 and 22 respectively, so that the mean age of the population (μ) is 18.[1] A sample of 2 is to be drawn ($n = 2$) with the object of estimating μ.

Suppose that the draw results in the selection of the members aged

[1] I am ignoring the possibility that this may in itself not be the "true" value, since people may give wrong information etc. All that matters here is that it is the value we would get if the survey covered everybody.

15 and 18. The sample mean (denoted by $\bar{x}$) is therefore 16·5, and this is taken as the estimate of μ, the population mean. Since, in this constructed example, we know that μ is 18, we are in a position to say that the estimate is *inaccurate*.[1] Had the selection fallen upon the two members aged 18 and 22, the estimate of μ would have been 20, which is even less accurate. Had it been the two aged 17 and 18, the estimate would have been 17·5 which is very close. The accuracy of a sample estimate refers to its closeness to the correct population value and since, normally speaking, the latter is not known, the actual accuracy of the sample estimate cannot usually be assessed, though its *probable* accuracy—which we term "precision" can be. This is explained below.

Let us now consider *all* the samples of size $n = 2$ that could have been selected from this population. It is assumed that sampling is *without replacement:* having selected the member aged 15, we select the second sample member from the remaining three (the first member is not "replaced in" the population and given a chance to be selected a second time). Here are the six possible samples and the estimate of μ derived from each:

Possible samples of $n=2$ (Ages of members selected)	$\bar{x}$ (*i.e.* EST *of* μ)
15 and 17	16
15 and 18	16·5
15 and 22	18·5
17 and 18	17·5
17 and 22	19·5
18 and 22	20
Total	108·0

If we imagine this process continued indefinitely, each of the above samples will be drawn over and over again. The distribution formed by the value of $\bar{x}$ derived from this infinite number of samples is called *the sampling distribution of the mean*—a logical enough term since it is a distribution of the means obtained from an infinite number of samples. Now, with simple random sampling, each of the six samples by definition has an equal chance of being selected and, therefore, in the long run occurs an equal number of times; the average of the estimates derived from all the possible samples is then $108/6 = 18$, which is equal to the population mean μ.

The average of the estimates of a population parameter derived from an infinite number of samples is called the *expected value of the estimate* (to be denoted by m). If this expected value is equal to the

[1] The term "accuracy" is sometimes used to refer to the size of the standard error (see below), but for this the term "precision" seems preferable and is used here.

population parameter—as in this case—the sampling procedure is called *unbiased;* if not, it is called *biased.*[1] The difference between the expected value and the true population value is termed the bias. An example of biased sampling would be the case where the population member aged 15 can never be found. The possible pairs would then be 17 and 18, 17 and 22, and 18 and 22, giving values of $\bar{x} = 17 \cdot 5$, $19 \cdot 5$ and 20 respectively. The expected value—still assuming simple random sampling—is now 19 which is higher than the true mean; the bias is 1.

It is important to understand that any one sample may give an inaccurate estimate of the population value, even though the sampling procedure is unbiased. Indeed, in the above example, every one of the six estimates was inaccurate although the process was unbiased: *on average*, however, the sample estimates equalled the population mean. It was correct to speak of the estimate of the population mean derived from the first sample ($\bar{x} = 16$) both as *inaccurate* (because $\mu = 18$) *and unbiased* (because the expected value of the estimate equalled the population mean). Conversely, a procedure that is biased may produce an individual sample that gives an accurate estimate. The term bias, in this statistical sense, refers to the long run, not to the correctness of a single sample.

I now pass on to another principle illustrated by the simple model. Although the sampling was random and unbiased, the estimates all differed somewhat from each other and from μ. This is not surprising for, as each estimate rests on only a sample of the observations, they are almost certain to differ from each other. Now, in practice, the estimate of the population parameter is of course based on only *one* sample and, at first sight, the fact that any two samples are likely to produce different estimates, makes this sound a risky procedure. In fact it is not, since one can estimate *from any one randomly selected sample* (as long as it contains at least two items) how big these differences, or sampling fluctuations as they are called, are likely to be *on average*.

What is needed is a measure of the extent to which the estimates derived from different samples are likely to differ from each other; in other words, a measure of the spread of the sampling distribution. The most usual measure of the spread of any distribution is the standard deviation (or its square, the variance).[2] The standard de-

---

[1] The "unbiasedness" here is due to the fact that simple random sampling was assumed.

[2] If there are n values x_i—$x_1, x_2 \ldots x_n$—then the standard deviation is defined as

$$\sigma = \sqrt{\frac{\sum\limits_{i=1}^{n}(x_i - \bar{x})^2}{n}}$$

where $\bar{x}$ is the arithmetic mean of the n values.

viation of the sampling distribution above, calculated from the figures on p. 59, is therefore

$$\left\{ \sqrt{ \begin{aligned} [(16-18)^2 + (16 \cdot 5 - 18)^2 + (18 \cdot 5 - 18)^2 + (17 \cdot 5 - 18)^2 \\ + (19 \cdot 5 - 18)^2 + (20 - 18)^2]/6 \end{aligned} } \right\}$$
$$= \sqrt{2 \cdot 16} = 1 \cdot 47$$

This important measure is called the *standard error of the mean* and is a suitable criterion of the variability of the various sample estimates, that is of the probable accuracy or *precision* of any one estimate. We shall henceforth call it $S.E._{\bar{x}}$ and its square, the sampling variance of the mean, $V_{\bar{x}}$.[1]

$S.E._{\bar{x}}$ can be represented by the following formula, and it can be estimated from a single sample:

$$S.E._{\bar{x}} = \sqrt{ \frac{\sigma^2}{n} \cdot \frac{N-n}{N-1} } \qquad \ldots(5.1)[2]$$

where $\sigma =$ the standard deviation (of ages, say) in the population[3]

$N =$ the number of units in the population
$n =$ the number of units in the sample.

If the population is very large relative to the sample, the factor $\sqrt{\dfrac{N-n}{N-1}}$, which is called the finite population correction (f.p.c.), approximates to unity and can reasonably be omitted. If the entire population is included in the "sample", the f.p.c. becomes zero and so, logically, does the standard error. Generally speaking, the f.p.c. can be ignored without much loss if the sample does not exceed about 10 per cent of the population.

In the present example, it clearly cannot be ignored and we calculate the standard error from (5.1), with $N = 4$, $n = 2$ and

$$\sigma^2 = \frac{(15-18)^2 + (17-18)^2 + (18-18)^2 + (22-18)^2}{4} = 6 \cdot 5$$

Therefore $\qquad S.E._{\bar{x}} = \sqrt{ \frac{6 \cdot 5}{2} \cdot \frac{4-2}{4-1} } = \sqrt{2 \cdot 16} = 1 \cdot 47$

which agrees with the previous result.

To summarise the distinction between accuracy, bias, and precision:

---

[1] The terms "sampling error" and "standard error" are often used interchangeably. It seems preferable to use the former to describe the *class* of errors caused by sampling, and the latter (or sampling variance, as the case may be) for the actual measures defined above.

[2] This is the formula for a simple random sample and has to be modified for more elaborate sample structures.

[3] In the present constructed example σ happens to be known. Normally it has to be estimated from the sample—see p. 66.

(i) The estimate derived from any one sample is *inaccurate* to the extent that it differs from the population parameter. In our notation, $(\bar{x} - \mu)$ measures the accuracy of an estimate of the mean. In practice, μ is generally unknown so that the *actual* deviation of a sample estimate from it cannot be measured. What can be measured is the *probable* magnitude of the deviation—see (iii) below.

(ii) A sampling procedure is *unbiased* (*biased*) if the mean of the estimates derived from all possible samples equals (does not equal) the population parameter. The former is called the expected value of the estimate and is here denoted by m; $(m - \mu)$ is the measure of bias. In practice, although m can always be calculated theoretically, μ is generally unknown, so that it may be difficult or impossible to assess the bias.

(iii) The sample designer will try to use unbiased methods of selection and, generally speaking, of estimation.[1] But even if he succeeds, the individual sample may result in an *inaccurate* estimate and, as noted above, the actual extent of inaccuracy will almost certainly not be known. This would be rather an unsatisfactory situation were it not for the fact that one can estimate from the sample how *probable* it is that the degree of inaccuracy is of any particular magnitude. This is a much simplified definition of what is meant by the *precision* of an estimate, further discussed below.

Bias and precision thus relate to distinct aspects of a sampling procedure, a point which is well illustrated in diagrammatic form (Fig. I), as adapted from Deming [50, p. 20].

In (A) and (B) there is large bias, the expected value of the procedure differing considerably from the population value: the difference between (A) and (B) is that in the former the estimates vary widely around their mean, as would be reflected in a large standard error, while in (B) they are more closely bunched around it. (C) and (D) are both unbiased, since the expected value is equal to the population value; they differ in that (C) has relatively lower precision. It can be taken that (D), which is unbiased and relatively precise, is the ideal while (A) is to be avoided. In practice, the choice is not as simple as this and there are circumstances in which a sample designer might be prepared to put up with some bias if thereby he can markedly increase precision.

The diagram shows that the standard error measures the fluctuations of the estimates around their own mean, that is around the expected value, not around the population value. If the two coincide, as in (C) and (D), it comes to the same thing; but, if they do not—if

[1] See Yates [291] or Cochran [36] for a discussion of different methods of estimation. Here it is assumed throughout that unbiased methods are used.

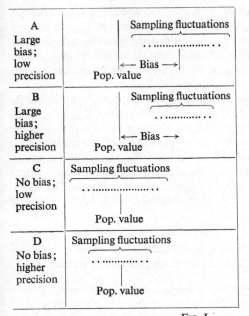

NOTE

(1) The dots represent estimates (of whatever variable is under consideration) derived from repeated application of the given survey procedures; i.e. they represent the sampling distribution of the estimates and their mean is the expected value.

(2) The population value is what the survey is trying to estimate.

(3) The terms "large", "low" etc. used in the panels are, of course, relative.

Fig. I

the method is biased (either through the selection or the estimation procedure)—such bias will *not* be included in the standard error.

There is a measure, called the *mean square error*, which combines sampling variance and bias; in our notation this is

$$MSE = V_{\bar{x}} + (\mu - m)^2 \qquad \ldots(5.2)$$

showing that the variability around the population value, (i.e. *MSE*) is equal to that around the expected value ($V_{\bar{x}}$) plus the square of the bias. If the latter could be estimated, *MSE* would be a better measure than the standard error for assessing the efficiency of a sample.

The avoidance of bias in the sampling procedure is discussed later and we must now look more closely at the question of precision. To extend the discussion of sampling distributions and standard errors, we abandon the small-scale model and use a more life-like illustration.

5.4. Sampling Distributions and Standard Errors

Let us suppose that the population to be covered consists of the 3,000 students in a college and that the purpose of the survey is to estimate their average age (μ). A sample of 150 students is randomly selected and their mean age ($\bar{x}_1$) calculated. The 150 cases are then "returned to the population" and a second sample of 150 students is drawn by the same procedure and their mean age ($\bar{x}_2$) calculated. Both means are estimates of μ. If this process is continued for an infinite number of samples, the distribution of all the estimates is the so-called sampling distribution of the mean, which we have already encountered.

But how does this theoretical concept of the distribution of an infinite number of samples help in assessing the precision of an estimate derived from a single sample, which is all one would have in practice? To answer this, let us assume that 1,000 samples of 150 students each have been taken and a value of $\bar{x}$ obtained from each; although this is not an infinite number of samples, the distribution for such a large number of samples will closely approximate to the sampling distribution. It might look something like column (a) in Table 5.1, showing

TABLE 5.1

Three hypothetical distributions of estimates of the mean age of 3,000 students, obtained from 1,000 random samples of 150 students each

Estimate of mean age	Number of samples (a)	(b)	(c)
18–	10	60	—
19–	10	70	—
20–	30	80	—
21–	100	90	—
22–	190	100	200
23–	290	140	600
24–	240	130	200
25–	70	120	—
26–	50	110	—
27–	10	100	—
Total	1,000	1,000	1,000
Average	23·5	23·5	23·5
Standard Deviation	1·6	2·6	0·6

that ten samples produced estimates between 18 and 19, ten samples gave estimates between 19 and 20 and so forth. The average of all the estimates is 23·5 which, with simple random sampling, would be very close to μ (not necessarily equal to it since only 1,000 samples were taken, not an infinite number). We see that some of the samples give results far away from this value, others are close to it; some err on the high side, some on the low. Our one real-life sample may be any one of these and we would not know where in the sampling distribution it fell, i.e. how inaccurate its estimate was. But what our theoretical knowledge of the sampling distribution does tell us is what deviations from its mean—that is, to all intents and purposes, from the population parameter—are likely in the long run. In other words, it enables us to assess the probability of a deviation of any given size.

Column (a) is fairly typical of the sampling distribution of a mean, with a strong peak at the centre and a fair spread on either side. Columns (b) and (c) show other distributions that might have been obtained; in (b) the estimates derived from the samples differ very widely, in (c) they are closely bunched together. It is evident from these that the chance of any one sample estimate being close to μ depends on how widely dispersed all the estimates are, in fact on the spread of the sampling distribution. If this spread is high, as in (b), any one estimate is likely to be a long way out. If, to take the opposite extreme, the estimates are closely bunched around their mean, as in (c), no one estimate is likely to be far from μ.

What is here called the *precision* of a sample estimate thus depends on the spread of the sampling distribution, and this is conveniently measured by its own standard deviation, i.e. by the standard error. If the sample statistic in question is the mean, then the relevant distribution is the "sampling distribution of the mean", the relevant standard error the "standard error of the mean"; if it is a proportion, the terms are "sampling distribution of the proportion" and "standard error of the proportion". We will for the moment continue to keep the discussion to the case of the mean.

The formula for the standard error of the mean was given on p. 61; leaving aside the f.p.c., we note that it is based on the two factors on which one would expect the precision of a sample estimate to depend:

(a) the value of *n*, i.e. *sample size*. Common sense suggests that one will get more precise results from a large than from a small sample; formula (5.1) shows that the standard error varies inversely to the square root of *n*—that is, to halve the standard error requires (other things being equal) four times as big a sample.

(b) the value of σ, i.e. *variability in the population*. This also accords with common sense. If the 3,000 students are all aged exactly 23, any sample will estimate the population mean with complete precision. The population standard deviation, σ, would be zero and so, from formula (5.1), would the standard error. If, on the other hand, the ages of the 3,000 vary over a wide range, the estimation of the population mean from one sample is much more "chancy"; this will be reflected in a widely spread sampling distribution (say, like (b) in Table 5.1) and therefore a large standard error.

There remains one difficulty in the use of formula (5.1), that we rarely know the value of σ. We get around this problem by substituting for σ the standard deviation of ages calculated from the *sample* (to be called s), and then estimating the standard error from the formula accordingly.[1] One must keep a clear distinction, though, between the true sampling error and this, its estimate. We shall generally give the latter, denoting it by expressions like

$$(\text{EST})\ S.E._{\bar{x}} \quad \text{or} \quad (\text{EST})\ \text{Var}_{\bar{x}}$$

The question now is how estimates of standard errors are to be interpreted. Suppose that we have a sample of 150 students, that their mean age is 21 and that s (calculated as shown in the footnote) is 12; the standard error of the mean is then estimated by

$$(\text{EST})\ S.E._{\bar{x}} = \sqrt{\frac{144}{150}} = 0{\cdot}98$$

(ignoring the finite population correction). What does this figure tell one about the precision of the sample estimate? A standard error measures the average (squared) deviation of all possible estimates from their mean; we are interested, as noted above, in the probability of deviations of particular size occurring or, in other words, in the probability that the one sample mean we happen to have obtained falls in any particular range of the sampling distribution. Before we can utilise the standard error concept, therefore, something needs to be said about the shape of sampling distributions and about what are termed confidence (or probability) levels.

The hypothetical distribution of column (*a*) in Table 5.1 closely approximates to the shape of what is called the *normal distribution* as shown in Fig. II. It is an important fact that, with reasonably large samples, the sampling distributions of many statistics (e.g. the mean, the proportion) approximate to the normal distribution and that this approximation holds even when the population itself is asymmetrical. That is, even if the ages of the 3,000 students were distributed quite asymmetrically (there being, say, a very large number at the young ages and small numbers at all the higher ages), the distribution of *means* from an infinite number of samples from this population will still be approximately normal in shape. The larger the samples, the closer will this approximation tend to be.

[1] If the sample observations are $x_1, x_2 \ldots x_n$, then $s^2 = \frac{1}{n}\sum_{i=1}^{n}(x_i - \bar{x})^2$; it can be shown that, though this is not an unbiased estimator of σ^2, $s^2 = \frac{1}{n-1}\sum_{i=1}^{n}(x_i - \bar{x})^2$ is. Therefore, in making the convenient substitution mentioned in the text, s should be calculated by using the divisor $(n-1)$ rather than n. If the samples are at all large, this makes virtually no difference.

The approximation of many sampling distributions to normality is highly convenient, since the characteristics of the normal distribution are precisely known. It is distributed symmetrically about its mean, with a large number of small deviations from the mean and few large ones. If its standard deviation (let us call it σ') is calculated and perpendicular lines are drawn at a distance of σ' on either side of the mean, then we know that the area enclosed between these lines will comprise approximately 68 per cent of the total area under the curve. Similarly, the area enclosed by lines drawn at a distance of $2\sigma'$ either side of the mean is approximately 95 per cent of the whole, that between the mean and $\pm 2 \cdot 6\sigma'$ approximately 99 per cent of the whole area. This is illustrated in Fig. II.

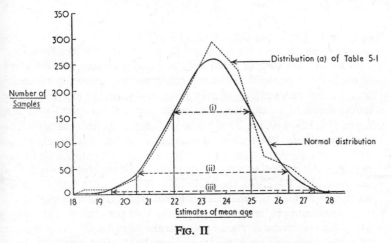

Fig. II

(i) These vertical lines are drawn at *one* standard deviation either side of the mean and enclose approx. 68 per cent of the area under the curve.
(ii) These vertical lines are drawn at *two* standard deviations either side of the mean and enclose approx. 95 per cent of the area under the curve.
(iii) These vertical lines are drawn at 2·6 standard deviations either side of the mean and enclose approx. 99 per cent of the area under the curve.

What is the relevance of all this in the present context? If a particular sampling distribution is known to be approximately normal in shape, we are able to say that about 68 per cent of the sample estimates of which it is comprised will lie between its mean and one standard error, about 95 per cent between its mean and twice the standard error, and so on. Tables enable us to look up the exact figures for any limits chosen.

In practice, this knowledge is utilised by putting our statement about population estimates in the following form: given that the sample mean, $\bar{x}$, is an unbiased estimator of the population mean, μ, one can be "68 per cent confident" that the range

$$\bar{x} \pm \text{Standard Error of the Mean}$$

i.e.
$$\bar{x} \pm \frac{\sigma}{\sqrt{n}} \qquad \ldots(5.3)$$

includes the population mean. Similarly, one's confidence would be approximately 95 per cent that the range

$$\bar{x} \pm 2\left(\frac{\sigma}{\sqrt{n}}\right) \qquad \ldots(5.4)$$

includes μ, and approximately 99 per cent that

$$\bar{x} \pm 2 \cdot 6\left(\frac{\sigma}{\sqrt{n}}\right) \qquad \ldots(5.5)$$

includes μ. The limits defined by (5.3), (5.4) or (5.5) are called *confidence limits*. If $\bar{x} = 21$, $n = 150$, $s = 12$, we would draw the following conclusion[1]: the sample mean is 21 and this is an unbiased estimate of the population mean. Since it is based on only a sample, we know that it is not necessarily—or even probably—equal to the true population mean. We can, however, be 68 per cent confident that the range $21 \pm 12/\sqrt{150}$, i.e. 20·02–21·98 includes μ; 95 per cent confident that the range 19·04–22·96 covers μ; and virtually certain—i.e. 99 per cent confident—that μ is within the range 18·05–23·95. Or to put the same thing another way: if we make the statement that μ lies in the interval 19·04–22·96, the probability is 95 per cent that the statement is correct, i.e. the chances are 1 in 20 that it is incorrect.

The different probabilities—68 per cent, 95 per cent, 99 per cent—are called *confidence levels*. In practice, the 95 per cent level is spoken of as the 5 per cent level, the 99 per cent level as the 1 per cent level and so on. (These figures are approximate; reference to standard tables will show, for instance, that the precise figure for the 95 per cent level is not 2 *S.E.*, but 1·96 *S.E.*) There is nothing magic about the three particular confidence levels here used for illustration and, although these—in particular the 5 per cent level—are the most commonly used, any others might do equally well. The researcher's choice of confidence level will depend, to put it simply, on what is more important to him: a narrow range of error or a high probability of being correct.

If he wants to be able to say with high confidence that the range given does include the population mean, he will go for the 1 per cent rather than the 5 per cent level, since the former corresponds to greater

---

[1] Here s is used in place of σ; see p. 66. In making these calculations no account has been taken of the finite population correction.

confidence. The price he pays for this is that the range—i.e. the limits either side of the estimate—is relatively wide. If he wishes to have a narrow error band around his estimate, his confidence in stating that this band includes the population mean must be correspondingly lower. It is only reasonable that, in drawing inferences from sample to population, one should have to compromise between setting very narrow error margins around the estimate and having very high confidence that the margins will include the population parameter; one cannot expect to have it both ways.

5.5. Significance Tests

Earlier in this chapter a distinction was drawn between two purposes of surveys, estimation and the testing of hypotheses, but so far the treatment has been entirely in terms of the former. This is not unreasonable since surveys are mostly concerned with estimation, but something must now be said about the reasoning involved in testing hypotheses. To illustrate this, I will take what is a typical application of hypothesis-testing in surveys: the comparison of two (or more) population groups.

Two independent random samples of 400 individuals each are taken in towns A and B, and of these 45 per cent and 52 per cent respectively say they are pro-Labour politically. We may express this by saying that $p_A = 0.45$ and $p_B = 0.52$, p standing for proportion *with* the given attribute. The layman might conclude at once that town B has a higher pro-Labour proportion than town A. In fact this does not necessarily follow since both proportions are sample results and therefore subject to sampling error; the difference of 7 per cent may be no more than would be expected as a result of sampling fluctuations and, if this were so, one would call the difference "not statistically significant

The test procedure is broadly as follows. We set up the so-called "null hypothesis" that there is *no* difference between π_A and π_B, where π stands for the proportion with the attribute in the respective *population*. We then estimate the standard error of the difference between the proportions and compare the observed difference with it. If this difference exceeds 2.6 its standard error we conclude that the probability of a difference as large as this occurring as a result of sampling fluctuations is only about 1 per cent (for reasons analogous to those explained on pp. 66–68), so that either something very unusual has happened or the original hypothesis must be regarded as discredited. With a difference as large as this, one would probably prefer the second alternative. If the difference were, say, twice the standard error, the situation would be less clear-cut, since a difference of this size would occur by chance about five times out of a hundred and is therefore not so unusual an event. Whether it is unusual enough for the researcher to reject the hypothesis is for him to decide; we shall return to this point.

To continue the above example, it can be shown that the standard error for the difference between two sample proportions is estimated by

$$\text{(EST)}\ S.E._{p_A - p_B} = \sqrt{\frac{p_A(1 - p_A)}{n_A} + \frac{p_B(1 - p_B)}{n_B}} \qquad \text{...(5.7)}$$

In the present case $p_A = \cdot45$, $p_B = \cdot52$ and both n_A and n_B (the sample sizes) are 400. The standard error is estimated to be $\cdot035$ and the observed difference of $\cdot07$ has to be set against it. As it is twice its standard error, we would regard it as significant at the 5 per cent, but not at the 1 per cent, level.

The general topic of significance tests is beyond our scope here (see Chapter 15 for some remarks on interpretation) but one other point must at least be mentioned. In drawing conclusions from a significance test, the researcher runs two risks: (1) of rejecting the hypothesis when in fact it is true; and (2) of accepting the hypothesis when in fact it is false.

In the above example, we are testing the null hypothesis that $\pi_A = \pi_B$ and we may suppose that the alternative hypothesis being considered is that π_A is not equal to π_B.[1] The first type of risk is measured by the confidence level. Suppose that the null hypothesis is in fact true and that we are testing at the 5 per cent level; this means that five out of every hundred times we would expect to get, purely through sampling fluctuations, a difference between p_A and p_B big enough to lead us to reject the null hypothesis; in these cases we should draw the wrong conclusion. Why, then, does one not simply use more stringent significance levels—say the 1 per cent level or even the $0\cdot1$ per cent level—so as to decrease the risk of this kind of error? The answer is that, by so doing, one would increase the risk of the second kind of error, of accepting the null hypothesis when it is *not* true. The statistician tries to balance the two types of error in accordance with his particular problem and with the risk attending each kind of wrong decision.[2]

5.6. Summary of Simplifications

In order to introduce the ideas of sampling with the minimum of complication, a number of simplifications were made in this chapter:

[1] A different alternative hypothesis would be that $\pi_A < \pi_B$.
[2] See the statistical texts recommended at the end of this chapter for full accounts of the subject.

(a) *Different statistics.* With the exception of the last section, only one type of statistical measure—the mean—has been used in the presentation. It should be understood that similar reasoning applies with other statistics. Particularly common is the estimation of a population proportion π (or a percentage), and here the standard error, based on a sample of size n (and ignoring the f.p.c.) is $\sqrt{\dfrac{\pi(1-\pi)}{n}}$. This can be estimated from $\sqrt{\dfrac{p(1-p)}{n}}$, where p is the proportion with the particular attribute in the sample. Suppose that one wished to estimate what proportion of the 3,000 families in a district had motorcars and that, in a sample of 400, it was found that 40 had them. Hence $p = \cdot 1$, $n = 400$, and

$$(\text{EST}) \; S.E._{p} = \sqrt{\frac{\cdot 1 \times \cdot 9}{400}} = \cdot 015$$

One would then say that one's confidence was about 95 per cent that the range 10 per cent ± 3 per cent included π, the population proportion; or translated into absolute numbers, that between 210 and 390 of the families had cars.

(b) *Sampling distributions.* We have dealt with the subject of sampling distributions very briefly. For many statistics, they are known and defined exactly, for others they have only been deduced in approximate form. Furthermore the above treatment has assumed that the sampling distribution approximates to the normal distribution. While this is often true, it is not necessarily so, and the closeness of the approximation will depend on the statistic in question, the size of the sample and the nature of the population. If the statistic is the mean, a sample size of 50 or so is generally enough—for most populations—to ensure an approximately normal sampling distribution. For estimating variances, the sample size would have to be greater to ensure such a distribution; for correlation coefficients greater still. In short, "normality" of the sampling distribution cannot be taken for granted, although for the situations most commonly encountered in social surveys, this complication need not cause much worry.[1]

(c) *Estimating procedures.* Nothing has been said about different ways of estimating a population parameter from the sample statistic. A mean or proportion calculated from a simple random sample is always an unbiased estimator of the corresponding population para-

---

[1] However, to the extent that a surveyor wants to make estimates for subgroups of the population (say, men of a particular age/social class group) rather than the population as a whole, the problem may be important. For the sample numbers in the relevant cells may be small enough to cast doubt on the normality assumption. See the technical literature for a discussion of alternative courses in such a situation.

meter, but the situation is not necessaily as straightforward as this with more complex designs. The choice of estimating procedure has an important bearing on the efficiency of a sample, but the subject is beyond the scope of this book (see references at the end of the chapter).

(d) *More intricate designs*. It has been convenient to explain the theoretical background with reference to simple random sampling, and all the formulae have been based on this. In practice, as the next chapter will show, more complex designs (always incorporating the element of randomness) are usually to be preferred; and for these different and more elaborate formulae apply.

NOTES ON READING

1. Most text-books on statistics carry chapters on sampling theory. Readers will find suitable introductions in BROOKES and DICK [22], DAVID [47] and HILL [119]; more advanced treatments in YULE and KENDALL [294], TIPPETT [263] and WALLIS and ROBERTS [280].

2. Readers with a fair knowledge of statistics, who want to study the theory of sample surveys thoroughly, are recommended to use COCHRAN [36] and YATES [291], both excellent modern texts.

3. Two very good accounts of the basic ideas of sampling are the introductory chapter in the first volume of HANSEN, HURWITZ and MADOW [112] and the chapter by KISH in FESTINGER and KATZ [78]. Another good treatment is the paper by COCHRAN, MOSTELLER and TUKEY [39], which is part of a methodological review of the Kinsey report.

CHAPTER 6

TYPES OF SAMPLE DESIGN

6.1. Introduction

Two MAJOR principles underlie all sample design. The first is the desire to avoid bias in the selection procedure, the second broadly to achieve the maximum precision for a given outlay of resources. Bias in the selection[1] can arise:

(i) If the sampling is done by a non-random method, which generally means that the selection is consciously or unconsciously influenced by human choice.

(ii) If the sampling frame (list, index or other population record) which serves as the basis for selection does not cover the population adequately, completely or accurately.

(iii) If some sections of the intended population are impossible to find or refuse to co-operate.

Any of these factors will cause systematic, non-compensating errors which are not eliminated or reduced by an increase in sample size. If the sample is taken from an inadequate list, no increase in size will correct its unrepresentativeness or eliminate the bias in the characteristics of an infinite number of samples so selected. An example is the famous 1936 *Literary Digest* débâcle. The *Digest* took a mammoth sample of 10,000,000 individuals, yet its forecast of the U.S. Presidential Election went disastrously astray because (*a*) the sample was picked from telephone directories and the like which did not adequately cover the poorer section of the electorate; and (*b*) only 20 per cent of the (mail) ballots were returned and these probably came predominantly from the more educated sections.

---

[1] Bias can enter through sources other than the sample selection—faulty measurement, interviewing, question wording and, as noted in the previous chapter, through the estimation procedure. Here we are concerned only with selection bias.

Bias arising from unsatisfactory frames and from non-response is discussed in the next chapter, but it is worth noting here that neither bias is peculiar to sampling. A 100 per cent coverage of a list covering only part of the intended population would equally be biased and so would the "complete" enumeration of a population in which some of the members either could not be found or refused to co-operate. Our concern in this chapter is with bias arising through the sampling method and there is only one sure way of avoiding this, namely to use a random method. Randomness lies at the base of all sound sample designs; these differ chiefly in the refinements introduced to minimise sampling errors for a given expenditure or, conversely, to achieve a certain precision at minimum cost. We begin, therefore, with a discussion of simple random sampling and then go on to designs which, while retaining the essential element of randomness, manage to increase precision by various restrictions and refinements.

6.2. Random Sampling

A *random* method of selection is one which gives each of the N units in the population to be covered a calculable (and non-zero) probability of being selected. In the American literature the term *probability sampling* is used in place of random sampling and this has much to commend it; sampling methods which do not embody the feature of randomness—such as quota and purposive sampling (both discussed below)—are called judgement samples.

The use of the term "random" has given rise to a certain amount of confusion in the literature, due to a looseness in distinguishing between random sampling and *simple random sampling*. The latter, as noted in Chapter 5, means that each possible sample of n units from a population of N units has an equal chance of being selected, which in turn implies that every member of the population has an equal chance of selection into the sample.[1] Equality of chance of selection is a characteristic of simple random sampling; for random sampling generally, what matters is only that the chance is calculable and not zero.

If we number the N members of the population and pick n of them by random numbers (see below), this will be a simple random sample; if we place N numbered discs in a hat, mix them well and pick out n at random, this will again be a simple random sample; if we take a list of the N population members, arranged in *random* order, and pick

[1] This is evident from the list of possible samples on p. 59. The member aged 15 is picked three times, so is the member aged 17 and so is each of the other two. Each population member appears 3 times out of 6, illustrating that the chance of selection is simply $\frac{n}{N} = \frac{2}{4} = \frac{1}{2}$.

out every $\frac{N}{n}$th name, this will also be a simple random sample. But in practice, one often has to proceed differently. One may, for instance, choose to divide the population into a number of strata (say age-groups) and select a random sample from each stratum. The sample as a whole is not then a simple random one. Since some sample members must be selected from each stratum (this being the point of the stratification) a sample consisting entirely of members of one stratum could not be chosen; which illustrates that all the theoretically possible samples of n would *not* have the same chance of selection. This is a form of restricted random sampling; but the vital point is that the method of selection within each stratum is still random.

The importance of randomness in the selection procedure cannot be over-emphasised. It is an essential part of the protection against selection bias and the whole theoretical framework described in the last chapter rests on it. If it is not possible to assign to each population unit a calculable probability of selection, then the theory is not applicable and standard errors cannot be calculated; in other words, the precision of the sample estimate cannot properly be assessed.

The layman tends to think of "random" as being equivalent to "haphazard" and to believe that, as long as the investigator does not exercise conscious selection and avoids obvious dangers, randomness is ensured. This is far from correct. It has been repeatedly shown that the human investigator is not a satisfactory instrument for making random selections, that he tends, however unconsciously, to "favour" some of the population units in his selection. In the field of social surveys it is easy to see how bias can arise. Interviewers told to select a random sample of people in the street may tend to pick people of their own social type or may unconsciously go for "average" people, thus getting a sample with too little variation in it. If instructed to select a sample of housewives at home, they may avoid the dirtier-looking houses and top-floor dwellers. One could not legitimately assign probabilities of inclusion to the people in the street or to the houses, nor assume that these probabilities were equal.

To ensure true randomness the method of selection must be independent of human judgement. There are two basic procedures:

(i) The "lottery method". Each member of the population is represented by a disk, the disks are placed in an urn and well mixed, and a sample of the required size is selected (either with or without replacement—see below).

(ii) The use of random numbers (see the tables by Kendall and Babington-Smith [140], Fisher and Yates [82] and Tippett

[262]). The members of the population are numbered from 1 to N and n numbers are selected from one of the tables in any convenient and systematic way. These become the sample.

Both procedures are independent of human judgement and ensure randomness; the first, because the population can be regarded as arranged randomly, the second because the numbers used for making the selection have been generated by a random procedure (see section 7.2).

The practicability of either procedure depends in the first instance on the size of the population. Let us suppose that a sample of individuals is to be selected in a town with a population of 250,000. Most probably, one would decide to concentrate the interviews in a few areas, so the first step may be to pick some of the wards in the town and then a few polling districts in each of the selected wards; both selections could be made by the lottery or the random number method. It now remains to take a sample of individuals in each of the selected polling-districts. Let us consider a polling-district containing 5,000 people and suppose that there is an adequate list covering them. We could number the individuals on the list and then use random numbers to make the selection, but this would be laborious. An alternative is simply to calculate the desired sampling fraction for the district (let $k = N/n$) and select every kth individual throughout the list, starting with a randomly chosen number between 1 and k inclusive. If 250 individuals are to be selected in the polling district, $k = 20$. We select at random a number less than 20 and this determines the first sample member. If this number is 6, the sample is composed of numbers 6, 26, 46. . . . The procedure is easy and convenient. The question is, is it equivalent to simple random sampling?

Strictly speaking the answer is "No", unless the list itself is in a random order. But no ordinary list is. Whether it is in street order, alphabetical order, house number order—there is invariably some systematic arrangement. This method of selection is therefore not simple random sampling, nor does the choosing of a random starting point—although important—make it so. It is sometimes called *quasi-random* sampling, and this differs from simple random sampling in that it does not give all possible samples of size n from the population of size N an equal chance of selection. Once the sampling fraction is determined, then the random selection of the starting point determines the whole sample, i.e. if number 6 is chosen, numbers 26, 46 . . . automatically follow. There are 20 such samples that could be chosen, not the vast number that could result from a simple random method. In quasi-random sampling, the selection of one sample member is dependent on the selection of a previous one, while with simple random sampling (with replacement) all the selections are independent of each other.

The use of quasi-random sampling is generally justified by the argument that the list can be regarded as arranged *more or less at random,* or that the feature by which it is arranged is not related to the subject of the survey. Thus, selecting at regular intervals from a list is often reasonably accepted as equivalent to random sampling.

This type of list sampling is sometimes called *systematic sampling,* but this usage should be avoided, at any rate without qualification. The adjective "systematic" has generally been used for sampling methods—especially in agriculture and forestry—where the population is explicitly ordered in some way and then every kth unit is selected. With quasi-random sampling the justification for applying random sampling theory lies in the belief that any order in the arrangement of the frame can be ignored and the arrangement treated as more or less random. The theory for systematic sampling aims to take account of the systematic arrangement of the population, which is quite a different matter. A compromise in terminology (see Yates [291]) is to use the term "systematic sampling from lists" in place of quasi-random. This indicates that the process of selection is, in the literal sense, systematic; the extent to which it approximates to random or systematic sampling theory then depends on the nature of the list.

The sampler has always to be cautious in taking systematic samples from a list, in case there is some trend or periodicity in its arrangement that may affect the accuracy of his sample and increase sampling errors.[1] But apart from this, the method offers by far the most practical approximation to random sampling. In Great Britain, where lists rather than maps predominate as sampling frames, it is used for the vast majority of samples.

It will have been noted that the characteristic of randomness applies to the mode of selection, not to the resultant sample. A randomly-chosen sample may look most "unrandom" and in fact be unrepresentative (leading to inaccurate estimates). Our sample of 250 people in a polling district may by chance contain no women, although the sexes are in fact about evenly divided in the population. So, if the survey is concerned with opinions on equal pay for men and women, this sample would hardly reflect the true state of opinion in

---

[1] Suppose the 5,000 people happened to be arranged in order of income. Then the sample consisting of numbers 1, 21, 41 . . . would have a much lower average income than that composed of numbers 10, 30, 50 . . . etc., illustrating that there would be considerable sampling variability; this would not be reflected in the standard error, if this is calculated by the simple random sampling formula. A similar situation can arise through a periodic arrangement.

the district. All one can say is that "an extraordinarily unlikely event has occurred", this sample being close to one of the tails of the sampling distribution. The surveyor has been "unlucky" but the fact remains that if he went on taking a large number of such samples in precisely this way, then *on average* the estimates of opinion derived from them all would correspond to the true opinion in the district.

In such a situation, there is often some temptation to reject the sample and start afresh. In a survey some years ago, the selection of towns was being carried out by picking names out of a hat, and the play of chance served up a sample composed predominantly of seaside towns. For the subject under study this seemed fatal, and it was no consolation to the surveyor to know that if he went on selecting an infinite number of samples by this method, his results would be right on average. One could sympathise with his desire to start again, while pointing out its unsoundness and emphasising that the chance of his getting such an extreme sample was reflected in the confidence limits he would attach to his estimates. To reject some samples is clearly unsound because it introduces an element of judgement into the selection and because it deprives these samples of their due probability of being selected. The proper solution to this problem—stratification—is introduced in the next section.

But it must be understood that the unrepresentativeness of a single sample does not throw doubt on the randomness of the sampling method. If the surveyor took another sample and again found far too many seaside towns in it, he would begin to have grounds for suspicion. The randomness of the process can be gauged by studying the results of repeated samples, not by the appearance of a single one.

6.3. Stratification

It is clear from the few formulae of standard errors given in Chapter 5 that one way of increasing the precision of a simple random sample is to increase its size. This is not, however, the only way and we now turn to a method for increasing precision—stratification—which is used in virtually all sample designs. Stratification is a means of using knowledge of the population to increase the representativeness and precision of the sample. Thus, in the example just mentioned, if the surveyor had wished to *ensure* that different types of town were adequately represented in the sample he could have stratified by town-type. Town-type is then called a stratification factor.

Stratification does not imply any departure from the principle of randomness. All it means is that, before any selection takes place, the population is divided into a number of strata; *then* a random sample is selected within each stratum. This is almost certain to be an improvement on a simple random sample because it makes sure that the different strata in the population (sexes, age-groups, regions, town-types and the like) are correctly represented in the sample. This reduction of the play of chance is reflected in a reduction of the standard error—which, after all, is simply a measure of the influence of chance on sample composition. Thus stratified random sampling tends to have somewhat greater precision than simple random sampling, and it is also generally convenient for practical reasons. But it is of course vital that the selection within strata is made randomly.[1]

The gain due to stratification

Let us take as an example a college population of 3,000 students and suppose that, in order to study their views on the subject of degree reform, we interview a random sample of 300 students. A simple random sample would provide unbiased estimates of measurable precision, but it could almost certainly be improved upon. A student's views on degree reform are probably related more to his special subject of study than to any other factor; commonsense suggests then —and theory confirms—that the special subject groups should be correctly represented in the sample.

Suppose that the 3,000 students are distributed as in Table 6.1.

TABLE 6.1

Distribution of the 3,000 students by special subject

Economics	950
Sociology	430
Statistics	250
Political Science	390
Law	320
History	660
	——
Total	3,000

The chances are that a simple random sample would produce a proportionate distribution of the 300 students something like this, but it would not be exactly the same. Stratifying by special subject ensures that it is so (ignoring the influence of non-response) and will tend to increase the precision of the results. Within each of the six strata the students are selected at random; and if we have a list of them arranged by strata and decide to take a uniform sampling fraction

[1] On no account should stratified random sampling be confused with purposive sampling—in which the selection is made by human choice; one might pick a couple of seaside towns, a light-industry town etc. Such a method suffers from all the defects of leaving the selection to human judgement and sampling theory cannot be applied to it. In stratified random sampling, although the stratification factors and the actual strata are fixed purposively, the selection of units is made at random; this makes all the difference.

throughout we can simply take every tenth name, starting with a random number between 1 and 10. If there is no such list but there is one (ordered in some other way) on which the stratum to which each unit belongs can be identified, we could select every kth name, allotting it to its stratum and continuing until all the strata are filled. Once the required number for a stratum is attained, further names selected for it are rejected; it is usually necessary to go through the list more than once.

The reason why stratification nearly always results in some gain in precision can be explained as follows. The total variation (regarding any variable or attribute) in a population may be regarded as composed of two elements: variation between strata and variation within strata. Thus of our 3,000 students those specialising in one subject may have different views from those specialising in another; and there will also be variation of opinion *within* each special subject group. In stratified random sampling, variation *between* strata does not enter into the standard error at all, because one ensures that this component of variation in the population is exactly reflected in the sample. There is no chance about it. Sampling, and therefore the play of chance, only takes place within strata. Consequently, since only the variation within strata enters into the standard error, the greater the proportion of the total variation in a population that is accounted for by between-strata variation, the greater will be the gain due to stratification. The object therefore is so to arrange the strata that they differ as widely as possible from each other and that the population within each stratum is as homogeneous as it can be. A little thought will show that this is achieved by selecting stratification factors closely related to the subject of the survey (see p. 83).

I stated in the previous chapter that the standard error of a proportion (p) based upon a simple random sample of size n is estimated by

$$\text{(EST) } S.E._{p\,(\text{ran.})} = \sqrt{\frac{p(1-p)}{n}} \qquad \ldots(6.1)$$

It can be shown that the standard error of a proportion in a stratified random sample (a uniform sampling fraction being taken throughout the strata) is estimated by

$$\text{(EST) } S.E._{p\,(\text{st./uni.})} = \sqrt{\frac{\Sigma n_i p_i (1-p_i)}{n^2}} \qquad \ldots(6.2)$$

[1] Throughout this section I will for simplicity ignore the finite population correction.

[2] Strictly, the N_i (population numbers) rather than the n_i (sample numbers) should be used in formulae 6.2–6.3. But since, with a uniform sampling fraction the latter are in proportion to the former, one can—and more conveniently—use the n_i.

where Σ = summation over all the strata

$\quad n_i$ = sample number in ith stratum

$\quad p_i$ = proportion of sample in ith stratum possessing attribute (in this case, proportion favouring degree reform)

$\quad n$ = total sample size.

The calculations for the above example are shown in Table 6.2, the numbers in column (1) representing the sample distribution that would be obtained from taking the same proportion (1 in 10) in each stratum,[1] while those in column (2) are the hypothetical values for p_i.

TABLE 6.2

Estimation of standard error of a proportion for stratified random sample with uniform sampling fraction

(Data of Table 6.1)

Special Subject	(1) n_i	(2) p_i	(3) $n_i p_i$	(4) $n_i p_i(1 - p_i)$
Economics	95	0·9	85·5	8·55
Sociology	43	0·5	21·5	10·75
Statistics	25	0·7	17·5	5·25
Political Science	39	0·8	31·2	6·24
Law	32	0·6	19·2	7·68
History	66	0·5	33·0	16·50
Total	300		207·9	54·97

(A) *To provide an estimate of the population proportion*

To estimate the proportion in the whole college who are in favour of the degree reform (π), we work out the proportion for each stratum and then combine these proportions into a weighted average (since sampling fractions are uniform, sample numbers can be taken in place of population numbers as the weights):

$$(\text{EST})\,\pi = p = \frac{\Sigma n_i p_i}{n} = \frac{207 \cdot 9}{300} = 0 \cdot 693 = 69 \cdot 3 \text{ per cent}$$

(B) *Estimate of S.E. for a simple random sample*

With $p = \cdot693$ and $n = 300$ we have

$$(\text{EST})\,S.E._{p\,(\text{ran.})} = \sqrt{\frac{\cdot 693 \times \cdot 307}{300}} = \cdot 0266$$

[1] The application of the overall sampling fraction to the strata populations may not give whole numbers. If it had been 1 in 15, for instance, the sample in the Economics group would have been 63·3. It is convenient simply to take the nearest whole number. The sampling fractions can still to all intents and purposes be regarded as uniform.

(C) *Estimate of S.E. for a stratified random sample* (uniform sampling fraction)

The computation of $\sum n_i p_i (1 - p_i)$ is shown in column (4). With $n = 300$ we have according to formula (6·2)

$$\text{(EST) } S.E._{p \text{ (st./uni.)}} = \sqrt{\frac{54 \cdot 97}{300^2}} = 0 \cdot 0247$$

This shows some gain due to stratification; the variance (i.e. square of the *S.E.*) in (C) is about 7 per cent smaller than that in (B), suggesting that a simple random sample of size $n = 320$ (i.e. $300/\cdot 93$) would be needed to get the same precision as this stratified random sample.

This illustration has been in terms of an attribute, but analogous formulae exist for variables. Suppose, for instance, that the purpose of the survey—as in the example of Chapter 5—is to estimate the mean (age) of a population. The standard error of the sample mean based on a stratified random sample of size n with uniform sampling fractions (and ignoring the f.p.c.) is

$$S.E._{\bar{x}(\text{st./uni.})} = \sqrt{\frac{\sum n_i \sigma_i^2}{n^2}} \qquad \ldots(6.3)$$

where n_i = sample number in the ith stratum

$\qquad \sigma_i$ = standard deviation for the variable in question in the population in the ith stratum.

$\qquad \Sigma$ and n as for (6.2)

To estimate (6·3), s_i, the strata standard deviations in the sample are used in place of the σ_i; I shall illustrate the calculations in another context on p. 85. It is in any case clear from formulae (6.2) and (6.3) that the computation of standard errors for stratified random samples essentially means working out a standard error separately for each stratum and then combining the results into a weighted sum for the whole sample (equally for the population parameters—one first makes an estimate for each stratum, then combines them to give an overall estimate).

I must not give the impression that gain in precision is the only, or even the most important, reason for stratification. In the first place, the surveyor may be as interested in the results for separate strata as in those for the population as a whole. Figures for areas, town-size groups, age-groups and so on are likely to be of paramount importance, and stratification—if necessary, with variable sampling fractions (see below)—ensures that these sub-groups are represented in adequate numbers for the analysis. Secondly, it often helps administratively to divide the population into strata; it is convenient, for instance, to divide a national sample geographically, each area being allocated to a separate supervisor and so forth. Thirdly, many sampling frames are divided into broad groups or areas which it is then convenient to use as strata.

The choice of stratification factors

Ideally one wishes to stratify a sample by the factors believed to be most closely related to the subject of the survey; but in translating this ideal into practice difficulties do occur.

It is, for instance, only possible to stratify by a factor for which the population distribution is known and which is individually identifiable for every population member. (For a discussion of stratification *after* selection, see below.) In the above example, stratification by special subject is possible only if we know how the 3,000 students are distributed over the special subjects *and* to which group each student belongs. That this is an important limitation in practice is made clear if we think of trying to stratify a sample of individuals within a town by sex and age. The distributions of these factors in the population are almost certainly known and the only difficulty is to identify the sex and age of each individual at the time the sample is drawn. If the electoral register is used as a frame, sex can usually be inferred from Christian names, so this stratification presents little problem. But age is not given on this register so one could not incorporate an age-stratification into the design.

There is no gain in precision from stratifying by a factor unrelated to the subject of the survey, for then the characteristics of the different strata would not differ—except through chance—from each other and nothing would be gained by excluding from the sampling error the between-strata variation.[1]

The question now arises, what should be done if the survey is concerned—as all surveys are—with a number of variables and not just a single one. A stratification factor related to one variable may not be related to another; one factor may suggest itself for the income question, another for, say, television viewing, a third for gardening and so forth. There is no simple way around this difficulty. Apart from factors chosen because they seem relevant to most questions, one

[1] Going back to the example on pp. 81–2, it can be shown that the gain in precision of a stratified random sample (unif. fraction) over a simple random sample is estimated by

$$\text{(EST)}\, V_{p\text{(ran.)}} - \text{(EST)}\, V_{p\text{(st./uni.)}} = \frac{\Sigma n_i (p_i - p)^2}{n^2}.$$

The reader can check that this comes to ·000097, agreeing with the result obtainable directly. The expression shows that if the strata are all alike (i.e. the stratification factor is unrelated to the variable studied), the numerator becomes zero and there is no gain from stratification. The greater the differences between the p_i the greater the gain.

D

can only decide which questions have first priority and select the stratification factors to suit these (see Cochran [36, p. 84]).

Fortunately the difficulty is often of theoretical rather than practical importance. There is not generally a wide choice of available stratification factors and the size of sample is often not sufficient to allow for many simultaneous stratifications.[1] Besides, with reasonably large samples, stratification by a factor unrelated to a particular variable will not result in a *loss* of precision. Broadly speaking, the worst that can happen is that it will bring no gain.

If little is known about the survey population and suitable stratifications are not apparent, the pilot survey can be helpful. Alternatively, the stratification factors can be chosen on common-sense grounds, a fairly safe procedure for the reason noted in the last paragraph.

Variable sampling fraction

So far it has been assumed that the same proportion will be taken from each stratum, i.e. that the sampling fraction is uniform over the whole population. There are, however, situations in which it is preferable to use a variable sampling fraction.

One such situation arises where the populations in some strata are much more variable than those in others. Suppose we are studying labour conditions in industrial firms of widely varying sizes. This would lead us to stratify by size. There will be a stratum containing a few giant combines, then one with a somewhat larger number of very big (but not giant) firms, and so on right down the scale. It is likely that the small firms differ much less among themselves than the large with respect to size, labour conditions and many other features.

It is also evident that the more mixed or variable the firms constituting any stratum are, the more difficult it is to "represent" that stratum by a sample of a given size. It would be sensible in this case to take a larger sampling fraction in the more variable strata, thereby increasing overall precision. Again if the cost per sampling unit is greater in one stratum than in another, one could increase precision by taking a smaller sampling fraction in the former. It can be shown that the optimum precision is attained if the sampling fractions in the different strata are made proportional to the standard deviations in

---

[1] Occasionally, it is appropriate to use what Yates has called "multiple stratification without control of sub-strata". We might stratify by sex, age, and social class, for instance, in such a way that the *over-all* proportions for each of the three variables separately are equal to those in the population, but without trying to equate the sample proportions in the individual cells (e.g. working-class males aged 15–20) to those in the population. Readers are referred to Yates [291] for a discussion. See also the discussion of quota sampling—p. 103—below.

those strata and inversely proportional to the square root of the costs per unit in the strata; in other words, if the

$$\frac{n_i}{N_i} \text{ are proportional to } \frac{\sigma_i}{\sqrt{c_i}}$$

where n_i = sample size
N_i = population size
σ_i = standard deviation
c_i = cost per unit
$\left. \right\}$ in the ith stratum

If the cost per unit can be assumed to be constant throughout the strata, the sampling fractions can be made proportional to the standard deviations. The question of allocation in stratified sampling is discussed fully by Yates [291] and by Cochran [36] among others.

To illustrate the estimation of population parameters and standard errors from stratified samples with variable sampling fractions (and, for comparison, with uniform sampling fractions), I shall consider a population of 5,000 firms, stratified into three size-groups (according to number of workers). The sample will comprise 200 firms and the purpose is to estimate mean turnover μ (stated in artificial units) per firm; the sample means ($\bar{x}_i$) and standard deviations (s_i) for the three groups are given in columns (3) and (4) of Table 6.3. The allocation resulting from a uniform sampling fraction is shown in column (5).

TABLE 6.3

Estimation of population parameters and standard errors—stratified random sample with uniform and variable sampling fraction

					Uniform Sampling Fraction			Variable Sampling Fraction		
	(1)	(2)	(3)	(4)	(5)	(6)	(7)	(8)	(9)	(10)
Group	Size (No. of workers)	No. of firms	Mean Turnover (in sample)	Standard deviation of turnover (in sample)	Sample size			Sample size		
		N_i	$\bar{x}_i$	s_i	n_i	$n_i\bar{x}_i$	$n_i s_i^2$	n_i	s_i^2/n_i	$N_i^2 s_i^2/n_i$
A	over 1000	50	100	90	2	200	16,200	10	810	2,025,000
B	100–999	1,250	50	40	50	2,500	80,000	110	14·5	22,656,250
C	under 100	3,700	10	10	148	1,480	14,800	80	1·25	17,112,500
		N=5,000			200	4,180	111,000	200		41,793,750

(i) *Uniform sampling fraction.* The first step is to estimate the mean turnover for all the firms. This is given by the sample mean, $\bar{x}$, i.e.

$$(\text{EST})\, \mu = \frac{\Sigma n_i \bar{x}_i}{n} = \frac{4{,}180}{200} = 20{\cdot}9$$

Next we can estimate the standard error of the mean, still on the basis of uniform sampling fractions. The appropriate formula (see p. 82) is

$$(\text{EST})\, S.E._{\bar{x}[\text{st./uni.}]} = \sqrt{\frac{\Sigma n_i s_i^2}{n^2}} = \sqrt{\frac{111{,}000}{200^2}} = \frac{333{\cdot}2}{200} = 1{\cdot}67$$

(ii) *Variable sampling fraction.* Alternatively, one might have decided to allocate the sample disproportionately to the strata, since they appeared to be of very different variability. Let us suppose for simplicity that we had estimated the standard deviations for the three strata to be roughly in the proportions A : B : C : : 9 : 4 : 1 (as they in fact turned out to be in the sample). If the sampling fractions were to be in proportion to these, we would have proceeded as follows: Let the fraction in stratum A be $1/k$. The fractions in strata B and C then become $4/9k$ and $1/9k$ respectively. With a total sample of 200, this gives

$$\frac{50}{k} + \frac{1250 \times 4}{9k} + \frac{3700}{9k} = 200$$

from which $k = 5{\cdot}08$; the sample numbers should therefore be *approximately* 10, 110 and 80. (They are recorded in column (8)). This allocation has assumed that the cost of sampling is the same in these three strata.

In order to estimate the mean turnover in the population from a stratified random sample with a variable sampling fraction, the means obtained in the different strata (which we still assume to be those in column (3)) have to be weighted by the strata populations :[1]

$$(\text{EST})\, \mu = \frac{\Sigma N_i \bar{x}_i}{N} = 20{\cdot}9 \text{ as before.}$$

In order to estimate the standard error of the mean, we require the following formula :

$$(\text{EST})\, S.E._{\bar{x}[\text{st./var.}]} = \sqrt{\frac{\Sigma N_i^2 s_i^2 / n_i}{N^2}} \qquad \ldots(6.4)$$

The necessary figures are given in columns (8) to (10) of Table 6.3, and the result is

---

[1] As mentioned earlier, with uniform sampling fractions, it is convenient and valid to weight by the sample numbers rather than the population numbers, since the former are in proportion to the latter. Here we must, however, use the population numbers.

$$(\text{EST})\ S.E._{\bar{x}[\text{st.}/\text{var.}]} = \sqrt{\frac{41{,}793{,}750}{5000^2}} = 1{\cdot}29$$

In terms of variances, the use of variable sampling fractions has reduced the estimated sampling variance from $1{\cdot}67^2$ to $1{\cdot}29^2$, i.e. from $2{\cdot}79$ to $1{\cdot}66$, a reduction of about 40 per cent. This was an extreme case (i.e. with very large differences in variability between the strata) and so substantial a gain would be unusual. I should remind the reader that no account has been taken of the finite population correction: in practice this would probably have been used here.[1]

In the above example, the strata standard deviations, on which the allocation was based, were taken as given. The practical situation is not as convenient, since one generally does not know what the relative variability in the strata is (nor usually the relative costs). There are several ways of overcoming this difficulty. In the first place, previous surveys dealing with the same or a similar population may give guidance. Or it may be possible to study a few firms in each stratum in order to make rough estimates of the standard deviations and costs. More formally, a pilot survey can give guidance on both these points. All such sources are likely to produce approximations rather than exact figures, but these are sufficient. If the sampling fractions are somewhere near the "best" fractions, there is still likely to be almost as much gain as if the "best" fractions had been used. If it is quite impossible to estimate the strata standard deviations, an alternative is to relate the sampling fractions to some other measurement which is itself known or expected to be related to the standard deviations. Where stratification is by size, for example, the standard deviations are sometimes roughly proportional to the means of the size groups or, even more simply, to their width. The sampling fractions can then be made proportional to the means or widths of the strata.

There is additional labour involved in using variable sampling fractions, owing to the need to weight strata results in order to arrive at overall population estimates. Whether this is justified by the gain in precision is for the sampler to judge in each case, taking into account the number of questions involved and how many strata, with different sampling fractions, there are.

One general difficulty in choosing sampling fractions is that fractions which are best for one variable (or attribute) being studied may not be so for another. If one variable predominates in importance, then this can govern the sampling fractions but, where no such

---

[1] It would certainly have been used in stratum A (where the sampling fraction is 1 in 5), but its omission is not serious since this stratum makes by far the smallest contribution to the sampling error.

priority exists, the problem of allocation is complex. The subject is discussed by Cochran [36] and by Yates [291, Section 10.4].

Finally we must recognise that, although gain in precision is an important reason for using variable sampling fractions, it is not the only one. Results are usually wanted separately for the various strata, so that it is important to have sufficient sample numbers in each of them and this in itself may call for variable sampling fractions. With a uniform fraction of 1 in 25 for instance, the sample in stratum A above had only 2 firms, so that no meaningful results for this stratum separately could have been given. Even with the variable fractions chosen, it only had a sample of 10 firms. If more than this were required for the analysis, the sampling fractions would have had to be fixed accordingly. An interesting discussion of the determination of sampling fractions in a national survey is given by Lydall [165].

Stratification after selection

I have noted that the possibility of stratification by a given factor depends on knowing the distribution of the population with respect to that factor and on knowing to which stratum each population unit belongs. Ignorance of the latter is often a limiting factor, even when the population distribution is known. If one wanted to stratify a sample of individuals in a town by age, one could easily get figures of the age distribution but, if there is no general population list showing the age of each individual, prior stratification would not be possible.

In such a case, one can "stratify after selection". Suppose the survey is to estimate mean income for the population (μ) and that one wants to stratify by age, but cannot do so for the reason given. A random sample is selected and each person's age ascertained at the interview. The resultant sample is then grouped by age and the mean income ($\bar{x}_i$) computed for each age stratum. The numbers (N_i) in the age groups in the population are known and the mean income for the population is estimated by

$$(\text{EST})\, \mu = \frac{\sum N_i \bar{x}_i}{N}, \text{ where } N = \text{total size of the population} \quad \ldots(6.5)$$

Providing that the sample provides a sufficient number of cases for each stratum, stratification after selection is theoretically as good as prior stratification with a uniform sampling fraction. The re-weighting, however, may be something of a nuisance at the computing stage, so that the normal form of stratification is to be preferred where possible.

6.4. Clustering and Multi-stage Sampling

A population can generally be regarded as being made up of a hierarchy of sampling units of different sizes and types. To take our simple example of the student survey, the population in the college (and within each special subject stratum in that college) can be regarded as being composed of a number of classes, each of which is itself composed of a number of students. In the discussion so far it has been taken for granted that, within each stratum, the students would be picked separately, one by one, from the population of that stratum. In practice it is often desirable to proceed differently. One might, for example, first select a sample of classes, each single selection leading to the choice of a whole cluster of units, and then, within each of the selected clusters, one can either include all the individual units which it comprises or only a sample of them. The principle here involved is called *clustering;* situations where there is any subsampling within the clusters chosen at the first stage are covered by the term *multi-stage sampling*, the case where there is complete enumeration of these clusters being usually denoted by *cluster sampling*. Actually the latter can be regarded as the special case of multi-stage sampling, where a 100 per cent sample is taken at the second stage.

Cluster sampling

Let us begin by illustrating this special, and in practice very important, case. Suppose that a survey is to be done among the inhabitants of a town and that the unit of enquiry, i.e. the unit about which results are to be obtained, is the individual household. Suppose further that the town contains 20,000 households, all of them listed on convenient records, and that a sample of 200 households is to be selected. One way would be to pick the 200 from the entire list by some random method, but this would spread the sample over the whole town, with consequently high fieldwork costs and much inconvenience. One might decide therefore to concentrate the sample in a few parts of the town and, if it may be assumed for simplicity that the town is divided into 400 polling districts with 50 households in each, a simple course would be to select at random 4 polling districts (i.e. 1 in 100) and include all the households in them in the sample. The over-all probability of selection is unchanged but, by selecting clusters of households, one has materially simplified and cheapened the fieldwork of the survey.

In this illustration it was the desire to lower the field costs that supposedly led to the use of a cluster sampling design. Another good reason for clustering arises where no satisfactory sampling frame for the whole population exists so that a listing of some kind has to be made specially. It is then obviously advantageous to be able to confine the special listing to a few areas or groups. This is a vital consideration in "under-developed areas" where there are rarely satisfactory sampling frames. American sampling practice also confirms that where adequate population lists are lacking, pre-listing is an inescapable necessity.

Three general points about clustering should be noted. In the first place, whether or not a particular aggregate of units should be called a cluster depends on circumstances. In the above example a polling district was the sampling unit and was appropriately called a cluster since it contained a number of households, the household here being the unit of enquiry. In another survey, the polling district might be the unit of enquiry, in which case one would not call it a cluster. Equally, in another survey, the household might properly be called a cluster, if it was itself the sampling unit but if results were to relate to individual members of the household.

Secondly, clusters need not necessarily be natural aggregates, as they were in the above examples. In area sampling (see section 6.9) one occasionally makes up artificial clusters by imposing grids on to maps. More commonly clustering takes advantage of existing groupings of the population, so that clusters do not usually contain equal numbers. However, for the sake of simplicity, the present discussion will be confined to the case of equal-sized clusters.

Thirdly, in any one sample design several types of clusters may be used. One may begin by dividing one region of England and Wales into its political constituencies and pick a number of these for the sample. Within each chosen constituency, one may pick a sample of the wards comprising it; within each chosen ward a sample of its polling-districts; and then finally within these a sample of households. Here, constituencies, wards and polling-districts are clusters at the first, second and third sampling stages respectively.

To illustrate the working of cluster sampling (with equal-sized clusters) let us return to the example of Table 6.2, taking the *History* stratum for illustration. The population in this stratum numbered 660 students, of whom 1 in 10, i.e. 66, were randomly selected from a list; half of them, that is 33 students, were found to be in favour of degree reform. This was in fact a simple random sample within the stratum but we will imagine for the moment that it was a clustered one: that the 660 students had first been divided into their 110 classes of 6 students each, that a sample of 11 of the 60 classes had then been randomly chosen, and that all the students in each of these were included in the sample. It may be supposed that the numbers favouring degree reform in the eleven classes or clusters were: 3, 5, 2, 3, 4, 1, 4, 2, 6, 1, 2 (total 33).

To estimate the proportion for the stratum as a whole we would, of course, simply divide 33/66 = 0·5, but it is worth noting that the same result would be achieved if we worked out the proportion for each cluster and then took an average:

$$\tfrac{1}{11}(\cdot500 + \cdot833 + \cdot333 + \cdot500 + \cdot666 + \cdot166 + \cdot666$$
$$+ \cdot333 + 1\cdot000 + \cdot166 + \cdot333)$$
$$= \tfrac{1}{11}(5\cdot496) = \cdot5$$

The next step is to calculate the standard error of this estimate. The appropriate formula is

$$(\text{EST}) \; S.E._{\bar{x}\text{(clust.)}} = \sqrt{\left(1 - \frac{m}{M}\right)\frac{s_b^2}{m}} \qquad \ldots(6.6)$$

where m is the number of clusters in the sample, M the number of clusters in the population, and s_b^2 the variance between the means of the sample clusters, i.e.

$$s_b^2 = \frac{1}{m-1}\sum_{i=1}^{m}(\bar{x}_i - \bar{x})^2$$

(where $\bar{x}_i$ is the mean of the ith cluster, $\bar{x}$ the mean of the whole sample and $\sum\limits_{i=1}^{m}$ summation over all the clusters).

Here $m = 11$, $M = 110$ and

$$s_b^2 = \tfrac{1}{10}[(\cdot5 - \cdot5)^2 + (\cdot833 - \cdot5)^2 + (\cdot333 - \cdot5)^2 + (\cdot5 - \cdot5)^2 +$$
$$+ \ldots (\cdot333 - \cdot5)]^2$$
$$= \cdot072$$

Hence $(\text{EST}) \; S.E._{\bar{x}\text{(clust.)}} = \sqrt{\dfrac{9}{10} \cdot \dfrac{\cdot072}{11}} = \sqrt{\cdot0059} = \cdot077$

If the stratum result in Table 6.2 (i.e. $p = \cdot5$ for the history students) had been based on a simple random sample—as we supposed in Section 6.3 to have been the case—the standard error of this estimate would itself have been estimated[1] as ·059. In other words, the clustered sample has resulted in a considerably higher standard error as compared with the simple random case. This is typical of real-life surveys and we must now consider how this "clustering effect" comes about.

To do this, let us make the very reasonable supposition that the division of the 660 students into 110 classes was not a random one, but that it had some relation to the characteristics of the individual students. There might have been an age criterion involved, or the division might have been connected with ability or with special interests within the field of history; the result in any case would have been to make the members within a cluster more like each other than

---

[1] By the formula

$$(\text{EST}) \; S.E._p = \sqrt{\left(\frac{N-n}{N-1}\right)\frac{p(1-p)}{n-1}},$$

where n = sample size, N = population size, p = sample proportion with attribute —all in the one stratum.

like members of other clusters. In statistical language there would have been a positive *intra-class correlation*.

Intra-class correlation is of the utmost importance in sample design and nearly always, in the field of social surveys, the correlation is positive. People living in a particular district of a town tend to have characteristics which make them *more* like each other than like people living in other districts; individuals in a household will on many—though not all—characteristics be more like each other than like members of other households, and so forth. The importance of this to the sample designer is that, if he selects clusters, he will tend to include or exclude (to put the point in extreme form) whole classes of units and this increased "riskiness" in the representativeness of the sample will be reflected in an increased sampling error. The population is "patchy" and, whereas the simple random sample will tend to be spread over all of it, the clustered sample risks missing whole sections. If, of course, the entire population were thoroughly "mixed", cluster sampling would be as precise as simple random sampling; but human populations tend to be anything but thoroughly mixed.

The effect on the sampling variance can be expressed as follows. If the population consists of a given number of clusters, each of size N, and m of these clusters are chosen and fully enumerated, then the sampling variance, on any attribute or variable, can be written as

$$\text{Var}\,(C) = \text{Var}\,(R)\,[1 + (N - 1)\rho] \qquad \ldots(6.7)$$

where Var (R) is the sampling variance for a simple random sample of size mN and ρ is the intra-class correlation. It is to be noted that

(i) If $N = 1$, that is each cluster only contains one unit, Var (C) = Var (R). This is as expected since there is then no clustering.

(ii) A value of $\rho = 0$ means that there is no intra-class correlation. In other words, each cluster is just as heterogeneous as the population at large. Then Var $(C) = $ Var (R).

(iii) The greater the "resemblance" of members of the same cluster, the closer will ρ approach 1 and the greater will be the difference between Var (C) and Var (R), the former always being in excess.

(iv) Even a small value of ρ might result in a substantial difference between Var (C) and Var (R), since it is multiplied by $(N - 1)$. Suppose $\rho = \cdot 1$ for a certain variable and each cluster numbers 100 persons, then the variance from a sample of clusters would be about 11 times that from a sample of individuals.

In the present case, Var (R) was $\cdot 0035$ and Var (C) $\cdot 0059$. Hence we can estimate ρ to have been $+ \cdot 14$. In practice correlations are often much higher than this, and are very rarely negative (ρ can never be less than $-1/N-1$). The important principle established by this discussion is that the more heterogeneous the clusters are within themselves (i.e. the smaller ρ is), the less precision will be lost by clustering. Thus whereas, for stratification, the aim is to make the strata as homogeneous within themselves as possible, in the formation of clusters the opposite holds. It also follows from the formula that a large number of small clusters is better—other things being equal—than a small number of large clusters. In practice, of course, the choice of clusters is often dictated by natural groupings but one must be prepared for the very considerable increase in sampling error that often results from the clustering. This point applies to multi-stage as much as to single-stage samples.

Multi-stage sampling

So far in this section I have discussed the case where there is only one stage of sampling, all members of each selected cluster being included in the sample. In practice it is usually desirable and often essential to carry out the sampling in two or more stages. The population is regarded as being composed of a number of first-stage units, each of them made up of a number of second-stage units and so forth. A sample—with or without stratification—is taken of the first-stage units; then a sample—again with or without stratification—is taken of the second-stage units in each *selected* first-stage unit; and so the procedure continues down to the final sampling units, with the sampling ideally being random at each stage.

The necessity for multi-stage sampling can be easily demonstrated. Suppose a random sample of 2,000 individuals is required to cover the civilian adult population of Great Britain. From a theoretical viewpoint, it would be admissible to select a single-stage sample with or without stratification from a sampling frame covering the entire population. Not only would it be admissible but, if cost and other practical considerations did not come into the picture, it could hardly be improved upon. In real life, however, these considerations are necessarily of prime importance and such a sample, thinly spread over the whole country, would be out of question for an interview survey; almost invariably, samples for interview surveys of widely spread populations are designed on a multi-stage basis. In this country, the first-stage units for national surveys are often administrative districts (county boroughs, boroughs, urban districts, rural districts etc.) or parliamentary constituencies.

Within the selected first-stage units, one may go direct to the final sampling units, such as individuals, households or addresses, in which case one would have a simple two-stage sample. But even to spread a sample of, say, 30 households over a town is expensive and it would be more usual to concentrate the sample by introducing one or more intermediate sampling stages. Since individual administrative districts consist of a number of wards, each of which in turn consists of a number of polling districts, either (or both) of these types of unit can be used at intermediate stages.

Before going further, it may be useful to emphasise the respective roles of stratification and of spreading a sample over several stages. Although these two features of design fulfil quite different functions, the newcomer to the subject often has difficulty in distinguishing them. Continuing with our illustration, suppose that there are suitable lists of districts and of individuals within districts from which we can draw the sample of 2,000 adult civilians. Let us look at four possibilities:

Design I. Unstratified, single-stage sample

This would involve taking the list of adults for the entire country and extracting from it a sample of the required size, either by random numbers or by some quasi-random procedure.[1]

Design II. Unstratified, two-stage sample

Sample I would be too thinly spread over the country to be practicable. We may decide instead to concentrate the sample in a certain number of administrative districts, selecting, say, 50 such districts from a complete list of districts. We then turn to the list of individuals for each of the selected districts, and from it select the required number (40 on average).

Design III. Stratified, single-stage sample

Either because the regions are believed to differ markedly from each other with regard to the subject of the survey or purely for convenience, we may decide to stratify by region (say, with uniform sampling fractions). The first step is then to allocate to each region its appropriate number of interviews. If South-West England has 10 per cent of the population of England and Wales, 200 out of the sample of 2,000 individuals would be selected from this region. Up to this point *no sampling has taken place*. Stratification is merely a way of dividing the population into a number of sub-populations. Once this is done, the sampling begins and, with a single-stage sample, we would select the number of individuals required in a region from the entire list for that region.

---

[1] In this latter case there might in fact be an element of stratification because of the arrangement of the list.

Design IV. Stratified, two-stage sample

The stratification by region is as in Design III. But in order to concentrate the interviewing, we select first a sample of administrative districts in each region and then a sample of individuals from each of the selected districts.

For purposes of illustration, the above has been confined to one stratification at the first stage and to two sampling stages. In practice, the most common type of design is (IV), but with several stratifications and more than two sampling stages.

The crucial advantages of multi-stage sampling are that it results in a concentration of fieldwork and consequently in a saving of time, labour and money, and that it obviates the necessity of having a sampling frame covering the entire population. As was clear from Designs II and IV, one needs a frame of the second-stage units *only for those first-stage units which have been selected at the first stage.*

There are many ways of distributing a sample over various sampling stages and in the choice between them both practical considerations and the effect on sampling errors must weigh. Suppose the survey population numbers 240,000 individuals grouped, geographically or otherwise, into 800 clusters of 300 persons each (I still assume that clusters are of roughly equal size). A sample of 2,400 persons is to be drawn, that is the sampling fraction is 1/100. The following are a few of the ways in which the sample could be allocated:

Allocation	Number of clusters	Number of persons taken per cluster
A	800	3
B	240	10
C	120	20
D	60	40
E	40	60
F	20	120
G	8	300

These can all be looked upon as two-stage designs: in (A) a "100 per cent sample" is taken at the first stage, in (G) a "100 per cent sample" is taken at the second stage (our special case of a cluster sample). From a cost and convenience point of view the designs get increasingly attractive as one goes from (A) to (G): the spread becomes smaller and smaller and so, broadly, does the cost per unit. But, at the same time, the designs become *less* attractive in terms of the precision achieved—in other words, the standard error increases as we move towards a smaller number of very large clusters (see p. 93). In practice, a national interview sample of 2,000–3,000 interviews would typically be spread over 80–100 first-stage units.

The sample designer's aim is to achieve the highest precision per £1 spent, that is to find some optimum point along the scale from design (A) to design (G). The decision is not always easy, since it requires estimates of costs and variances per unit associated with the different allocations. If the designer is aiming at a given precision, the problem is to find the cheapest design that will attain it; if he must keep to a given maximum cost, the task is to find the design that will give maximum precision at that cost. In either case, the necessary estimates have to be based on previous experience, pilot surveys or guesswork. The multi-purpose problem—see p. 87—arises here too and some priority among the variables of the survey has to be established. The reader is referred to the text-books on sampling for a full discussion of procedures.

As regards the estimation of standard errors for multi-stage samples, the important part to note is that each sampling stage makes its own contribution to the total sampling error. Consider a two-stage sample and suppose that, at the first stage, we select (at random, with or without stratification) m out of a possible M districts and that, in each of the selected districts, n out of N individuals are then chosen (again at random, with or without stratification). Both the selection of m out of M first-stage units and of n out of N second-stage units in each of the selected first-stage units gives rise to sampling errors.

This is brought out by formula (6.8) which shows the estimate of the sampling variance of the mean (income, let us say) based upon such a sample:

$$\text{(EST) Var}_{\bar{x}} = \left(1 - \frac{m}{M}\right)\frac{s_b^2}{m} + \left(\frac{m}{M}\right)\left(1 - \frac{n}{N}\right)\frac{s_w^2}{mn} \quad ...(6.8)$$

This estimate is composed of two parts, the first of which—the between-district variance—has already been encountered in the general discussion on p. 91. But added to this variation between districts, the n sample members *within* each district vary among themselves and a measure of this variation has to be calculated for each district. These measures are then pooled for all districts and the result is s_w^2, a criterion of variation *within the first-stage units*. As it is based on n cases in each of m districts, it is divided by mn and multiplied by *its* corresponding finite population correction.[1]

The sum of the two components constitutes the estimate of the sampling variance. It is a fairly general finding that the sampling of clusters, of the first-stage units, contributes the major part of the

[1] The reason for the additional multiplication by m/M is not self-evident. Since s_b^2 is calculated from those second-stage units actually included in the sample, the variation between these units is already reflected in the first term of (6.8). Therefore, the variation within districts should only contribute in part to the total and this is why the second term is multiplied by the first-stage sampling fraction m/M.

total and one can sometimes reasonably approximate to the total sampling error by working out only the first-stage component. Durbin [64], extending a result due to Yates, has shown that if the sampling at the first stage is done *with* replacement (i.e. any district selected is "returned to the population" and given a further chance of inclusion) then the sampling error is properly estimated from the first term of (6.8) only.

Two extremes of formula (6.8) are of interest:

(i) If *all* the first-stage units are included, then $\left(1 - \dfrac{m}{M}\right)$ becomes zero and so does the first term of the variance. This is design (A) in the scheme on p. 95 and is equivalent to a stratified random sample with a uniform sampling fraction, in which the first-stage units have become the strata. In order to minimise the overall variance, now consisting only of the second term in (6.8), s_w^2 must be minimised. In other words, the districts (strata) should be as *internally homogeneous* as possible. This was noted before, when we discussed stratification.

(ii) At the other extreme, if all second-stage units in each district are included, i.e. $\left(1 - \dfrac{n}{N}\right)$ is zero, only the first-stage contribution remains. This is logical, since there is now no second-stage sampling. We have here design (G) above and, to minimise $\mathrm{Var}_{\bar{x}}$, we aim to minimise s_b^2. This means that districts (clusters) should be as *internally heterogeneous* as possible, which is the feature of cluster sampling noted earlier.

Between these extremes, the general approach is that strata should be as homogeneous as possible and that, in forming clusters *within these strata*, the more mixed the membership of each cluster the better. This is a theoretical desideratum. In practice, the choice of cluster is much influenced by purely practical factors: costs, fieldwork convenience, nature of sampling frame, areas for which data are required and so on.

The discussion throughout has been in terms of two-stage sampling, but all the principles can be generalised to more stages.

6.5. Sampling with Varying Probabilities

The preceding discussion was simplified by the assumption that the clusters of sampling units were of more or less equal size. If they are not, various complications arise, most of them beyond the scope of this book. One approach, that of sampling with varying probabilities, is of such general importance, however, that it must at least be mentioned. Suppose that, at the first sampling-stage, administrative districts are to be selected. As these vary greatly in size, it would be appropriate to stratify by size and select a sample of districts in each size group, probably with variable sampling fractions. An alternative is to make the selection with probability *proportionate* to size (say, of population). If district A has twice as large a population as district B, it is given twice the chance of being selected. If the *same* number of second-stage units is then selected in A as in B, the over-all probability of selection of any individual will be the same. This can be demonstrated by a simple example, in which the over-all probability of selection is to be 1/20.

TABLE 6.4

Illustration of sampling with probability proportionate to size

District	(1) Popu- lation	(2) Prob. of selection of district $= P_D$	(3) Size of sample selected in each district	(4) Prob. of selection for any individual within district $= P_I$	(5) Over-all prob. of selection $P_D \times P_I$
A	20,000	10	100	100/20,000	1/20
B	2,000	1	100	100/2,000	1/20

District A, having a population ten times that of district B, is given ten times as great a chance of selection as the latter, and the same size of sample is selected in each. The product of the probabilities in column (5) shows that each individual has the same chance of selection.

Sampling with varying probabilities has a number of convenient features. One of the most important applies when a few out of a large number of sampling units of very different sizes are to be selected and there are a number of other useful stratification factors. If the units are selected with probability proportionate to size, rather than stratified by size, these other stratifications can more easily be utilised. An additional advantage is that second-stage samples of equal size are convenient for the fieldwork planning.

The selection procedure is worth illustrating, since it figures in most present-day random samples. If there are 20 districts in a stratum—from which 2 are to be selected with probability proportionate to size—the 20 are listed in some order (possibly according to another stratification) and the population of each is recorded together with the cumulated population figures. Table 6.5 shows the scheme.

We now select from a Table of Random Numbers two numbers between 1 and 560 and the districts corresponding to these numbers are included in the sample. Thus the chance of any district being selected is in proportion to its population. When the first district has

TABLE 6.5

Scheme for selecting districts with probability proportional to size[1]

District	Population (000's)	Cumulated Population (000's)
1	50	50
2	63	113
3	28	141
4	16	157
.	.	.
.	.	.
.	.	.
16	.	(say) 428
17	17	445
18	43	488
19	39	527
20	33	560

been chosen, it should strictly be "replaced" in the population and given a second chance of selection, otherwise the probabilities of selection vary from draw to draw with consequent theoretical complications. Sampling with replacement is unpopular with the survey practitioner since he does not like the idea of having to include the same district twice, but the seriousness of this can be exaggerated; by and large, sampling with replacement is to be recommended.

6.6. Multi-phase Sampling

Multi-phase sampling is best explained by looking at an example—say a household expenditure survey. Having decided what information is wanted and selected a sample of households, one can question them on *all* the matters being covered; but this may impose a considerable burden on the respondents. The question is: Can this burden be reduced? Basic data like the size and composition of the household, occupation of its head, income etc. may indeed be needed from every sample unit; and on others, such as distribution of expenditure over the main items, one may want to analyse the results in so much detail that the whole sample must be questioned to give the required precision. But there will be less important matters on which the surveyor does not require detailed analyses or such high precision. In regard to these, and also to factors known to be fairly constant in the population, adequate precision may perhaps be achieved by questioning a smaller sample. Finally, some information may be so costly or troublesome to collect that one can only consider collecting it from a small part of the entire sample. In all these situations multi-phase sampling is worth considering.

Briefly it is a type of design in which some information is collected

[1] An alternative procedure is given by Gray and Corlett [102]. See also section 10.8 in Yates [291]; Chapter 7 in the latter should be consulted on the matter of sampling errors for this type of design.

from everybody and additional information is—either at the same time or later—collected from sub-samples of the full sample. It should not be confused with multi-stage sampling (with which it can indeed be combined). In the latter, different types of sampling unit (administrative districts, wards, individuals) are sampled at different sampling stages; in multi-phase sampling, the same type of sampling unit is concerned at each phase, but some units are asked for more information than others.

Multi-phase sampling can result in considerable economies and reduce the burden on respondents. In addition, it offers a way of utilising the main sample as a sampling frame for later-phase samples. Once a first-phase sample is selected, it is a simple matter to take all kinds of sub-samples from it. Further, this main sample can provide information useful for deciding on suitable stratifications, and gives a basis for determining optimal sampling fractions.[1] A final point is that the information available from the initial main sample is useful in estimating the effect of non-response in the later-phase samples. Basic data about many of those who fail to give the later-phase information will have been collected and the unrepresentativeness (or otherwise) of the remainder can thus be gauged.

An illustration of multi-phase sampling in this country was the survey on intelligence conducted by the Population Investigation Committee and the Scottish Council for Research in Education [209], in which a sample of about 80,000 children was used for group intelligence tests and for the main questionnaire. A more detailed questionnaire was then addressed to a sub-sample of children born on the first three days of each month. A further sub-sample comprising those born on the first day of each alternate month was used for individual intelligence tests.

As suggested earlier, multi-phase sampling could effectively be used for the Population Census in this country. Even if it is necessary to question everybody about certain *basic* items, such as sex, age, household composition and so forth, some questions—concerning, say, items like baths and kitchen sinks—might be confined to samples of the population, and yet give adequate accuracy. The sample sizes necessary to give the required accuracy for different questions could be estimated and it would not be administratively difficult to confine some questions to these samples. Multi-phase sampling was used in the United States Population Censuses of 1940 and 1950.

6.7. Quota Sampling

The types of design discussed so far have all embodied the feature of randomness, thus ensuring that every member of the population

[1] For the estimation of sampling errors with multi-phase sampling see Yates [291].

had a calculable chance of being included in the sample; which in turn is a necessary condition for the estimation of sampling errors.

Quota sampling differs from random methods in several minor ways, but most fundamentally in that, once the general breakdown of the sample is decided (e.g. how many men and women, how many people in each age-group and in each "social class" it is to include) and the quota assignments are allocated to interviewers, the choice of the *actual* sample units to fit into this framework is left to the interviewers. Quota sampling is therefore a method of stratified sampling in which the selection within strata is non-random. It is this non-random element that constitutes its greatest weakness.

The issue of quota versus random sampling has been a matter of controversy for many years. Some experts hold the quota method to be so unreliable and prone to bias as to be almost worthless; others think that, although it is obviously less sound theoretically than random sampling, it can be used safely on some subjects; still others believe that with adequate safeguards quota sampling can be made highly reliable and that the extra cost of random sampling is not worth while. In general, statisticians have criticised the method for its theoretical weakness, while market and opinion researchers have defended it for its cheapness and administrative convenience.

Before we look at these pros and cons, the method must be described in a little detail.

The quota controls

Let us suppose that a national opinion survey is to be based on a quota sample. The first step will probably be to stratify by region, by urban/rural area and perhaps by town size, just as in a stratified random sample. Nor do the two methods necessarily part company when it comes to selecting, say, administrative districts (e.g. towns) within these broad strata. In either case, this selection may be made at random (often, in quota samples, it is in fact made purposively—see section 6.8). The essential difference between random and quota sampling lies in the selection of the final sampling units, say individuals.

In quota sampling, each interviewer is given an assignment of interviews, laying down how many of them are to be with men and how many with women, how many with people in various age-groups, social classes and so forth. These *quotas* are so arranged that, for the whole country and possibly even for each region, the sexes, age-groups and social classes are represented in the sample in the right proportions—fixed on the basis of available data. In other words, the total sample, as well as being stratified by region, urban/rural area, town size and so forth, is stratified also by sex, age and social class.

These three latter factors (which, incidentally, can rarely be used for stratifying random samples) are known as *quota controls* and are used universally since they are—reasonably enough—believed to be useful stratification factors for virtually all surveys. Neither the sex nor the age control presents much difficulty as there are statistics on which to base them and as interviewers can without trouble decide to which group a respondent belongs.

The social class control,[1] which is a vital part of quota sampling, is more difficult on both counts. First, there is no reliable statistical basis for setting the quotas, since the definition of "social class" usually involves a combination of objective factors, such as occupation and income, and subjective factors like appearance, speech and so forth. Secondly, the definition of the control is generally vague, leaving some play to the interviewer's subjective judgement and bias. It is true, of course, that the "social class" grouping is always broad (often into only three or four strata) so that inaccuracies in the quotas or in the interpretation of the definitions may not cause major bias; but even so this is an aspect of quota sampling open to criticism.

The three main controls are often supplemented by special controls (housewife/not housewife; head/non-head of household; occupation and industry; marital status) when the subject under study seems to call for them. The tendency is, however, against the use of many extra controls since they render the interviewer's task more difficult.

The assignment schemes

Once the controls and quotas have been fixed, the next step is to give each interviewer her assignment. The difference between the two common types of assignment schemes, respectively called "independent" and "interrelated" controls, is illustrated by the following hypothetical assignments:

Independent controls

SEX		AGE		SOCIAL CLASS	
Male	9	20–29	4	Highest	2
Female	11	30–44	6	Middle	4
Total	20	45–64	7	Lowest	14
		65 +	3	*Total*	20
		Total	20		

[1] Alternatively called income grade, economic group, social status, socioeconomic status etc.

Interrelated controls

	SEX	SOCIAL CLASS						Total
		Highest		Middle		Lowest		
		Male	*Female*	*Male*	*Female*	*Male*	*Female*	
AGE	20–29	1	–	–	1	1	1	4
	30–44	–	1	–	1	3	1	6
	45–64	–	–	1	1	2	3	7
	65 +	–	–	–	–	1	2	3
Totals		1	1	1	3	7	7	20
		2		4		14		

With independent controls, only the marginal quotas for sexes, ages and social class groups are set; there is no formal attempt to relate these controls to each other, to ensure for instance that a given number of the interviews in each age-group are with women, a certain number with men.[1] With interrelated controls, the numbers to be interviewed in all the sub-groups are assigned.

There are advantages in both schemes. Independent controls are simpler for the interviewer and, on the whole, less costly; they are also easier to set accurately since a statistical basis for the marginal quotas is more readily found than for the sub-groups. But they are less likely to ensure sample representativeness. Thus interviewers may so select respondents that all or most of the women are elderly and the men young, and so on. True, they are instructed to avoid such "pairing" of controls, but instructions cannot ensure that the resultant sample is equivalent to the proportional spread over the sub-groups which interrelated controls would ensure. Some findings on this point are given by Moser and Stuart [194].

Whatever type of scheme is used, it is up to the interviewer, aided by instructions, to approach people she thinks will fit into her quotas, interview them if she finds they do, otherwise politely reject them.[2] Unless instructed to the contrary, she may interview anywhere—at homes, in offices, factories, parks, public places or the street. Some organisations allow no street interviewing and insist that housewives are interviewed at home, working men in offices and factories. Some

[1] This is analogous to stratified sampling without control of sub-strata—to which I referred on p. 84—except that here selection within strata is non-random.

[2] Contrast this with the task of the random sample interviewer, who is given the address and (usually) name of every respondent, told not to take any substitutes and to continue her efforts—within stated limits—until she has secured an interview with the pre-selected respondent.

place-of-work interviewing is obviously desirable (unless the field-work is done in the evenings or at weekends) if important sections of the population are not to be missed.

This is one of the crucial worries with quota sampling—does it end up with representative samples of the population? For instance, un-less special controls are set to ensure that different occupations are correctly represented, they may easily not be. Interviewers, being human, may tend to select people who are readily at hand (subject to instructions and controls), and thus favour certain groups. A clear-cut illustration is the following occupational distribution achieved by two comparable surveys, one based on a national quota, the other on a national random, sample.

TABLE 6.6

Percentage distribution by occupation/industry

Quota and random samples

	Men		Women	
Occupation/Industry	Quota Sample	Random Sample	Quota Sample	Random Sample
Manufacturing	6·5	24·9	4·3	7·2
Clerical	3·8	5·0	4·2	4·6
Distributive	15·7	5·9	9·0	3·0
Transport and Public Services	18·3	7·6	1·3	—
Professional and Managerial	18·1	20·0	5·4	3·2
Mining and Quarrymaking	1·4	4·6	—	—
Building and Road-making	14·3	6·3	·2	—
Agriculture	2·4	2·8	·3	·8
Other Industries	15·5	8·1	10·3	5·5
Housewives	—	2·0	64·8	69·2
Retired, unoccupied, part-time	4·0	12·6	·2	6·6
Not stated	—	·2	—	—
Total	100·0	100·0	100·0	100·1

Source: Quota sample—British Market Research Bureau; Random sample—Government Social Survey. See Moser and Stuart [194, p. 352].

This shows a large excess in the quota sample of persons employed in distribution, transport, the public service and building and road-making and a correspondingly small proportion of persons employed in manufacturing. Comparisons with other data showed the random sample proportions to be broadly correct.

It does not necessarily follow that this maldistribution in the quota sample would bias its results: that depends on whether the questions studied were closely related to occupation. But it does illustrate the dependence of quota sample composition on the ways and whims of interviewers. Even allowing for the controls and instructions usual in quota surveys, interviewers retain considerable freedom in deciding where, when and whom to interview.

The main arguments against quota sampling

(a) The use of random selection, as already explained, makes it possible to attach estimates of standard errors to the sample results. This is not possible with quota sampling which does not meet the basic requirement of randomness.

It is sometimes argued that sampling errors are so small compared with all the other errors and biases that enter into surveys that it is no great disadvantage not to be able to estimate them. There is no denying the importance of other kinds of errors or the fact that, in most surveys, we do not know their magnitude and direction. But the point is that, with random sampling, at least one type of error, sampling error, is under control and measurable. One does not have to worry about it. With quota sampling, this security is lacking.

(b) Within the quota-groups, interviewers may fail to secure a representative sample of respondents. They may, for instance, fill the top age-group of 65 and over mainly with persons of 65 and 66, so that the very old are under-represented. This is a crucial problem of quota sampling: given that all the quotas are correctly filled—i.e. that every sampling unit is in the group to which it belongs—is the spread within groups such that a representative sample emerges? Are the extremes sufficiently represented? Quota samplers generally claim that instructions to, and constraints on, interviewers are sufficient to guard against the main dangers of selection bias, but this is a matter of belief rather than fact.

(c) The social class control, which is an inevitable part of quota sampling, can be criticised on two grounds: it is based on a hazardous statistical foundation and, as generally defined, leaves a great deal to the interviewer's judgement.

(d) The method makes strict control of the fieldwork more difficult. In particular, it is not easy to check to what extent interviewers place respondents in the groups where cases are needed rather than in those to which they belong.

The main arguments for quota sampling

(a) Quota sampling is economical. Travelling costs are much lower since there is no need to travel all over a town in order to track down pre-selected respondents. Also call-backs are avoided. No accurate figures are available but it seems likely that, on average, a quota interview costs only a half or a third as much as a random interview. This is one of the main reasons why quota sampling continues to be used in spite of its theoretical weakness.

(b) It is easy administratively. The labour of random sample selection is avoided and so are the headaches of non-contacts and call-backs. Quota sampling does not of course *avoid* non-response. There are no non-contacts, in the sense of pre-selected respondents being out when the interviewer calls; but just as such persons tend to be missed in random sampling so other kinds of people (perhaps those who are most at home) tend to be missed by quota sampling. Refusals occur in both methods: an experiment by Moser and Stuart [194] showed a refusal rate for the random samples of about 3 per cent, for the quota samples of about 8 per cent.

(c) If the fieldwork has to be done quickly, perhaps in order to reduce memory errors, quota sampling may be the only possibility. This is the situation with the B.B.C. Audience Research surveys, which take a national sample of 3,100 people each day and question them about the previous day's programmes.

(d) Quota sampling is independent of the existence of sampling frames and is often the only practicable method of sampling a population for which no frame is available.

An experiment on quota sampling

The debate on the merits of quota and random sampling has been carried on over a number of years, little aided by experimental evidence. When survey results obtained by the two methods could be compared, sometimes they have been remarkably close, at other times quota sampling appeared to have gone astray. To secure evidence on the subject the Division of Research Techniques at the London School of Economics undertook a research programme on quota sampling. The results have been published [192, 194], and only some general conclusions will be mentioned here.

On two important factors the quota samples were shown to be unpresentative: occupation and education. These were among the questions which could (with qualifications) be checked against the 1951 Population Census figures. The occupation results largely confirm the findings shown on p. 104. The education question was that asked in the Census: "At what age did you finally stop receiving full-time education?", and the results showed a pronounced tendency in the quota samples to under-represent those who finished education before the age of 15. It has often been suggested that quota samples obtain too educated a cross-section of the population, and the results here confirmed this view. On most of the other comparisons between the random and quota sample results, the differences were slight; there seemed little evidence of other selection biases in the quota samples.

The experiment was designed to make it possible to estimate the sampling variability of the quota samples,[1] and the results showed that, while this varied from question to question, it was generally between one and three times as great as the theoretical variability of random samples of the same size. The authors suggested that this difference was mainly due to "between-interviewer" variability in the selection of quota samples, i.e. that pairs of interviewers given the same assignment (in the same town and so forth) selected markedly different samples and that it was this factor, not present in random sampling, that accounted for the large difference. Some support for this view was provided in a subsequent experiment by Durbin and Stuart [68, p. 409].

It must of course be remembered that the cheapness of quota samples has to be weighed-up against their higher variability. If the cost per interview was half that of random samples and the variance on average over twice as great, quota sampling would not pay—quite apart from the danger of bias in it.

That the experiment revealed relatively few major differences between the quota and random sample results does not contradict the fact that quota sampling is theoretically unsound; rather does it provide one more observation that, in the hands of practitioners of long experience—the quota setting and fieldwork were done by leading market and opinion research organisations—the method can give reasonably accurate over-all results. Nor is this surprising. The three controls of sex, age, and social class together account, as they are designed to, for a great proportion of the variation in the answers to many questions. By arranging that the sample is broadly representative on these factors, the quota sampler makes sure that the results will not be dangerously out of line.

But although quota sampling skilfully done can succeed in practice, it is not suitable for surveys in which it is important that the results are derived from theoretically safe methods. Only random sampling fulfils this requirement. In saying this, I am not forgetting the non-response problem, which quota sampling proponents hold up as a theoretical weakness in random sampling on a par with the known weakness of quota sampling. This point of view is hardly supportable. In random samples, the surveyor knows that, as regards about 70 to 90 per cent of the sample (response rates on most professional surveys fall in this range) he is on safe theoretical ground; even as regards the remainder he is only partially in the dark since it is often possible broadly to assess the effect of the non-response upon the results. The quota sampler does not reach such comparative safety;

---

[1] It must be stressed—the point is explained at length in the paper [194]—that this was possible only because of a special feature of the design and does not contradict the fact that, in an ordinary quota sample, one cannot compute standard errors.

he is—to use the words of Yates—"continually looking over his shoulder and wondering whether some extraneous factor exists which will vitiate the conclusions based on his results" [194, p. 398]. It is doubtful, in spite of this, whether quota sampling will ever disappear; there will always be the practitioner to whom the discomfort of "continually looking over his shoulder" is compensated by the saving of money.

In conclusion, I must mention the attempts to combine random and quota sampling. Some opinion pollsters have, for instance, used designs in which each interviewer is assigned to a district or block and is given—in addition to the usual quotas—exact instructions on how to proceed. She may be told to call at every second house and interview everyone (or one person) in it until her quota is filled. Such a design restricts the interviewer's influence but it still does not yield a random sample.

6.8. Other Types of Design

It remains to say a few words about a mixed assortment of designs which are of fairly general interest: interpenetrating samples, area sampling and master samples.

(a) *Interpenetrating samples.* It is occasionally useful to split a sample into two or more independent parts, each forming a self-contained and adequate sub-sample of the population. These are called interpenetrating samples (replicated samples is perhaps a better term) and they can be used with any basic sample design: with stratified or non-stratified, single- or multi-stage, single- or multi-phase samples. In terms of the student survey illustration, the sample of students within each special-subject stratum could be split randomly into, say, two halves, each being an independent sample of the college population.

Interpenetrating samples have two main merits. The first is practical. If the size of the total sample is too large to permit the survey results to be ready in time, it can be split and one part be used to get out advance results.

The second advantage of interpenetrating samples lies in the light they can throw on *non-sampling errors* (see Chapter 13). Each of the sub-samples produces an independent estimate of the population characteristics; so if each is carried out by, for instance, a different interviewer or set of interviewers, one obtains an estimate of between-interviewer variation. Interpenetrating samples were first regularly used for this purpose by Mahalanobis [169].

It must be stressed that each of the samples has to be a random sub-sample of the whole, otherwise they cannot be regarded as comparable and the difference between them taken as an unbiased estimate of between-interviewer variation. It would not do, for instance, to divide the total sample of students into two halves according to special subject-group, i.e. to put economics, sociology . . . students into one sample, the remainder into the other. Even if this were done so that each sample contained the same number of students and was covered by a different interviewer, the difference between the results for the two samples would not constitute a criterion of the differences between interviewers. It would be mixed up with differences between special-subject groups and there would be no way of knowing how much of the difference was due to this and how much to interviewers.

Interpenetrating samples, although a valuable means of investigating non-sampling errors, must not be treated as a substitute for careful fieldwork supervision and control. For one thing, numbers in the separate sub-samples tend to be small so that detailed investigation of interviewer errors is rarely possible, only the major sources of variation being discovered; for another, interpenetrating samples do not disclose systematic errors common to all interviewers, for these will appear equally in the separate sub-samples. Some doubts regarding the value of interpenetrating samples as a regular feature of sample surveys are expressed by Sukhatme [256].

(b) *Area sampling.* In this method the area to be covered by a survey (e.g. a country, a county or a city) is divided into a number of smaller areas, of which a sample is selected at random; within these areas, either a complete enumeration is carried out or a further sub-sample is taken. Area sampling is basically a form of random sampling in which maps, rather than lists or registers, serve as the sampling frame. It is discussed separately because the student of the American literature will encounter the term very frequently.

Suppose we wish to make a survey of living conditions in a sample of dwellings in a city and that we can get no list of the dwellings which could serve as a sampling frame. If there is an accurate map on which clusters of dwellings—such as blocks bounded by streets—can be identified, this could provide a convenient frame. The city area is then divided into these blocks (if possible, of approximately equal population), the blocks are numbered and a random sample of them is selected. If a sample of 1 in 1,000 dwellings is required, a random sample of 1 in 1,000 blocks could be taken and every dwelling in the selected blocks included in the sample.

In practice, multi-stage sampling is usually preferred. Thus one might select, on the usual principles, 1 block in 100 and then a 1 in 10 sample of dwellings within each block. For sub-sampling there are basically two alternatives, the choice depending on what maps are available. If these are detailed enough for the smaller units—say dwellings—making up each block to be identifiable, then the second stage selection can be done on the map. The dwellings in the selected block can be given serial numbers and a random sample of 1 in 10 chosen. If maps of such detail are not available, investigators have to go to the selected blocks and list all the dwelling-units before the sub-sample can be drawn (occasionally the listing and interviewing are combined). All three methods—complete enumeration of a sample of blocks, sub-sampling from the maps, and sub-sampling from special lists—have been used in the United States.

The boundaries defining individual areas may be natural ones, such as streets; and in the United States, where cities are commonly laid out in regular patterns, this is usually convenient. Even if they are not regular, as for instance in rural areas, natural boundaries have great advantages from the point of view of identification. The alternative is to impose a grid on the map, numbering the squares and taking a random sample of them; but such a grid will cut across the sampling units and raise problems of allocation and listing.

No personal choice of sampling units enters into area sampling (although biases may arise in the listing; see Mannheimer and Hyman [172]) and every population unit, being associated with one and only one area, has a calculable and non-zero chance of inclusion. Nor is any prior information about the population needed to design the sample; shifts of population and other changes will be disclosed by the sample results.

Area sampling was developed principally in the United States where it remains, and is likely to remain, the predominant method. Its value there and non-use in Great Britain are both easy to understand. In the United States there are no convenient general population lists, while here there are two or three. Conversely, while detailed and convenient maps have been prepared in the United States, in this country none of the available maps would be adequate for area sampling and there is at present little incentive to anyone to undertake the high initial cost of preparing them. An exception is in the sampling of shops and similar establishments, where the absence of a suitable list or register is a serious difficulty.

(c) *Master samples*. If repeated samples of the same area or population are to be taken, there are advantages in preparing some sort of master sample, from which sub-samples can be taken as and when required. This was first done on a big scale in the U.S. Master Sample of Agriculture, described by King and Jessen [143], for which the country was divided into a large number of small areas and a master sample of 70,000 constructed, representative of every county. Sub-samples from this could be drawn to give whatever regional or national coverage was required for a survey. The main advantage of master samples is that they simplify and speed up the selection procedure.

The sample-units into which a master sample is divided should be relatively permanent. There would be little point in constructing a master sample of individuals or households since, owing to deaths, births and removals, it would quickly become out-of-date; a master sample of dwellings would be of more long-term usefulness, although even here the construction of new homes would be a major cause of out-of-dateness.

Whether or not the trouble of preparing a master sample of, say, dwellings in Great Britain would be worth while is difficult to say. It certainly seems uneconomical for survey bodies to have to select a fresh sample for each survey; there may be scope (i) for the procedure of sample selection to be centralised, and (ii) for this selection to be simplified by the use of a master sample.

5.9. Panels

This is the most convenient point at which to discuss the panel method, in which the aim is to collect data on broadly the same questions from the same sample on more than one occasion. Problems of initial sample design are no different for panels than for single surveys, but there are special problems of maintaining sample representativeness.

The panel begins as a randomly selected sample of the survey population. Information is then sought from this sample at regular intervals, either by mail or by personal interview. Volunteer panels are excluded from this discussion.

The advantages of panels

The attraction of panels is that they offer a particularly good way of studying trends, whether of behaviour or attitudes. If a market researcher wants to study how brand preferences change from month to month a panel enables him to do so conveniently (and the sampling error of the change between the two dates will be smaller than if a different sample is taken on each occasion). The researcher can study the buying habits and views of a fixed sample of people, judge how stable these are and what circumstances lead them to change.

This last point is particularly important. Panels are useful for studying the effects of specifically-introduced measures, such as advertisements; and in this respect they are certainly superior to the single survey, in which one would have to ask respondents to recall their views before the time of the advertisement, thus placing undue reliance on memory.

Panels have another important advantage. Suppose that in period 1,

48 per cent of the panel members favour Brand X, while in period 2 the proportion is 54 per cent. It is then possible not only to measure the net amount of change (which independent samples could do also) but to identify and study the "changers": those who no longer favour Brand X and those who did not previously favour it, but now do so. Panels of shops, as opposed to panels of consumers, can also be valuable in showing up trends and the function of retail audit panels has already been noted. The value of panels in official and in social research is discussed by Wilson [288].

Administratively, panels have the advantage that the overhead costs of sample selection can be spread over many surveys and that they make for easy fieldwork planning. Further, once people have agreed to give information it is generally possible to obtain fuller and more reliable data than in the single survey.

The problems of panels

The chief problems of panels are the achievement of the initial sample, sample mortality and conditioning.

To recruit a representative panel is clearly no mean task. It is one thing to ask a housewife a few questions on the doorstep; it is quite another to ask her to supply information regularly over an extended period. In the case of the original Attwood Consumer Panel,[1] about 80 per cent of the contacts agreed to be enrolled on the panel. This would be a satisfactory enough figure but, by the time the first reporting period came round, 1 in 5 of these failed to co-operate. This left 64 per cent of the initial sample and even these did not all stay the course. It is the experience of researchers that the first few weeks (or months or quarters, depending on the reporting period) always take a heavy toll of panel membership and that it then settles down. The Attwood panel lost a further 16 per cent of the total in the first 6 weeks so that 48 per cent of the original sample remained. Those who refused or dropped out were replaced by households with similar demographic characteristics. What is difficult to ascertain is how typical those who refused to co-operate or who dropped out were of the remainder; they may have been less literate, busier, had bigger families, less interest in the survey and so on. True, the composition of the remaining sample can be checked against known data on some factors, but this is only partial reassurance; its representativeness with regard to the behaviour and attitudes which are the subject of the survey must remain in doubt.

Panels are not, of course, alone in suffering from non-response but because the burden on respondents is greater than in single interviews, the problem is bigger.

[1] See Wadsworth [279] and Le Mesurier [157] for a description of this Panel.

By "panel conditioning" one means the risk that the panel members may become untypical as a result of being on the panel. This is not as fanciful as may at first appear. Members of a radio listening panel may gradually become more critical of programmes, more conscious of defects, more interested and more attentive. Those on a consumer panel may with time become more aware of different brands, of advertisements and of different forms of presentation; they may also become growingly conscious of their spending habits and in sheer horror tighten their belts. Members of a panel studying political opinions may try to appear consistent in the views they express on consecutive occasions. If such things happen, the panel becomes untypical—not in composition but in its characteristics—of the population it was selected to represent.

Panel operators are conscious of this danger and keep a watchful eye for signs of conditioning. There are several possible checks, the best being the expensive one of selecting independent samples of the population at regular intervals and comparing their characteristics and results with those of the panel. Another safeguard is to give members only a limited panel life, and then to replace them with persons taken randomly from a reserve list (perhaps from within strata of family composition, social status and so on).

There is a strong case for using some form of partial replacement on every panel, but it has to be rigorously applied. The method has been theoretically developed (see Yates [291]) and the chief objection, from the panel operator's viewpoint, is that it goes against the grain to replace panel members who are co-operative and reliable. However, this method of partial replacement would help to anticipate both the difficulties of panel mortality and conditioning and is worth some experimentation.

6.10. Concluding Remarks

In this chapter I have sought to introduce the basic sampling designs in use today. I noted at the beginning that if bias in selection is to be avoided and the precision of the results to be calculable random methods of selection must be employed. Thus randomness forms the base of the entire structure of sample design. This assured, a number of refinements are possible to meet both practical and theoretical requirements. Of these, multi-stage sampling, with equal or varying probabilities of selection, and stratification are the most important. In an introductory account, all these aspects of design must perforce be described separately, although in practice the sampler calls on them in combination. It is the purpose of Chapter 8, in which a national design is given in detail, to show how a sampler goes about his task.

One other point. I have noted repeatedly how the designer of a sample needs information about the population he is sampling to do the job most effectively. To fix sample size (see Section 7.1) he must estimate the variability in the population; in order to decide on the most appropriate sampling fractions for the various strata, he ideally needs some knowledge of their respective variability and of their respective costs; in order to decide how to distribute a sample over various sampling stages, he requires information on the variabilities within and between first-stage sampling units, and again about the different cost components involved. There are often approximate methods of making these estimates, but few better than to use information available from previous sample surveys of the same, or a similar, population. Sample design is a task in which one learns from experience: in which the results of one sample can and should be used to improve the design of the next.

NOTES ON READING

1. There are several excellent text-books which describe in detail modern methods of sample design. The best non-mathematical descriptions are to be found in Chapter 3 of YATES [291], in Chapter 1 (Vol. I) of HANSEN, HURWITZ and MADOW [112]. Both books, in later chapters, give theoretical treatments of the designs and, for the reader wishing to pursue the subject at this level, we should add the book by COCHRAN [36]. Other good single-chapter introductions are those by McCARTHY in JAHODA, DEUTSCH and COOK [129] and by KISH in FESTINGER and KATZ [78]. For those who read German, a good introduction is the book by KELLERER [135]; for readers of French, THIONET [259] is recommended.

2. The paper by GRAY and CORLETT [102], of the Government Social Survey, gives a full account of the use of many of the basic designs in national surveys in this country.

3. On quota sampling, readers may refer to papers by MOSER [192] and by MOSER and STUART [194]. On area sampling the book by HANSEN, HURWITZ and MADOW [112] gives by far the most complete treatment. Other useful papers on this subject are by KEYFITZ and ROBINSON [142] and by HANSEN and HAUSER [110].

4. On panels, a publication by the U.S. DEPARTMENT OF AGRICULTURE [274] is well worth studying. So are the articles by LAZARSFELD [156] and WILSON [288].

CHAPTER 7

FURTHER ASPECTS OF SAMPLING

7.1. Sample Size[1]

WE HAVE now looked both at the basic ideas of sampling and at the designs which are commonly used. It remains to discuss a few other aspects of sampling of general importance —the question of sample size, the use of random sampling numbers, sampling frames and the problem of non-response—before giving a detailed illustration of one particular sample design in the following chapter.

Anyone who ever has to advise on sample designs will know that almost invariably the first question he is asked is: "How big a sample do I need?" He will also know how disappointed the researcher usually is when told that an accurate answer is hardly possible until he himself has provided a good deal of information relating to the survey and the population it is to cover.

Most people who are unfamiliar with sampling probably over-rate the importance of sample size as such, taking the view that "as long as the sample is big enough, or a large enough proportion of the population is included, all will be well". The fallacy in this is clear as soon as one looks at any standard error formula, say (5.1) on p. 61 above. If the population is large, the finite population correction $N-n/N-1$ practically vanishes and the precision of the sample result is seen to depend on n, the size of the sample, not on n/N, the proportion of the population included in the sample. Only if the sample represents a relatively high proportion of the population (say, 10 per cent or more) need the population size enter into the estimate of the standard error.

Although an increase in sample size will increase the precision of the sample results (as is made clear by any standard error formula) it will not eliminate or reduce any bias in the selection procedure.

[1] Sample size and design are so intimately connected that I chose to postpone this discussion until the designs had been explained.

Therefore, the size of the sample is not in itself enough to ensure that "all will be well" (as the *Literary Digest* débâcle referred to on p. 73 above proved).

Returning to the researcher's opening question ("How big a sample do I need?"), if cost and other practical limitations do not enter into the picture there is no basic difficulty in determining the desired sample size (we assume throughout this section that the f.p.c. can be ignored). To illustrate the principle of estimating sample size, let us recall the formula for the standard error of a proportion p based on a simple random sample of size n. The purpose of the survey is to estimate the proportion π in the population with some particular attribute. The standard error of the estimate is

$$S.E._p = \sqrt{\frac{\pi(1-\pi)}{n}} \qquad \ldots(7.1)$$

and, inverting this formula, we obtain

$$n = \frac{\pi(1-\pi)}{S.E._p^2} \qquad \ldots(7.2)$$

which is an expression for n in terms of π, the population proportion, and the $S.E._p$. In other words, *if* we can form some rough estimate of what π is likely to be and *if* we can decide how small a $S.E.$ we wish to end up with, we can estimate from (7.2) the required sample size.

Suppose we are trying to estimate the proportion of smokers in a given population, and we believe that it is about 40 per cent. If we decide that a standard error of more than 2 per cent would be undesirable, we can use formula (7.2) to solve for n. A sample of 600 would be necessary to meet the case.

If we were estimating a population mean, we could similarly use formula (7.3)

$$S.E._{\bar{x}} = \frac{\sigma}{\sqrt{n}} \qquad \ldots(7.3)$$

where σ is the standard deviation of the variable under study in the population. Inverting we have

$$n = \frac{\sigma^2}{S.E._{\bar{x}}^2}; \qquad \ldots(7.4)$$

in order to calculate n, we require some idea of the standard deviation in the population or, as an estimate of this, of the standard deviation in the sample. We also must decide how big a standard error can be tolerated. These simple formulae (7.2) and (7.4) merely illustrate the principle involved; in practice the task of deciding on sample size is more complicated than they would suggest.

The first difficulty concerns the precision required. The surveyor himself must decide how precise he wants his sample results to be, that is how large a standard error he can tolerate. Most researchers have not thought about this enough to give a confident answer; but some answer *must* be given. It requires thought as to how, and by whom, the results are to be used and how much hinges on the decisions which they will determine. Since every set of survey results may be used for several different purposes, some of them unforeseeable, this is no easy task—especially as the researcher must think not only of the precision required for the overall results but also for the sub-group analyses. It is most unlikely that an estimate of the proportion of smokers in the total population is all that is required, or that it is even the result of chief interest. As much interest will lie in the proportions for men and women separately, for different age-groups, for different age-sex groups and so forth. If, say, 50 of the sample of 600 fall into a given age-group, the estimate of the proportion of smokers for that group will be based on $n = 50$ and, will be subject to a much larger standard error than the over-all estimate based on $n = 600$.

The decision on sample size will in fact be largely governed by the way the results are to be analysed, so that the researcher must at the outset consider, at least in broad terms, the breakdowns to be made in the final tabulations. He can then work out roughly what numbers are needed in *each sub-group* to give the desired precision for that sub-group and hence what total sample size would be desirable—it may, of course, be well beyond what is practicable. But it must be clear that, without some guidance from the surveyor as to the analysis and precision required, the statistician can be of little help.

This leads to the second complication. No survey is confined to one purpose: nearly always it seeks information on a number of different variables (or attributes) and a sample that is quite big enough for one variable may be inadequate for another which requires greater precision. Perhaps different clients are involved; perhaps we know that the results for one question are to be put to particularly vital use; perhaps some of the questions are of only marginal importance. But even if the same precision *is* required for all questions, a smaller sample might achieve it for some than for others, since the size necessary to achieve a *given* precision depends on the variability in the population. We note from formula (7.2) that the smaller $\pi(1 - \pi)$ is, the smaller a sample is needed to achieve a given standard error; similarly from formula (7.4) that, the less variable the population, the smaller the sample necessary to represent it with a given precision.

How can this problem of the "multi-purpose" of surveys be dealt with? Short of taking a sample large enough to give the desired precision for *all* the variables—which would rarely be possible—there is no perfect solution. Some order of priority for the different objectives has to be established, so that at least the principal ones are achieved with satisfactory precision. The reader is referred to Cochran [36] for a thorough discussion of this problem.

Let us suppose these difficulties are overcome: the researcher has stated what precision he requires and has established some order of priority for the survey's various purposes. Now, in order to use formulae (7.2) or (7.4) to calculate n, we need some estimate of π or σ respectively. For the simple random samples to which these formulae apply it may not be difficult to make the necessary estimates (they need only be approximate), but few practical designs are as straightforward as this.

Suppose the sample embodies some stratification. The above formulae then no longer apply but are replaced by others, such as that on p. 82. If this formula is to be used to estimate the required sample size, one needs to estimate not the variability for the population as a whole, but *for each of the strata*. With this information, one could work out the numbers required in the individual strata and thus in the whole sample. Or again suppose that the sample is a multi-stage one; formula [6.8] on p. 96 shows that, in order to estimate the required size for such a sample, some estimate of the variances between and within first-stage units should be made.

What this amounts to is that for normal designs the proper estimation of sample size may be quite complex, and require a good deal of knowledge, or shrewd guesswork, regarding the population.

In practice, this complexity is sometimes by-passed by the following kind of reasoning (rationalisation is perhaps a better word): "The formulae (7.1)–(7.4) apply to a simple random sample; ours is a stratified one and stratification serves to reduce the standard error; it is also a clustered sample and this serves to increase the standard error. We will assume that the two effects will roughly cancel out and use the simple random sampling formulae." What evidence there is suggests that stratification often brings rather little gain while clustering tends to increase standard errors considerably, so that this assumption tends to cause sample sizes to be fixed too low (and, generally, sampling errors to be under-estimated).

Up to now we have looked at only one side of the decision on sample size: what size would be necessary to achieve a given precision. In practice the sample designer's aim is either to get the maximum precision at a given cost or, conversely, to attain a fixed precision at the lowest cost; so his decision on sample size is influenced as much by his rough estimate of costs as by standard error estimates. Of course, in many social research surveys the desired size is unattainable in any case, because of financial, time or personnel limitations. In such a situation, it is best to take the largest sample financially possible *and* to discard questions on which a much larger sample would be needed to give useful results. One must accept the limitations imposed by a shortage of resources and try to utilise the available sample to best advantage, i.e. to attain the highest precision possible by statistical ingenuity in the design.

This section may be summarised as follows. The researcher must think out what use is to be made of the results, broadly what subtabulations he intends to make and how much precision he requires for these as well as the over-all results. Given certain facts about the population, the statistician can then work out roughly what sample size is necessary to achieve these aims, taking account of the nature of the sample design, the costs and the money available. In finally deciding on the sample size, the fact of non-response must not be lost sight of. If a sample of 2,000 is to be the aim, and it is estimated that some 20 per cent of the sample will not be "achieved", it is advisable to start off with a sample of 2,500. This ensures adequate numbers, but is of course in no way a safeguard against the risks of non-response bias (see Section 7.4).

7.2. Random Numbers

We saw in the last chapter that there are many occasions in sample selection when random numbers can be helpful and their use will now be briefly illustrated.

Using an earlier example, let us suppose that a random sample of 1 in 10 is to be selected from a college population of 3,000 students stratified into six special subject groups of which one, the "Economics" group, numbers 350. How can tables of random numbers help us to select the 35 Economics students?

The procedure is first to number the 350 students 1, 2 . . . , 350, the order being quite immaterial. We then turn to one of the sets of random numbers, say that of Kendall and Babington-Smith [140]. This contains 100,000 random numbers arranged in 100 separate thousands and printed in pairs and fours. The first 200 numbers are as follows:

TABLE 7.1

Extract from a table of random numbers

23 15	75 48	59 01	83 72	59 93	76 24	97 08	86 95	23 03	67 44
05 54	55 50	43 10	53 74	35 08	90 61	18 37	44 10	96 22	13 43
14 87	16 03	50 32	40 43	62 23	50 05	10 03	22 11	54 38	08 34
38 97	67 49	51 94	05 17	58 53	78 80	59 01	94 32	42 87	16 95
97 31	26 17	18 99	75 53	08 70	94 25	12 58	41 54	88 21	05 31

Source: Kendall and Babington-Smith [140].

It does not matter from what section of the tables the numbers are picked, though in repeated sampling it is as well to avoid continually using the same section. As the population contains 350 members, we have to select three-digit numbers. We start in the left-hand top corner and go systematically down sets of three-digit columns, rejecting numbers over 350 and any that come up for a second time. The first 35 of the numbers accepted would then represent our 1 in 10 random selection from the 350 students. With the above numbers, it would look like this:

231–55–148–126–35 and so on.

In one sense this is rather inefficient. Three-digit numbers range from 001 to 999 and, if we only use those from 1 to 350, we would reject something like two out of every three numbers in the table. This wastes time and a more efficient procedure is: when a number between 351 and 700 comes up, subtract 350 and accept the number corresponding to the difference; thus the number 389 would select population member 39; 575 would select 225 and so forth. Numbers over 700 would still be rejected and the reader may wonder why, when a number over 700 is drawn, we do not deduct 700 and accept the resultant number. The reason is that the "population" of 999 three-digit numbers contains only two complete sets of 350 consecutive numbers (1–350 and 351–700). The third set (701–999) contains only 299 numbers, so if we used it the numbers 300–350 would be underrepresented in the sample and we would have failed to give all the 350 population members equal chances of selection.

There is no basic difficulty in using random numbers although a number of refinements are possible in practice (see Yates [291]). What is less easy to explain is why we are entitled to say that random numbers are random. The trouble is that the concept of randomness is itself complex and we must here content ourselves with a simple answer. Various devices are employed for constructing tables of random numbers. Kendall and Babington-Smith obtained theirs by a randomising machine, Tippett got his by extracting figures from volumes of official statistics. But what matters more than the source is how the tables stand up to the tests of randomness to which they are subjected—tests to check whether individual digits appear with equal frequency (allowing for sampling fluctuations), whether pairs of various digits do so, and so on. The tables mentioned above have stood up to these tests and can therefore be used with confidence. Many other sets of numbers—e.g. telephone numbers—do *not* satisfy these tests of randomness (see Kendall and Babington-Smith [140]).

The question might be asked: Is anything gained by using this random-number procedure? Could not the sampler himself number the 350 students at random and then pick any 35 numbers (even the first 35 on the list would do)? The argument against this procedure is that it is basically unsound to throw the onus for securing randomness on the sampler. So we take the alternative course of ordering the population in whatever is the most convenient way and using random numbers for the selection; the randomness is ensured by the arrangement of the numbers not by that of the population.

7.3. Sampling Frames

One of the decisive factors in sample design is the nature of the sampling frames available—the lists, indexes, maps or other population records from which the sample can be selected at each sampling stage. The population coverage, the stages of sampling, the stratifications used, the process of selection itself—every aspect of design is influenced by the sampling frames.

The qualities looked for in a sampling frame

In discussing the qualities looked for in a frame, I follow the useful distinctions made by Yates [291, Section 4.8]:

(*a*) The first desideratum is that the frame should be *adequate*, in the sense that it should cover the whole of the population to be surveyed. This is, of course, relative to each survey, not a general characteristic of the frame. A frame which is adequate for one purpose may be very inadequate for another. If the special subject "Economics" in the student survey is supposed to cover Accountancy students, the frame is inadequate if it excludes them, and this inadequacy will be reflected in the sample. If a frame does not range over the entire population to be surveyed, it can still be used for the part it does cover and a sample of the remainder obtained from other sources.

(*b*) The sampling frame should be *complete*. By this I mean that all the population members who are supposed to be on it are in fact on it. If some of the Economics students who are supposed to be on the list fail to register, the list is incomplete. These students have no chance of being selected, so that the sample will be unrepresentative to that extent. Incompleteness can be a serious defect, especially if the people excluded tend to be a particular type—quite a possibility if inclusion on the list is a matter of personal responsibility.[1] Incompleteness is the more serious because, generally speaking, it is not easily discovered.

(*c*) A frame should *not be subject to duplication*. If certain members are included more than once, they can get into the sample more than

[1] An important practical example of incompleteness arises through dwellings which are unoccupied when the frame is constructed but occupied by the time of the survey. They should thus be included. See Yates [291, p. 67] for a description of the "half-open interval" method for dealing with the situation.

once. This may happen, for instance, if people who move from one area to another are immediately included in the list for the new area, but not so quickly deleted from the old.

(*d*) The information for each sampling unit listed on the frame should be *accurate*. In addition the frame ideally should not include "non-existent" units. This source of inaccuracy is met with in many population lists, houses being included which have been demolished, addresses which do not exist, and people who are dead.

(*e*) As a particular aspect of (*d*), the frame should be as *up-to-date* as possible. It may, when first constructed, be complete, free from duplication and accurate; but may be deficient in all these respects some months later—for instance, through people moving home.

(*f*) Finally, it is *convenient*, though not essential, to have the frame available in one central place. It is helpful if it is arranged in a way suitable for sampling—if stratification by polling districts is desired, a frame which is arranged by polling districts is a great help. It is convenient if the units are numbered, and essential that the information given enables the units to be identified with certainty.

These are stringent requirements and no sampling frame meets them all. Most of the frames used for large-scale surveys are constructed for administrative purposes and it would be pure coincidence if they happened to be ideal for sampling. However, the first thing a sample designer needs is to know what frames are available and how far they enable him to sample his population completely, accurately and conveniently. If no suitable frame exists, one may have to be constructed. In the Unites States, for example, where area sampling is facilitated by excellent maps, a field listing of the units living in, say, city blocks is usually necessary before the final selection can be made.[1]

The national frames in Britain

We are fortunate in Great Britain in possessing two national lists, one of dwelling-units and one of individuals, which make suitable frames for samples of the general population. These are the Rating Records and the Register of Electors. The Maintenance Register (the list deriving from national registration) and the sets of reference leaves of the Ministry of Food Ration Books were occasionally used as a sampling frame, but are now a matter of history and will not be discussed further.

The Rating Records

Local authorities throughout the country are responsible for preparing and keeping up-to-date records of the property in their areas.

[1] The problems of constructing a list in the field are discussed by Hansen, Hurwitz and Madow [112].

The records are kept locally and permission to use them for sampling purposes is at the discretion of Rating Officers. Usually—there are some regional differences—the records for a local government area are arranged by wards, within these in alphabetical street order and within streets by street number. For any given property, the records note the type (house, flat, cinema, shop), rateable value, the name of the owner and the name of the occupier.

The rating records are a suitable frame for sampling dwelling-units as long as care is taken to exclude non-dwelling property. In practice, the records are often used for selecting households rather than dwellings, and this causes some minor difficulties, which it is instructive to examine.

Suppose that the records show a given area to contain 1,000 dwellings and that we wish to draw a sample of 100 households. Three alternative procedures for drawing the sample may be considered, bearing in mind that some dwellings contain more than one household. Gray and Corlett [102] estimated that about 5 per cent of dwellings in England and Wales contain two households and about 1 per cent contain three or more.

(a) One could select every tenth dwelling, starting at a randomly chosen point, and include the household it contains; if there are two or more, one of them could be selected at random. This procedure, however, is unsound, since the resultant sample would under-represent households living more than one to a dwelling. A simple example shows why. Using Gray and Corlett's estimates, the chances are that of the 1,000 dwellings in the area about

    940 will contain 1 household, i.e. a total of 940 households
    50 will contain 2 households, i.e. a total of 100 households
    10 will contain 3 or more households, i.e. a total of 40 households.[1]

If the sample is to be representative of these classes of households, it should include them in the ratio 94 : 10 : 4, that is 87 per cent : 9 per cent : 4 per cent. In fact, our procedure results in a ratio of 94 per cent : 5 per cent : 1 per cent, so that the sample will under-represent households living more than one to a dwelling.

(b) To overcome this difficulty, one might take all the households in each selected dwelling. This would give the correct distribution of households, but we would end up with more than 100 households, as is clear from the above example (which would have selected a total of 108). The excess would differ from area to area, depending on the proportion of dwellings in the area containing more than one household,

[1] Assuming that the average is 4 households per dwelling (this is probably on the high side).

and the net effect would be to over-represent in the final sample those *areas* which have a high proportion of multiple-household dwellings. Accordingly, if the sample is to have the correct representation of all the areas, the results would have to be corrected by re-weighting. This is acceptable but a nuisance.

(*c*) A system that avoids the problems of both (*a*) and (*b*) is used by the Government Social Survey and has also been employed else-where—for instance in the official Household Expenditure Survey of 1953. If the dwelling at which an investigator calls contains two households, *both* are included and the investigator then omits the next dwelling on the list, proceeding to the next-but-one; if a dwelling contains three households the investigator includes them all, and omits the next two and so forth. Gray and Corlett [102], to whom this system is due, show that it works well and gives the correct distribution of households.

In practice the biases caused by either (*a*) or (*b*) might be small, but the sample designer has to be aware of their possibility and take precautionary action.

The Register of Electors

For samples of individuals the Register of Electors generally offers the most convenient frame. The Register is compiled every October and published in the following February and, as there is no revision between one October and the next, not only is the new Register 4 months out of date when it appears, but the old one it is replacing is 16 months out of date. The Register of Electors aims to list all those entitled to vote in parliamentary and local elections, which effectively means British subjects aged 21 and over.[1] The exclusion of foreigners may be a serious drawback for some surveys and in some areas.

The arrangement of the Register is as follows. There is one booklet for each polling district, and the Register belonging to any one ward, constituency or administrative district can be identified. Within polling districts the order is similar to that of the Rating Records,[2] but the entry for any address names all those in it who are entitled to vote (and have registered). Order of names is alphabetical by sur-name and, within surname, by Christian name. The names in a polling district are serially numbered.

A considerable convenience is that the Register is centrally

---

[1] Actually it also includes those who, though not 21 on the October qualifying date, will become 21 before the following 1st June. These persons are marked "Y". The Register thus covers persons aged 20 years 5 months and over. Certain groups of electors (e.g. Service men) are also specially marked. For full details of the Register, and its use as a sampling frame, the reader is referred to Gray, Corlett and Frankland [103].

[2] Except in rural districts, where it is arranged entirely in alphabetical name order.

available. The British Museum has a complete set; the Government Social Survey has a set for England and Wales; and a separate set for Scotland is housed in Edinburgh.

At one time, the Register was greatly distrusted as a sampling frame, being thought incomplete and out of date; it is widely used now because, since the Maintenance Register was discontinued, the Register of Electors has become the only national sampling frame of individuals available and an empirical study of the Register, published by Gray, Corlett and Frankland [103] in 1950, was fairly reassuring as to its completeness and accuracy.

Now a word about the use of the Register for sampling. To obtain a sample of individuals, the sampling interval $(k = n/N)$ is determined, a starting point is picked at random and then every kth name is chosen. Every individual on the Register has the same chance of being selected and minor difficulties, such as eliminating Service voters, are easily disposed of.

To take a sample of addresses or households is more complicated. If we selected every kth individual and included the address to which he belonged, the probability of any address being selected would be proportionate to the number of registered electors in it, so the results would have to be re-weighted. An address with 5 registered electors would have 5 times as much chance of being selected as a single-person address and, in arriving at final results, the former would have to be given a weight of $\frac{1}{5}$ and the latter a weight of 1 in order to equalise the probabilities. There is no objection to this except that re-weighting is a nuisance which practitioners prefer to avoid.

An alternative is to make a preliminary selection of every kth individual (starting at a random point), noting the address and the number of electors registered at it. This latter gives the probability of that address's selection. Then, if we compose from this a final sample of *every* selected address containing one registered elector, every *second* address containing two electors and so on, the result is a sample of addresses selected with equal probabilities.[1] It can then be converted into an "equal-probability" sample of *households* in the manner described for the rating list above.

With sufficient care, both the rating records and the Register of Electors can be used effectively for sampling purposes. Whatever their defects, these two frames certainly exercise a determining influence on British sampling practice.

These two lists are most often used for national samples of the

---

[1] Another alternative method is suggested by Yates [291, p. 67], namely to examine every kth name and include the address if the name refers to the first listed member at that address.

general population, and the question arises how useful they are for sampling special sections of the population. This will largely depend on the identifiability and size of the section. If, for example, one required a sample of British Males aged 30–44 in Bristol, the Register of Electors would serve as a convenient frame, and the main decision would be to determine the appropriate sampling interval. Suppose that the total population on the Register for Bristol is 400,000 and we estimate that 40,000 are males in the required age-group. If the sample is to be 1,000, then the actual sampling fraction is to be $\frac{1,000}{400,000}$, but in order to allow for those on the register who are not in the required group we would use the fraction $\frac{1,000}{400,000} \times \frac{400,000}{40,000}$, i.e. we would pick out 1 in 40 not 1 in 400.

As the Christian name is given on the register, we could at the selection stage eliminate (nearly all) women who are selected, leaving us with, say, 5,000 names. The register gives no clue to a person's age, so there is no alternative but to contact these individuals, find out whether they fall into the required age-group, interview those who do, and reject the others.

This process is tedious and uneconomical, especially if the section to be sampled covers a small proportion of the population covered by the frame; but, barring the construction of a new frame, there is no real alternative.

Other sampling frames

Sampling frames of some kind can usually be found for special populations but exceptions might be: people on holiday, housewives who saw a certain film or bought a particular product last week, people who read a given paper. With such difficult populations, either a frame must be constructed or methods like quota sampling be used.[1] (It is worth noting that sampling frames of institutions —e.g. manufacturing establishments, offices, farms—are often difficult to come by—quite a serious obstacle to market researchers.)

I have mainly discussed sampling from lists of names, but there are many other situations. Sometimes, for instance, it is convenient to sample dates, as was done in the enquiry into the trend of intelligence mentioned on p. 100. The main sample was an entire age-group of children and sub-samples by dates were taken from this for special purposes. One such consisted of all children born on the first three days of every month (the 36-day sample); another was of the children born on the first day of every second month (the 6-day sample).

[1] A paper by R. Tulse [266] offers a rigorous solution to the problem of sampling small sub-sections of a population.

When the population to be covered is already represented by cards or schedules, serial-number sampling is often convenient. In a current survey among university students, each of the (approximately) 20,000 students is given a serial number. Later sub-samples can easily be drawn with the aid of these. For a 10 per cent sample, for instance, a digit between 0 and 9 (inclusive) would be chosen at random and all the cards with serial numbers ending in that digit selected. A 1 per cent sample could be obtained by selecting all students whose numbers end in a randomly chosen *pair* of digits. An example of this was the 1951 Population Census in which a 1 per cent sample of the schedules was selected for early analysis. The frame was provided by the complete set of schedules and selection was based on the household serial numbers. In enumeration districts with odd reference numbers, all household schedules ending in 25 were selected; for those with even reference numbers, all ending in 76 were chosen.

7.4. Non-response

Designing a sample is a matter of technical knowledge and ingenuity, and the expert can usually design as precise a sample as the client or research worker can afford. If the sample is selected at random, the principles of sampling theory sketched in Chapter 5 apply, enabling the precision of the sample results to be estimated. But there is one weak link in this chain. The theory is based essentially on the text-book situation of "urns and black and white balls", and while in agricultural and industrial sampling the practical situation corresponds closely to its theoretical model, the social scientist is less fortunate. He has to sample from an urn which some of the balls properly belonging to it happen not to be present at the time of selection, while others obstinately refuse to be taken from it. This is not quite the random sampling of the text-books.

Non-response is a problem no investigator of human populations can escape; his survey material is not, nor ever can be, entirely under his control and he can never get information about more than a part of it. This applies as much to complete-coverage surveys as to sample surveys. Fortunately a good deal of knowledge has been accumulated on how to deal with the problem and it would be quite wrong to imply that non-response vitiates the scientific nature of sampling. Mail surveys apart, it is usually possible to keep non-response down to a reasonable level and to estimate roughly what biasing effects it may have upon the results.

At the risk of explaining the obvious, I will first show explicitly why non-response cannot simply be ignored, why one should not regard the, say, 80 per cent of the sample who respond as a satisfactory final sample and leave it at that. Suppose that a random sample has been selected to cover a given population and that, for one reason or another, answers are obtained from only a part of it. If this *part* were similar, in all characteristics that matter, to the *whole* sample, there would be nothing to worry about apart from the sheer reduction in sample numbers. Experience shows, however, that the missing part does often differ materially from the rest and certainly one should never *assume* that it will not do so.

It is helpful to think of the survey population as composed of two sub-populations or strata: respondents and non-respondents.[1] The survey succeeds in getting information about the former, not about the latter. This is, of course, an over-simplification since, whether a population unit belongs to the one stratum or the other, itself depends on the nature of the survey; but for purposes of illustration this simple model suffices.

Let us suppose now that the population consists of N units, of which N_1 belong to the "response stratum", N_2 to the "non-response stratum", and let $N_1/N = R_1$ and $N_2/N = R_2$. The purpose of the survey is to estimate μ, the mean (age, say) of the entire population. The question is, how much bias is there in using as an estimate of μ the mean of a simple random sample drawn from this population. The sample, by definition, will consist of respondents only and we suppose that their mean age is $\bar{x}_1$; the expected value of this estimate— i.e. the average of the estimates derived from an infinite number of samples from the "response stratum"—we can call μ_1. The unknown population mean of the non-response stratum we term μ_2. The bias due to non-response is then $\mu_1 - \mu$, and this can be written as follows:

$$\mu_1 - \mu = \mu_1 - (R_1\mu_1 + R_2\mu_2)$$
$$= \mu_1(1 - R_1) - R_2\mu_2$$
$$= R_2(\mu_1 - \mu_2) \qquad \ldots(7.5)$$

This result demonstrates two points about non-response, both in accordance with common sense. First, that its biasing effects will be the greater, the greater is R_2, the non-response proportion. Secondly, that the biasing effect will be the greater, the greater is the difference between μ_1 and μ_2, i.e. that the seriousness of the non-response bias depends on the extent to which the population mean of the non-response stratum differs from that of the response stratum.

Suppose that a survey is to find out how often, on the average, people go to the cinema each week. A simple random sample of 1,000 is selected and answers are obtained from 800. Then[2] $R_1 = \frac{4}{5}$,

---

[1] The formulation of the non-response problem in the next paragraph or two follows the treatment of Cochran [36].

[2] I continue to simplify by assuming that the non-response proportion in the sample is an exact reflection of the proportion in the population belonging to a fixed "non-response" stratum.

$R_2 = \frac{1}{5}$. The 800 respondents on the average go to the cinema once a week, so that $\bar{x}_1 = 1$. This is an unbiased estimate of μ_1 but, if we use it to estimate μ, that is if we ignore the possibility of non-response bias, we might be seriously in error. If, for instance, $\mu_2 = 2$ (one would expect non-respondents to be the more frequent cinema-goers), then the true population average is

$$\mu = R_1\mu_1 + R_2\mu_2$$
$$= 1\frac{1}{5}$$

and not 1, as estimated. If the difference between the two strata, or the non-response proportion, were larger, the bias would be much more marked.

This simple analysis points the way to methods for dealing with non-response. These amount, first, to efforts to reduce its proportions to a minimum and, second, to trying to get some information about the characteristics of the non-response stratum. For once one knows *something* about μ_2, one is able to assess the likely extent of non-response bias and to improve the sample estimates accordingly. Before we turn to prevention and cure, however, we must examine the different kinds of non-response and their relative importance.

Types of non-response

It is useful to distinguish six sources of non-response:

(i) *Units outside the population.* First, we may clear out of the way one category which is not, properly considered, non-response at all. The sampling frame may include units that field investigation proves do not exist: demolished houses, non-existent addresses, and people who have died, are examples. These units should be considered as outside the population and not as non-response; the number (of non-existing units) should be subtracted from the sample size before calculating the non-response rate. Substitutes—randomly selected—may reasonably be taken for such units in order to keep the sample up to the required size.

(ii) *Unsuitable for interview.* Every selected sample is likely to include some people too infirm, deaf or unfamiliar with the language to be interviewable. Interviewers must be instructed as to what is to pass as "interviewable". If a respondent claims a headache in excuse for not co-operating, this is a case for calling back at another time, not for giving him up as "uninterviewable".

(iii) *Movers.* Any pre-selected sample of persons or households at given addresses will include a number who have moved, either within the same or to another area. Durbin and Stuart [68], for instance, found that 10 per cent of their initial sample of individuals (drawn from the register of electors) had moved from their address. At the time of fieldwork, the register was 10 months out of date.

(iv) *Refusals*. Some people invariably refuse to co-operate and critics of surveys often protest that they do not see why people should answer survey questions. There is indeed no formal reason. Very few enquiries (the Population Census is one) carry compulsory powers; but, as a matter of fact, few people ever do refuse. Most are extraordinarily willing to talk to strangers about their personal affairs, their likes and dislikes, their opinions. Interviewers more often report difficulty in stopping people talking than in persuading them to co-operate.

(v) *Away from home*. Every interview sample will include persons or households away from home for longer than the fieldwork period, so that ordinary re-calling is inapplicable.

(vi) *Out at time of call*. Some people are out when the interviewer calls, but could be contacted by re-calling. Included in this category are people who, though in, find the time inconvenient for interview and on whom a call-back can be made at another time.

In this classification, I have had in mind mainly random sample surveys in which informants are pre-selected and to be interviewed at home. Where interviewing is done in factories, colleges, offices and so forth, some of the above categories do not apply; similarly, when mail questionnaires are used. In quota sampling, since there is no pre-selection, categories (iii), (v) and (vi) do not appear in the same sense. In practice, quota sample interviewers usually do have to make some home interviews and undoubtedly not all their attempts meet with success. But these failures are not on record since the interviewer simply goes on to the next house. Similarly, a quota interviewer may approach someone who turns out to be "uninterviewable" but—unless the organisation specially demands the information—this will not show in the non-response analysis.

The magnitude of non-response

How important are the various components of non-response in ordinary random sample interview surveys? The following sets of figures come from (*a*) a newspaper readership survey of the British Market Research Bureau (see Chapter 8) and (*b*) a Government Social Survey sample. The respective sizes of the two samples were 3,600 and 8,000 adults.

The main differences between the figures derive from some special features of the B.M.R.B. survey. The interviewer, for instance, had to list all the members of a household before interviewing one of them. Of the refusals, nearly 30 per cent were due to unwillingness to give the information necessary for the listing; the remainder were refusals of the selected member to be interviewed. The over-all refusal rate was thus higher than usual.

TABLE 7.2

Sources of non-response in two national random sample surveys

	B.M.R.B. Sample	Social Survey Sample
	per cent	*per cent*
Unsuitable for interview	1·7	1·7
Refusals	6·2	2·8
Away from home	2·4	2·0
Out at time of calls	1·6	3·9
Miscellaneous	·4	·5
Total	12·3	10·9

Sources: B.M.R.B. sample, Edwards [72]. Social Survey sample: Gray and Corlett [102].

In both sets of figures, units "outside the population" and movers are excluded.

The "Out at time of call" rate in the B.M.R.B. survey, on the other hand, was uncommonly low because up to eight calls were made before the possibility of an interview was abandoned. In most surveys, three or four calls represent the limit of recalling. The Government Social Survey proportion of 3·9 per cent was after a minimum of three calls and represents a more typical figure.

Whether or not the above figures as a whole are reasonably representative is difficult to say; my guess is that they are below average. In any case, they refer only to straightforward interview surveys. Where anything more than answering a few questions is required, the non-response is always higher. In surveys on family expenditure, which require the household to keep accounts, a response of 60 per cent is considered good. In the official 1937–8 household-expenditure survey [269], budgets were requested at four quarterly intervals; by the end of the year only 45 per cent of the initial sample remained. In the 1953 enquiry, 67 per cent of all the sample households completed records: an unusually good response. The Ministry of Food [268] tried to obtain budgets of food expenditure from the same households at four quarterly intervals but abandoned the attempt because only 35 per cent of the sample were left at the end of the year. In mail surveys, it is doubly hard to get a satisfactory response.

We may assume that, in the average interview survey, there will be no information through non-response from something like 10 to 20 per cent of the selected sample, and there is much evidence in the survey literature that non-respondents and respondents differ in important respects. Housewives with large families are more likely to be found at home than those with few or no children; daytime interviewing will fail to find many young people and working men at home; keen cinema-goers or greyhound enthusiasts are less likely to be found at home in the evenings than others. Nor is willingness to co-operate likely to be spread evenly over the whole population. In an experimental survey, Moser and Stuart [194] found the following refusal rates:

TABLE 7.3

Refusal rates in an experimental survey—by sex, age and social class
(Percentages)

Sex		Age-Group		Social class	
Males	6·1	20–29	4·6	Upper	12·2
Females	8·9	30–44	6·1	Middle	9·7
		45–64	11·0	Lower	6·3
		65 +	7·5		

Source: Moser and Stuart [194].

The above figures referred to quota sampling and the over-all refusal rate was high; but the differentials may not be too untypical.

TABLE 7.4

Response rates analysed by rateable value of dwelling and size of town (successful interviews expressed as a percentage of total possible interviews in each group)

Rateable value of dwelling	Great Britain	Size of town		
		Conurbation	Other urban	Rural
Under £10	84	73	84	90
£10 to £19	79	74	81	84
£20 to £29	68	64	69	83*
£30 to £39	63	62	63	81
£40 to £49	55	51	55	80*
£50 and over	51	46	56	57
All dwellings (weighted)	75	66	77	86

* Based on a sample of less than 50.

Source: Lydall [165].

The Oxford Institute of Statistics' National Savings Survey provided further findings on differential response rates. Table 7.4 shows these analysed by the rateable value of dwellings and the size of towns.

The differences in response rates between town and country are striking; so are those between the rateable value groups (similar differences have been found in the Cambridgeshire Social Accounting Survey—see Utting and Cole [277]). The major share of this non-response was caused by direct refusals, but as the survey dealt with personal savings this was not surprising.

How should one deal with this problem—the danger of bias through non-response? Taking substitutes is no solution because the danger arises from the possibility that non-respondents differ significantly from respondents. If substitutes are taken, all that happens is that non-respondents are replaced by respondents, so that the risk of bias remains the same. The only argument in favour of substitution is that the final sample is kept up to the desired size; this may well be necessary to ensure that the numbers are adequate for the intended analysis and to keep sampling errors to their estimated magnitude (they would be inflated by the reduction in sample size).[1] Where these considerations weigh heavily, and it is felt that substitutes must be taken, they should be taken at random, e.g. from a reserve list drawn together with the initial sample. But it must be understood that this in no way helps to solve the problem of non-response bias.

The first approach to this problem is to try to increase the response rate, different steps being suitable for the different types of non-response. There is little to be done about people who are *unsuitable for interview*. A particularly good interviewer may manage to interview people who are, say, partially deaf or do not speak the language where another, less determined, would have failed; but it is not worth making an issue of this.

People who have *moved* are a rather special category. The logical procedure, if a pre-selected household has moved, is to track it down; but this is usually impracticable. In the 1954 Readership Survey, conducted by the Institute of Practitioners in Advertising, out of a total sample of about 17,000 individuals, 2,400 were found to have moved; of these, about 1,400 had moved to a known address in the area covered by the survey and were followed up (see [127]).

Another way of dealing with movers is to substitute for the moved household the new one that has taken its place. With a sample of individuals, one has to select an individual from the new household by some rigorously-defined procedure (as in Durbin and Stuart [68]). This method appears sound since it would still correctly represent movers in the final sample. A re-weighting procedure for dealing with the problem is used by the Government Social Survey (see Gray, Corlett and Frankland [103]).

[1] One other point is sometimes advanced in favour of substitutes (see Gray and Corlett [102, p. 186]). If interviewers know that, in cases of non-response, they will be expected to interview a substitute, they may try more determinedly to secure a response in the first place. Thus substitution acts as an incentive.

The steps a surveyor can take to minimise *refusals* are in the main matters of common sense.[1] It always helps to keep the questionnaire as brief as possible so that the burden on the respondent is at a minimum; to help him in giving information, perhaps with the inducement of financial rewards. But much will depend on the sponsorship and purpose of the survey itself, on the interviewers, on the questions and on the general approach. Some people will always refuse, whatever the survey or the interviewer, but their number is small; certainly smaller than the group of people who, although unwilling, can be won over, i.e. whose co-operation will depend on the survey itself and on the interviewer's approach.

Durbin and Stuart [66] in an experiment found that experienced professional interviewers had 3 to 4 per cent refusals as against the inexperienced amateurs' 13 per cent; also, that with a questionnaire on tuberculosis, a subject of urgent public importance, the refusal rate was only about 4 per cent, but doubled for questionnaires on reading habits and on saving. The fact is that the refusal rate depends a good deal on the researcher's and the interviewer's skill; but, as in most general interview surveys it is not more than 3 to 5 per cent—and even the most strenuous efforts generally fail to reduce it below the hard core of 1 or 2 per cent—it is not worth spending much thought or money on.

People who are *away from home* for the period of the fieldwork can be contacted after it is over, and should be if practicable. But generally it is not, and these non-respondents must then be written off as lost.

People who are *out at time of call* form a sizeable but not insoluble problem. Common sense must be used to make calls as productive as possible. For instance in a sample drawn, say, from the electoral register, the interviewer knows from her list the sex of nearly all sample members, so she will try not to make her calls on men in working hours. She can also, in preparation for second or later calls, find out when people are likely to be at home or arrange appointments. There is the risk that appointments may prove a two-edged weapon, in that some people may make doubly sure of being out or not answering the door when the interviewer calls; but scattered evidence shows that they do result in increased response rates. Thus Durbin and Stuart [66] showed that, when an appointment had been made, 71 per cent of second calls resulted in interviews, as against 40 per cent when none had been made.

Re-calls

However sensibly timed and arranged the first calls are, no surveyor would risk basing his results on these alone. The following figures,

[1] For a discussion of interviewing and securing co-operation see Chapter 11.

taken from the B.M.R.B. newspaper readership survey described in the next chapter, show one aspect of this:

TABLE 7.5

Distribution of interviews obtained at successive calls. Men and women

Number of effective interviews if a limit had been laid down of	Total	per cent	Men	per cent	Women	per cent
1 call	1,243	40	367	27	876	50
2 calls	2,389	77	962	71	1,427	81
3 calls	2,880	93	1,227	90	1,653	94
4 calls	3,023	97	1,313	97	1,710	97
5 calls	3,089	99	1,348	99	1,741	99
6 calls	3,109		1,357		1,752	
7 calls	3,116		1,359		1,757	100
8 calls	3,117	100	1,360	100		

Source: Edwards [72].

If interviewing had been confined to one call, only 40 per cent of the final sample would have been obtained and only 27 per cent of the final interviews with men. It is relevant to note that, in this survey, interviewers did not know the sex of informants in advance, so the low percentage of successful first calls on men is not surprising. But, a sample based on first calls alone would also have been entirely unrepresentative with regard to sex and many other factors.

Some re-calling is in fact standard practice. The Government Social Survey insists on a *minimum* of three calls (i.e. two re-calls) and encourages further calls if there is hope of an interview; other organisations take three calls as their maximum. Practitioners, on the whole, do not like too much re-calling on account of its costliness. True, the *total* cost of a survey does go up as more re-calls are made, but re-calling may not raise the average cost of an interview as much as is usually supposed. See Durbin [65] and Durbin and Stuart [68] for a discussion of this. The latter paper reports an experiment on call-backs, the results of which broadly support the common practice of making only two re-calls.

Complete re-calling on a sub-sample of "not-at-homes"

An alternative to calling back a few times on all the initial "not-at-homes" is to call back persistently on a sub-sample of them. This was first suggested by Hansen and Hurwitz [111] in connection with mail surveys; the theoretical basis is beyond the scope of this discussion, but the general idea should be explained.

The method was intended primarily for situations where following up "not-at-homes" is more expensive than original contacting (for instance, in mail surveys if the follow-up is by personal interview). Hansen and Hurwitz provide a theoretical framework by which the optimum sub-sampling ratio for a given survey, i.e. the proportion of the non-respondents to be included in the sub-sample, with minimum variance at a given cost, can be calculated. The solution involves estimating the likely "not-at-home" proportion, the variability (with regard to the main question or questions under study) in the entire population and in the "not-at-home" stratum. If reasonable estimates of these quantities can be made, the method is certainly useful for mail surveys.

Its value for interview surveys is more questionable. Durbin [65] has shown, for instance, that if the "not-at-home" rate is 60 per cent and the ratio of the cost of a re-call interview to that of a first-call interview is 2 : 1, the relative gain in efficiency over 100 per cent recalling on the "not-at-homes" is only 2·6 per cent. When the latter ratio is 3 : 1, the relative gain is 5·8 per cent. In practice, the ratios are unlikely to be as great as this, so the gains to be expected from this method in ordinary interview surveys are not large.

The Politz-Simmons method

We come next to an ingenious method of overcoming the "not-at-homes" problem in interview surveys, which was suggested by Hartley [116] and developed by Politz and Simmons [208], by whose names it is generally known.

The essence of the PS method (as it will be called here) is that the members of the survey population are regarded as being grouped into strata according to the probability of their being found at home by the interviewer. Then suppose that all interviews are made in the evenings and that *only one call* is made on each sample member—all that is necessary in the PS method. The interviewer asks each respondent on how many of the previous five evenings (usually weekday evenings) he was at home at about this time.[1] Some of the population members were in every evening so that the probability of their being found in by the interviewer was 1. Others were in no other evening apart from the one of interview, so for them the probability was $\frac{1}{6}$. The population can thus be thought of as divided into seven strata from $P = 1$ to $P = 0$, the last comprising the few people who were not in on any of the six evenings.

Now the achieved sample will contain members from each of these

---

[1] The period covered can just as well be any other. In the experiment referred to above [68], a complete week was taken (including Sundays). But, if the PS question covers Sundays, then interviews also should take place on Sundays, at the same rate as on other days.

strata except the last; with the interviews spread evenly over the six weekdays, one would find at home about $\frac{1}{6}$ of those who are in only one evening a week, $\frac{2}{6}$ of those who are in about two evenings a week .., and all those who are in every evening. One would in fact obtain a sample selected with different sampling fractions from the various "at home" strata and, in order to derive unbiased estimates from it, the results for each stratum should be weighted by the reciprocal of the sampling fraction, i.e. the reciprocal of the probability of being at home. These probabilities are unknown and must be estimated from information obtained at the interview. The only qualification to the statement that the procedure here described will result in unbiased estimates is that the people with probability 0 are never found in, which may cause slight bias. But with evening interviewing the zero proportion is so small that one need hardly worry about it.[1]

A constructed example will illustrate the working of the method:

TABLE 7.6

An example to show the working of the Politz-Simmons method

(1) Proba- bility of being at home P	(2) Intended sample size n	(3) Achieved sample size n'	(4) Sample means for survey variable*	(5) Calcula- tion of population mean $(4) \times (2)$	(6) Estimation of popu- lation mean from achieved sample $(4) \times (3)$	(7) Re- weighted estimates $(6) \times \frac{1}{P}$
1	180	180	1	180	180	180
$\frac{5}{6}$	180	150	1·2	216	180	216
$\frac{4}{6}$	180	120	1·4	252	168	252
$\frac{3}{6}$	180	90	1·6	288	144	288
$\frac{2}{6}$	180	60	1·8	324	108	324
$\frac{1}{6}$	180	30	2·0	360	60	360
Total	1,080	630		1,620	840	1,620

* Assumed equal to population means in the respective strata.

A sample of 1,080 is to be drawn from a population and we assume for convenience that in this population the strata containing people at home one evening a week, two evenings a week, and so on contain equal numbers, and that there are no people who are never at home at the relevant times. The intended sample numbers in the six strata are

[1] See the original Politz-Simmons paper [208] for a suggestion on how the extent of this bias can be gauged.

shown in column (2) and the achieved numbers—caused by the effect of the "not-at-home" proportions—in column (3).

The assumed strata means for the variable to be studied are given in column (4), and the calculations of the population mean as well as its estimation from the achieved sample are shown in columns (5) and (6). We find that

$$\text{the population mean} = 1620/1080 = 1\cdot 5$$
$$\text{the sample estimate} = 840/630 = 1\cdot 3$$

This under-estimation is due to the fact that the "low-probability" strata, which are under-represented in the sample, are the ones with the highest values of the variates (as might well happen in practice, e.g. if frequency of cinema-going were the subject of the survey). The PS method now involves multiplying the estimate from each stratum —i.e. the figures in column (6)—by the reciprocals of the probabilities and then combining the figures for all strata. The results are shown in column (7) and lead to a re-weighted sample mean = 1620/1080 = 1·5, which is equal to the population mean. I repeat that the stratum with zero probability of being at home has been ignored.

Theoretically the method is sound, and unbiased estimates of sampling errors can be made. Durbin [65] has shown that it does not require—as is sometimes suggested—that the times of the calls, and the choice of the previous occasions about which respondents are asked, be chosen at random. What is necessary is that the same number of calls be made on each evening of the fieldwork period, preferably by each investigator but certainly over the sample as a whole. The attraction of the method is that it enables unbiased estimates to be made on a one-call sample. Whether it is more efficient than recalling depends on the cost of re-calls and on the degree of correlation between the variables studied by the survey and the probability of respondents being at home. The method is subject to relatively high sampling errors as it rests on the use of the at-home probabilities, which, being themselves based on sample estimates, are subject to error. Furthermore, as its use is restricted to evening interviewing, it may be expensive and inconvenient.

There remains the question whether it is feasible to get from respondents the information on which the estimates of the probabilities have to be based? Will people tell, and accurately, on which of the previous five evenings they were at home? Practitioners have been sceptical about this, feeling that respondents might resent the intrusion into their affairs and refuse, or answer inaccurately. But in the Durbin-Stuart experiment already mentioned [68] only 19 out of 374 (i.e. 5 per cent) first-call respondents failed to give a complete answer to the "times-at-home" question; only two of these refused information. Whether the replies were accurate is another matter. People may not remember when they were in or they may wilfully mislead the interviewer, perhaps fearing that the information might be useful to burglars as well as to market researchers. The low refusal rate suggests that such fears are not widespread, although of course some people might find it easier to give wrong answers than to refuse altogether. How accurate their memories are is again difficult to say, but there seems no reason why the answers to the PS question should be any less accurate than those to any other of the many survey questions involving memory.

Adjusting for non-response bias

It follows from formula (7.5) that any success in correcting for non-response bias hinges on the possibility of gaining some knowledge, however meagre, about the non-respondents. There are several possibilities. Often the interviewer can find out something about the people she fails to interview. In the case of personal refusals, she can note the informant's sex, approximate age, perhaps broad social grouping. If she has failed to find the person, others in the house may be able to tell her something about him—his age, occupation and the size of his family; anyway, she can see and record the type of house. Interviewers should be asked to produce as much information about non-respondents as they can collect without snooping.

The composition of the achieved sample should be compared with known population data, including information available on the sampling frame, so as to give a clue to the extent and direction of non-response bias (see Lydall [165] for a discussion of the problems of checking survey results against external data). In a multi-phase design, the first-phase sample provides information about some of the later-phase non-respondents. Finally there are various methods of "follow-up". People who have refused to answer a lengthy questionnaire may yet be willing to complete a postcard asking for a few simple facts, and these may be sufficient to enable the surveyor to judge what kind of people his sample has missed.

One or more of these sources are open to most researchers and they make possible some comparison of respondents and non-respondents. Such comparisons, however, can never prove the *absence* of bias; at best, they can reassure the researcher that the final sample is not badly out of line. He may be able to deduce that, as regards the sex ratio, age distribution, social class grouping and various other characteristics, the non-respondents are broadly similar to the respondents but, while this gives him confidence, it does not mean that the two groups are similar in respect of whatever it is the survey is studying.

As an illustration of the practical approach to the question of non-response bias, let us return to the B.M.R.B. sample, for which the non-response figures were given in Table 7.2.

There were 483 non-respondents out of a sample of 3,600.[1] Did their absence cause any marked unrepresentativeness in the sample—for instance in its sex composition?

The sex of 33 of the 483 non-respondents was known: 58 per cent of these were men and the reasonable assumption was made that the percentage was roughly the same for the other 150. The probable sex composition of the initial sample of 3,600 was then estimated, as in Table 7.7.

TABLE 7.7

Sex composition of B.M.R.B. sample—successful interviews and non-respondents

(1) Sex	(2) Successful Interviews		(3) Non-Respondents		(4) Initial Sample constructed from (2) + (3)	
	No.	*per cent*	*No.*	*per cent*	*No.*	*per cent*
Men	1,360	43·6	280	58·0	1,640	45·6
Women	1,757	56·4	203	42·0	1,960	54·4
Total	3,117	100·0	483	100·0	3,600	100·0

Source: B.M.R.B. memorandum.[2]

The achieved sample had too few men (the population proportion was 47 per cent), but this under-representation was virtually corrected by allowing for the non-response factor. A similar calculation was made for the age distribution, although on a less secure basis; and for distribution by family size. It was also done for the social class composition to correct for the under-representation of the higher social classes.

Having found that an achieved sample is in some respects unrepresentative, is one entitled, and well advised, to adjust the results? The answer is certainly Yes—but one must be quite clear what this adjustment achieves and does *not* achieve.

The aim of a sample is to estimate certain population characteristics as accurately as possible and it would be irrational to leave a sample wrongly constituted when one has the knowledge and resources to

[1] This does not agree with the percentage of 12·3 in Table 7.2; that table excluded, while the figure 483 includes, units "outside the population".

[2] See footnote on p. 145.

improve it. Take the case of the sex ratio. The achieved sample contained 43·6 per cent men as against the estimated 45·6 per cent in the sample as selected (I shall use this latter figure as the correct one, rather than the population figure of 47·0 per cent, so that the figures in Table 7.7 can be used for illustration. In practice, one would of course adjust by the most accurate data available.) Now suppose that, among the respondents, men and women differ considerably in respect of the variables under study; suppose, say, that the *Daily Tabloid* is read by 80 per cent of the men, but by only 10 per cent of the women. Without re-weighting, the estimate of readership for the two sexes combined would be

$$\frac{(43 \cdot 6 \times 80) + (56 \cdot 4 \times 10)}{100} = 40 \cdot 5 \text{ per cent}$$

Knowing that the sample contains too few men—too few in the "heavy readership" group—we re-weight according to the correct proportions

$$\frac{(45 \cdot 6 \times 80) + (54 \cdot 4 \times 10)}{100} = 41 \cdot 9 \text{ per cent}$$

The difference is slight since the weights themselves—43·6 and 45·6—differ little. If the population sex-ratio (47 : 53) were used for re-weighting, the estimate would be 42·9 per cent. What must be clearly understood is that the re-weighting only ensures that the sexes are correctly represented in the sample; it does not reduce any bias arising from unrepresentativeness *within* the strata, that is within each sex group.[1]

There is a superficial resemblance between this re-weighting and "stratification after selection" (see Section 6.3), but the difference between the two is much more vital than the resemblance. In that method, the sample members found to belong to each stratum are a random sample of the population of that stratum. In the present context, the sample members in any stratum are a random sample only of the "response-population" in that stratum; hence the estimates based upon them are biased to the extent that respondents and non-respondents in that stratum differ from each other. This is best seen if we look at the calculation of the re-weighted result in a slightly different form. We first calculate the readership proportion for the respondents (as above), obtaining the result of 40·5 per cent. Next we calculate the readership proportion for the non-respondents

---

[1] It may even accentuate it. If the sample in the stratum that is given additional weight in the process is particularly unrepresentative of the population in that stratum, the biasing influence on the results may be increased. If the men respondents were a very unrepresentative sample of all men, while the women were a representative sample of all women, this could happen here.

assuming that here too 80 per cent of the men and 10 per cent of the women are readers. The result is

$$\frac{(58 \cdot 0 \times 80) + (42 \cdot 0 \times 10)}{100} = 50 \cdot 6 \text{ per cent}$$

Combining the results for the two strata, respondents and non-respondents, we obtain

$$\frac{(40 \cdot 5 \times 3117) + (50 \cdot 6 \times 483)}{3600} = 41 \cdot 9 \text{ per cent}$$

as before. This method of arriving at the result shows clearly the assumption underlying such re-weighting: that the men who are non-respondents are similar to those who are respondents, that in each group the readership proportion is 80 per cent.

An alternative, if there is no information about the composition of the non-response group, is to calculate the potential non-response bias on the most extreme assumptions possible:

(1) *Assumption that none of the non-respondents read the "Daily Tabloid"*

$$\frac{(40 \cdot 5 \times 3117) + (0 \times 483)}{3600} = 35 \cdot 1 \text{ per cent}$$

(2) *Assumption that all the non-respondents read the "Daily Tabloid"*

$$\frac{(40 \cdot 5 \times 3117) + (100 \times 483)}{3600} = 48 \cdot 5 \text{ per cent}$$

These are wide limits, but then they are based on the most extreme assumptions. Many other possibilities suggest themselves: one might assume that the readership among men non-respondents is 100 per cent, among women non-respondents 0 per cent, figures which are closer to the proportions in the respondent group and more reasonable than the extreme assumptions; they would give a result of 42·8 per cent. But this is a matter of judgement and the result is worth no more than the judgement. Taking the extremes has certain theoretical advantages,[1] but the resultant limits are usually too wide for comfort; besides, when one is dealing with a variable rather than an attribute, as here, there are no theoretical limits in the same sense. In practice, in assessing the likely influence of non-response, one usually bases the calculations on a mixture of common sense and empirical evidence. The more knowledge about the non-respondents one can gain, the more realistic will the calculations be. Whatever is done, the potential influence of non-response bias has to be acknowledged and any re-weighting done to correct for it fully described in the survey report; preferably the weighted *and* the unweighted figures should be

[1] See Cochran [36, p. 294].

given side by side. To many people, any adjusting or weighting of results denotes something a trifle shady and it is up to the researcher to allay such misgivings by a thorough explanation.

A sound way of adjusting for non-response bias was used in the Family Census of the Royal Commission of Population [93]. Out of a sample of approximately 1,353,000 women, 230,000 did not respond to the initial request for information, a non-response rate of 17 per cent. These were sent further letters asking them to co-operate and 50,000 of them did so. These 50,000 were then treated as a sample of all the 230,000 non-respondents and the results weighted accordingly. In actual fact, only the first 12,000 of the follow-up replies were analysed and combined with the remainder of the sample with a weight of 230/12. While the initially achieved sample had contained considerably too few women with no or very few children, the results, after the non-response had been allowed for in this manner, corresponded well with known figures. It seems very reasonable to treat the respondents to follow-up appeals as representative of all the non-respondents, rather than of the initial respondents. This applies to all follow-up methods, including call-backs in interview surveys. If there are several follow-up waves, the results to each wave can be analysed separately, permitting any trend to be discerned. If, for instance, people who are enthusiastic about a product are more likely to respond than others, one might find the proportion (expressing itself favourably on it) going down with each batch of respondents to the various waves. If such a trend is discernible, it is reasonable to assume that it would continue for the non-respondents remaining at the end.

The importance of some following-up, wherever non-response is of sizeable proportions, can hardly be exaggerated. The scale, procedure and the amount of information demanded in a follow-up, are matters to be decided in the individual survey; but there are various possible economies. It is not, for instance, necessary to go all out for complete information from follow-up contacts; a few key items may do. Again, the follow-up sample need not be spread over a wide geographic area; one can concentrate it in a few carefully selected areas, and use the differences between initial respondents and follow-up respondents found in *these* areas to correct the results for the entire sample.

Concluding remarks

I have distinguished various types of non-response and discussed ways of reducing their magnitude and of dealing with the core of non-response that invariably remains. There are several methods, both of prevention and of cure, which serve to reduce the seriousness of the problem and the survey planner should at the outset lay down the procedure to be followed in dealing with it. Certainly he can never afford to ignore it. Indeed some authors (see, especially, Cochran [36] and Deming [51]) have suggested that non-response bias may often be so serious as to dwarf the ordinary sampling error; in this case it might well pay to aim at a smaller sample and to spend the resources thus freed on efforts to secure a high response rate.

NOTES ON READING

1. The subject of sample size is discussed in all the text-books on sampling mentioned in previous chapters. For those whose algebra is adequate the chapter on sample size in Cochran's book [36] is particularly recommended.

2. On sampling frames, the book by Yates [291] and the paper by Gray and Corlett [102] are most useful. The former describes all types of frames, not only those used for sampling human populations; the latter gives a detailed account of the lists used in this country. On the register of electors, Gray, Corlett and Frankland [103] should be consulted.

3. There is a considerable literature on non-response. Among the text-books, those mentioned in the two preceding paragraphs both have good accounts of the subject. The main journal references I have already noted in the text.

CHAPTER 8

AN EXAMPLE OF A NATIONAL
RANDOM SAMPLE DESIGN

TO CONCLUDE the discussion of sampling, I am going to describe in detail a random sample design used in a national market research survey in 1952.[1] No single design can illustrate all the problems and refinements of practical sampling, since so much depends on the population to be covered, the resources available and the subject-matter of the survey. However, this sample will serve as well as any to illustrate the process which links the initial decisions on design with the final allocation of names and addresses to the interviewers.

The subject of the survey—the readership of newspapers and periodicals—is fairly typical of the general run of market research surveys; but in one respect this survey did differ from many others. Its prime purpose was to check the accuracy of the results achieved by a quota-sample survey on the same subject and its own reliability was therefore vital. Broadly speaking, the limits to the size and precision of this sample were time (only four weeks were allowed for the fieldwork) and the number of interviewers available, rather than financial resources. I may add that the results from this random sample showed those of the quota survey to have been substantially correct.

Population

The sample was to cover the adult civilian population aged 16 and over in Great Britain and the question immediately arose whether

[1] The sample was designed and used by the British Market Research Bureau, with Mr. J. Durbin and myself acting as consultants. Thanks are due to Mr. T. Cauter, then Managing Director of B.M.R.B., for permission to reproduce details of this sample; and to Mr. F. Edwards and Mr. P. Parkinson for allowing me to draw on their memoranda on the survey. All the Tables in this chapter derive from this source. The population figures used in them derive from the 1951 Census.

certain remote areas—like the Highlands of Scotland, the Southern Uplands of Scotland, Central Wales and islands other than the Isle of Wight—should be included. Interviewing in such areas is time-consuming and the cost always tends to be out of proportion to the value of the results. But because the sample had to be beyond criticism, it was decided to include these areas.

Sample size

The sample size was fixed with regard to the time and interviewers available and the detail and precision required in the analysis. As we saw in Section 7.1, for a simple random sample the size required to achieve a given precision is fairly readily determined, but this simplicity disappears with the more complex samples usual in large-scale surveys. The sample in this case was to be stratified by several factors and to be spread over four sampling stages. Little about the population, about the relative variability in different strata, and between and within clusters, was known in advance and the computation of *desired* sample size was a very approximate one. It was agreed that the sample should be of the order of 3,000–4,000; the actual number finally decided on—3,000—was determined mainly by the number of interviewers available and how many interviews could be managed in the time at the survey's disposal.

Estimating from past experience that the response rate would be about 84 per cent, an initial sample of 3,600 was selected. The actual response rate was 86·6 per cent (there being 3,117 successful interviews). Details of the non-response figures relating to this survey were given in Section 7.4.

Type of design

Like most national random samples, this one was a multi-stage stratified design:

Stage	Sampling unit	Stratifications
I	Administrative district	Geographical region, urban/rural, industrialisation index, zoning.
II	Polling district	
III	Household	
IV	Individual	

At stages I and II, selection was to be made with probability proportionate to population size. All towns over a certain size were included in the sample so that, for this "large town" stratum, there were only three sampling stages.

Sampling frame

No existing sampling frame exactly corresponded to the population to be covered. The most suitable was the register of electors, which was also centrally available in London—an important advantage since time was short. The sample had to be drawn in March and April, at a time when the new (i.e. November 1951) register was just being issued, and the old register was 15 to 16 months out of date. The new register was used wherever possible, namely for 60 per cent of the addresses; the remainder were taken from the old. It is worth noting that the non-response rate was no higher for the latter than for the former.

Sampling stage I

The choice for first-stage units lay principally between administrative districts and constituencies. The former lent themselves to convenient stratification by the industrialisation index (see below) and were therefore preferred.[1] The 1,500 or so administrative districts varied considerably in size, so the choice was either to stratify them by size or make the selection with probability proportionate to size. The latter alternative was adopted; it had the advantage that, while achieving the same end as stratification by size, it left more scope for additional stratifications.

The districts were first stratified by geographical region, then by urban/rural district within region. For the first stratification, the Registrar-General's twelve Standard Regions were used. (In fact, the results were wanted for a different set of six regions; but these were easily derived by adding together Standard Regions.) The distribution of the population at the 1951 Census was as shown in Table 8.1.

These figures refer to the total population, whereas the sample was to be of the population aged 16 and over; strictly the stratification should have been based on population figures for this latter age-range. Unfortunately, at the time, the Population Census results by age-groups were not available, but as it was known that the age group 16 and over forms a fairly uniform proportion of the total population over the different regions, the allocation of interviews was made according to the figures in Table 8.1. They were undoubtedly close enough to serve as a satisfactory basis for the stratification.

The over-all sampling fraction was $\frac{3,600}{48,840,000} = 1/13,567$. It was decided to use a uniform sampling fraction throughout, on the grounds

---

[1] Constituencies have the advantage that they are of roughly equal population size; if one stratified them by some index related to social/economic condition—such as per cent voting for a given party or the J-index (see below)—they might be preferable to administrative districts.

TABLE 8.1

Distribution of the population of Great Britain by region and urban/rural area. 1951

Standard Region		Urban 000's	Urban %	Rural 000's	Rural %	Total 000's	Total %
I	Northern	2417	4·9	723	1·5	3140	6·4
II	East and West Ridings	3562	7·3	534	1·1	4096	8·4
III	North Midland	2271	4·6	1107	2·3	3378	6·9
IV	Eastern	1945	4·0	1151	2·4	3096	6·4
V	South-Eastern	1779	3·6	777	1·6	2556	5·2
VI	Southern	1721	3·5	927	1·9	2648	5·4
VII	South Western	1870	3·8	1151	2·4	3021	6·2
VIII	Wales	1812	3·7	785	1·6	2597	5·3
IX	Midlands	3689	7·6	733	1·5	4422	9·1
X	North West	5927	12·1	517	1·1	6444	13·2
XI	Greater London	8346	17·1	—	—	8346	17·1
XII	Scotland	3564	7·3	1532	3·1	5096	10·4
Total		38903	79·5	9937	20·5	48840	100·0

that the advantages of a variable sampling fraction would be outweighed by the complications of weighting in the tabulation, computation and presentation. This is an arguable point. There may be something to be said for, say, sampling the rural areas less intensively than the urban; they are more costly per interview and may be less variable on some subjects. But in this case there was no firm evidence either way, so the simpler course was followed. With a uniform sampling fraction, each stratum was allotted a number of interviews approximately equal to $\dfrac{\text{population in stratum}}{13,567}$. The resulting distribution is shown in Table 8.2.

The next question was: over how many administrative districts should the sample be spread? The answer was determined by three practical considerations:

(i) The fieldwork was to be distributed over four weeks in such a way that in each district the interviews were spread over at least two "parallel" weeks—either weeks 1 and 3, or weeks 2 and 4 (in districts entitled to a sufficient number of interviews they were to be distributed over all four weeks). In the intervening weeks, each interviewer covered another administrative district.

(ii) Approximately 40 interviewers were to be used.

(iii) It was estimated that an interviewer could do about 20 to 25 successful interviews per week in an urban district and rather less in a rural district.

The combination of these factors suggested an aim of about 45 interviews per urban district and 26 per rural district. This in turn led to the decision to use a total of 90 administrative districts, which was the maximum the field staff could manage in the time and therefore preferable to any more clustered sample.

TABLE 8.2

Distribution of interviews over the regions and urban/rural areas

Region	Urban	Rural	Total
I	178	53	231
II	262	40	302
III	168	81	249
IV	143	85	228
V	131	57	188
VI	127	68	195
VII	138	85	223
VIII	134	58	192
IX	272	54	326
X	436	39	475
XI	615	—	615
XII	263	113	376
Total	2,867	733	3,600

As is usual, it was decided to group into one stratum the "large towns" and to include all of them in the sample; here "large" was taken to mean any town with a population big enough to be entitled to about a week's interviewing. These towns are listed in Table 8.3, together with population figures and number of interviews allocated. (London is not included; it figures as a separate region—No. XI.)

Subtracting the "large town" allocation from the respective regions, the distribution of interviews was as shown in Table 8.4.

The number of administrative districts selected in the various sub-strata of the sample is shown in brackets in Table 8.4 and the number of interviews in any sub-stratum was divided about equally among the selected districts. Generally, there is much to be said for selecting the same number of districts per stratum, since it greatly simplifies the standard error calculations, but here the complicated fieldwork pattern argued against this procedure.

In addition to these regional and urban/rural stratifications, the administrative districts (other urban and rural) were stratified by the industrialisation index in England and Wales, and by rateable value per head in London and Scotland. It has always seemed desirable to stratify administrative districts by some factor related to their economic or industrial character and it was to fill this need that

TABLE 8.3

The "large towns" by region, with population figures and number of interviews

Town	Region	Population (000's)	No. of Interviews
Newcastle	I	292	22
Leeds	II	505	37
Sheffield	II	513	38
Hull	II	299	22
Bradford	II	292	22
Nottingham	III	306	23
Leicester	III	285	21
Bristol	VII	442	33
Birmingham	IX	1,112	82
Liverpool	X	790	58
Manchester	X	703	52
Glasgow	XII	1,090	80
Edinburgh	XII	467	34
Total		7,096	524

TABLE 8.4

Allocation of interviews to regions, "large towns", other urban and rural districts

(Number of administrative districts included in sample shown in brackets)

Region	Large Towns		Other Urban		Rural		Total	
I	22	(1)	156	(3)	53	(2)	231	(6)
II	119	(4)	143	(3)	40	(2)	302	(9)
III	44	(2)	124	(3)	81	(3)	249	(8)
IV	—		143	(3)	85	(3)	228	(6)
V	—		131	(3)	57	(2)	188	(5)
VI	—		127	(3)	68	(2)	195	(5)
VII	33	(1)	105	(2)	85	(3)	223	(6)
VIII	—		134	(3)	58	(2)	192	(5)
IX	82	(1)	190	(4)	54	(2)	326	(7)
X	110	(2)	326	(6)	39	(2)	475	(10)
XI	—		615	(13)	—		615	(13)
XII	114	(2)	149	(4)	113	(4)	376	(10)
Total	524	(13)	2343	(50)	733	(27)	3600	(90)

the Government Social Survey first used the industrialisation index. The index is the "ratio of industrial to total rateable value in each district" and is undoubtedly useful for stratification; it is fully explained by Gray and Corlett [102].

The method of selecting administrative districts was that illustrated in the same paper. To show its working, I give in Table 8.5 an extract from the list of other urban districts in Region I, together with population and cumulated population figures.

TABLE 8.5

Extract from the list of other urban districts in Region I

Number	Name of District	Industrialisation Index	Population (000's)	Cumulated Population
1	Billingham	430	24	24
2	Melburn	164	23	47
.	.	.	.	.
.	.	.	.	.
.	.	.	.	.
25	Blyth	044	35	637
26	Newbiggin by Sea	043	10	647
27	Jarrow	042	29	676
.	.	.	.	.
.	.	.	.	.
.	.	.	.	.
72	Gosforth	001	24	2,122
73	Scabby	000	6	2,128

The first number (falling between 0 and 2128) drawn from a table of random numbers was 638 and Newbiggin was therefore included in the sample. The other two districts were selected by adding to 638, ($\frac{1}{3}$ of 2128) and ($\frac{2}{3}$ of 2128) respectively, resulting in the choice of Tynemouth and Windermere. This procedure for selecting districts ensured that the three districts were chosen at intervals along the industrialisation index scale and thus achieved a stratification by this index. In one or two regions, a further stratification by geographical zoning—conurbation/non-conurbation—was used in addition.

Greater London—for which the industrialisation index is not available—was divided into a North-East, a North-West and a South section, each with roughly the same population; and the districts in each of these three sections were listed in order of residential rateable value per head. The required number of districts was then selected with probability proportionate to population size. In Scotland, too, rateable value per head had to be used instead of the industrialisation index, but the selection procedure was broadly similar to that employed for the rest of Great Britain.

Summarising the design so far: administrative districts were stratified by geographical region, by urban/rural district, by industrialisation index (or rateable value per head) and, in a few regions, by geographical zoning. Within strata, districts were selected with probability proportionate to size, a systematic-random selection method being used.[1]

Sampling stage II

In deciding how to sample within each of the 90 administrative districts, the relevant considerations were:

(a) How much clustering was desirable for the fieldwork.
(b) What possibilities of stratifying the units into which administrative districts are divided—wards and polling districts— were available.

To have gone straight to a sample of households in each district would have unduly spread the fieldwork and at least one intermediate sampling stage was advisable. Wards and/or polling districts were the possibilities. Since both vary considerably in economic and social characteristics, some form of stratification related to these characteristics was highly desirable.

Two indices for stratification were considered. One was the percentage voting, say, Labour in a ward at the last election, but this was ruled out because time was insufficient to get the necessary data. The second was the so-called J-index, which is worth describing although it was not in fact used here. It is due to the Government Social Survey and is explained by Gray, Corlett and Jones [104]. On the electoral register, electors liable for jury service are marked with the suffix "J" and, since qualification for jury service is a function of the rateable value of the premises occupied by the elector (as well as of his age), it seemed reasonable that the "percentage of registered electors with this suffix in any area might serve as an indicator of the economic status of the area" [104]. Tests of the index showed this to be the case. The index has been calculated for all polling districts and can thus also be ascertained for larger areas. It is used as a regular stratification factor by the Government Social Survey and frequently by other organisations.

[1] I should note—the point is too technical to be developed here—that this method has disadvantages, leading in particular to awkwardness in estimating the standard errors. It will also tend to produce an over-estimate of the standard error and in this survey it might have been better to have selected districts randomly (as in the procedure illustrated on p. 99) and with replacement.

The index would certainly have been a good basis for stratification in this survey, but unfortunately it was not at the time available for more than a few areas. In the event stratification of wards or polling districts was thus ruled out; even so, in view of the shortness of time and the need to concentrate the fieldwork, it was decided to use an intermediate sampling stage. A non-stratified sample of four polling districts was selected in each administrative district, the selection being made with probability proportionate to electoral populations. (Where an administrative district had less than four polling districts, all were included.)

For this sampling operation, it was necessary to find out which polling districts belonged to each administrative district, then to search out the respective booklet of the register of electors (one for each polling district) and to list all the polling districts in the 90 administrative districts. As there were 4,700 polling districts involved, this was no mean task. The number of interviews to which any administrative district was entitled was divided about equally among the four (or fewer) polling districts. Thus, any elector in the population had the same chance of inclusion in the sample. The reader can convince himself—by a calculation similar to that given for a two-stage sample in Section 6.5—that this is in fact so.

Sampling stage III

The main complication of this sample arose from the age-range it had to cover. The register of electors includes electors aged 21 and over,[1] while the sample was to cover adults aged 16 and over. One possibility was to use the register for drawing a sample of individuals aged 21 and over, and to obtain a sample of persons aged 16–20 from some other source; another was to take a sample of households from the register, list all their members and then make a selection in the office. Neither was practicable and the best alternative was to use the electoral register for drawing a sample of households and then, *in the field*, to use some rigorous procedure for selecting one individual from each sampled household. This was the method adopted.[2]

The required number of households in a polling district was first selected by taking every *n*th name from the register, using a random starting point; the household to which this person belonged was the one from which an individual was to be selected. The chance of selection for any given household was thus proportionate to the number of electors in it listed on the register. The name chosen on the register served as the "guide" for finding the right household, and it

[1] See footnote on p. 124.
[2] See the I.P.A. national readership survey [126] for an alternative and very ingenious way of dealing with the problem discussed in this paragraph.

and the address were recorded at the drawing stage. Thus a list of 3,600 households spread over some 320 polling districts in 90 administrative districts was obtained.

Sampling stage IV

To convert this list of households into a sample of individuals the method used was that due to Kish [146], by which the interviewer is given simple and rigorous rules for selecting one person from a given household, the system being so devised that all individuals have an equal chance of selection. Having identified the correct household with the help of the "guide" name (this needed some care where there were several households at the address) the interviewer had to list on a "selection questionnaire" all the persons aged 16 and over in that household. In doing so, she followed a systematic pattern, first listing the males and then the females, both in descending order of age. The n persons listed within the household were then given serial numbers 1, 2, ... n, and the interviewer made the selection by referring to two lines of figures printed on the questionnaire. The following is an example:

If total number of persons is:	1	2	3	4	5	6	or more
then interview person numbered:	1	2	2	3	4	4	

This system uniquely determined the person to be interviewed. If he or she was not at home, re-calls had to be made in the usual way and no other person in the household or elsewhere was to be substituted. The interviewer's selection task was thus reasonably simple; she did not incidentally have to find out the ages of most of the household members, as only their *age-order* needed to be known. For the re-weighting (see below) it was, however, necessary to record whether a person fell into the 16–20 or the 21 and over age-group. The main fieldwork difficulty with the method is that the person who supplies the household listing is not usually the one to be interviewed. With skilful interviewers, however, this need not be serious and in this survey the method worked smoothly.

So much for the practical operation of the Kish method. It is now important to see how it achieves sample representativeness. The two lines quoted above are an extract from the full selection table below.

As the household addresses were brought to the office—having been taken from the registers—they were given serial numbers from 1–60. Each selection questionnaire then had its appropriate selection lines printed on it in the office.

Inspection of the table will show that the method results in a representative sample of individuals for the different household sizes. For three-person households, for instance, the person listed first will

TABLE 8.6

The Kish selection table used in the B.M.R.B. survey

Serial number of address	If total number of adults in household is:					
	1	2	3	4	5	6 or more
	then select					
1–10	1	1	2	2	3	3
11–15	1	2	3	3	3	5
16–25	1	2	3	4	5	6
26–30	1	1	1	1	2	2
31–40	1	1	1	1	1	1
41–45	1	2	3	4	5	5
46–55	1	2	2	3	4	4
56–60	1	1	1	2	2	2

be interviewed in addresses numbered 26–30, 31–40 and 56–60, that is in 20 out of 60 addresses; similarly the persons listed second and third will be interviewed in a third of the cases. The same even spread over the household members applies in households with 1, 2 and 4 members. In five-person households, there will be a slight over-representation of persons listed 3 and 5 and, in the largest-household size group, persons numbered 7 or over are not interviewed. Both biases are extremely small and can be ignored in practice.

This selection method had one complicating effect, in that it necessitated re-weighting of the survey results. The probability of any *household* being selected into the sample was in proportion to the number of registered electors in it, while the probability of any *individual* being selected from that household was in inverse proportion to the number of persons aged 16 and over listed on the selection questionnaire. Unless the two figures—number of persons on electoral register and number of persons listed on the selection questionnaire—were the same, the results had to be re-weighted.[1] Details of the procedure used were given by Edwards [72].

Sampling errors

Sampling errors were not calculated at the time of the survey, partly because the calculation by the appropriate formulae would have been a forbidding task, and partly because the users of the results were satisfied with very approximate estimates of the sampling errors.

[1] For instance, households for which one person was listed on the electoral register but three on the selection questionnaire (presumably because they contained two persons aged 16–20) had only ⅓ of their correct chance of getting into the sample and respondents from them had to be given a weight of 3 to equalise the probabilities.

It does seem that all too little attention is paid to sampling errors in the social survey field, especially in market research. When quota sampling is used, sampling errors cannot legitimately be calculated and this is one of the sacrifices made for its economic advantages. But, when the sample is a random one, sampling errors can and should be calculated, and presented together with the survey estimates.

Among market researchers it is a fairly common practice to estimate sampling errors (if they are dealt with at all) by means of the simple random sampling formulae. Thus the standard error of a proportion is estimated by $\sqrt{p(1-p)1n}$, a formula which can be calculated on the back of an envelope, but which is inappropriate to anything but a simple random sample. When a multi-stage stratified design has been used, more complicated expressions are involved and it is difficult to say with confidence how good a guide the figure derived from the simple formula is to the correct one.

In the present survey, the calculation of the standard error was complicated by the selection features noted on p. 152 and I shall confine the calculations to the first stage of sampling; this is likely to give a fairly close approximation to the true standard error.[1] The formulae for the estimates of the first-stage component of the sampling variance[2] of a sample proportion p are as follows:

Large towns. The component for a particular town is

$$\left(1 - \frac{r}{R}\right) \frac{\sum\limits_{i=1}^{r} (p_i - p)^2}{r(r-1)} \qquad \ldots(8.1)$$

where r is the number of polling districts (p.d.'s) selected (4 in our case), R is the number of p.d.'s in the town, p_i is the observed proportion in the ith p.d. and $p = \frac{1}{r}\sum\limits_{i=1}^{r} p_i$, that is the unweighted mean of the proportions in the 4 polling districts.

Remaining districts. The component for a particular stratum is

$$\left(1 - \frac{n}{N}\right) \frac{\sum\limits_{j=1}^{n} (p_j - p)^2}{n(n-1)} \qquad \ldots(8.2)$$

where n is the number of administrative districts (a.d.'s) selected, N is the number of a.d.'s in the stratum, p_j is the observed proportion in

---

[1] If the administrative districts had been selected at random (not systematically) and with replacement, the standard error estimation could properly be based on the first-stage estimate only. To use this approximation here will lead to a slight over-estimate of the standard error, which is at least to err on the right side.

[2] It is easier to present the calculations in terms of sampling variances rather than their square roots, the standard errors.

the jth a.d. and $p = \dfrac{1}{n} \sum\limits_{j=1}^{n} p_j$, that is the unweighted mean of the proportions in the n administrative districts.

It was necessary to calculate a variance component for each large town and for each stratum of the other districts and then to combine them in a weighted sum to give the over-all sampling variance.

To illustrate, let us take the following question: "Have you a car or cars in your family?" Some 17·1 per cent of the sample[1] answered "Yes", so the "back-of-the-envelope" standard error for a simple random sample would be

$$(\text{EST}) \ S.E._{p} = \sqrt{\frac{p(1-p)}{n}} = \sqrt{\frac{\cdot 171 \times \cdot 829}{3243}} = \cdot 66 \text{ per cent}$$

Let us now calculate it according to formulae (8.1) and (8.2).

Large towns

Leeds will be taken as our example of a large town. Leeds has 155 p.d.'s ($R = 155$) of which 4 were included in the sample ($r = 4$). Thus

$$\left(1 - \frac{r}{R}\right) \bigg/ r(r-1) = \cdot 0812.$$

It remains to calculate $\sum\limits_{i=1}^{r} (p_i - p)^2$. The proportions ($p_i$) who answered "Yes" in the four polling districts were:

$$p_1 = \tfrac{1}{8} = 0 \cdot 125$$
$$p_2 = \tfrac{2}{9} = 0 \cdot 222$$
$$p_3 = \tfrac{0}{7} = 0$$
$$p_4 = \tfrac{0}{8} = 0$$

p is therefore $= \tfrac{1}{4}(\cdot 347) = 0 \cdot 087$, and

$$\sum\limits_{i=1}^{r} (p_i - p)^2 = (1 \cdot 125 - \cdot 087)^2 + (\cdot 222 - \cdot 087)^2 + 2(0 - \cdot 087)^2 = 0 \cdot 0349$$

Multiplying (·0349) by (·0812) = 0·002834, which is the component for Leeds. This gives an estimate of the standard error = 0·053: the "back-of-the-envelope" formula $\sqrt{p(1-p)/n}$ would have given a result of 0·051 for Leeds, a slight underestimate. This is due to the clustering effect not being allowed for in the simple random sampling formula.

The above calculation is repeated for all the large towns, giving the following table:

[1] This is based on $n = 3243$, not $n = 3117$ given for the achieved sample size above. The difference is accounted for by the number of cards reproduced in re-weighting the sample (see p. 155).

TABLE 8.7

Calculation of components of sampling variance for the large towns

(1) Name of Town	(2) R	(3) $\dfrac{(1-r/R)}{r(r-1)}$	(4) $\overset{r}{\underset{i=1}{\Sigma}}(p_i-p)^2$	(5) $(3)\times(4)$ Var p_j	(6) N_j (000's)
Newcastle*	77	·0790	—	—	292
Leeds	155	·0812	·0349	·00283	505
Sheffield	208	·0817	·0062	·00051	513
Hull*	89	·0796	—	—	299
Bradford	132	·0808	·0275	·00222	292
Nottingham	105	·0802	·0208	·00167	306
Leicester	125	·0807	·1773	·01430	285
Bristol	135	·0807	·0093	·00075	442
Birmingham	926	·0830	·0167	·00138	1112
Manchester	309	·0818	·0496	·00406	790
Liverpool	211	·0822	·0133	·00110	703
Glasgow	155	·0812	·0068	·00055	1090
Edinburgh	83	·0793	·0221	·00176	467

* Here the terms in column (4) become zero, since all the p_i in the town were zero.

The figures in column (5) are the contributions of the various large towns to the estimate of sampling variance; they are termed Var p_j. In order to estimate the contribution for all the large towns combined, we use the formula for the estimate of the sampling variance of a proportion for a stratified sample

$$\text{(EST) Var}_{p\,(\text{strat.})} = \frac{\overset{k}{\underset{j=1}{\Sigma}} N_j^2\,\text{Var}\,p_i}{(\overset{k}{\underset{j=1}{\Sigma}} N_j)^2} \qquad \ldots(8.3)$$

where N_j is the population in the *j*th town and $k = 13$ (there being 13 towns). It may be asked why the strata variances are weighted by the population rather than the sample totals, since the two sets of figures should be in proportion to each other (a uniform sampling fraction having been used) and the sample totals, being smaller figures, would be simpler to use. The reason for preferring the population totals arises from non-response. This varied from town to town; so, although a uniform fraction of the sample in the towns was *selected*, the fraction actually achieved varied somewhat. The best figures for weighting are, therefore, the population totals.

The N_j are given in column (6) and it is now only necessary to square each of these, multiply the result by the corresponding figure in column (5), add these products together and divide by $(\Sigma N_j)^2$, i.e. $7,096^2$. The result of these operations is

$$\text{Var}_{p\,(\text{LT})} = \cdot000166$$

This is the estimated first-stage sampling variance for large towns. The standard error, its square root, in terms of a percentage is $1 \cdot 29$ per cent. If we had used the simple formula $\sqrt{p(1-p)/n}$ for the group of large towns we would have obtained

$$S.E._p = \sqrt{\frac{\cdot079 \times \cdot921}{484}} = \cdot0122 = 1 \cdot 22 \text{ per cent}$$

Once more, the simple random sampling formula gives an underestimate.

Remaining districts

The procedure for calculating (8.2) is similar to that above, and can be illustrated for the stratum of "other urban" districts in Region I. As Table 8.4 shows, 3 administrative districts were selected from the 73 in this stratum (i.e. $n=3$, $N=73$): Newbiggin by Sea, Tynemouth and Windermere. $\left(1 - \frac{n}{N}\right) \Big/ n(n-1)$ is therefore $0 \cdot 159$. We now have to calculate $\sum_{j=1}^{n} (p_j - p)^2$. Here are the figures:

$$\begin{array}{lll} \text{Newbiggin} & p_1 = & 4/50 = 0 \cdot 080 \\ \text{Tynemouth} & p_2 = & 8/47 = 0 \cdot 170 \\ \text{Windermere} & p_3 = & 11/54 = 0 \cdot 204 \end{array}$$

Therefore $p = \frac{1}{3}(\cdot 454) = \cdot 151$ and $\sum_{j=1}^{n} (p_j - p)^2 =$
$$(\cdot080 - \cdot151)^2 + (\cdot170 - \cdot151)^2 + (\cdot204 - \cdot151)^2 = \cdot008211$$

Multiplying $(\cdot008211)$ by $(\cdot159)$, we get $\cdot00131$, which is the component for this particular stratum. We then

(i) carry out the same calculation for each of the other strata, both those containing the "other urban" districts and those with rural districts;

(ii) combine these components in accordance with a formula of type (8.3). The over-all results for the "other urban" and the rural strata are $\begin{Bmatrix} \text{Var}_{OU} = \cdot000142 \\ \text{Var}_R = \cdot000644 \end{Bmatrix}$; the standard errors, as percentages, are therefore $S.E._{OU} = 1 \cdot 19$ per cent
$$S.E._R = 2 \cdot 54 \text{ per cent}$$

The following table brings together these results and compares them with those obtained by the simple random sampling formulae.

We thus see that the first-stage standard error of the estimate of $17 \cdot 1$ per cent (the proportion saying they own a motor car) is $\cdot 95$ per cent, so, in accordance with the discussion in Chapter 5, we can say that our confidence is approximately 68 per cent that the range

TABLE 8.8

Results of computation of standard errors for "car question"

(1)	(2) Sampling variance as obtained above	(3) Standard error in per cent terms	(4) Achieved sample n	(5) Stratum sample proportion p	(6) $\sqrt{\dfrac{p(1-p)}{n}}$ in per cent terms
Large Towns	·000166	1·29	484	·079	1·22
Other Urban	·000142	1·19	2060	·156	·79
Rural	·000644	2·54	699	·277	1·69
Entire Sample	·000090	·95	3243	·171	·66

$(17 \cdot 1 \pm \cdot 95)$ per cent includes the correct population proportion. For statements commanding greater confidence, limits at, say, 2 or 3 standard errors could be taken.

The important thing to notice is that the "back-of-the-envelope"

TABLE 8.9

Estimated standard errors of selected characteristics in the total sample

(Oxford Institute of Statistics: National Savings Survey)

Description of characteristic	(1) Mean or proportion given by sample	(2) Estimated standard error of actual sample	(3) Standard error of simple random sample of same size	(4) Col. (2) as per cent of Col. (3)
Mean amount per income unit	£	£	£	
Gross income	424	12·1	11·5	105
Liquid asset holdings	225	24·7	21·3	116
Total saving	+4	3·9	3·4	115
Proportion of income units who:	per cent	per cent	per cent	
Own a car	8·2	0·76	0·54	141
Own a television set	7·2	0·61	0·51	120
Expect income to rise	26·8	1·12	0·87	129
Expect to save	27·1	1·20	0·88	136

Source: Lydall [165].

formula would have underestimated the standard error by over 43 per cent. In other words the *sampling variance* as calculated from the first-stage component is nearly twice as high as would be estimated by the simple random sampling formula. This is because the latter does not make allowance for the clustering effect.

Similar results were given in the analysis of the National Savings Survey conducted by the Oxford Institute of Statistics. Lydall [165] presents standard errors for seven of the items estimated from the survey, three variables and four attributes. These standard errors were also estimated from the first stage component and are given in column (2) of Table 8.9. The next column gives the standard error for a sample of the same over-all size calculated from the simple random sampling formula. Column (4) expresses the former as a percentage of the latter.

These results show, as of course follows from the theory, that the practice of estimating standard errors of complex sample designs by means of the simple random sample formulae is to be deprecated; it will generally result in a substantial under-statement of sampling errors. An excellent paper on this point is by Kish [147].

NOTES FOR READING

1. A detailed discussion of the practical aspects of the sample described in this chapter is given by EDWARDS [72].

2. The reader should read descriptions of other sample designs for comparison. Among recent surveys, particularly complete accounts of random sample designs were given in the report on the *I.P.A.* readership survey [126]; in a paper on the Cambridge household budget enquiries by UTTING and COLE [277]; in the paper by PEAKER [204] describing a Ministry of Education school enquiry; in the book by LYDALL [165] on the Oxford Savings surveys, and in the Family Census report [93] by GLASS and GREBENIK.

3. It will be obvious that the design described in this chapter owes much to Government Social Survey sampling, as described by GRAY and CORLETT [102]. Readers are therefore advised to study this reference.

4. The reader interested in examples of sample surveys in other countries might consult (a) the pages of the *Journal of the American Statistical Association* for examples of American applications; (b) the reports on the large-scale *Indian National Sample Survey* [125]; and (c) the journal *Population Studies* for a number of articles on sample surveys in "underdeveloped" territories. For a more general picture, the series of pamphlets on Current Sample Surveys issued by the UNITED NATIONS STATISTICAL OFFICE [271] should be consulted. The bibliography in YATES [291] contains many other references.

5. For the practical sampler it is worth noting the SOCIAL SURVEY publication [240] which brings together the values—for administrative districts, constituencies and smaller units—of the most generally needed stratification indexes.

CHAPTER 9

METHODS OF COLLECTING THE INFORMATION
I—DOCUMENTS AND OBSERVATION

9.1. Introduction

IN THE last few chapters we have been concerned with the coverage of surveys and particularly with methods of sampling. The collection of the information to which we now turn brings us up against difficulties much more serious, in one sense, than those of sampling. The selection of samples rests on well-developed theories and the surveyor can, broadly speaking, make the sample as precise as resources permit. Methods of collecting the information are not so developed and systematised. There is a wealth of experience and a formidable literature describing it, but few would claim that this amounts to a coherent set of principles or to a theoretical framework. Every survey expert has his own ideas but however well grounded in past experience these are, they have neither the certainty nor the objectivity as his choice of sampling design. Perhaps matters like interviewing and questionnaire design can never achieve a theoretical basis in the sense that sampling has one, but research on methods of data-collection must be given priority if the development of this aspect of surveys is to catch up with that of sampling and analytical techniques.

Methods of obtaining data about a group of people can be classified in many ways. For our purpose, the following grouping is convenient:[1]

    (a) Documentary sources
    (b) Observation
    (c) Mail questionnaire
    (d) Interviewing

[1] In the United States telephone interviewing is also of some importance, especially in radio research; the method is not discussed here.

162

Documentary methods and observation are discussed in this chapter; mail questionnaires and interviewing will be studied in Chapters 10 and 11.

9.2. The Use of Documentary Sources

The value of documentary sources in the *planning* of surveys was discussed in Chapter 3. The researcher was warned not to "hurry into the field" without first consulting the necessary book and journal literature, past and present investigations of relevance, official reports and statistics, records of institutions and so forth.

In this chapter the interest is in documents in a more restricted sense and we will now discuss how different types of documents can supplement data obtained by observation, mail questionnaire and interviewing.

(*a*) *Sources giving information about the survey population*. It is usually possible to answer some of the questions a survey is intended to cover from available data. For example, in planning a social survey of a town's population, one *could* omit questions on, say, marital status or occupation in so far as the figures are available from the Population Census or other official sources. This must not be misinterpreted. In practice one almost certainly would *not* omit these questions because (i) the answers would provide a check on the accuracy of the survey and (ii) the answers to other questions in the survey are probably to be related to those on marital status and occupation, and this can only be done if all these pieces of information are ascertained for each individual.

In a survey on the structure of National Health Service practices, some information about the population of practitioners operating it could be obtained from the British Medical Association, the Ministry of Health or Regional Hospital Boards. It could form a statistical background against which to judge the significance of the survey results. An enquiry concerned with the leisure activities of a town's population may usefully begin by getting statistical data about the use made of the local libraries, attendances at cinemas, membership of clubs and societies and so forth. A good example of such use of statistical material appears in the book on *The Communication of Ideas* by Cauter and Downham [32].

In short, a mass of information about the populations studied by social surveys is available in historical documents, statistical reports, records of institutions and other sources; it is up to the surveyor to derive what help he can from it.

(*b*) *Sources giving information about individual "units of enquiry"*. It is much more difficult to supplement the information about indi-

vidual survey units from documentary sources.[1] Not that there is any
lack of information; the difficulty is in gaining access to it if it was
collected for quite another purpose. Government departments possess
a mass of information relating to individuals (census schedules, employment records, insurance cards, health records, income tax returns, family budget records, and so on) but this has generally been
collected with at least the implied assurance that it would not be used
for purposes other than that for which it was requested, so it is not
generally available to the outside researcher.

Nor is it only Government departments that possess data relating
to individuals or groups. Institutions like hospitals and prisons,
adoption societies, professional institutes, business firms—all have in
their files information which a surveyor might on occasion like to use;
but, save in very special circumstances, he can hardly expect to gain
access to it.

(c) *Case records.* Much material collected in the form of case records by, for instance, probation officers, psychiatric social workers
and almoners is of interest to the sociologist and psychologist; nor can
one doubt that it deserves more widespread dissemination and systematic analysis than the original social worker can give it. But such
material has limitations for the research worker in that it can only
represent a highly specialised population, the cases that happen to
come before social workers. Also, if the records are written without
any thought of subsequent classification and analysis, they may not
readily lend themselves to these purposes. And they are, and must
always be treated as, subjective statements; the comparison and
aggregation of the findings of different workers is, to say the least,
difficult.

This last problem, the individuality and subjectivity of a case
record, is the most fundamental. The value of case records to the researcher is diminished by the extent to which they are reflections of
the social worker as well as of the case being studied. I shall discuss
this later in relation to interviewing, for the great objection to the informal interview is that the results "contain too much of the interviewer", so that it is often difficult to compare and to aggregate.

It is relevant here to recall an aspect of Booth's classic survey [13]
of half a century ago. Booth wanted information about the living
conditions of a large number of families and obtained the bulk of it
through the school attendance officers. These officers—like social
workers—obtained in the course of their work a wealth of information about living conditions and kept detailed records in their notebooks. Booth recognised the danger of individual biases in these

---

[1] I say "supplement" since we are not concerned here with researches which are
entirely documentary.

reports, even of the possibility that the mere choice of words and expressions might colour the impression they gave; to overcome these drawbacks he interviewed the school attendance officers, making their notes the basis for the discussion of each individual family. To use the words of Beatrice Webb, he "would extract from the school attendance officer, bit by bit, the extensive and intimate information with regard to each family, the memory of these willing witnesses amplifying and illustrating the precisely recorded facts in their notebooks". She goes on to suggest that "what was of greater significance . . . than any of the facts revealed was the way in which this method of wholesale interviewing and automatic recording blocked the working of personal bias" [281, p. 230]. Although the social worker's caserecords and these notebooks are in many respects dissimilar, the principle of using the records as a documentary basis for interviews is a sound one. In a survey of problem families, for instance, caserecord material thus treated could be a valuable supplement to data obtained by direct study.

(d) *Personal documents.* So far I have considered documents which could provide the surveyor with information originally collected for another purpose, so that their contents, reliability and representativeness have been beyond his control. What about those personal documents which come directly from the informants, such as diaries, letters, autobiographies and essays? The term "personal document" is sometimes used in a wider sense to include interview and questionnaire data but this is clearly not appropriate in our context.

Like case records, personal documents provide a richness and detail not achieved by the more standardised methods of social surveys. They can give an insight into personal character, experiences and beliefs that formal interviewing can rarely, perhaps never, attain and, as long as they are unsolicited, the possibility of any investigator bias colouring their contents is eliminated. At their best, they give a personal and authentic picture of how people see themselves and their environment. But the use of personal documents in social surveys has many difficulties.

There is, first of all, the question of how to get them. When they are produced spontaneously they may be highly revealing, but this fortuitous source of data has little relevance to the methods and approach dealt with in this book. As soon as one tries to *solicit* personal documents from someone being interviewed, problems appear. Not that essays or diaries are more difficult to secure than, say, family budgets. Susan Isaacs for instance, in her Cambridge Evacuation Survey [128], obtained from child evacuees essays describing their experience in Cambridge and their attitudes to it. Or, to take another case, Mass Observation collects from its volunteer panels personal documents of various kinds. Other examples within the framework of social surveys could be given.

But what is always hard is to get a representative collection of documents: some people are more able and ready to write letters, diaries, essays and so forth than others and, if one wants to reduce such bias through selection, one must select the sample first and then request the documents. Even then not everybody will produce them. In any case, the step of *asking* people for personal documents is a crucial one. The more the investigator comes into the picture, the more danger there is of personal distortion by the respondent. It is fair to add that this risk exists even when the document is spontaneously produced and that its value will always hinge on the person's true motive in producing it. One is more ready to trust the truthfulness and completeness of a diary than of a letter, of a private document than one intended for publication, certainly of one that has been written spontaneously rather than at request. The children in the Cambridge Evacuation Survey were asked to write on a given subject, in a particular context of time and place and by an investigator known to them; the essays had to be studied in this light. The presence of the researcher on the scene, of someone *for whom* the document is written, in fact takes us one stage nearer to the formal interview—the next stage being informal interviewing, in which the researcher, not the informant, does the writing. By and large, personal documents are at their most valuable when unsolicited and this means that they are less helpful in collecting data about a population than in gaining an insight into particular individuals. But, even in the typical social survey, they can be illuminating in the exploratory stages as a means of orientation and a source of hypotheses.

9.3. Observation

Observation can fairly be called the classic method of scientific enquiry. The accumulated knowledge of biologists, physicists, astronomers and other natural scientists is built upon centuries of systematic observation, much of it of phenomena in their natural surroundings rather than in the laboratory. On the face of it, the relatively infrequent use of observational methods by social scientists is surprising, especially when one reflects that they are literally surrounded by their subject-matter, that they have only to open their eyes to observe their fellow-men and women, and the institutions and societies they have created, in action. Looked upon as a means of general orientation, observation certainly plays as much part in the social as in any of the sciences. A social scientist can hardly avoid being influenced in his choice of research problem, his ideas and his theories, by what he observes around him. Observation as a *systematic* method of collecting data is, however, quite another matter. For this it is not sufficient that the subject-matter is there to be observed. The method must be suitable for investigating the problems in which the social scientist is interested; it must be appropriate to the populations and samples he wishes to study; and it should be reasonably reliable and objective.

On all these scores, the observational method presents problems. It is suitable for only a small fraction of the subjects the social scientist wants to study; it is often not easily combined with random sampling and it gives all too much scope to the subjective influence of the individual investigator. In consequence one need not be surprised that social scientists have come to rely increasingly on their main alternative method of collecting information, that of asking questions. Yet this also has serious limitations as a research method, so that the advantages are by no means all on one side.

In some parts of the field covered by surveys the observational approach is quite unsuitable. One limitation is brought out if we consider something like a family budget or nutrition survey, where detailed information, extending over time, is required from each family. An observer could live with a family and study its expenditure pattern but, if this is possible at all, it can only be done on a very small scale; record-keeping or interviewing are more appropriate methods in such a case. For similar reasons, data on *frequency* of behaviour can hardly ever be obtained by observation. One can ask a person how often he goes to church, but one cannot observe the frequency of his attendance.

There are other circumstances in which observation offers little help. A researcher interested in events or activities that belong to the past will have to rely on documents or more probably on what people tell him, although he knows that the latter information will be subject to memory errors. For predicting future behaviour observation of present behaviour is of limited use; but then answers to questions are hardly a less precarious guide. Finally, observation is rarely the most appropriate method for studying opinions and attitudes. There are situations where the link between opinion and behaviour is so close that observation of the latter affords a good clue to the former (e.g. observation of what goods people buy in shops) but generally direct questioning is the better way.

On the other hand, observation is invaluable for studying small communities and institutions in action and for seeing how people live and how they behave in given situations. Instead of asking people what they *did*, one can observe what they *do*, and avoid biases of exaggeration, prestige effects and memory errors. Observation of this sort can provide a first-hand and authentic picture, without being as dependent as interviewing on securing peoples' co-operation.

One point of terminology must here be mentioned. In the strict sense, observation implies the use of the eyes rather than of the ears and the voice: the *Oxford Concise Dictionary* defines it as "accurate watching and noting of phenomena as they occur in nature with regard to cause and effect or mutual relations". In social science, the term is often used in a much wider sense. The participant observer, for example, shares in the life and activities of the community, observing—in the strict sense—what is going on around him but supplementing this by conversations, interviews and studies of records. Again, Mass Observation, though of course it collects observational material in the strict sense, includes in its survey reports much else besides. In what follows, both the strict and the extended sense of the term will be used as the context requires and I do not think that any confusion will result.

Our concern is with observation as a method of empirical enquiry, whether it be used in studying the life of a community or in investigating some particular activity, like newspaper-reading or shopping. The two applications are very different. In studying the life of a community the question of the observer's participation in the activity of the "observed" arises, as also does that of "observer-observed interaction". In investigating an activity the researcher often relies on a comparatively superficial use of observation, involving neither participation nor, except in very slight measure, interaction.

Let us first consider the role of the observer in studying the life of a community as a whole, the relationship between its members and its activities and institutions—the type of study typical of social anthropology. The community may be as small as a family or as large as a city; it may be a "closed" community, like a family or a tribe, or an "open" one, such as a factory, a town or a village. An important difference between the two is that in the "open" community an observer can sometimes remain unnoticed, while in the "closed" this is impossible.

The observer's task is to place himself in the best position for getting a complete and unbiased picture of the life of the community and this at once raises the question: is the best observation post inside or outside the community? In the language of sociology, to what extent should the investigator assume the role of a participant observer?

There is no general answer to this, for so much depends on the nature and size of the community, on what the observer wishes to observe and on his own personality and skill. Sometimes the question will answer itself. If the community is very small or "closed"—say a family—the researcher may live with it and share in its activities, but he cannot become a full member of it; he must remain to a certain extent an outsider.

With a bigger and less naturally restricted community, the extent of participation is largely a matter of choice. If the observer can become so accepted as part of the community that its members are unaware of being observed, he will naturally get a more authentic, because less self-conscious, picture of its behaviour. He may, for instance, be able to take a job and work in a factory without disclosing his true purpose.[1]

Where complete integration is impossible, this is not necessarily a handicap; there is much to be said for being a partial outsider able to ask questions a member of the community would not ordinarily ask (or expect a frank answer to if he did). The observer has what Whyte (in Jahoda *et al.* [129]) calls "stranger-value".

Much will depend of course on how he introduces himself to the community and how good a relationship he builds up with its members. He must be able to explain what he is trying to do in a way that is acceptable to the key people and show genuine interest in what is going on.

The risk in participant observation is that the observer's very closeness to the community he is studying may, so to speak, impair his vision: the spectator can usually see more of a game than the players. If the players are sufficiently at ease to play the game unselfconsciously, much is gained by watching from the edge of the field.

A participant observer may need to avoid becoming too closely associated with one particular group in the community he is studying. Miller [187] notes a case in which the observer established such good relations with one section of the community under study—the worker's leaders—that they prejudiced his relations with the rank and file and he was forced to abandon parts of his intended field of enquiry for fear of antagonising the leader group. The ideal of being able to enter into the life of a community at several different levels, so as to get a complete picture, is rarely attained.

It hardly needs emphasising how much the success of the participant observer's approach depends on his skill and personality. If these command the respect and friendship of the community, and if they are combined with an ability to interpret and describe what he sees, the method enables him to present a picture at once more vivid, complete and authentic than is possible with other procedures. But any defects in his approach and ability can easily arouse suspicion and so undermine his position and its possibilities. Participant observation is a highly individual technique.

The best example of the use of observation—in the widest sense—

---

[1] Robb, as part of a recent study of anti-semitism in the East End of London [214], worked for some time as a bar-tender in a public house in the area.

in studying an advanced community is the famous pair of surveys of Middletown by Robert and Helen Lynd [166, 167]. The authors lived in a mid-Western American city for a considerable period, observed the community at work and play, participated in many of its activities, talked with all types of people, and studied all kinds of documents—newspapers, historical papers, records of institutions and so on. The result was a well-rounded picture of a community seen as a whole, which stands as a model of empirical sociology. It was such a successful utilisation of observational methods that we should note some of its features.

First, the observers were skilled sociologists with years of practice and thought behind them; and were fully aware of the risks of getting a biased and unrepresentative picture. Such awareness may not in itself ensure that these risks will be avoided, but it is a necessary step towards that goal. They possessed a maturity and skill in observation, understanding and reporting that could not be expected in an average team of fieldworkers, even if specially trained.

Secondly, since Middletown was a large city, there were none of the problems met with in using participant observation in small communities. There was no likelihood that the observers would be constantly noticed and that the behaviour of the community would become self-conscious and untypical.

Thirdly, to collect their material the Lynds made a prolonged stay in the community. This was no quick, superficial survey.

Lastly, the material obtained by observation was supported where necessary by other methods, which gave the observers an unusual insight into past events, into the "why" as well as the "how" of particular actions, into the working of institutions and the like.

In this country, there have been no comparable surveys, although smaller-scale studies have similarly made use of observation as one tool among several. An example is Rees' study of a Welsh village [212]. The Tavistock Institute of Human Relations frequently uses participant observer methods in its researches on human relations in industry,[1] and some of the earlier Mass Observation researches used the technique (see, for instance, its study of pub-going and drinking habits [181]).

We must now ask how useful observation can be in surveys concerned with investigating special problems, situations and activities— of which many examples were given in Chapter 2. Suppose that one wants to know what kind of people read certain papers, smoke certain brands of cigarettes, drink certain drinks; how much can one learn by observation?

Provided the activity takes place "in public", there is no basic

---

[1] See its journal, *Human Relations*.

difficulty. Observers can sit in trains, buses and library reading rooms, station themselves in shops or public houses and note what they see. And since the facts thus collected are free from prestige and memory effects, such as can undermine the reliability of answers to questions, they may be more accurate than these.

A straightforward example of such a use of observational methods is the enquiry into *The Effects of a Local Road Safety Campaign on the Behaviour of Road Users* [195] carried out by the Government Social Survey. Rather than find out by question-and-answer methods whether people knew more about road safety after than before the campaign, the Survey studied by observation whether the campaign had had any marked effect on their road behaviour. The enquiry, which took place in a provincial town in 1951, is described by Moss :

"It was necessary as a preliminary to train investigators to observe accurately and this was done by having them watch road safety films and make recordings of actual behaviour in the films. Those who were unable to give accurate recordings of the activities on the roads in the films were not put into the field for this study. The selected investigators were given a series of observations to make with a sample of sites in the chosen town; the investigators at each particular site observing only one particular form of behaviour during a particular selected time in the day. Observations were repeated on a sufficient scale to take account of random variation in road behaviour. Twenty-six different kinds of behaviour were observed in this controlled way before and after the publicity campaign. The conclusion from the survey was that the campaign in this particular town had had no measurable effect on actual road behaviour" [195, p. 488].

Observation of people going about their everyday activities can provide the sociologist with data difficult to obtain reliably by any other means; but there are serious problems in this method, which must be looked at.

Representativeness

If the characteristics of a population are to be inferred from those of a sample, the sample should ideally be randomly selected. With interview and questionnaire methods this is readily ensured; not so with observation. To instruct investigators to observe people of all types, men and women, of different ages, social classes and so on, does not make the sample a random one; it does not even ensure that the resultant group is representative.

Unrepresentativeness in another sense may also arise with "over-heards". These provide the researcher with a valuable, but uncontrollable, source of data, rather like unsolicited personal documents, in interpretating which it is always necessary to remember that some people are more self-expressive than others. "Overheards" may give an unrepresentative picture of the attitudes of a group rather as an M.P.'s mail gives an unrepresentative picture of the views of his constituents.

Skill and objectivity

In many respects, observation is a particularly difficult method of obtaining information. A community survey, like that of Middletown, very obviously requires the skill and understanding of the sociologist or anthropologist. But, even with less ambitious projects, the observer needs more skill and discernment than is normally required of the interviewer.

Efficiency in observation and recording may be attainable through training,[1] but objectivity is more elusive. The social investigator, unlike his natural science colleague, has to observe something of which he is himself a part. The situations or activities to be observed are so familiar that it is hard for him to view them with the sort of detachment a biologist achieves in observing the behaviour of animals. Even the social anthropologist studying a primitive society fundamentally different from his own is at an advantage, compared to the investigator studying his fellow-men in his own environment.

The problem of objectivity has several facets, first among them being that of *selection*. In any complex situation, the observer can hardly be expected to observe and note everything relevant to his subject, and his selection of the aspects of behaviour and environment which he notes may follow certain channels. Because what he is studying is so familiar, he may fail to note the obvious; extreme forms of behaviour, deviations from the normal, may catch his eye most easily and, unless he takes care to give the normal its due place, the over-all picture may be false. We all tend to note the unusual more readily than the normal.

On the other hand, the observer's *preconceptions* of how people normally behave may also colour his picture; not, I trust, of what he sees but of what he thinks he sees. In other words, instead of recording what he actually observes, he may fit this into the stereotypes to which he is accustomed. Such a tendency would counteract that suggested in the previous paragraph.

This brings us to the difficulty of distinguishing between *observation and inference*, vividly brought out in the remarks of Bertrand Russell:[2]

"You say 'What can you see on the horizon?' One man says, 'I see

---

[1] See the chapter by Heyns and Zander in Festinger and Katz [78] for a discussion of different types of schedules for recording observations.
[2] Quoted by Madge [168, p. 122] who discusses this point in detail.

a ship.' Another says, 'I see a steamer with two funnels.' A third says, 'I see a Cunarder going from Southampton to New York.' How much of what these three people say is to count as perception? They may all three be perfectly right in what they say, and yet we should not concede that a man can 'perceive' that the ship is going from Southampton to New York. This, we should say, is inference. But it is by no means easy to draw the line; some things which are, in an important sense, inferential, must be admitted to be perceptions. The man who says 'I see a ship' is using inference. Apart from experience, he only sees a queerly shaped dark dot on a blue background. Experience has taught him that that sort of dot 'means' a ship" [225].

Three observers seeing the same thing describe it differently, failing to make the subtle distinction between observation and inference. It is difficult enough when the object of observation is inanimate, like a ship; how much more so, when the observer is studying his fellow-men and women! Striving for observation untinged with inference and interpretation is perhaps striving for the impossible, but at least researchers must be conscious of the problem.

I have suggested that observers are so much part of their subject-matter that they may fail to see it objectively; that their vision may be distorted by what they are used to seeing or what they expect to see; and that they may find it hard to present a report in which observation is satisfactorily distinguished from inference and interpretation.

Observation of human behaviour is, as we have seen, a somewhat individual method. One cannot expect it to yield the faithful and objective picture that a camera would achieve, nor suppose that several observers studying the same situation would bring back identical pictures. The same difficulties do not of course arise in observing physical environment (always a valuable supplement to interview data) or in carrying out simple counts.[1]

I must emphasise that this discussion has been largely confined to the observational method in the context of social surveys and that I have not attempted to cover controlled laboratory observation or observation in the study of intra-group behaviour (e.g. committees, management-worker meetings).

NOTES FOR READING

1. Among the text-books, MADGE [168], FESTINGER and KATZ [78] and JAHODA, DEUTSCH and COOK [129] are the most useful on the subject-matter of this chapter. The last contains three chapters on observational methods—Nos. 5, 14, 15— of which the middle one, by WHYTE, is a par-

---

[1] For a discussion of the "moving observer" method in counting the number of people in a street (or shop), see Yates [291], Section 3.16; and Section 10.15 for a discussion of road traffic censuses.

The use of mail questionnaires has been widely condemned for some years on account of the difficulty of securing adequate response. Though serious, this difficulty should not blind one to the merits of the method. On occasion these merits may be substantial enough to weight the balance in favour of the mail questionnaire *as long as* some estimate can be made of the effect of the non-response. The problem can, like many others in survey methodology, be reduced to simple economics. Mail questionnaires are cheaper to send out than interviewers; but they achieve a much less adequate coverage. Is the saving in cost sufficient to justify this loss? Let us look at the points for and against mail questionnaires and, in particular, the non-response problem.

10.2. The Advantages of Mail Questionnaires

Without doubt, the mail questionnaire is generally quicker and cheaper than other methods. In the startling words of Jahoda, *et al.* [129]: "Questionnaires can be sent through the mail; interviewers cannot." Little is known (or, at any rate, published) about interviewing costs in this country; but it is likely that the cost of using mail questionnaires, in which postal charges take the place of interviewers' salaries and expenses, is often only a small fraction of that of a field survey, certainly if the latter is based on a random sample. Sometimes the population to be covered may be so widely spread, and the time or funds available so limited, that the mail questionnaire is the only feasible approach. This was the position in a recent survey on 2,000 women graduates, described in *Graduate Wives* [207]. As the questions to be asked were simple and the respondents an educated group, the researcher had no need to regret her forced choice of method. But even if limited resources alone do not dictate the choice of the mail questionnaire, its economy and potential efficiency must always be considered. Of course it is not *necessarily* a cheap method; the response to a mail questionnaire, especially with a sample of the general population, may be so low that the cost per completed questionnaire is higher than with an interview sample.

Similarly, a mail questionnaire is not necessarily a quick method of conducting a survey It takes little time to send out or to get the bulk of the eventual returns; but time must be allowed for late returns and perhaps responses to follow-up attempts. In one experience of a market research agency, however, two-thirds to three-quarters of the total returns to a series of mail questionnaires were received within one week of mailing and hardly any came in later than three weeks after mailing.

The mail questionnaire does of course avoid the problems associated with the use of interviewers. As we shall see, there are several sources of interviewer errors which may seriously undermine the reliability and validity of survey results and it is reassuring not to have to worry about them.

Mail questionnaires also have something to commend them when information concerning several members of a household is required. The housewife might be hard put to it to give accurate figures of the earnings of individual members of the household, their average weekly expenditure on meals out or even their exact ages (e.g. where lodgers are included) and in such situations a mail questionnaire, allowing some "intra-household consultation", may lead to more accurate data than a doorstep interview.

The same holds with questions demanding a considered rather than an immediate answer. In particular, if the answer requires—or would be more accurate as a result of—consultation of documents, a questionnaire filled in by the respondent in his own time is preferable. Examples are questions like: "When was this house built?" and "How much ground rent do you pay?" (and, of course, the sort of questions asked of firms, shops etc.).

Some people may answer certain questions—perhaps those of a personal or embarrassing nature—more willingly and accurately when not face to face with an interviewer who is a complete stranger to them. Isolated results quoted in the survey literature suggest this. Whether the mail answers give a more truthful picture is another matter, and one on which no research evidence has been published in this country.

Finally, the problem of non-contacts, in the strict sense of respondents not being at home when the interviewer calls, is avoided.

10.3. The Limitations of Mail Questionnaires

Apart from the vital question of non-response (dealt with separately in section 10.4), there are five main disadvantages to the mail questionnaire method.

First, the method can only be considered when the questions are sufficiently simple and straightforward to be understood with the help of the printed instructions and definitions. Ambiguity, vagueness, technical expressions and so forth must be avoided even more sedulously than when the questionnaire is to be filled in by an interviewer.[1] A mail questionnaire is most suited to surveys whose purpose is clear enough to be explained in a few paragraphs of print; in which the scheme of questions is not over-elaborate (not too many questions depending on answers to previous ones—e.g.: "If 'No' to section (i) of Q. 3 (b), answer Q. 6 but not Q. 7"); and in which the questionnaire can be kept reasonably short. It is unsuitable where the objective and purpose of the survey take a good deal of explaining, where the respondent is being asked difficult questions or where it is desirable to probe deeply or get the respondent talking.

Secondly, the answers to a mail questionnaire have to be accepted as final, unless re-checking or collection of the questionnaires by interviewers can be afforded. There is no opportunity to probe beyond the given answer, to clarify an ambiguous one, to overcome unwillingness to answer a particular question or to appraise the validity

---

[1] This is sometimes referred to as a *recording schedule* to distinguish it from a *questionnaire* filled in by the respondent. See Chapter 12.

of *what* a respondent said in the light of *how* he said it. In short the mail questionnaire is essentially an inflexible method.

Thirdly, the mail questionnaire is inappropriate where spontaneous answers are wanted; where it is important that the views of one person only are obtained, uninfluenced by discussion with others; and where it is essential that one particular person in each household (say, the chief wage-earner) fills in the questionnaire, and no one else.

Fourthly, when the respondent fills in the questionnaire, he can see all the questions before answering any one of them, and the different answers cannot therefore be treated as independent. In an interview, an early question might be: "Can you name any detergents currently on the market?" and a later one: "Do you ever use WISK, DREFT, . . .?" In a mail survey, the previous question would be pointless.

Fifthly, with a mail questionnaire there is no opportunity to supplement the respondent's answers by observational data. An interviewer can describe the respondent's house and neighbourhood, his appearance and manner, his attitude to the survey and the way he reacted to different questions; all this is valuable background material.

It may be noted that some of the disadvantages of the mail questionnaire can be overcome by combining it with interviewing. Thus questionnaires can be sent by mail and collected by interviewers, who can clear up difficulties, check answers and ensure completeness. Conversely, questionnaires can be delivered in person and returned by mail, the visits being used to explain the purpose and methods of the survey and to elicit co-operation.

10.4. Non-response in Mail Surveys

The vital limitation of mail surveys is the difficulty of getting an adequate response. Non-response in general has been discussed in Chapter 7; its especial importance in mail surveys arises from the fact that the response-rate tends to be very much lower than when interviewers are used. It is not of course the loss in sample numbers that is serious, but the likelihood that the non-respondents differ significantly from the respondents, so that estimates based on the latter are biased.

The proportion replying to a mail questionnaire depends on the population, the subject of the survey, its sponsorship and the success of the covering letter in arousing interest.[1] Surveys with a response of as low as 10 per cent are not unknown, while occasionally a rate of 90

[1] All non-response is not due to lack of co-operativeness. A number of the sample members may have died or moved away from the address. The latter category can be large if an out-of-date mailing list is used. This should always be checked.

per cent has been obtained. If the sample is of the general population, rather than of a special group, strenuous efforts are usually needed to bring the response rate above about 30 or 40 per cent. In such cases, it is difficult to know how to interpret the results or whether indeed to attach any value to them. We thus face two general questions: what steps can be taken to increase response to mail questionnaires; and how can the effects of the remaining non-response on the accuracy of the results be estimated?

Three of the main influences on the response rate in a survey must be taken as fixed—its sponsorship, its subject-matter and its population. A survey with official backing will normally get a bigger response than one emanating from, say, a university or a research agency. Most favourable is the situation where the sponsoring body is in some way connected with the population members—e.g. a magazine publisher carrying out a survey among its subscribers, a professional organisation circulating its members. Subject matter is equally important. The survey of women graduates mentioned on p. 176, secured a response of 55 per cent; if the subject, instead of being the interference of household tasks with the respondents' other interests, had been, say, their attitude to the United Nations, the response would certainly have been much lower. One of the highest response rates quoted in the survey literature (81 per cent—see Gray and Corlett [102]) was in a pilot survey of midwives, the questionnaire being concerned with matters relating to their profession. The sample was a special and educated group, the subject-matter of interest to them all and the sponsors (The Working Party on Midwives) a body charged to consider their future, and enjoying high prestige among them. A similar experience was provided by a current investigation of the teaching profession, conducted by the Nuffield Research Unit at the University of London Institute of Education. Here the pilot survey, based on a mail questionnaire, received a response of over 80 per cent. The mail questionnaire is very suitable for such circumstances.

Even then, and more so in less favourable conditions, the question is: what can the researcher do to ensure getting the maximum response? Occasionally legal sanctions are available and then no problem arises. Sometimes a payment or gift can be offered for completed questionnaires; but if the payment is more than nominal, this may offset the chief advantage of the method—its cheapness. In commercial surveys concerned with product testing, people may agree to fill in questionnaires simply because they like receiving free samples. Among other common-sense steps for increasing response are enclosing stamped addressed or business reply envelopes (the former are said to produce a relatively higher response), assurance of anonymity and confidentiality,[1] a good covering letter and, of course, a reasonably short and simple questionnaire. Only the last two points need further discussion.

The covering letter takes the place of the interview opening and, as such, it must try to overcome any prejudice the respondent may have against surveys. It should make clear why and by whom the survey is being undertaken, how the addressee has come to be selected for questioning and why he should take the trouble—for such it is—to reply. This last point is crucial. Surveyors are all too ready to *expect* people to answer their questions without being told what it is hoped to gain from the survey.

The researcher in each case must decide what tone to adopt in the covering letter. If the survey is genuinely expected to lead to changes beneficial to the respondents, the mention of this will be a strong inducement. But this is rarely the case. With most surveys the changes (if any) expected as their consequence are too distant and indirect to constitute a "selling point". Should one then appeal to the respondent's sense of duty or spirit of helpfulness? Should one plead or persuade; be authoritarian or excessively polite? No general answer can be given, nor are there any published comparative results to quote for this country. The best approach is to explain in simple terms why the survey is being undertaken and why, and by whom, it is considered important. In the case of a research survey, one may begin by saying that: "We (The Research Institute) want to find out . . .", or: "This information is needed by a professor writing a book" or: "We hope that this information will lead to public recognition of . . . problem . . . and to action. . . ." One published research result of relevance is worth noting [257]. In an experiment by the Bureau of the Census two types of covering letter were compared. One was short, somewhat curt and authoritarian; the other, polite and diplomatic. The former achieved a slightly higher response rate!

The response will also, of course, be influenced by the form and contents of the questionnaire itself and the designer of a mail questionnaire must be particularly alive to its appearance and length, to the clarity of the questions and to the instructions and explanations given. The questionnaire used for the teachers' survey, mentioned above, had a short paragraph explaining the purpose of each group of questions. A good example of an official questionnaire was that used in the Family Census of the Royal Commission on Population (attached to p. 211). The shorter the questionnaire the better. The order of questions is less important than if an interviewer is used,

---

[1] It is impossible to follow-up non-respondents, unless each questionnaire carries an identifying mark or number and this may tend to make people suspect that the enquiry is not confidential.

since the respondents can look at them all before starting to answer. Nevertheless, first impressions count and it is best to start with the harmless and least awkward questions, and to arouse interest by opening with one or two questions of close concern to most people.

The points for increasing response mentioned so far accord with common sense and experience, but there is an evident need for research. Common sense may suggest that people will more willingly answer a short questionnaire than a long one; but how long is "short"? And is there a steady decline in response as the number of questions increases, or a sudden drop if the questionnaire exceeds a certain length, perhaps one page? Such questions can never be answered in general but some accumulation *and publication* of research findings would give the surveyor a more secure basis for decision. In any case, in a pilot mail survey, different formats and designs of the questionnaire, different covering letters, different kinds of response encouragement, can always be compared experimentally.

Non-response is a problem because of the likelihood—repeatedly confirmed in practice—that people who do not return questionnaires differ from those who do. Suchman and McCandless [255], for instance, showed that better educated people are more likely to respond than others and many others[1] have found that mail questionnaires addressed to a general population sample tend to result in an upwards-biased social class composition; this is only what one would expect.

It has also been shown frequently that response is correlated with interest in the subject of the survey. On a radio-listening survey, enthusiastic listeners reply more readily than others; on the survey of women graduates mentioned above, women who felt strongly about the interference of housework with other interests probably replied more readily than those who felt less strongly. Filling in a questionnaire takes time and trouble and people are obviously more likely to afford both if they are interested in its contents.

For all such reasons, it is clear that in mail surveys every effort must be made to judge the extent of unrepresentativeness of the response and to take account of it in making the final estimates.

This may seem easy: all one need do is to include in the questionnaire one or two questions for which the results can later be checked with population figures, e.g. on the geographical spread of the sample, its age and sex breakdowns, the distribution of household composition and occupation. It is true that obvious unrepresentativeness can thus be revealed, but such checks can never *prove* the representativeness of the sample. Even if the sample were judged

[1] See some of the references on p. 184

satisfactory by all the above criteria, it might still be seriously unrepresentative on others, including the one that matters most—the subject of the study. On this no check of representativeness is possible, for otherwise there would have been no need for the survey.

As suggested in Section 7.4, a survey population can be regarded as made up of two strata: respondents and non-respondents. Assuming that the sample was selected randomly in the first place, the former sub-population is adequately sampled. The problem is how to sample the latter, how to obtain *some* information about the people who do not complete questionnaires. There are several possibilities which can be applied singly or in combination:

1. Follow-up requests, enclosing a copy of the questionnaire and covering letter, can be sent to the non-respondents. This invariably produces further returns and these not only increase the numbers available for analysis but can be used to improve the over-all results. Suppose that 40 per cent of the sample members return the questionnaires in the first instance, that follow-up letters are sent to the remaining 60 per cent and that a further 15 per cent (of the total) return questionnaires as a result. It is then reasonable to regard these 15 per cent as more representative of the non-response population than of the 40 per cent initial-response population; in other words, the figures for the 15 per cent group should be given a weight of 60 per cent in arriving at the over-all results.[1] This is preferable to either (*a*) treating the initial 40 per cent as representative of the whole population and not bothering with follow-up attempts at all, or (*b*) combining the 15 per cent with the 40 per cent without giving them any extra weight (which would be tantamount to assuming that the still remaining non-respondents—45 per cent—are no closer in characteristics to those who responded to the follow-up effort than to those who responded in the first place).

The procedure can be repeated for further follow-up waves, but there obviously comes a point when the cost of the follow-up is not rewarded by a sufficient response.

Fairly typical of the effect of follow-up methods (though not, unfortunately, of the response rate) is the survey of midwives mentioned above. Replies to the first letter and questionnaire were requested within a fortnight. "When after three weeks the returns began to decline, a reminder letter was sent to those who had not

---

[1] This is the method used in the Family Census and mentioned on p. 143 above. As we there noted, it was clear that the later respondents were unlike the early respondents in important respects. Findings leading to the same conclusion—this time a radio survey—have been given by Suchman and McCandless [255] and by many others.

returned the questionnaire. After a further three weeks a second copy of the questionnaire was sent, together with both the original covering letter and the reminder letter" [102, p. 184]. The results of these efforts are shown in Table 10.1.

TABLE 10.1

Returns to a Government Social Survey postal enquiry

	per cent
Returned before first reminder	38·0
Returned after first and before second reminder	31·7
Returned after second reminder	7·3
Returned from alternative address	1·4
Information received of death, illness or emigration	2·4
Returned by Post Office (person no longer living at address)	9·2
No information received	10·0
Total to whom final questionnaire was sent (16,124)	100·0

Source: Gray and Corlett [102, p. 185].

2. Reasons for non-response range all the way from complete refusal or inability to respond (where informant has died, moved to a different address, gone on holiday) to mislaying the questionnaire, forgetfulness and reluctance to take the trouble. Ordinary follow-up methods will recruit their successes from the latter end of this range. As an alternative, or supplementary, method interviewers can be sent to all or some of the non-respondents. They can be sent either to the initial non-response group or only to those who did not respond to the follow-up. This procedure will often be ruled out on grounds of expense but it is an excellent way of combining the economy of mail questionnaires with the higher response obtained by interviewers. The method of Hansen and Hurwitz [111], mentioned on p. 135, develops a theoretical basis for such a combination; it enables one to estimate how many mail questionnaires to send out and how many of the non-respondents to follow-up by interview in order to achieve optimal efficiency.

3. Follow-up attempts need not necessarily use the entire original questionnaire. Non-respondents can be sent a shorter version of the questionnaire or even a postcard asking for only a few key items. The replies may indicate how different the non-respondents are from the rest. A more sophisticated method is to send one (short) questionnaire to one set of non-respondents, a different one to a second set and so forth. In this way, data covering the entire range of the original questionnaire might be collected—each part (set of questions) being based on a small

sample of the non-respondents. This is an application of multi-phase sampling, discussed in Chapter 6.

One remaining possibility is to use interviewers for that part of the sample which is expected to have a low response rate (say, the less educated or the "lower social class" respondents) and mail questionnaires for the rest. This deserves some study but, as with any of the methods combining mail questionnaire and interview data, there is the over-riding problem: can answers to questions put on paper and asked in person be regarded as comparable?

We have seen that the mail questionnaire as a data-collecting technique has its advantages and its limitations. Among the former, relative cheapness and speed are the most important; among the latter, the problem of non-response stands out. If the seriousness of this could be satisfactorily overcome, the economies of the method would undoubtedly bring it much more into favour.

NOTES ON READING

1. Good accounts of the practical aspects of mail questionnaire surveys —form of mailing and covering letter, timing and method of follow-up approaches—are given by GOODE and HATT [97] and by PARTEN [202].

2. SLETTO [236] reports the results of some pre-tests, in which different forms of a covering letter, of the questionnaire, of the follow-up approach were compared. MARKS and MAULDIN [176] report other results of close relevance, as do CLAUSEN and FORD [35].

3. There are many papers reporting differences between respondents and non-respondents to a mail questionnaire. The reader might like to look at those by BAUR [5], EDGERTON, BRITT and NORMAN [71], FERBER [76], LAWSON [153], MANFIELD [171], REUSS [213], STANTON [243] and SUCHMAN and McCANDLESS [255].

the completely informal approach, but between means for combining them in varying degrees. Indeed, interviews that are formal and informal may be combined in the same inquiry.

11.2. The Interviewer's Task

The interviewer has a complex task. Not only has she to find and make contact with the people selected in the sample, persuading them to give her the information she is after, but also she has to do the actual interviewing in a competent manner.

CHAPTER 11

METHODS OF COLLECTING THE
INFORMATION
III—INTERVIEWING

11.1. Types of Interviewing

THE METHOD of collecting data most usual in social surveys is personal interviewing. Without doubt this is generally the most appropriate procedure, even though it introduces various sources of error and bias. These errors are the subject of Chapter 13 and the present chapter discusses the interviewer's task, the selection and training of interviewers, and various points of organisation. It also deals with informal interviewing.

Many situations merit the description "interview", but we can in the present context confine ourselves to that in which the interviewer is neither trying to help the informant nor to educate him, neither to gauge his suitability for a job nor to get his expert opinion: the situation where she[1] is simply seeking information from, and probably about, him and where he is likely to be one of many from whom similar information is being sought. This does not mean that the discussion is confined to the typical "doorstep interview" which comes immediately to mind. Formal interviewing, in which set questions are asked and the answers are recorded in a standardised form, is certainly the norm in large-scale surveys, but we must also consider the less formal variants, in which the interviewer is at liberty to vary the sequence of questions, to explain their meaning, to add additional ones and even to change the wording. Less formal still, she may not have a set questionnaire at all but only a number of key points around which to build the interview.

In practice, the choice is not between the completely formal and

---

[1] Since most interviewers are women, I shall refer to them throughout as of the female sex.

the completely informal approach, but between many possible degrees of informality. Social surveyors tend to keep to the formal end of the scale and so we will examine this first.

11.2. The Interviewer's Task

The core of the interviewer's task is to locate (or select) her sample members, to obtain interviews with them and to ask the questions and record the answers as instructed.

Finding the sample members

In considering characteristics desirable in interviewers, one easily overlooks how much of their working time is spent in simply finding the respondents. An applicant may express a strong "interest in people" and be enthusiastic about interviewing; but, if she is going to hate walking around a town or cannot read maps, she will be a liability to her employer and will probably soon give up the work. How difficult or responsible a task the finding of respondents is depends on the sampling method. In quota sampling, as shown in Section 6.7, interviewers themselves make the selection and, while their freedom of choice is limited by the quotas, it is still considerable. With random sampling, interviewers are given lists of the persons to be interviewed. Often the names and addresses[1] of these are inserted on the questionnaires themselves or on record sheets, together with any other information about the respondent—such as sex—deducible from the sampling frame. Interviewers are usually required to record the results—e.g. questionnaire completed, refusal, non-contact—of the first and subsequent calls and are instructed how to deal with various kinds of non-response.

The sample allocated to any one investigator may be spread widely over a town or district and interviewers are generally left to arrange their own itinerary. Perhaps the most distressing part of their work is having to call back, perhaps several times, on people whom they do not find in. Some evening work is unavoidable with random samples of the general population.

---

[1] Occasionally—as in the sample described in Chapter 8—the interviewer is assigned a sample of *households* and has to select an individual from each, according to a pre-determined scheme. There is also the situation, important in area sampling, in which the interviewer is sent to a small area, say a block, and has to list the population in the area before making a selection. This listing operation involves its own difficulties and hazards; see Hansen, Hurwitz and Madow [112].

In some organisations in this country, interviewers themselves make the selection of the random sample from local lists; thus the British Institute of Public Opinion (for its random surveys) sends each interviewer instructions consisting of (*a*) a tabular scheme for selecting a polling district in the constituency she is covering; and (*b*) a tabular scheme for selecting from the electoral register for that district a given number of electors. Both schemes are based on random numbers.

Obtaining an interview

Having located the respondent, the interviewer's problem is to obtain an interview. How should she go about this? She will usually begin by stating what organisation she represents (though in commercial surveys the sponsor's name can often not be disclosed) and perhaps showing an authorisation card. In many cases this, together with a brief statement of why the survey is being done, is enough to secure co-operation. Most people are only too ready to talk about themselves and to air their views, and common politeness, mixed with curiosity, does the rest.

The form of the interview opening is crucial, nevertheless, to win those who are less willing to co-operate. The time may be inconvenient, the subject of the survey may be one they are not prepared to talk about or they may be antagonistic towards surveys in general. Then it is that the interviewer's, and also the researcher's, attitude counts. Both should recognise that the call *is* an encroachment upon people's time, although one which many do not resent. The request for information needs justification. There is no need for excessive diffidence or apologies, or for lengthy introductions; but it should be the interviewer's duty to explain precisely why, and for whom, the survey is being done, what is expected to emerge from it, to whom the results will be of interest and so on.

There are many satisfactory ways of doing this and only a few general principles need be suggested. First and foremost, the "sales talk" should not be anything but entirely honest. There is no excuse for implying that a survey will lead, directly or indirectly, to concrete benefits or indeed to any action, when such is not expected; nor should its urgency or importance be overstated. Many surveys are done simply because someone wants some information, and most people will co-operate with an interviewer who asks for it pleasantly and unpretentiously, even if at heart they think the survey a futile one. Indeed perhaps the respondent's view of the survey matters less than the interviewer's. Dorothy Cole's findings [40] suggest that the interviewer's interest in the survey, and her conviction of its value, can materially affect the response rate.

When the survey answers are to be treated as confidential or anonymous, this should be made clear to the respondent. It is often worth explaining, in simple terms, how the sample was selected and that lack of co-operation would make it less representative. The interviewer should remove any suspicion that she is out to ask test questions (e.g. to find out how much the respondent knows), to educate, to advertise or to sell something. Some interviewers are no doubt better than others at establishing what the psychologists call "rapport" and some may even be too good at it—the National Opinion Research Center studies [124] found slightly less satisfactory results from the highly extrovert and sociable interviewers who are "fascinated by people"!

Asking the questions

In most large-scale surveys, the aim is to attain uniformity in the asking of questions and recording of answers. In consequence the training of interviewers is orientated towards efficiency in following instructions. They are expected to ask *all* the applicable questions; to ask them in the order given and with no more elucidation and probing than is explicitly allowed; and to make no unauthorised variations in the wording. If complete uniformity could be achieved and interviewers act like machines, answers could be regarded as independent of the way the questions were asked.

But interviewers are not machines. Their voices, manner, pronunciations and inflections differ as much as their looks, and no amount of instruction will bring about complete uniformity in technique. Every interviewer will be tempted on occasion to add a word of explanation or make a change in the wording and sequence of the questions, but the researcher can minimise the temptation by intelligent design. If questions are phrased in everyday language, interviewers will be less inclined to re-phrase them. If interviewers are allowed to probe on some questions, the danger of unauthorised probing becomes less. If the order of questions is such that, with occasional linking phrases, the interview flows logically and conversationally, there will be less temptation to omit questions or change their sequence.

The importance of interviewing uniformity itself varies with the type of question. Opinion questions are more "sensitive" than factual ones to variations in wording, phrasing or emphasis by the interviewer. Questions such as "How many children have you?" or "How much did you spend on vegetables yesterday?" are less vulnerable in this respect than "Do you believe the Government is doing a good job?" or even "Do you like Rownbury's milk chocolate?" In questions of the latter type, exact wording is of utmost importance. If an interviewer inserted the word "really" before "like" in the last question, she would immediately alter its tone and affect the way it was answered. She should be warned of this and told to keep to the prescribed wording and not to give any lead by explanations.

The surveyor must also decide to what extent interviewers should be allowed to probe: that is, to repeat or paraphrase a question in order to make it clear to the respondent; to ask the respondent to enlarge on his answer in order that this should not be misunderstood;

and to request further data if there are gaps in the answer. A reasonable scheme is that adopted by the Government Social Survey and described in its *Handbook for Interviewers* [239]. The Survey distinguishes three types of questions: factual, opinion and knowledge (an example of the last type would be: "Can you tell me what is meant by convertibility?"). With factual matters, the interviewer is allowed to repeat or explain the question so as to make sure the respondent properly understands it; and to ask for clarification of answers she finds vague, ambiguous or not to the point. Even then probing has its risks. For one thing, it must not be allowed to confuse the intended definitions (a vital aspect of factual questions). Secondly, answers should not be *forced* into categories to which they do not belong. If a person's genuine answer is "Don't know", it would be most undesirable if probing were to result in a different answer being given. One aspect of the interviewer's art is indeed to recognise when answers are genuinely, rather than evasively, vague, ambiguous and non-committal. A "Don't know" can be a way of refusing to give a definite answer, can indicate genuine lack of knowledge, a fear of giving the "wrong" answer, an inability to decide, a failure to understand the question, or just a lack of interest. The interviewer must try to sense what lies behind the answer.

On opinion questions (marked "O" on their questionnaires), the Government Social Survey allows no deviation from the printed wording, nor any probing. The only assistance permitted is a repetition of the question. If the answer is not clear, the interviewer may ask the respondent to "explain a little more fully what you meant by that" [239]. On no account must she give an indication of her own views; for thus respondents of an argumentative disposition might be led to take the opposite view, while others might give the replies they think the interviewer would favour. In either case the answers would misrepresent the respondent's true opinions.

With knowledge questions, also, there is a danger that explanations may influence answers by "educating" the respondent, and leading him to give a substantive answer where "Don't know" would have been more accurate. Respondents should be made to feel that a "Don't know" answer is not only in order but that many people give it; otherwise they may hesitate to admit ignorance. By intelligent probing—always, of course, neutral—the interviewer can make the respondent feel at ease about the opinions he is revealing, can ensure complete and meaningful data and can make the interview flow interestingly.

On some questions, interviewers are instructed to "prompt", i.e. to make the respondent aware of the possible answers. For instance, with the question "What do you think is the proportion of entitled people who will apply for their medals?" [286] the interviewer was told to offer various answers—one quarter, one half, three quarters, nearly all, all. The same idea is involved in the "aided recall" method. Thus a B.B.C. Audience Research interviewer investigating which programmes a person listened to on the previous day will help by reminding him what the programmes were.

A form of prompting which is increasingly popular is to show the respondent a card listing the possible answers, so that he simply has to indicate which one applies.[1] This method was used, for example, in a recent survey (see questionnaire on p. 215) when the following question was asked: "Where are you living? Would you show me on this card which applies to you?" The card read

At home	1
As a lodger or a boarder with a family	2
In a hotel/hostel/boarding house/hospital/institution	3
Elsewhere	4

Further details were asked only from those answering 4. Visual aids are also much used. In the I.P.A. readership survey [126] carried out by Social Surveys Ltd. (The British Institute of Public Opinion), respondents were asked about their reading of all kinds of newspapers and periodicals and, to help them to remember, they were shown reproductions of title headings of all the publications.

Recording the answers

In most interview surveys, the interviewers themselves have to record the answers. The exceptions are those in which questionnaires are left or collected by interviewers, but filled in by the respondents and the rare cases in which a secret ballot is used (see Cantril [28]).

The recording of answers would seem a simple enough task and one which interviewers might be expected to perform with accuracy. That they sometimes make substantial errors is due to several factors. First of all, their task is a fairly tiring one. With random sampling, the interviewer may have travelled and walked a good way before getting to the respondent. Once there, she has to go through what is often a lengthy, and always a somewhat repetitive, operation. She might well be forgiven, then, if she is harassed or bad-tempered—especially if the respondent is unhelpful. Secondly, the interviewer often has to code answers according to complicated instructions. Thirdly, she is rarely able to confine her entire attention to one task: while recording the answer to one question, she is perhaps preparing

---

[1] Care has to be taken in interviewing illiterate respondents and those with poor eye-sight! It is a good rule in any case to read out, as well as show, such card lists.

to ask, or actually asking, the next. At the same time, she has to be on the alert for vague and qualified answers, for "red-herrings" and for signs that the question has been misunderstood.

In discussing the recording of answers, the distinction between open and pre-coded questions,[1] treated fully in Chapter 12, must be mentioned. Examples—taken from the questionnaire[2] on p. 215— will show the difference:

An open question

"What kinds of things would you like to spend more time on in your leisure hours?"

A pre-coded question

"When did you last go to the pictures?"

Within last 7 days......	1
8–14 days ago	2
15–28 days ago	3
More than 28 days ago	4
I never go	5
Don't know	6

In the open question, the interviewer's job is to record the answer as completely as possible and in the respondent's, not her own, words. With pre-coded questions the interviewer's task is to decide on the appropriate code and to ring it; errors may arise through faulty judgement and carelessly ringing the wrong code. Many pre-coded questions, of course, hardly require judgement. The question "Are you married?" admits of a "Yes" or "No" answer and there is no problem of judgement so long as the interviewer knows the definitions —e.g. how to code a divorced person. The question on cinema-going similarly provides little room for the exercise of judgement. The risks of more difficult pre-coded questions are discussed in Chapter 13.

At the close of the interview, the interviewer must check that she has asked all the questions and recorded all the answers, that she has ringed the right codes and that there is no inconsistency between answers. She should also record her impressions and observational notes on the interview. It may be useful at the analysis stage to know in what kind of environment the respondent lives and what type of person he is; to know his attitude to the survey and the interviewer's assessment of the validity of his answers. The more the interviewer adds by way of comments to the bare skeleton of a completed questionnaire, the better it is.[3]

---

[1] Alternative terms for open are free-answer or free-response; closed or check-answer are sometimes used in place of pre-coded.
[2] This comes from the experiment on quota sampling [94] mentioned in Section 6.7. It will be used for illustration in this and ensuing chapters.
[3] See Sheatsley [230] for a discussion of interviewer report forms.

11.3. Selection and Training

The description of an interviewer's task suggests a number of desirable personal characteristics. She should make a pleasant impression at first meeting and possess tact and some social sense; she should be accurate, reliable and honest and able to stand up to what is often tiring work; and obviously she should be available for the sort of routine and hours demanded in surveys. What more does one require of her? Need she be particularly intelligent and educated? Does it matter what kind of social background she comes from? Is the age—and, for that matter, the sex—of the interviewer relevant?

Such questions are not easy to answer. Survey experts have their own views on the relative importance of various characteristics, but little systematic evidence has been published in this country. Logically the desirable characteristics should be those that are found to be associated with good interviewing ability. But what is "good" interviewing? Is it to be measured in terms of the truthfulness of the answers the interviewer brings home? If so, we must resign ourselves to being able to measure interviewing quality on only a small fraction of survey questions. Or is it to be gauged by the proportion of refusals, of "Don't know" answers, of recording errors and so forth? If so, it would have to be admitted that we were only measuring part of the whole. There is a real difficulty in measuring "good" interviewing and in deciding what interviewer characteristics are desirable.

Added to this, the importance of any one characteristic naturally varies from survey to survey. Sometimes an expert knowledge of the survey subject is an advantage, sometimes it is unnecessary. Evident racial characteristics are undesirable in certain surveys, but irrelevant in others. Often one tries to avoid using interviewers with strong opinions and prejudices on the subject of the survey since they may influence answers. All in all, it is impossible to lay down any specification to suit all surveys. The trend is to select interviewers according to their performance on certain clearly defined tasks, rather than on personal characteristics.

Selection

There is, however, an astonishing range of practices regarding the selection of interviewers, only some of it explained by differences in the work of the organisations. Representative of one type is the procedure used by the *British Institute of Public Opinion* (the Gallup Poll). Everyone who applies (or is recommended) is sent a lengthy application form on the basis of which certain categories of people are turned down (those who are likely to be available only for a short period, salesmen, students and some others are rejected). The only other hurdle is the request to make 5 unpaid trial interviews; anyone who fails to make them is rejected straightaway. About 1 in 4 of all applicants get accepted.

Except in the case of special projects, there is no personal training. B.I.P.O. has a panel of some 1,500 interviewers all over the country, none of them depending on interviewing as their main source of income. They are sent occasional assignments of, typically, 15–20 interviews, which they may refuse. On any one survey a large number of interviewers do a small number of interviews each. The basis for B.I.P.O.'s policy is the belief that most people can make reasonable interviewers, that full-time interviewing leads to low morale and bad work, that too much training may make interviewers over-conscious of errors and perhaps better able to cover them up; and that, with the above system, it is more likely that interviewer differences will cancel out than if a few interviewers do many interviews each. This set-up further makes it possible to do large-scale surveys cheaply and quickly.

The *B.B C. Audience Research Department* also has a large staff of interviewers—about a thousand—spread over the country. For them, too, interviewing is a spare-time job, consisting of occasional assignments of about three weeks a time; about 200 of them are actively engaged at any moment. They are trained and supervised by full-time members of the Audience Research staff.

By way of contrast, there is the *British Market Research Bureau* which has a permanent staff of 25 to 30 interviewers, who are engaged on the work full-time and travel around the country. Additional interviewers are engaged when needed. A good deal of attention is given to selection and to training.

The *Government Social Survey* employs about 200 part-time investigators, spread over the country, trained and supervised by five regional organisers. Its selection procedure is probably the most rigorous in this country, and is worth describing. Before being interviewed, applicants are scrutinised on the basis of their written applications. (Some applicants may live in an area where no interviewers are needed.) In one particular batch,[1] 21 per cent of the applicants dropped out at this stage (including 6 per cent who withdrew). The remainder were given a lengthy interview designed to find out what kind of people they were, what they expected the work to be like, their availability and so on. It also served to give them a clear picture of the nature of the work. A further 41 per cent of the original applicants failed to pass this stage, about 6 per cent withdrawing of their own

[1] The figures refer to a batch of 170 applicants in a six-month period in 1953; they were quoted by Fothergill and Willcock [86]. The procedure described is general Government Social Survey practice.

volition. For the 38 per cent now remaining there followed a clerical test, designed to test accuracy in recording, summarising, checking and classifying data and in carrying out the kind of elementary arithmetic which features on many questionnaires. A quarter of those tested failed, a third passed but withdrew. The remainder, about 16 per cent of the original batch, were passed on to training and all but a few of them completed it.

This is a complex scheme, which the *ad hoc* survey team, let alone the solitary researcher, cannot hope to adopt. Its underlying principle is, however, worth following: it is to give applicants every opportunity to withdraw if they begin to get dubious about their suitability or enthusiasm for the work. Thus many potential misfits are kept out of the field from the beginning and the researcher's time and money are not wasted on training people who will not stay the course. Even so, interviewer turnover remains a major problem; in recent experience, some 60 per cent of the Government Social Survey's investigators left within a year of commencing work, in spite of these efforts in selection and training.

A noteworthy feature of the scheme is the emphasis on testing performance on routine tasks. It is no good engaging people who will send in slipshod or illegible work, who cannot do simple arithmetic or follow instructions. Fothergill and Willcock, in discussing the Survey's policy, say: "It is believed that whilst it may be possible to teach some people interviewing ability, it is much less possible to teach accurate recording and unbiased summarising" [86, p. 72]. Clerical tests, dummy interviews (with the research staff) and observed interviews in the field are among the most useful tools in the selection process. The value of intelligence and aptitude tests of various kinds remains under debate and offers considerable scope for research.

Amidst all this uncertainty, the researcher can at least seek comfort in the knowledge that there is no such being as an ideal interviewer. Many personal qualities may be desirable, but few of them are so vital that an applicant could be rejected solely for not possessing them. The following are among the least controversial:

(*a*) *Honesty*. There can be no dispute about this: interviewers must be honest and scrupulous. Cheating, in the sense of complete fabrication of a questionnaire response, is fairly easily detected, unscrupulousness in following instructions is not. Honesty and integrity are not characteristics that can be easily assessed at the selection stage, but interviewers who are later found deficient on these scores can and should be quickly dismissed.

(*b*) *Interest*. Interest in the work is highly desirable. Errors and poor quality work are much more likely if the interviewer is bored and regards the work as valueless. The quality of most interviewers' work deteriorates after a time—an important consideration to remember when they are being engaged for a lengthy period. For this reason, some experts believe in occasional assignments rather than full-time work.

(c) *Accuracy*. Interviewers should be accurate in their recording of answers, in the way they follow instructions, apply definitions and carry out their administrative duties. Everyone makes mistakes sometime; what one tries to avoid is the person who tends to make them habitually.

(d) *Adaptability*. If an interviewer is likely to be employed on a variety of surveys, including different types of questions, subjects and respondents, she should be a person who easily adapts herself to varying circumstances; who happily carries out a survey on living conditions in the slums of Glasgow one week and one on chocolate preferences in Mayfair the next. In engaging interviewers for a single survey this is not so relevant, although even here interviews with many different *types* of people will probably be required.

(e) *Personality and temperament*. The danger of "over-rapport" between interviewer and respondent has already been noted and there is something to be said for the interviewer who, while friendly and interested, does not get too emotionally involved with the respondent and his problems. Interviewing on most surveys is a fairly straightforward job, not one calling for exceptional industry, charm or tact. What one asks is that the interviewer's personality should be neither over-aggressive nor over-sociable. Pleasantness and a business-like manner is the ideal combination.

(f) *Intelligence and education*. Ordinary survey interviewing does not call for very special intelligence. Persons of the highest intelligence and education will be the most easily bored by its repetitiveness and the least happy to follow instructions allowing little room for discretion. What is needed is sufficient intelligence to understand and follow complicated instructions and to be adaptable, within given limits, to each respondent and situation.

Occasionally it may be desirable to use specialist interviewers. A good example of this was the Survey on Maternity conducted by the Population Investigation Committee [130], in which the interviewing was done by Health Visitors. Their work gave them a close professional interest in the survey and a natural access to the respondents, circumstances at least partly responsible for the survey's remarkable success.

In small-scale social research studies, where the interviewing is done by perhaps a handful of investigators, it is the rule, rather than the exception, for these to be sociologists, anthropologists, social workers and the like, rather than professional interviewers. For the formal interviewing used in most large-scale surveys, although the interviewer must know enough about the subject to be able to answer the questions the more curious of her respondents will ask, she does not require the knowledge or skill of the specialist.

Training

On the training of interviewers there is as much diversity of opinion and practice as on the selection. Some organisations give virtually none, relying on a quick dismissal of those whose performance fails to come up to scratch; others take the utmost trouble in training their new staff. Some favour formal training, others training by field experience, while still others regard good working conditions as more important than either.

In the Government Social Survey's training programme (see Fothergill and Willcock [86]) recruits are first asked to read, and to take a test on, the *Handbook for Interviewers* and then to attend a two-day seminar on survey methods; after this, the recruits carry out practice interviews on each other and on the training officer. During the next 10 to 20 days, they have their first taste of fieldwork, accompanied by a training officer. First, interviews are done by the officer, then by the new interviewer watched by the officer, finally by the interviewer alone. Later on the interviewer may again conduct some interviews under observation and, after 3 to 6 months in the field, she is given a test, on the result of which she is graded into one of five groups to determine her future payment and the type of assignment she will be given. Those graded into the lowest of the five groups are dismissed.

The main ingredients of any sound training scheme are here: a training manual, talks and discussions in the office, observation of expert interviewers at work, trial interviews. The manual itself is comprehensive, including a description of the Survey's work, of the methods used in all stages of its surveys and of how the interviewer's job should be done. It also gives standard definitions used in its questionnaires.

To illustrate another training scheme, I quote Utting and Cole, writing on the social accounting enquiry of the Department of Applied Economics at Cambridge: "All our interviewers have been recruited by local advertisement, and although mostly women they have varied backgrounds. They all receive an initial 15 to 20 hours' training which covers the general objects of the survey, survey methods and interviewing technique. This is followed by practice interviews in the field which are discussed afterwards. In the last course of training we made considerable use of recorded interviews . . ." [277, p. 308].

To summarise, a researcher wishing to train a team of interviewers might proceed as follows. New interviewers should be given some insight into the general work of the organisation and told why the survey is being done, by whom and how the results are to be used and how the rest of the survey (apart from interviewing) is going to be handled. The importance of the interviewer's role should be explained to her so that she is made to feel, as is indeed the case, that the value of the survey depends on the accuracy and completeness of the information she and her colleagues collect.

Then could follow some instruction on interviewing methods. A manual or, more modestly, a sheet of general instructions would serve as the basis of talks by selected members of the research team. Films and recordings, showing how interviews should and should not be handled, are valuable; and experienced interviewers can give demonstration interviews which are afterwards discussed. If time permits, the new interviewers might try their hand at interviewing each other in the presence of experienced investigators (in turn taking the part of respondent and interviewer); if these dummy interviews can be recorded for subsequent re-playing, all the better. Next, the interviewers can be given their first taste of fieldwork on pre-testing the questionnaire and instructions; they should also be asked to code, edit and analyse some of the test questionnaires to show them how mistakes can arise.[1]

A scheme of this sort, though allowing for talks and discussions, emphasises *learning by experience*, and one concrete study of the value of experience is worth quoting. Durbin and Stuart [66] conducted an experiment to compare the success of experienced professional and inexperienced student interviewers in *obtaining* interviews. Three groups of interviewers took part in the experiment: professionals from the Government Social Survey and British Institute of Public Opinion, and students from the London School of Economics. Some of the results are given in Table 11.1.

By "success" was meant that the questionnaire was wholly or partially completed (regardless of the number of calls). The striking difference in the success rates between the experienced and inexperienced interviewers was maintained through the three districts sampled (Bermondsey, Tottenham and Wandsworth) and was independent of which questionnaire was used (Tuberculosis, Reading

---

[1] Not everyone would agree with the wisdom of the last step; there is a risk that interviewers will gain not only an insight into their errors, but an insight into how to hide them on future surveys.

TABLE 11.1

Results of attempted interviews. Experienced and inexperienced interviewers

	Social Survey per cent	B.I.P.O. per cent	L.S.E. per cent
Success	83·7*	81·3*	69·6*
Refusal	3·8*	3·2*	13·5*
Non-contact	5·0	6·7	5·8
Gone away	5·4*	7·5*	10·1*
Other	2·2	1·2	1·0
Total	100·1	99·9	100·0
Sample size	(504)	(504)	(504)

* Significant at the 1 per cent level.

Source: Durbin and Stuart [66, p. 173].

or Saving) and of the age and sex of the respondents. It is worth noting that the two professional organisations hardly differed in their response rates, which suggests that the additional training to which the G.S.S. interviewers are subjected (as against the B.I.P.O. group) did not affect the response rates to any extent.

The authors suggested in their conclusions that "though the enquiry has demonstrated the inferiority of the students in obtaining interviews when compared with professional interviewers it tells us nothing of the causes of the differences and whether they can easily be remedied. Is it simply a matter of inexperience, or are the differences due in part at least to deeper causes such as students' youthfulness or the personality characteristics of people who go to universities?" [66, p. 184]. These questions remain unanswered and it is still open to someone to investigate the effect of training on success in obtaining interviews.

One would also like to know to what extent training and experience improve the *quality* of interviewing, but this is much more difficult. Certain aspects, however, can be checked. The Bureau of the Census has reported an experiment[1] in which two groups of interviewers were given the full (1950 Census) training course of 16 hours, while two other groups were given a five-hour course plus a two-hour review session after two days' interviewing. The questionnaires were then analysed regarding "the proportion of entries which were blank or not acceptable"—"not acceptable" meaning that occupation was too vague to be coded, that there was an entry in the labour force block

[1] In the report on a conference held at Michigan in 1951 [257].

for persons 13 years or under (for whom no entries were required) and so on. Table 11.2 shows the results of the analysis:

TABLE 11.2

Percentage of total entries required which were not reported or not acceptable

	Long Course per cent	Short Course per cent
Occupation—not acceptable	3·5	7·2
omitted	1·9	1·8
Industry—not acceptable	7·5	16·8
omitted	2·0	2·5
Worker classification—not acceptable	2·4	2·8
omitted	3·3	4·0
Sample line information omitted	18·4	31·0
Migration	1·5	2·7
Labour force, incorrect patterns	2·0	4·2
Household composition incorrect	·2	·4

Source: University of Michigan Conference Report [257, p. 62].

The report on the experiment felt it reasonable "to conclude that exposure to the complete training did improve the quality of the enumeration. On the other hand, the gains for some items were not particularly startling and for other items even the complete training does not show too encouraging a picture. Since the complete training course meant a training expenditure by the Bureau more than three times the training expenditure for the short course, the question of whether the training technique used gave the Bureau the most for its money is still an open one. The abbreviated training course was prepared in considerable haste and did not by any means represent the best utilisation of the 5 hours allocated to it. It is possible that a course of this length might have been just as effective as the complete training with a better distribution of the points of emphasis" [257].

These conclusions stress the vital point that both selection and training cost money and that the operative point to the researcher is the extent to which this expenditure is repaid in terms of increased efficiency. Some money is worth spending, but how much? The answer depends on the relation of this outlay to interviewer turnover, on the one hand, and to the quality of interviewing, on the other. Our knowledge on all this remains scanty and what there is, at least in this country, is largely unpublished. Each survey expert takes his stand on the basis of experience and resources. The social researcher, with no permanent organisation and fund of experience behind him, must be guided by such considerations as have been mentioned in this section, by common sense, and by whatever experimentation he can afford in preparing his enquiry.

11.4. Some Practical Points

This section brings together a few practical aspects of interviewing, which arise whatever the nature of the survey and however modest the scale of the organisation.

Interviewer instructions

An important part of any interview survey are the fieldwork instructions and briefing. What ground they cover depends on the training the interviewers have already had, but they generally indicate how the respondents were, or are to be, selected and how they are to be found (e.g. "the names and addresses of your respondents are given in columns 1 and 2 of the record sheet; no substitutes may be taken"), how many re-calls are to be made, how to deal with various types of non-response, to open the interview, ask the questions and record the answers. The instructions should explain any documents issued for the survey and deal with the administrative routine.

Most important perhaps are the questionnaire instructions. These may be printed on the questionnaire or issued as a separate document; in either case, they should state whether any deviation from the printed order and wording of questions is permissible, and what probing is to be allowed. They must further give the definitions needed for the interpretation of questions and tell the interviewer what to do in the case of vague or doubtful answers. Thus question 6 in the questionnaire on p. 215 asked: "Roughly, how long does it take you to get to work? (Record as stated)" and interviewers were instructed: "If the informant says that 'it varies', find out what is most usual for him or her and record this." However complete and clear the instructions, they must always be supplemented by one or more briefing meetings. An hour's personal briefing and discussion of doubtful points can do more than many pages of instructions to impress upon interviewers the operational details of their task.

Field supervision

Some supervision of interviewers is essential, both to detect bad work and to keep fieldworkers up to the mark. With a small mobile field staff, one or two centrally located supervisors may take care of all supervision; with a large field staff spread throughout the country, a localised organisation is more usual, each region being in the charge of a supervisor. In either case, the supervisor is the main link between field staff and head office. She may do the briefing locally, having first been briefed herself at the office; she may have to direct the sample selection if this is done from local lists; and she will have to decide which interviewers are to participate and to give them their sample assignments. Queries and difficulties are referred to her, and she is expected to keep in touch with interviewers during the field-work period, and to receive their completed questionnaires. Checks on individual interviewers are usually carried out by her. No need to emphasise, then, how important the supervisor's task is in a survey organisation. For the researcher engaged on an *ad hoc* survey, personal supervision on this scale is usually out of the question but some attempt to see that interviewers are doing their work efficiently, scrupulously and pleasantly, should be made.

Fieldwork checks[1]

As has been said before, interviewers are human beings and there-fore liable to make mistakes. However sound the selection procedure, not all who get on to the field staff will prove satisfactory, while some of those who start well, will deteriorate. It is therefore advisable to keep the quality of the fieldwork constantly under review and to in-vestigate any case where an interviewer appears to be doing unsatis-factory work.

The main objects of fieldwork checks are (a) to test whether an interviewer in fact made all the interviews claimed; (b) whether her response rate is satisfactory; (c) whether she is asking the questions, and interpreting and recording the answers, in accordance with in-structions.

The first check can be made by sending postcards to all or a sample of the respondents, asking them whether they were interviewed. (It is becoming standard practice in quota sampling to obtain names and addresses, so that such checks are not confined to random sampling.) The main problem with postcard checks is that they are themselves subject to non-response. In a recent survey [68] by the Research Techniques Unit of the London School of Economics, 70 per cent of the check cards were returned, an unusually high rate. No case was found of an interviewer having dishonestly recorded an interview, but no information was available, of course, regarding the remaining 30 per cent. Might people who had in fact not been interviewed be less likely to return the cards?

An experiment conducted by the U.N.E.S.C.O. Institute for Social Sciences in Cologne is relevant here.[2] This was based on a sample

[1] A fuller discussion of interviewer errors and biases, and the checks used to detect them, will be found in Chapter 13.

[2] The following details were communicated by Dr. E. Reigrotzki, of this Institute, and are quoted with his permission.

of 3,500 interviews; and in order to check on these, check cards were sent to approximately 1,070 reported contacts, asking a few questions and requesting the person to put a cross if no interview had taken place. Of these cards, 396 (37 per cent) were returned, and 10 were marked with a cross. The question now was whether people who had been interviewed were more or less likely to have returned the card. In either case, the proportion 10/396 would give a false impression.

To check on this, similar cards were sent to 100 people randomly selected from the same population, but who had definitely *not* been interviewed. Only 9 were returned, all marked with crosses. The experimenters then reasoned that the bias could be measured by the ratio of percentage replies from the "interviewees" and the "non-interviewees", i.e. 37/9: "the rate of interviews reported as having been made but yielding a negative check is thus, if we believe the estimate of the bias, in the neighbourhood of

$$\left(\frac{10}{396} \times 100 \times \frac{37}{9}\right) \text{ per cent} = 10 \text{ per cent.}"$$

The experiment was felt to have been too small to be conclusive (taking account of the sampling error, one would get very wide limits around this estimate) but it did suggest the existence of a bias. In any case the idea is ingenious and worth pursuing in future studies.

Coming to the second type of check, the response rate[1] an interviewer achieves in successive assignments is worth studying. If she is consistently less successful than her colleagues, or shows signs of deteriorating, it may be time to dismiss her or to "rest" her for a while. A different guide to efficiency is provided by response rates on individual questions. If an interviewer is consistently getting more refusals than the average on difficult questions it is time to review her work. The same applies if she is getting an excessive number of "Don't know" replies. In short, the researcher can lay down certain operational standards (possibly on the basis of *average* performance) and check on the work of any "sub-standard" investigators.

The most difficult of all points to check is whether an interviewer is asking the questions in the right way, and correctly interpreting and recording the answers. Some inaccuracies in coding and recording may be spotted by a scrutiny of the completed questionnaires, but many types of error will not; one can rarely tell from the questionnaires whether the interviewer deviated from the printed wording or

---

[1] By which I mean the proportion of an interviewer's assigned interviews from which she gets completed questionnaires. A different point is "number of interviews a day". This is also worth keeping a check on, though the effect of size of town, region, travel facilities must be borne in mind. The Government Social Survey takes account of a "Population Density Index" in making this latter check.

sequence, whether she probed too little or too much and whether she recorded the answer incorrectly.

There are broadly six ways of checking upon the quality of interviewing, other than by scrutinising the completed questionnaires. One is to use high-grade interviewers or supervisors to re-interview some of the respondents and to compare the two sets of results, the presumption being that the high-grade interviewers are more likely to be correct. In spite of the obvious snags of re-interviewing, such quality checks can be useful (see Chapter 13). A second way is to have supervisors observing interviewers at work. This is useful when an interviewer is thought to be falling below the required standards, but one can never be sure that interviewers conduct all their interviews as they do those under observation. The same qualification applies to the third method, which is to have interviewers conduct test interviews in the office. The most that can be hoped for is that such interviews will disclose any persistent bad interviewing habits the investigators have got into. The fourth way is mechanically to record the interviews. This would be a good check, if the interviewers were left unaware that it was being done; but if they themselves carry and work the recording apparatus, their performance can again not be regarded as typical of everyday work. Fifthly, if the survey is designed on the basis of interpenetrating samples (see Section 6.8) major differences between interviewers, though not consistent biases, can be discerned. Finally, the quality of the interviewer's work can be gauged to the extent that the answers to survey questions can be checked against other data.

Working conditions

Selection and training are one side of interviewer efficiency, morale is another. Payments to interviewers, working conditions, hours of work, assignments, contacts with the research team—all these are related to morale and thus to efficiency.

Payment should be good enough to attract the right sort of people and to keep them satisfied. Payment is normally on a time-basis, since piece rates may easily lead to slipshod work; the Government Social Survey pays differential rates according to the grading of the interviewers, other organisations have systems of bonus payments. In general pay rates for interviewing are very low, and one cannot wonder that labour turnover is a problem of such magnitude in professional organisations.

Interviewers should be given reasonable assignments. If they are full-time workers they cannot be expected to do much at weekends or in the evenings; but part-timers are likely to do most of their work at these times. Frequent long journeys for dispersed interviews are discouraging, as are interviews in difficult localities. If an interviewer has been long in the field, a spell in the office or a complete rest from surveys is often beneficial. Interest is bound to flag after a time and the surveyor may be able to help by varying the types of assignments and by keeping in touch through news letters and so on.

Finally, it is worth making the obvious remark that researchers cannot expect interviewers to do a decent job if they produce overlengthy or ill-designed questionnaires and ask questions which most people find unintelligible, uninteresting or futile.

11.5. Informal Interviewing[1]

So far I have been concerned with formal interviewing, in which the questions that are asked, their sequence and wording, are worked out *beforehand* and the ideal is that the interviews should be conducted in a uniform way.[2]

The case for formal interviewing is simple. Only if all respondents are asked exactly the same questions in the same order can one be sure that all the answers relate to the same thing and are strictly comparable. Then, and then only, is one justified in combining the results into statistical aggregates.

The intention is understandable enough. The surveyor wants to feel confident that if a respondent had been questioned by interviewer B rather than by interviewer A the answers would have been the same; similarly, that were he to be *re-interviewed* by interviewer A, much the same set of answers would be obtained. The aim all the time is to maximise *reliability*—i.e. the extent to which repeated measurements (interviews) made on the same material (respondents) by the same measuring instrument (interviewer) would get the same result.[3] Without doubt formal interviewing succeeds in achieving higher reliability than informal techniques.

Reliability, however, is not everything. The other side of the picture is the *validity* of a response, that is its closeness to the truth which one is trying to ascertain. When the survey subject is complex or emotional, it may be that the greater flexibility of an informal ap-

---

[1] There are many other terms in use to distinguish between what I am calling formal and informal interviewing: structured and unstructured; mass and formative; inflexible and flexible; standardised and qualitative; controlled and uncontrolled; extensive and intensive.

[2] It is sometimes suggested that the "open" question is the first step towards informal interviewing. This is not in accord with the present use of the term, at any rate. In formal survey interviews, both "open" and pre-coded questions are supposed to be *asked* in a specified form; they differ only in the form in which the answer is recorded. But the interviewer has no freedom to alter the course of the interview, which is the essence of what I am calling informal interviewing.

[3] The term "reliability" is often used in the wider sense, to express the extent to which two (or more) *different* interviewers working under similar conditions get the same results.

proach succeeds better than set questions in getting to the heart of the respondent's opinion.

I do not intend to imply that there is no flexibility at all in formal interviewing; the interviewer can always adapt her opening remarks to the situation confronting her, and explain, probe, and adjust the speed of the interview within the defined limits. But these limits are fairly rigid. Probing, for instance, is usually allowed only on some questions and even then only according to instructions. And, except with factual questions, interviewers are hardly ever allowed to change the wording or order of questions or to ask additional ones.

This is where the contrast with informal interviewing is most striking, for here the conduct of the interview is largely in the hands of interviewer and respondent. Just how extensive their respective influence is varies with the type of interview.

These can be visualised along a scale of increasing formality. At one end there is the completely *non-directive* interview[1] which has more affinity to the psychoanalyst's approach than to the usual survey interview. The informant is encouraged to talk about the subject under investigation (usually himself) and the course of the interview is mainly guided by him. There are no set questions, and usually no pre-determined framework for recording answers. The interviewer confines himself to elucidating doubtful points, to re-phrasing the respondent's answers and to probing generally. It is an approach especially to be recommended when complex attitudes are involved and when one's own knowledge of them is still in a vague and unstructured form. Suppose we wished to study how a group of parents feel about the effects of "comics" on their children. In the early stages of the research, at any rate, one would probably treat the subject, not in terms of set questions, but by an informal approach which will show what points are worth attacking in the later and more structured stages.

Then we have the kind of *conversational* or *casual* interviewing used by Mayhew [182], and revived recently by Zweig in his various studies. In the introduction to his best-known book Zweig says: "I dropped the idea of a questionnaire, or formal verbal questions put forward in the course of research; instead I had casual talks with working-class men on an absolutely equal footing and in friendly intercourse. These were not formal interviews but an exchange of views on life, labour and poverty" [295, p. 1]. There is no doubt that, in Zweig's hands, this highly individual method was successful.

Moving towards more formal methods, we come to the situation in which the interviewer, whilst allowing the respondent a good deal of

[1] Other terms are depth or non-guided interview. One of the classic examples of this form occurred in the famous Hawthorne experiments [215.]

freedom, aims to cover a given set of topics in a more or less systematic way. This is best termed the *guided* or *focused* interview. Again there is no set questionnaire and most of the questions are open ones, designed to encourage the respondent to talk freely around each topic. A good example was given in a paper by Marriott [178], which described a survey among industrial workers aimed to study what factors made for satisfaction and what for discontent among them. The individual interview was guided around eight topics, which previous study had found to be crucial in the context: operation of the actual task performed; hours of work; shift system; amount of wages; payment system; firms and higher management and their policies; supervision and workmates. A few simple factual questions introduced each subject, and were followed by the open questions which formed the core of the discussion for every topic; finally, respondents were asked to assess their own contentedness as regards each topic.

Such interviewing gets away from the inflexibility of formal methods, yet gives the interview a set form and ensures that all the relevant topics are discussed. The respondents are all asked for certain information, yet they have plenty of opportunity to develop their views at length. Interviewers, on their side, are free to choose when and how to put their questions and how much to explore and probe, all the time keeping within the framework imposed by the topics to be covered. The focused or guided interview is thus more formal than the non-directive interview; there are numerous examples of its application in the literature.

Informal interviewing raises various issues, some on the debit, others on the credit side, and these will repay looking at.

Interviewer skill

Informal interviewing clearly calls for greater skill than the formal survey interview. More than a careful following of instructions is involved. The conduct of the interview calls for intelligence, understanding and tact, and for a deeper knowledge of its subject-matter than is required in formal interviewing. In the latter, the skilful part of the process is, as far as possible, taken out of the field and into the office. The less formal the method, the more skill is required in the field; and informal methods at their best demand the abilities, not of professional interviewers briefed by the sociologist, but of the sociologist himself. They do not, therefore, lend themselves well to the large-scale surveys which are the main subject of this book.

Interviewer bias

Informal interviewing gives much greater scope to the personal influence and bias of the interviewer than the formal approach. The investigator at least partly determines what form the interview takes, the questions that are asked and the details that are recorded. There is, in the report of an informal interview, "more of the interviewer" than on the standard survey questionnaire, which is another way of saying that the process is not so reliable.

Validity

The chief recommendation for informal methods is that they can "dig deeper" and get more valid data than the formal interview. The importance of this "digging" depends on the questions that are being asked. If a survey is designed to collect simple facts about individuals, such as their age, their marital status, the size of their family, their chocolate purchases and so forth, there is no need to look beyond the formal approach. But when it sets out to study more complex things, particularly attitudes, formal interviewing may limit the investigation to too superficial a level to be appropriate. A method which is suitable for ascertaining a person's age is not necessarily the best for discovering his attitude to homosexuality.

Survey experts have long recognised that simple poll-type questions are inadequate when complex attitudes are involved and have made increasing use of "attitude batteries" and scaling devices. A large number of questions relating to the subject-matter are asked, and the answers combined, by more or less sophisticated means, to give a wider picture of an attitude than could be obtained by a few simple questions. But the essential limitation of the formal interview, its inflexibility in the face of different situations and respondents, is still there. This becomes clear if we consider a hypothetical survey on attitudes to homosexuality. Most people have views on this subject. Some people feel strongly about it, others are little moved by it; some are too inhibited to talk about it, others only too glad to do so; the views of some are straightforward and rational, those of others complex and highly emotional. One cannot hope that any set of standardised questions, however well framed, will get to the core of the attitude of each respondent. Validity will vary from person to person. With informal interviewing, if skilfully done, the interviewer should be able to cut through any embarrassment and emotional inhibitions surrounding the subject and to "dig as deep" as may be necessary to get to the heart of each person's attitude. All the qualifications surrounding this attitude, its causes, implications, and intensity, should emerge, resulting in a fuller and more rounded picture than is attainable by formal methods.[1]

[1] Rose [217] even suggests that, in order to draw out the respondent's real attitude to a subject, the interviewer may find it useful to use biased words and leading questions, to express an attitude of her own (real or assumed), to give the

It does not of course follow that the fuller description is *necessarily* the more valid one. As was suggested in the National Opinion Research Center studies [124] some people may not have hidden depths, in which case a snap answer to a snap question may be a more valid response than a complicated picture arrived at by lengthy discussion! The latter may influence the respondent in the answers he gives, and may lead him to rationalise. Also, because in the informal interview the interviewer's personality and views tend to come more into the open, the respondent may be led to present a biased picture of his own views. An outstandingly interesting problem for research—and a difficult one to tackle—is the comparison of the validity and reliability of answers resulting from formal and informal interviewing techniques.

Analysis

A basic objection to informal methods is the difficulty of summarising and quantifying the material. There are essentially three facets to this. One is that, as interviewers are free to determine the run of the interview, different *items* of information may be obtained from different respondents, so that it is hard to compare and aggregate the results.

Secondly, even if interviewers have asked for the same items, differences in wording and so forth may make the answers not truly comparable. Thirdly, the results of descriptive, non-quantified interviews do not easily lend themselves to statistical analysis as answers to straight questions do. If quantification is desired, coding must precede it and this is relatively harder with descriptive interview material.[1] The material obtained from depth, non-directive or casual interviews has to be used quite differently from that obtained in formal surveys. The point of the informal approach is to obtain a more complete picture of, say, a person's attitude than a formal interview would. If this gain is not to be sacrificed, the analysis must retain a fair amount of detail and not merely be compressed into a series of statistical tables.

Conclusions

It can be seen that the choice between formal and informal methods depends on the character of the survey problem and the use to be made of the results. The formal approach achieves greater uniformity and this is a weighty factor when comparability between interviews is important and when the interest is in the characteristics

respondent—whose expressed attitude may be based on misinformation—any necessary information.
[1] See p. 287 for some references on the coding of non-quantified material.

of the aggregate more than in those of the individual. In any case the method is quite adequate for the simple type of questions involved in many administrative surveys and market research.

Its use becomes questionable when complex phenomena are under study: formal questioning is then often too superficial and crude for the task. For this reason alone, informal techniques will continue to be used in a good deal of sociological research. They will also remain invaluable at the pilot stage of even formal surveys, to provide guidance on what are the important questions and how they should be asked. They do, however, require more skill and alertness to the danger of personal bias than formal methods: they are also relatively slow and expensive.

NOTES ON READING

1. Perhaps the best way to get the "feel" of an interviewer's job is to read one of the manuals issued by professional bodies for their field staff. The GOVERNMENT SOCIAL SURVEY'S *Handbook for Interviewers* is the most detailed in Great Britain but, like those of commercial bodies, it is not published in the ordinary way. The paper by FOTHERGILL and WILLCOCK [86] has a good discussion of interviewing problems, in the context of the Social Survey's work

Among the text-books, GOODE and HATT [97] and PARTEN [202] discuss the interviewer's job in particular detail.

2. The SURVEY RESEARCH CENTER at the University of Michigan sponsored in 1951 a conference on *Field Methods in Sample Interview Surveys*. The report [257] summarises the proceedings, which ranged over the whole field of selection, training, instruction, supervision and so forth. It is a concise and very much to-the-point discussion of outstanding problems. SHEATSLEY's chapter on interviewing in JAHODA, DEUTSCH and COOK [129] is well worth studying; so is that by CANNELL and KAHN in FESTINGER and KATZ [78].

3. The classical article on non-directive interviewing is that by ROGERS [216]; on focused interviewing the best reference is the book by MERTON, FISKE and KENDALL [185]. Other interesting papers on informal techniques are those by LAZARSFELD [155] and ROSE [217]. MADGE [168] has a good summary of all these methods.

4. Numerous articles on interviewing are spread through the pages of the *Public Opinion Quarterly* and the *International Journal of Opinion and Attitude Research* (now discontinued).

5. Finally, for this chapter almost as much as for Chapter 13, the report on the National Opinion Research Center studies by HYMAN and others [124] must be regarded as a standard reference.

CHAPTER 12

QUESTIONNAIRES

12.1. General Principles of Design

IN THE last two chapters I discussed the principal ways of collecting survey data: mail questionnaires and personal interviews. I now turn to the instrument on which both approaches depend, the *questionnaire* or *recording schedule*.

As briefly noted above, these two terms are sometimes used to distinguish between the situation in which the respondent himself fills in the answers and that in which an interviewer asks the questions and records the answers.[1] To the survey designer the distinction is important, for in one case he is producing a document to be used and, he hopes, understood by the respondent unaided, while in the other the users will be persons especially trained to handle such documents. The Family Census questionnaire reproduced opposite is a good example of the former type.[2] It is true that in this case the questionnaires were collected by enumerators so that respondents could ask for assistance in answering the questions; but the design of the questionnaire was such as to minimise the need for assistance. That the answers will be treated in confidence is emphasised in the heading and not, as sometimes, in a remote corner. The sections applying to different parts of the household—the wife, children, husband—are clearly sign-posted. Introductions are simple and well-placed, the layout and printing are attractive and the explanations, definitions and instructions are clear. What is more, the questions themselves are simple and it looks as if a genuine effort was made to keep them to a minimum.

---

[1] I confine myself throughout this chapter to formal interviewing. The type of schedule used in some kinds of informal interviewing is best called an interview guide.
[2] Three illustrative questionnaires or schedules are reproduced in this book: the form used in the Family Census; a Gallup Poll questionnaire, and the questionnaire used in the quota sampling experiment [194] mentioned earlier.

The requirements for a recording schedule are in some respects different from this. Since it is handled by interviewers, it can be a fairly formal document, in which efficiency of field handling, rather than attractiveness, is the operative consideration in design. It can be in a highly codified form, with instructions and definitions printed on the schedule.

In designing either a questionnaire or recording schedule, the convenience of the office staff as well as that of interviewer and respondent must be considered. Layout and printing should be such that editing and coding can proceed smoothly. As it is often desirable to prepare punched cards (see Chapter 14) straight from the questionnaire or schedule it should be designed with this in mind; code numbers should stand out clearly so that punch-operators can spot them quickly. But of course it is the interviewer, rather than the office worker, who has to cope with the schedule under the most difficult circumstances, so it is her convenience that must be given top priority.

One of the skills in designing either type of document is to make clear which questions are to be answered by whom. Sometimes whole sections concern only a sub-class of respondents, in which case this should be quite plain to whoever is recording the answers. The schedule on p. 215 is a good example: here questions 4 to 7, for instance, were to be asked "only of informants with jobs".

Frequently, "a question" consists of a main question and one or more "dependent" or sub-questions. In the schedule just cited, question 3(a) is asked of all, question 3(b) only of those who answer "Has job" to the former. Again, in the B.I.P.O. schedule opposite question 9(a) asks all respondents about their voting intentions "if there were a General Election tomorrow"; question 9(b) asks those who answered "Liberal" or "Other" how they would vote if there were "only Conservative and Labour candidates", while question 9(c) asks all except the Liberals "whether, if a Liberal stood in their constituency, they might vote for him". Sub-questions can become complicated and clear layout and printing are essential.

Having made the distinction between questionnaires and recording schedules, I shall not labour it unduly. Where it is of particular relevance, I shall say so; otherwise, the more convenient term "questionnaire" will be used.

It has been said that "no survey can be better than its questionnaire", a cliché which well expresses the truth that no matter how efficient the sample design or sophisticated the analysis, ambiguous questions will produce non-comparable answers, leading questions biased answers and vague questions vague answers. Discussion on the questionnaire must begin right at the start of the planning stages and will not end until the pilot surveys are completed. It is fair to say

H

that question design is the survey director's most persistent headache, particularly since it is still so largely a matter of art rather than science.

There are admittedly a number of general principles guiding question design and some pitfalls to beware of (it needs no theorist for instance to point out that if uninfluenced answers are required it would be foolish to put a question in the form "You don't think . . . , do you?"). Yet for virtually every conceivable question there are several possible, and theoretically acceptable, forms; in choosing between them, knowledge of the survey population and subject-matter, common sense and past experience are at present the surveyor's main tools.

The value of these tools is not questioned, but clearly surveys would be greatly strengthened if there were a more scientific basis to question design; if the choice between the alternative forms of a question could more often be based on theoretical principles or on firm empirical evidence. By the latter I mean more than the surveyor's recollection that a particular question form was unsuccessful on a particular occasion; an alternative form might after all have been equally unsuccessful. If, on the other hand, different forms of questions were tried out experimentally or in pilot surveys, the comparison of their success—however judged—would be a solid basis for choice. The difficulties in all this are obvious, which is why surveyors continue to rely on common sense and hunches. It is easy enough to compare several question forms experimentally, but such comparisons always relate to a particular question, time and group of respondents; it is exceedingly hard to derive comparisons of *general* relevance. Apart from which, even if two question forms produce different results, it is often hard, and sometimes impossible, to judge which result—if either—is correct.

The first step in designing a questionnaire is to define the problem to be tackled by the survey and hence to decide on what questions to ask. The temptation is always to cover too much, to ask everything that might turn out to be interesting. This must be resisted. Lengthy, rambling questionnaires are as demoralising for the interviewer as for the respondent, and the questionnaire should be no longer than is absolutely necessary for the purpose. Certain questions will, so to speak, include themselves, but a problem of choice inevitably arises with marginal ones. Let us consider a hypothetical survey to ascertain what daily newspapers different kinds of people read. A number of newspaper questions, together with those asking for necessary personal data, automatically suggest themselves. Then, as the discussion on the planning of the survey warms up, many extensions of interest occur to those taking part. Would it be useful to include reading of periodicals and books? Would the main results be more meaningful if they could be viewed against the background of the respondents' leisure habits as a whole? Would it be wise to find out something about how much money and time different people have available for newspaper buying and reading? Should one ask a question or two about the use of libraries? Should one go beyond the facts of reading and ask people's opinions on the individual news-papers?

And so it goes on, with the questionnaire growing from a short list of questions to a document several pages long. Enquiries in the pro-fessional survey field, where the questionnaire is tailored to a client's precise requirements, usually avoid this process; but in social research, where a survey is often aimed to study a certain *field*, rather than to collect specific information, it is exceedingly common. Nor is there any simple way of deciding what limit to put on the range of a ques-tionnaire. The extra cost (in time and money) of adding further ques-tions can be estimated from trial interviews, but these are not the only variables. Length of questionnaire must be presumed to affect the morale of both interviewer and respondent, and probably also re-fusal rates and the quality of the data; these are unknown quantities unless special efforts are made in the pilot survey to estimate them. The difficulty again is to develop any general principles. Perhaps the only certainty is that the shorter the questionnaire the better the interviewer and respondent will like it, which is about as useful as saying that the bigger the sample the more precise will be the results. Both statements are unexceptionable, but neither suffices as a guide for action. An enormous sample may be desirable but financially out of reach; a short questionnaire may suit the respondent but not the purpose of the enquiry (nor does it *necessarily* suit the interviewer; too short a questionnaire gives little chance to create "rapport" and secure full co-operation).

It is obvious that the survey planner must rigorously examine every question, and exclude any which are not strictly relevant to the sur-veys's objectives. In this, the pilot survey is his most helpful tool. Here all the marginal questions can be tested out and dummy tabu-lations made from the results. Questions likely to prove of trivial importance in the final analysis can be spotted, as can those which turn out to be not worth asking unless a host of others is also included.

In settling the scope of a questionnaire, one other criterion should be applied, namely that the questions should be practicable. This merits emphasis, even though no amount of text-book admonition can take the place of common sense. It is no good asking a person's opinion about something he does not understand; about events too far distant for him to remember accurately; about matters which, although they concern him, he is unlikely to have accurate information on or that are so personal or emotional that valid answers cannot be expected by formal questioning.

12.2. Question Content

In considering any question, then, it is wise to ask oneself whether respondents are likely to possess the knowledge, or have access to the information, necessary for giving a correct answer. It is unsafe to *assume* that respondents will voluntarily admit ignorance. On the contrary it has often been shown that they will give some kind of answer to most questions, even if they are ill-informed and know it. Similarly, they will express opinions on matters they have given little thought to or which they barely understand.

Let us look at it from the viewpoint of the respondent. He finds himself confronted by an interviewer, who is a total stranger to him, asking his opinion on some matter and thereby implying, albeit subtly, that he has an opinion to offer. Why should he belittle himself by saying that he has never considered the issue, that he does not know what the question means or that he has no opinion to give? There is little reason for him to do so unless he is directly asked about the extent of his knowledge—in which case he is quite likely to admit ignorance, and may indeed welcome the opportunity in the hope of avoiding further questions.

Such difficulties do not apply only to opinion questions. In asking a respondent for factual information, one needs also to be sure that he is in a good position to give it. There is no difficulty in asking women about their husbands' incomes, or in obtaining answers from most of them, but such answers may have little accuracy. Again, to what extent is one entitled to expect accurate answers to the many survey questions involving memory? All too little is known about the role of memory errors in surveys (but see Gray [100]) and this is a corner of the survey field in which the psychologist should have something to offer.

To summarise, the surveyor should aim to ask questions only from those likely to be able to answer them accurately; to ask about past events only if he can reasonably expect people to remember them accurately (perhaps with the help of recall methods); and to ask their opinions only if he can be reasonably sure that they understand what is involved and are able to give a meaningful answer. It is always well to remember that most survey questions are addressed to people very differently qualified to answer them.

So much for taking account of the *ability* of people to give accurate answers. Quite as important is their *willingness* to do so. Except in the rare surveys in which people are compelled to give information, there

Number of

ant...........................

I am from the Survey Research Unit, and
we are trying to find out a few things about
what people do in their spare time. Would
you mind telling me, are there any things
which you would like to spend more
time on?

Yes	1
No	2
Don't know	3

If YES (1) to Q.1: What, for instance?
(Record fully)

....

....

....

For office use

Y	X	0	1
2	3	4	5
6	7	8	9

QUESTION 2 OF ALL WOMEN IN-
IANTS. FOR MEN GO ON TO QUES-
3.

e you a housewife—that is, the person who
mainly responsible for domestic duties in
ur household?

Yes	1
No	2
Not applicable	3

ALL.

I know that your job makes a lot of
difference to the amount of spare time you
get, so would you mind telling me whether
you have a paid job?

Has job	1
Has no job	2

es Job" to Q.3 (a):

What is your job? (Obtain fullest possible
description of occupation and industry.)

Occupation ....

....

Industry ....

....

Q.4–7 ONLY OF INFORMANTS WITH
. FOR THOSE WITHOUT JOBS GO
TO Q.8.

4 Is your job full-time or part-time? (part-time means less than 30 hours per week)

Full-time	1
Part-time	2
Not applicable	...3

5 On how many days a week are you at your
job? (Record as stated)

....

....

....

Not applicable 9

For office use

Y	X	0	1
2	3	4	5
6	7	8	

6 Roughly, how long does it take you to get to
work? I only mean going to work, not
coming home. (Record as stated)

....

....

Not applicable 9

For office use

Y	X	0	1
2	3	4	5
6	7	8	

7 (a) How do you generally get to work? (Ring
all mentioned)

On foot	1
Bicycle	2
Motor cycle	3
Car	4
Public transport (bus, tram, train, etc.)	5
Not applicable	6

(b) If PUBLIC TRANSPORT (5) to Q.7(a):
How much per week altogether do you
spend on fares to and from work? (Record
as stated)

....

....

Not applicable 9

For office use

Y	X	0	1
2	3	4	5
6	7	8	

8 (a) Will you tell me, when did you last go to the pictures?

Within last 7 days	1
8-14 days ago	2
15-28 days ago	3
More than 28 days ago	4
I never go	5
Don't know	6

(b) **If within last 7 days (1) to Q.8:** How many times have you been in the last seven days? (Ring number stated)

Don't know	Y
Not applicable	X

1	2	3	4
5	6	7	8

9 During this last football season did you go in for any football pools?

Yes (alone)	1
Yes (shared)	2
No	3
Don't know	4

10 (a) Do you smoke?

Yes	1
No	2

(b) **If YES:** How many cigarettes did you smoke yesterday? (Record as stated) (**Number SMOKED is asked for, irrespective of when or by whom they were bought**)

....

....

....

Not applicable 9

For office use

Y	X	0	1
2	3	4	5
6	7	8	

11 Do you hold a ticket in your own name for the public library?

Yes	1
No	2
Don't know	3

12 Did you read any daily morning newspapers **yesterday?** Which ones? (**If interview is on Monday, ask of previous Saturday**)

RING EVERY PAPER MENTIONED

None	Y
Don't know	X
Daily Mirror	0
Daily Graphic (Sketch)	1
Daily Express	2
Daily Mail	3
Daily Herald	4
News Chronicle	5
Daily Telegraph	6
Manchester Guardian	7
The Times	8
Daily Worker	9
Birmingham Gazette	91
Birmingham Post	92
Western Daily Press and Bristol Mirror	93

Scotsman	
Glasgow Herald	
Others (list below)	

....

....

13 Did you read any Sunday newspaper Sunday? Which ones?

RING EVERY PAPER MENTIONED

None	
Don't know	
News of the World	
The People	
Sunday Express	
Sunday Graphic	
Sunday Pictorial	
Sunday Chronicle	
Sunday Dispatch	
Reynold's News	
Empire News	
The Observer	
Sunday Times	
Birmingham Sunday Mercury	
Sunday Mail	
Sunday Post	
Others (list below)	

....

....

14 Now I would like to ask you a few about yourself and your household. A married?

("Divorced and married but living apart" should be coded "3")

Married	
Single	
Widowed and other	

15 Where are you living? Would you sho on this card which applies to you? (**Please call by number**)

At home	
As a lodger or boarder with a fam	
In a hotel/hostel/boarding house/ hospital/institution	
Elsewhere (give details below)	

....

....

16 (a) **If AT HOME:** What kind of house Would you show me on this card applies to you? (**Please call by number**)

Whole detached house	
Whole semi-detached house	
Whole terrace house	
Self-contained flat	
Other (give details below)	
Not applicable	

....

....

f whole house (5, 6, 7) to Q.16(a): Do you
ent your house, or is it your own?

Rented 1
Own 2
Other (give details below) 3
Not applicable 4

....

....

....

will you tell me who are the people living
ur household?

in first line for informant, whose age should
btained.   Other ages are only required if
r 21.

Relationship to Informant	Sex		Age
1. ...... INFORMANT......	M	F	......
2.	M	F	......
3.	M	F	......
4.	M	F	......
5.	M	F	......
6.	M	F	......
7.	M	F	......
8.	M	F	......
9.	M	F	......
10.	M	F	......
11.	M	F	......
12.	M	F	......

No. in Household aged:

0–4   ...   .

5–15   ...   .

16–20   ...   .

21 and over   ...   .

TOTAL   ...   ...

e any of you a motor   Yes 1
?   No 2
Don't know 3

you have a television   Yes 1
yet?   No 2

Have you a telephone?   Yes 1
No 2

(b) If YES: Is it in the   Yes 1
directory under your   No 2
(family) name?   Don't know 3
Not applicable ...4

21 At what age did you finally stop receiving
full-time education?

11 or under ....Y
12 X
13 0
14 1
15 2
16 3
17 4
18 5
19 6
20 or over 7
Don't know 8
Not yet finished 9

22 Now, one final question. Do you mind
telling me from this card which income grade
your own income last week fell into?

(a) **If Informant is working, add:** I mean, after
deducting income tax and National Insurance, but including overtime and
bonuses.

(b) **If informant is not working, add:** I mean,
income of your own.
(Housewives' housekeeping money should not
be included)
Group

None 1
Up to £3 2
Over £3, up to £5 3
Over £5, up to £7 10s. 4
Over £7 10s. up to £10 5
Over £10, up to £20 6
Over £20 7
Don't know 8
Refused 9

Name of Informant ....

....

Address of Informant ....

....

....

Interviewer's No. ..../........./........./.........

RING DATE OF INTERVIEW

	Sun.	Mon.	Tues.	Wed.	Thur.	Fri.	Sat.
APRIL	—	28	29	30	—	—	—
MAY	—	—	—	—	1	2	3
	4	5	6	7	8	9	10
	11	12	13	14	15	16	17
	18	19	20	21	22	23	24
	25	26	27	28	29	30	31
JUNE	1	2	3	4	5	6	7

is no formal reason why they should answer survey questions. That they generally do so is due in part to general helpfulness, in part to their liking to talk about themselves and their views and in part to the innocuous nature of the questions themselves.

But willingness is no guarantee that the answers will be accurate. If information is sought on a personal subject about which people are reluctant to talk, the surveyor must adapt his interviewing approach accordingly and be prepared to go to some length in checking on the accuracy of the replies.[1]

Any subject which is surrounded by strong social conventions, on which some types of behaviour and opinions are more "respectable" than others, demands from the surveyor sufficient subtlety of approach to overcome his respondents' temptation to mislead, to understate, to exaggerate. Even the ordinary factual questions on a schedule are exposed to the influence of prestige feelings: witness the case of a woman who impressively described her husband as "a man who knows about dust"—correctly enough, for he was a dustman; or, to quote from Payne [203, p. 185], the man who described himself as a "bank director"—again correctly, since it was his job to "direct" the bank customers to the proper official or window! More seriously, people might tend to understate their age and their alcohol consumption; and to exaggerate their education, their reading, their church-going and so forth.

Factual questions

Most survey questions are concerned with either facts or opinions. There are also questions dealing with motivation ("Why did you go to the cinema last night?") and knowledge questions ("What do the initials N.A.T.O. stand for?"), but the main points of methodology will emerge if we consider fact and opinion questions.

One major difference between them is the amount of latitude generally given to the interviewer to probe, explain, vary the wording and so on. With factual questions (whether the facts relate to the respondent, to people he knows or to events) interviewers—for instance, in the Government Social Survey—are allowed to take any reasonable steps to ensure that respondents have correctly interpreted the questions and that they, the interviewers, have correctly understood the answers.[2] With opinion questions, such latitude would

---

[1] See the reports of Kinsey's surveys on sex behaviour [144, 145] for an interesting illustration of accuracy checks. It is also worth looking at the papers by Cochran and others [38, 39] which contain an evaluation of Kinsey's methodology. The book by Hyman [123] contains, in Chapter 4, a thorough discussion of accuracy checks.

[2] This is not a general rule. Some organisations allow no more latitude for factual questions than for others, believing that the facts hinge so much on precise definition that this would be too risky.

be too risky and so is not permitted. It is well recognised that changes in wording, sequence and even emphasis may materially affect the answers.

Leaving aside public opinion polls, the majority of questions asked in surveys are probably concerned with facts. In saying this I am using the word "fact" in a wide sense. I would call the question "How much did you spend on beer last week?" factual, although the answers given by many would be a mixture of fact, wishful thinking, vague recollection, and a desire to give the answer the interviewer is believed to be looking for. But that is irrelevant here. The adjective "factual" refers to the type of information the question seeks, not to the accuracy with which it is given, so to describe a question as "factual" does *not* imply that the answers given are necessarily accurate.

Many examples of factual questions are contained in the questionnaire on p. 215—e.g. those on the respondent's work, the composition of his family, occupation, income; on his living conditions, possessions and leisure pursuits.

Some of these are so-called "classification" questions, asked chiefly to provide information by which the main groups of respondents can be distinguished in the analysis. Questions 14 (marital status) and 17 (household composition), amongst others, are of this type. Classification questions require careful definition, and these may be given in separate instructions or, in the case of a permanent organisation, the Interviewers' Manual. The Government Social Survey, for instance, has a "Standard Classification Section", consisting of about twenty items, which are asked for in most surveys, and for which definitions are laid down in the *Handbook for Interviewers*.

Classification questions are usually left to the end of the interview so as to avoid crowding the opening minutes with personal questions. An important exception occurs in quota sampling. At the beginning of an interviewer's assignment, virtually every person approached fits into the sample, but towards the end it becomes increasingly difficult to find people to fit the quota group. Many who are approached have to be rejected, and it would be wasteful (and a temptation to mis-classify) to go right through an interview only to find at the end that the informant does not belong to the required age-group or social class. Accordingly, the classification questions relevant to the quotas are usually asked at the beginning.

Wherever such questions are placed, they need a special introduction. After all, a respondent who agrees to answer questions about his leisure pursuits or to give his opinions about television, may legitimately wonder why he should supply details about his family, his age, his education and even his income. In the questionnaire on

p. 215 question 14, which opens this group, acknowledges that the content of the questions is shifting and leaves it at that.

Government Social Survey interviewers are told that, before passing on to the classification section, they should give the following explanation: "When the results of the survey are analysed we never mention the names of the people interviewed but we like to be able to classify each person according to such things as age, sex, occupation, etc." An alternative phrasing is "Because people's habits, needs and opinions sometimes vary according to their age, occupation and general living conditions we like to know a few facts of this kind about the people we interview " [239, p. 22].

Gallup Poll interviewers are told to introduce the classification section (see questionnaire at p. 211) by "Now may I ask you a few details so that my office can keep check on the sample of people I am interviewing?"

The chief difficulties with factual questions are to ensure that interviewers understand, and manage to convey to the respondents, precisely what facts are wanted. Some of the definitions may be tricky but, in most cases, the chances of either interviewer or respondent misunderstanding the question, not understanding it at all, or being influenced in his answer by the words chosen are much slighter than with opinion questions.

Opinion questions

With these the problems are much more fundamental. Though I would not venture into the psychologist's territory and discuss the concepts of opinion and attitude in any detail, some attempt must be made to analyse why the study of opinions is basically so much more troublesome than that of facts. Why would one be more confident with a question asking a respondent whether he owns a wrist-watch than with one asking whether he is in favour of capital punishment? There are several related reasons:

(*a*) A respondent either does or does not possess a watch, and one may reasonably assume that he knows whether he does or not. All the surveyor has to do is to make clear to the respondent what he wants to know, and to be sure he understands the respondent's answer. It may be that the respondent wishes not to give the correct answer but at least he knows what it is. With the opinion question it is not so simple. The respondent's attitude to capital punishment may be largely latent, and he may never have given the matter any conscious thought until he was confronted by the question. The first problem with opinion questions thus arises from the uncertainty whether the respondent, in any meaningful sense, "knows" the correct answers. To say whether he possesses a watch or not needs no "thinking" on the respondent's part; to give a genuine opinion on capital punishment may require thought and "self-analysis".

(b) A person's opinion on virtually any issue is many-sided. On capital punishment there are moral, medical, legal and other aspects; it is quite possible to be against it on moral grounds, in favour on legal ones. A person may be against it in all but certain circumstances, or against it whatever the situation. He may be in favour of abolishing it experimentally, or as an irrevocable step whatever the consequences. In short, there probably is *no one correct answer* to the survey question as there is to that on watch ownership. The answer the respondent actually gives will depend on the aspect of the issue that is uppermost in his mind—quite possibly because the wording of the question, or the context created by previous ones, has put it there.

(c) Closely related to this is the problem of intensity. On any given subject some people feel strongly, some are indifferent, some have settled and consistent views, others are highly changeable in their attitude. In any attempt to get more than snap answers, the problem of assessing the intensity of opinion or attitude must be faced.

(d) Finally, it must be repeated that answers to opinion questions are more sensitive to changes in wording, emphasis, sequence and so on than are those to factual questions. The pages of the *Public Opinion Quarterly* and of the *International Journal of Opinion and Attitude Research* are full of evidence on this point and the reader can also refer to Cantril [28], and Mosteller [196] for examples. This established sensitivity of opinion questions does not imply instability of opinion among respondents. Rather is it a reflection of the point made in (b) above. Opinion is many-sided and questions asked in different ways will seem to "get at" different aspects of the opinion: if they result in different answers, it is largely because respondents are in effect answering different questions.

There is a secondary difficulty here. With factual questions, it is often feasible to compare the merits of different forms of the same question by checking the answers against known data. With opinion questions, this is virtually impossible, the only exceptions being where opinions are closely related to checkable behaviour, as in election polls.

In the face of these problems, two quite distinct approaches are used in opinion and attitude enquiries. One, the most common in opinion polls, attempts simply to estimate what proportion of the survey population say they subscribe to a given opinion; the second goes further and tries to measure the strength of the opinions held. In the terminology of the survey literature, this is the distinction between asking for opinions and measuring attitudes.

The B.I.P.O. schedule at p. 211 has many examples of the former. Take Q. 2(a): "Are you satisfied or dissatisfied with Eden as Prime Minister?" The respondent's can answer "Satisfied", "Dissatisfied" or "Don't know" and there is no attempt to measure the strength of their opinions, to ascertain what aspects of the matter they had in mind or to find out to what extent they had thought about the issue. The pollster simply wants a snap answer to a snap question to enable him to count the number who react in a given way to that particular stimulus.

The second approach attempts to *measure* the respondent's attitude, which typically means asking a large number of questions bearing on the subject and combining the answers into some sort of score. This is the method of attitude scaling, discussed in Section 12.6.

12.3. Question Wording

The literature on the wording of questions is bewildering. Numerous papers have appeared showing the relative advantages of various specific questions, the danger of using a certain word or phrase, the sensitivity of answers to changes in wording and presentation; but it is exceedingly difficult to build out of them any general principles. I shall confine myself to those aspects of wording which are of general importance in social research surveys.

(a) *Questions that are insufficiently specific.* A common error is to ask a general question when an answer on a specific issue is wanted. The question: "Are you satisfied with your canteen?" is unsatisfactory if one is interested specifically in meal prices and the quality of service. Equally unsatisfactory, for a different reason, would be: "Are you satisfied with the service and with the prices charged in your canteen?", as it is generally desirable to confine a question to a single issue or idea.

It is also usually advisable to frame questions in terms of the respondent's personal experience rather than in general terms. An example comes from the penultimate chapter of Payne's book [203], in which he applies the principles outlined in his previous chapters to the question: "Which do you prefer—dichotomous or open questions?" In this form the question has obvious defects; so it does in the other 39 forms which Payne discusses, and dismisses, in turn. Only the 41st attempt finds his favour:

"Which questions did you like best—those stating two answers to decide between, those stating more than two answers, or those leaving the answers for you to state?"

This is essentially a different question from the first: respondents are now asked to state a preference between question-types in the context of immediate experience rather than to give a general opinion. All the answers will now refer to specific, well defined issues.

(b) *Simple language*. Technical words and jargon are obviously to be avoided. The hypothetical question quoted above included the word "dichotomous", and such a word would not of course be used in practice. The use of the common word "open" would equally have to be avoided, for its use in this technical sense is quite unfamiliar to the lay public. And obviously we would not ask a respondent whether his household is run on matriarchal lines, what he thinks about bilateral trading, amortisation of the National Debt or fiscal policy.

Much less easy to recognise and reject are words which, though everyday usage to the university-trained survey expert, are far from common in ordinary conversation. Words like hypothetical, irrespective, aggravate, deprecate and hundreds more are in this category.

Question designers try to put themselves in the position of their typical, or rather their least educated, respondents, but they are not always the best judges of the simplicity and clarity of their own questions. The reactions of typical respondents—not only of their professional colleagues—should be sought (informally and in pretests) to ensure that the questions are comprehensible. Payne [203] names a large number of words which analysis of American magazines has *shown* to be in common usage by writers; this does not necessarily mean that they are suitable for survey questions, but at least they are known to be much-used. Gowers [99] mentions many words which can often be replaced by simpler alternatives. The following are a few from his list:

acquaint	inform, tell
assist	help
consider	think
initiate	begin; start
major	important; chief; main; principal
materialise	come about; happen; occur
purchase	buy
sufficient	enough
terminate	end

The first principles in wording are that questions should use the simplest words which will convey the exact meaning, and that the phrasing also should be as simple and informal as possible. It is more natural to ask: "Do you think ... ?" than: "Is it your opinion ... ?";

"What is your attitude to . . . ?" than: "What is your attitude with regard to . . . ?" In fact the more the questions sound like ordinary conversation the smoother the interview will be. Of course, this should not be overdone. Bad grammar may be more common than good, but one would not advocate its deliberate use in survey questions. Nor are slang expressions advisable; as with technical jargon, not everyone uses the same. It is not indeed enough to know that a word or phrase is commonly used; one must equally be sure that it is used in the same sense by all groups of respondents. A simple case where this is not so is the word "book", which in some parts of the population is taken to include magazines. Hence the phrasing of the following question in a recent readership survey [253]: "During the past week roughly how many hours would you say you had spent reading *books*—I mean books not magazines or papers?"

Clarity can be still further ensured by remembering that a short and simple question is more readily understood than a long and complex one. Payne [203] has suggested that the more complex a question is, the more "sensitive" to changes in wording will it tend to be.

An instance of a question which is too complex for comfort occurred in the enquiry into Family Limitation, conducted for the Royal Commission of Population [158]: "Has it happened to you that over a long period of time, when you neither practised abstinence, nor used birth control, you did not conceive? YES/NO." This question is vague (what is "a long period"?), too formal ("Has it happened to you . . . ?") and complex, because of its length and double negative.

(*c*) *Ambiguity*. Ambiguous questions are to be avoided at all costs. If an ambiguous word creeps in, different people will understand the question differently and will in effect be answering different questions. The following example is taken from a university research survey: "Is your work made more difficult because you are expecting a baby?" The question was asked of all women in the survey, irrespective of whether they were expecting a baby or not. What, then, did a "No" answer mean? Depending on the respondent, it might have meant "No, I'm not expecting a baby" or "No, my work is not made more difficult by the fact that I'm expecting a baby."

(*d*) *Vague words*. Vague questions encourage vague answers. If we ask people whether they go to the cinema regularly or occasionally, the meaning of their answers will be vague (this common choice of alternatives is strictly illogical; the word "occasional" refers to frequency, the word "regular" does not. However, this may be a case where logic can give way to common usage). The meaning can easily be made more precise, as in the following question from the readership survey referred to above [126]: "Do you read any daily morning paper(s) regularly—that is on at least three days a week?"

Vague words and phrases like "kind of", "fairly", "generally", "many", "much the same", "on the whole" should be avoided, unless one is only seeking vague answers. If one asks "What kind of house do you have?" some people will answer that it is semi-detached, others that it is suburban, others that it is a very pleasant one and so on.

A similar type of vagueness occurs in "Why" questions. In answering the question: "Why did you go to the cinema last night?" some respondents will say that they wanted to see that particular film, some that they did not want to stay at home, others that "the wife suggested it", or that they hadn't been since last week. The word "Why" in this question—as the phrase "kind of" in the previous one —can mean so many different things that its use would produce a useless mixture of answers.[1] Lazarsfeld [154] discusses the problems of the "Why" question.

(e) *Leading questions*. A leading question is one which, by its content, structure or wording, leads the respondent in the direction of a certain answer. The question form: "You don't think . . . , do you?" as obviously leads to a negative answer as the form: "Should not something be done about . . . ?" leads to a positive one.

Equally, a question which suggests only some of the possible answers may lead in their direction. Take the question: "Do you read any weekly newspapers, such as the *New Statesman* or *Punch*?" Respondents, especially if they are not sure of the correct or complete reply, may seek refuge in the answers named; either all or none of the alternative answers should be stated.

There are numerous words which have been shown on occasion to have had a "leading" influence in survey questions (see Payne [203] and Cantril [28]). The word "involved" in a question like: "Do you think that the Government should get involved in . . . ?" may have a sufficiently sinister ring to lead people in the negative direction. Similarly, the wording: "Do you think that the Government should continue to stay out of . . . ?" or "Do you agree that the Government is right in staying out of . . . ?" invites a "Yes" answer. The "leading" nature of these examples is obvious, but more subtle leads can often creep unnoticed into survey questions.

In addition to "leading words", there is the risk that the general context of a question, the content of those preceding it and the tone of the whole questionnaire or interview can lead the respondent in a given direction. An interesting argument related to this was provoked

---

[1] There are exceptions to even this statement. The surveyor might want to see what type of reason each respondent produces when asked this question, what factors were uppermost in his mind.

by Kornhauser's article entitled "Are Polls fair to Organized Labour?" [150].

An example nearer home was the 1954 ballot on attitudes to the (Football) Pool Betting Bill.[1] It will be recalled that, as a result of a debate in Parliament, the Pools Promoters' Association conducted a ballot among their clients. A statement by the Association arguing against the Bill was circulated with the football pool coupons in a certain week and each client was asked to vote for one of the following alternatives by placing a cross against it.

(1) "I agree with what you say in the statement which you sent me and I am against the Bill."

(2) "In spite of what you say in the statement which you sent me I support the Bill."

As much as 75 per cent of the votes were cast for (1), 7 per cent for (2) and 18 per cent of the clients did not vote. At the same time, the Gallup Poll asked a sample of the population: "At present football pool promoters do not have to publish accounts. A Bill is being introduced to make it compulsory for them to show each week where the money goes. Do you think that this is a good or bad thing?" 63 per cent said it was a good thing, 15 per cent said it was a bad thing and 22 per cent expressed no opinion. Of those in the sample who filled in pools coupons, 66 per cent said it was a good thing.

That the two surveys produced such contradictory results must in part be attributed to the fact that the Pools Promoters' questions were printed on the weekly football coupon and were in no way secret or anonymous; for this reason alone, it is difficult to accept the results at face value. But, this point aside, the differences between the two surveys in the context and wording of the questions could account for some of the difference in results. The alternatives proffered by the Pools Promoters were preceded by a detailed and somewhat complicated statement on football pool finance, which stressed how the cost of complying with the Bill's requirements would affect the amount of money available for dividends. Finally, the phrase "in spite of" in the second alternative suggests that this would be a rather irrational view. The Gallup question was set in a more neutral context, but here the phrase "to show each week where the money goes" might be thought to carry a slight implication that this is a clear and obvious duty for a Pools Promoter.

There were, in this instance, several complicating features, and the difference in results cannot with certainty be attributed to the question-forms. Yet the example is instructive in that it shows how differently the same issue can be presented. Some issues are so clear

[1] Reported in *The Times*, 8th March, 1954.

and well-understood that such differences would hardly affect results. But when an issue is complex and many-sided, when its implications are not widely or easily understood, then one must expect answers to be sensitive to the way it is presented.

(*f*) *Presuming questions.* Questions should not, generally speaking, presume anything about the respondent. They should not imply that he necessarily possesses any knowledge or an opinion on the survey subject, or that he engages in the activity about which he is being asked. Questions like: "How many cigarettes a day do you smoke?" or "How did you vote in the last General Election?" are best asked only after a "filter" question has revealed that the respondent does smoke cigarettes and did vote in the last election.

On occasions, however, one deliberately departs from this procedure. Kinsey [144] did not first ask his respondents *whether* they had engaged in certain sexual practices, but went straight into questions about frequency and detail. Respondents were thus spared the embarrassment of admitting the experiences directly and were made to feel that these represented perfectly usual behaviour; thus they found themselves able to talk freely and give detailed answers.

The case for such an approach is obvious, but one cannot ignore the possibility that it may discourage "I never do" answers and thus cause an upward bias in the results.

(*g*) *Hypothetical questions.* Questions of the "Would you like to live in a flat?" type are of very limited value. Most people would like to try anything once, and an affirmative answer would have little value as a prediction of behaviour. It is another matter if one has first made sure that the person has experience of both flat and house dwelling. Equally, answers to the "What would you do if . . . ?" kind of question, although perhaps a good reflection of wishful thinking or of what people feel to be right and proper, are unsafe pointers to future behaviour.

Yet prediction of future behaviour on the basis of survey questions plays, and must be expected to play, a central role in survey applications. Market researchers would like—and try—to predict how people will react to a proposed change in the price of a product, to an alteration to its quality or packaging; how many people are likely to buy cars, radios or television sets in a given period, and so on. They may rely on straight questions (a Gallup Poll question in 1950 was: "Supposing the price of (a certain newspaper) went up from 1d. to 1½d. would you change over to another paper where the price hadn't gone up?") but the answers are recognised to be imperfect guides to future behaviour. People are not good at predicting their behaviour in a hypothetical situation and, as we shall see in Section 12.6, the prediction has somehow to be taken out of their hands and made by the researcher himself—naturally on the basis of the information he has obtained.

(*h*) *Personalised questions.* It is often necessary to decide whether a question should be asked in a personalised form or not. This is well illustrated by the following pair of questions which appeared, one after the other, in a schedule dealing with health matters (see David [48]): "Do you think it is a good idea to have everyone's chest regularly checked by X-ray?" and "Have you ever had yours checked?" Some 96 per cent of the respondents answered "Yes" to the first question, but only 54 per cent to the second. As the author suggested, the opinion given in answer to the first question "is more a pious hope for some vague corporate decision than a considered aim involving personal action".

(*i*) *Questions on periodical behaviour.* An interesting choice arises in studying the frequency of periodical behaviour. The main choice of questions can be illustrated with reference to cinema-going:

  (i) "How often have you been to the cinema during the last fortnight (or any other period chosen)?"
 (ii) "How often do you go to the cinema on the average?"
(iii) "When did you last go to the cinema?"

The first question covers a number of different possibilities corresponding to the period chosen, and answers will depend on the type of activity and on the extent to which one is willing to rely on the respondent's memory.[1] In any case, the three question-types might produce different results, and there is little evidence on which to choose between them. On first sight, (i) seems to be the most specific, but many people's answer might simply be an estimate of their average cinema-going rather than the actual figure; i.e. if they normally go twice a fortnight, they may give this as an answer, although they went only once during the last fortnight. The longer the period chosen, the more likely is this to happen.

Many survey questions involve this type of choice, e.g. questions on newspaper reading, radio listening, consumer purchases. It is a matter deserving research.

Concluding remarks

I have not attempted to deal comprehensively with the vast subject of question wording. The few points selected for discussion have been

---

[1] Whatever period is chosen, there is always the risk that people will include in their answer visits (or whatever it may be) which took place before the beginning of the period, so that the over-all figures will err on the high side. This effect is believed to operate in family expenditure surveys, for instance (see Prais and Hout-hakker [210], Section 4.32).

those thought to be of most interest to the student or researcher considering embarking on a survey. To the problem of question design in general, there is no easy solution. Even if one follows all the accepted principles, there usually remains a choice of several question forms, each of which seems satisfactory. Every surveyor tries to phrase his questions in simple, everyday language, to avoid vagueness and ambiguity, to use neutral wording. His difficulty lies in judging whether, with any particular question, he has succeeded in avoiding all these traps. He may appreciate perfectly that leading questions are to be avoided, but how can he know for sure which words will be "leading" with the particular question, survey and population that confront him, perhaps for the first time? Question designing remains a matter of common sense and experience, of having regard to known pitfalls and of rigorously testing alternative versions in pre-tests and the pilot survey. It is not as yet, if indeed it ever can be, a matter of applying theoretical rules.

12.4. Open and Pre-coded Questions

The relative merits of open and pre-coded questions have been the subject of a good deal of research and debate. In an open question the respondent is given freedom to decide the aspect, form, detail and length of his answer and it is the interviewer's job to record as much of it as she can. In the case of pre-coded questions, either the respondent is given a limited number of answers from which to choose or the question is asked as an open question and the interviewer allocates the answer to the appropriate code category.[1] Examples of the two types of question (in addition to those given on p. 191 above) are contained in the questionnaires reproduced on other pages:

(i) *Open questions*

> *S.R.U. schedule, p.* 215.
>> Q. 1 (*b*) is a typical open question, not only in its form and content, but also in that it opens the interview. It is often desirable to start the interview with an open question to get the respondent talking and make him feel at ease.

> *Family Census Questionnaire, p.* 210.
>> The question on occupation.

(ii) *Pre-coded questions, respondent given limited choice*

> *S.R.U. schedule*
>> With most of the questions here only a few answers are *possible.* Q. 2 asked women whether or not they are housewives; Q. 10 (*a*) asked respondents whether or not they smoked.

---

[1] Often several answers may have to be coded, e.g. in a question asking which newspapers the respondent reads.

B.I.P.O. schedule, p. 211

Most of the questions here are opinion questions in which respondents are given the choice between "Yes" and "No", "Good" and "Bad" and so forth (together with "Don't know"). This type of question is probably the most common in opinion research.

(iii) *Pre-coded questions, interviewer codes*

S.R.U. schedule

Q. 8 (*a*) here asks "When did you last go to the pictures . . . ?" The respondent answered in his own terms and the interviewer coded accordingly.

The essential difference thus lies in the stage at which the information is coded, whether in the office, by the respondent or by the interviewer. If the researcher wants a very detailed answer, or wishes to find out what aspects of an issue are uppermost in the respondent's mind, (i) is to be preferred. Even if it has subsequently to be summarised, all the detail is there, not merely a number representing the nearest code answer. Any summarising or coding can be carried out uniformly in the office, uninfluenced by the circumstances of the interview or the reaction of the respondent to the interviewer. But, of course, open questions have their problems. The detail obtained is partly a reflection of the respondent's loquacity, so that different *amounts* (as well as different items) of information will be available for different people. A second difficulty lies in the task of compressing a written, qualitative answer into code categories. Again, although the remoteness of the office from the interview situation ensures some gain in coding objectivity, it also has draw-backs. Just as questions can *sound* different if asked by different people, so the meaning of an answer is communicated partly by the *way* it is given, and this will not be reflected in the written record. Finally, there is the difficulty of getting a verbatim record of what is said. All interviewers probably exercise some selection in recording answers and, to the extent that this happens, bias may creep in.

Pre-coded questions may offer two or more alternative answers (referred to respectively as dichotomous and multi-choice—or "cafeteria"—questions) and their advantages are evident. To combine the recording and coding of answers in one operation simplifies the whole procedure; and, in a very real sense, the interviewer is the person best placed to arrive at an accurate coding, since she hears the answers in full and thus has more data to work on than the office coder. On the other hand, once she has ringed a code there is little hope of detecting errors of recording or judgement.

If the range of answers to a question is limited and well established, pre-coding is generally to be preferred. Most factual questions—

with regular exceptions like questions on occupation—belong to this category. If, however, one cannot reasonably determine in advance what the main answer categories will be, it is best to begin with open questions, progressing to pre-coded ones as the range and distribution of answers becomes clear. This is why open questions play such a valuable role in pilot surveys.

The alternatives offered in pre-coded questions must above all be exhaustive and mutually exclusive. (The code "Other" is usually added for rare or unthought-of answers.) In questions of type (ii) all the possible answers must be given. The following question occurred in an opinion survey: "What happens to the copy of the . . . (newspaper); for instance, does anyone take it to work?"

Stays in house	1
Regularly taken to work, left there	2
Occasionally taken to work, left there	3
Taken to work, brought home	4

It is likely that the form of the question disfavoured the first code-answer. If any of the answers are to be suggested, *all* should be. A respondent who has never considered the subject of the question carefully may seize upon any lead given by the mention of a possible answer.

A risk with pre-coded questions is that answers may be forced into a category to which they do not properly belong. Take the hypothetical question: "Do you think the present Government is doing a good or a bad job?" Many people will have clear views and will unhesitatingly say "Good" or "Bad". But what of those who are inclined to say "Yes, but . . ." or "No, except that . . ."? The coding demands a decision one way or the other and may result in qualified responses being forced into categories to which they do not genuinely belong. To try to avoid this, survey designers leave space for qualifications or allow in the codes for finer shades of opinion. But, without necessarily commending the straight GOOD/BAD/DK choice, I should point to two difficulties caused by a finer coding. First, the more codes there are, the more margins there are between them, and the greater the possibility of doubtful, marginal answers being coded inappropriately. Secondly, if people are given the choice between a number of answers, some extreme, some mild, many will go for the middle course and avoid extreme positions. The following question was included in a schedule on saving habits: "During the coming year do you think things will get much better or worse for people in your position or do you think there is not likely to be much change?" The last phrase offered a neutral escape and 44 per cent of the respondents chose it. These answers may of course express genuine opinions but there clearly is a risk in suggesting a non-committal answer to the respondent.

When answers are to be prompted (see Chapter 11), it may be preferable to show them to the respondent on a card rather than to read them out. In either case, the answers given may be affected by the order in which the alternatives are presented. It has been shown that alternatives stated at the beginning or end of the list are apt to be favoured (see, for instance, Mosteller [196, p. 170]) and one should consider randomising the alternatives over the sample. In the I.P.A. newspaper readership survey [126], as mentioned on p. 190, respondents were shown reproductions of the title-headings of all the newspapers and periodicals. To avoid bias arising from the order of presentation, the order of papers within any group (newspapers being one group, weeklies a second, monthlies a third, and so forth) was varied throughout the sample.

Several writers have proposed ways of combining open and pre-coded questions. The principle is generally to ask a series of questions, beginning with open types and going over to pre-coded ones as the subject-matter becomes more clearly structured, enabling more specific questions to be asked. Gallup's so-called *Quintamensional Plan of Question Design* [89] is of this kind.[1] It suggests that, for many issues, a series of five types of questions is useful:

Q. 1. Designed to find out whether the informant is aware of the issue at all, whether he has thought about it.
Q. 2. Designed to get his general feelings on the issue. Invariably of the free-answer variety.
Q. 3. Designed to get answers on specific parts of the issue. This is done by pre-coded questions.
Q. 4. Designed to find out reasons for the informant's views.
Q. 5. Designed to find out how strongly they are held.

12.5. Question Order

There is plenty of evidence that the order of questions may affect the answers obtained (e.g. Mosteller [196], Cantril [28], Whitfield [285]), especially so when one is concerned with opinions that are unstable or marginal.[2]

Looking at the problem statistically, there is certainly a case for randomising the order of questions over a survey sample. But this is more easily said than done for, in the average survey, scope for randomising questions is very limited. It is always desirable to ask questions in a logical sequence, to enable the interviewer to lead easily from one point to the next and to retain the respondent's

---

[1] See also Lazarsfeld [155].
[2] It has been suggested that one way of gauging the intensity of opinion is by the sensitiveness of answers to changes of question order and wording. This point deserves further study.

interest. Also, every researcher, if he has any choice, will start the interview with a few easy and generally interesting questions, leaving the difficult ones to the end.

There is another hindrance to randomising question order. It is no good asking: "Can you name any kind of washing powder?" if a previous question has mentioned "Tide" or "Dreft"; in other words knowledge questions must not be preceded by others giving relevant information. Often a schedule is so designed that one question or group of questions sets the context for later ones. Thus our illustrative question on the achievements of the present Government may be preceded by others on the work of the previous Government, so that respondents view the question from a standpoint of comparison between the two. But the reverse is more common: the schedule is designed so that the answers to a question are *not* influenced by what has gone before. These are the practical considerations governing question order. Whether, in view of them, randomisation is worth while in every-day surveys is a debatable point and one requiring further experimental study.

12.6. Scaling Methods

On virtually every subject ever tackled by a survey one could make a list of relevant questions far longer than any reasonable questionnaire could include—not merely because wording variations enable one to ring numerous changes upon a single question, but because there are generally so many aspects of the subject that could be explored. Suppose one wished to know the attitudes of a group of workers towards their management. At once a number of possible questions suggest themselves: "Do you think the management is making a good or a bad job of things?", "How well qualified do you think the managers are for their task?", "In what ways do you think the relationship between management and workers could be improved?", "What do you think of the management's part in improving working conditions?"

All these questions—a small sample from the vast number one could formulate—have a bearing on the "favourableness to management" attitude but they all approach different aspects of it. In a straightforward opinion survey one might include, say, ten or twenty questions, tapping different aspects of the subject and simply count the number of respondents giving various answers. One may argue that such an approach is superficial, but then its aim also is modest and unsophisticated. No pretence is made—or should be made— that it *measures* attitudes in the strict sense; it merely *counts* how many people choose to express certain views. To go further than this, to try to combine the answers a respondent gives to the various questions into a measurement of the extremity and intensity of his over-all attitude, requires a different analytical approach; and this is where scaling devices find their place. If we may assume that—for the population under study—there is such a thing as "attitude towards management", then we may proceed, by one of several techniques, to find out where along a scale ranging from extreme favourableness to extreme unfavourableness a particular attitude lies. This may properly be called attitude measurement.

The value of such an approach is at its most obvious where the subject-matter is complex or of strong emotional content, where people's feelings about it vary markedly or where it can be approached from many quite different angles. The opinion-counting approach then leaves much to be desired, even if it is useful in ascertaining people's snap reactions to snap questions. If we can get beyond these to a measurement of the extremity and strength of the underlying attitude, we should stand to gain a more complete and sensitive picture. In the same way scaling methods are valuable when we wish to make predictions of future behaviour from survey answers. One may certainly ask people whether they intend to buy a car next year, whether they would continue to take the *Daily Tabloid* if its price went up by a penny and whether they would like to live in a flat. But, as every surveyor knows, it would be hazardous to predict actual behaviour from the answers, which will be a mixture of intentions and wishful thinking. A person may, when talking to an interviewer, show no signs of anti-semitism, but may yet, in certain circumstances, act anti-semitically. When asked whether he would continue to buy the *Daily Tabloid* if its price went up, his snap reaction may be to say "Yes", whereas in the event the increase may cause him to change to another paper.

No method can, of course, take account of all the external events that affect behaviour, but at least one can build into the questioning a good number of the relevant factors. This, then, is the more sophisticated approach in prediction surveys: to determine by preliminary study what the relevant factors are and how they combine to determine behaviour, then to collect the necessary bits of information by a whole battery of questions, finally piecing the answers together into a score on which the predictions are based. In short, instead of asking the respondent himself to put all the relevant factors together in making the prediction—which demands effort, insight and self-analysis—one asks him merely to produce the bits of relevant information and then pieces them together (by scaling methods) in the office. This is analogous to the approach customary in the study of personality. One does not ask a respondent which of several personality types he belongs to any more than a doctor asks a patient to name his disease; instead various "symptoms" are noted and the diagnosis formed accordingly.

Essentially, then, scaling methods come into play when one wishes to utilise simultaneously a number of observations on each respondent. Individually the pieces may be of no more interest than the single pieces of a jig-saw puzzle. What matters is the total picture and the difficulty of the process is to decide what are the appropriate pieces (ensuring that they are logically related and all refer to the same attitude dimension), how to fit them together into a meaningful whole and how to test the properties (particularly the reliability and validity) of the scale thus constructed. An incidental advantage of basing survey interpretations on the combined answers to many questions is that the risk of bias through wording is thereby reduced.

Rating scales[1]

In brief, the idea of using scaling methods is that, instead of learning simply whether or not a respondent is favourably inclined towards management (as judged by his answers to specific questions), one gets a measure of the strength of his attitude: instead of being satisfied with differences in kind, one attempts to measure differences in degree. Before discussing scaling methods proper I must refer to some modifications of the YES/NO type of answer choice, which can be regarded as rough approximations to them.

The simplest way of "measuring" the strength of a person's attitude is to ask him himself to rate that strength. This can be done in a number of ways. The easiest perhaps is to present him with a number of attitude statements of varying intensity—e.g. "I feel very strongly that nationalisation of the coal industry is a bad thing", "I am not sure whether nationalisation of the coal industry is a good thing or not"—and to ask him which statement comes closest to his own attitude. Or one may ask the same question throughout but offer a number of possible answers, say ranging from "strongly against" to "strongly in favour".

Yet another way is to present the hypothetical range of attitudes, from extreme favourableness to extreme unfavourableness, graphically or pictorially. The "scale" may take the form of a straight line or of a picture of a thermometer, with regular divisions marked on it and the extremes indicated, so that the respondent can be asked to place his own attitude. The Gallup Institutes often use the scalometer method (designed by the Netherlands Institute of Public Opinion) in which the respondent is shown a diagram of ten squares

---

[1] I confine myself to rating—and self-rating—scales as part of the ordinary questionnaire approach. Applications such as the rating of occupational prestige by a panel of judges are not discussed.

placed one above the other. The top five are white and are marked with a plus sign, the bottom five are black and are marked with a minus sign. The respondent is asked to indicate his attitude-position by pointing to the square which he considers most appropriate, taking the ten blocks to range from extreme favourableness to extreme unfavourableness.

All these self-rating methods have the merits that they are simple to operate in the field, demand little effort of respondent or interviewer and that, in the case of the pictorial variants, they avoid dangers of verbal bias. Moreover, they are certainly more sensitive and informative than a straight YES/NO choice of answers. One must, on the other hand, recognise that they are entirely subjective, the assessment of attitude position being left to the respondent. This may not matter much with straightforward survey topics, but it makes one reluctant to rely on them with complex and emotion-laden subjects on which the respondent may not be able to assess his own attitude objectively.

Nor is it necessarily an improvement to substitute someone else's subjective judgement for the respondent's, e.g. to leave the assessment of attitude to the interviewer. It is true that the manner and tone of an answer often afford vital clues to how strongly a person feels, so that the interviewer is certainly better placed than any other outside judge to measure attitude. But even so, this is too subjective an approach to be a good substitute for scaling methods proper.

Types of scales

Underlying all these methods is the assumption—which can be explicitly tested with some—that there is a dimension or continuum along which the individual attitudes can be ranged and one of the tasks of scale construction is to try to ensure that all the questions "belong" to this same dimension. If there is no such thing (for the particular population) as "attitude to management", but only several separate dimensions such as "attitude towards the Board of Directors", "attitude towards the factory officials", "attitude towards the foremen" etc., then it would be not only artificial but misleading to combine them all into one scale.

Given a series of items or questions that are presumed or have been shown to belong to the same attitude dimension, several types of scales can be aimed at, mentioned here in increasing order of "measurement sophistication".[1] The crudest form is often called a *nominal* scale, which classifies individuals into two or more groups, the members of which differ with respect to the characteristic being

[1] For a rigorous discussion of different kinds of measurement, see the chapter by Coombs in Festinger and Katz [78].

scaled, without there being any implication of gradation or distance between the groups. Although this is a way of classification rather than of arrangement along a continuum, it is in a sense the basis of all more sophisticated methods.

The next major step is to the *ordinal* type of scale, which ranks individuals according to the characteristic being scaled, but again carries no implication of distance between scale positions—the step from position 1 to position 2 may be greater, smaller or the same as from position 4 to position 5.

Next, one may distinguish what is generally called the *cardinal* or *interval* type of scale, which uses equal units of measurement, thus making it possible to interpret not only the order of scale scores but also the distances between them. The position of the zero-point in such a scale is a matter of convenience so that, while one may add or subtract a constant to all the scale values without affecting the form of the scale, one cannot meaningfully multiply or divide them. In other words, one can say that two persons with scale positions 1 and 2 are as far apart as two persons with scale positions 4 and 5, but not that a person with score 10 feels "twice as strongly" as one with score 5. For this to be meaningful one would require a *ratio* scale— weights and lengths are obvious examples—in which there is a fixed zero point. However, most attitude scaling is less ambitious than this.

Now, given the many relevant questions that could be asked on a particular survey subject, some way must be found to arrive at a manageable and appropriate selection to constitute the scale. The best way to illustrate what is involved is to say a few words about each of four different types of scaling procedure. For details the reader must turn to the references cited at the end of this chapter.

Thurstone scales

One of the best-known approaches to attitude scaling is Thurstone's method of "equal-appearing intervals"—a clear example of an interval scale.

The first step in the procedure is to collect a large number of statements on the survey subject (say attitude to management), the statements ranging from one extreme of favourableness to the other. These are then reduced, by cutting out obviously ambiguous statements, duplicates and so forth, to somewhere near a hundred, each of which is written on a card. A large number of "judges"—perhaps 100 or so—are then asked independently to arrange the statements into eleven piles, corresponding to differing degrees of favourableness and considered to be about equally spaced. For each statement a median value is calculated—that value such that half the judges give the statement a lower position and half the judges a higher—and also the inter-quartile range, which measures the scatter of judgements (the extent to which the various judges place the statement at different parts of the scale). The list of statements is now reduced by (a) discarding those with a high scatter, for they are clearly in some sense ambiguous or irrelevant; and (b) selecting from the remainder some 20 or so which cover the entire range of attitudes (as judged by the medians) and which appear to be about equally spaced (again, as judged by the medians) along the scale.

The statements so selected are then embodied in a questionnaire, in random order, and each respondent is asked to endorse all the statements with which he agrees. The average (mean or median) of the median values of all the items he endorses is his scale score. From the respondent's viewpoint, the procedure is very simple, requiring no scoring or judging of distances, but merely a checking of the statements he agrees with; the judgement of distances is part of the construction process.

Thurstone scales are what are sometimes termed *differential* scales, in the sense that, given a sound and reliable scale, the individual will agree only with statements adjacent to each other on the scale—as distinct from *cumulative* scales, in which he would ideally be expected to agree with all statements less extreme than the most extreme one he endorses, and disagree with all those which are more extreme.

A frequent criticism of the method has been that the characteristics and attitudes of the people who judge the scale statements may be very different from those of the respondents whose attitudes are to be scaled, and that the former may affect the scale values. In fact, empirical evidence on this point is conflicting, but there are some fairly reassuring indications of the independence of the scale values of the judges' own attitudes.

Likert scales

The principle that the initial judging of the scale items should be done by people fairly typical of those ultimately to be studied underlies the method originated by Likert [160]. Here a group of people reasonably representative of those whose attitudes are to be scored are given a number of statements and are asked to respond to each in terms of one of (usually) five categories—ranging from "strongly approve" to "strongly disapprove". These categories are allotted scores, ranging, say, from 1 for strong approval to 5 for strong disapproval, and a person's total score is the sum of these individual scores. The list of statements is then reduced by eliminating those which fail to correlate highly with total scores or which have little discriminating power—in the sense of discriminating between people with very high and very low scores on the whole questionnaire. The 20 or so most discriminating statements are made into a questionnaire and now the actual respondents are asked to indicate their attitude by checking one of the categories of approval or disapproval for each question. The total score is derived as above, and we note that weighting is according to intensity of opinion, not according to the content of the question.

The method is somewhat simpler in construction than that of Thurstone and is likely to be a more reliable and sensitive mirror of attitudes, if only because each question allows five alternative answers, rather than the straight dichotomy of the Thurstone technique. On the other hand, it does not produce an interval scale, so no conclusions can be drawn about the meaning of distances between scale positions.

Scalogram analysis

As pointed out earlier, a crucial assumption underlying scaling methods is that the various attitude statements included in the scale all belong to the same dimension. With the Thurstone and Likert methods, as with some others, the only evidence on this point comes from the relative agreement of those who judged the scale position of the individual statements. This is clearly not very powerful evidence and, for that reason alone, the scaling method originated by Guttman —which results in an ordinal scale—presents a major development.

The scalogram method, as it is called, starts out by defining the total attitude (technically called the "universe of content") being scaled. A "sample" of questions representing this universe is selected for possible inclusion in the scale and then—this being the central feature of the method—these questions are tested for "scaleability". This is meant in the technical sense that the questions should belong to the same attitude dimension and it is important to emphasise that the criterion for this unidimensionality lies, not in the views of outside judges, but in the pattern in which the respondents' answers arrange themselves. Since the Guttman scales are of the cumulative type (see p. 238) the requirement of the *perfect* scale is that the respondent endorses all the items to one side of the most extreme one with which he agrees, and none that are more extreme. To illustrate this point, I quote the simple example given in *Measurement and Prediction* [252], where the method is fully described. It is there pointed out that, for a hypothetical scale of stature, the three questions:

1. Are you over 6 ft. tall?   — YES — NO
2. Are you over 5 ft. 6 in. tall?   — YES — NO
3. Are you over 5 ft. tall?   — YES — NO

are scaleable in the scalogram analysis sense, since anybody who answers (1) affirmatively, should also answer YES to the other two questions.[1] Thus only four patterns of answers are possible (assuming that accurate answers are given).

	Says "YES" to item			Says "NO" to item		
Score	1	2	3	1	2	3
3	x	x	x			
2		x	x	x		
1			x	x	x	
0				x	x	x

This diagram is called a scalogram. If one secures a set of attitude data items that is *perfectly* scaleable in the above sense, then—as this scalogram shows—from the total score for an individual one can infer precisely what individual items he agreed or disagreed with. This is fundamentally different from the Thurstone and Likert techniques, with both of which a final score of a given magnitude can result from quite different patterns of responses, so that it is impossible to tell from the score what the individual answers were. With the Guttman technique, the perfect scale implies that a person who answers a given question favourably will have a higher total score than a person who answers it unfavourably. In this situation the *number of items* endorsed by a respondent gives a complete picture as to *which* items he agreed with.

Now, of course, this assumes a perfect scale, which is a rarely-found phenomenon. The extent to which a scale approximates to this ideal is measured by the *coefficient of reproducibility*, which is the percentage of question responses that can be correctly predicted (reproduced) from knowledge of the total scores of the individuals taking the test. Certain standards have been suggested in the literature for what shall be regarded as a satisfactory degree of reproducibility. It should be added—this is sometimes criticised as a weak, because subjective, aspect of the method—that one or two other criteria are generally used in addition to this coefficient for judging the scaleability of the suggested scale items.

In practice, several sets of questions are often tested before an acceptable combination is found, every effort being made to achieve uni-

---

[1] Whereas the questions: "Are you over 6 ft. tall?", "Are you between 5 ft. 6 in. and 6 ft. tall?", "Are you between 5 ft. and 5 ft. 6 in. tall?" etc., are not scaleable in this sense. Only one affirmative answer is possible and it would not be evident from the answers alone whether a person who answers, say, the first question affirmatively is taller than one who answers the second question affirmatively.

dimensionality.[1] Guttman claims that if the universe of content is unidimensional, then any sample of questions from it will be scaleable and will result in the same ranking of individuals. This has the important corollary that from a scaleable set of items quite a small number—perhaps only three or four—may be selected and a broad ranking of respondents' attitudes based on these.

Criticisms of the method have centred on its relative complexity, on the danger that the throwing out of unscaleable items may entail a certain loss and may lead to a tendency to eliminate deviant cases, and on a certain degree of subjectiveness in the selection of statements for inclusion in the scale. It has also been pointed out that the coefficient of reproducibility, on which the final composition of the scale largely depends, is a function not only of the degree of multi-dimensionality embodied in the items, but is also affected by the split of opinions on each of the items selected, the fineness of the steps between them and the degree of reliability in the scale. However, in spite of the various criticisms, the idea at the core of the method undoubtedly represents a major advance over earlier techniques.

One extension from it is worth noting, because it seems to go some way towards reducing certain dangers of question bias. This involves an ancillary device, by which the respondent is not only asked to say whether he agrees with a given statement but how strong his agreement—or disagreement—is, this intensity usually being classified into five categories. We thus get for each respondent not only a content score (as indicated by the number of questions he has answered favourably) but also an intensity score; and these two may be plotted against each other on a graph. The result is often, though not always, an approximately U-shaped curve, the more extreme views in either direction being held with greatest intensity. Guttman suggests taking the content score at the lowest point reached by this curve as the dividing line between favourable and unfavourable responses. It is claimed that this lowest point, and therefore the percentage estimated to feel favourably on the issue, will not be affected by the form or wording of the individual questions; and that this method therefore provides an objective way of dividing respondents into "Pros" and "Cons". The argument is developed at length by Suchman and Guttman [254]. Some doubts on it have been expressed by Peak in Festinger and Katz [78].

Latent-structure analysis

Finally, I may just mention one of the latest advances in scaling

[1] Such unidimensionality, it must be realised, is always specific to the particular population; there is no guarantee that it will apply to others or, for that matter, to the same population at another time. Unidimensionality is not an invariant feature of a scale.

methodology, and one that is still the subject of development and, to some extent, controversy. This is the technique of latent-structure analysis due to Lazarsfeld and his colleagues.

The method postulates that there exist a number of latent classes—with reference to the characteristic being scaled—such that the relationship between the answers to the various items on the questionnaire can be entirely accounted for by these latent classes. Any one item is thus conceived of as being made up of two components, one associated with the latent factor, the other specific to the item. The specific component is assumed to be independent of the latent factor, as well as of the specific component of any other item. Taking the simplest case of two classes, the aim of the method is to divide the sample into two groups, those who possess the latent attribute (say, favourable attitude to management) and those who don't. But, of course, the existence of a latent attribute underlying the various items has to be demonstrated and the criterion is that—ideally—all the relationship between any two items on a questionnaire can be explained by that attribute. This would be achieved if there were no correlation between the question-responses *within* the class possessing the latent attribute, or between the question-responses *within* the class not possessing that attribute. In practice, one can never fully realise the ideal, but one can find the pattern of responses that best approaches it. Readers familiar with the technique of factor analysis will recognise the resemblance to it of Lazarsfeld's scaling method. The details of the method are far too intricate to be explained here and readers interested in them must turn to the reference cited below.

Reliability and validity

Whatever approach to attitude scaling one cares to adopt, there always remains the question (which, ideally, should be answered before a scale is put to research use) to what extent the scale is reliable and valid?

A measuring instrument is *reliable* to the extent that repeat measurements made with it under constant conditions will give the same result (assuming no change in the basic characteristic—e.g. attitude—being measured). Ideally one would wish to gauge reliability by repeating the questions on the same people using the same methods. The practical difficulty of this is self-evident; and even if people were to submit themselves to repeat questioning, a comparison of the two sets of results would hardly serve as a valid test of reliability, since they could not be regarded as independent. The first questioning may have made respondents think more about the survey subject; they may try to be consistent in their two replies, they may make less effort the second time to give accurate answers and so on. In any of these circumstances, the first measurement has affected the second, so the difference between the two is a mixture of unreliability and change in the characteristic itself and no proper evaluation of reliability is achieved.

A different possibility is to give two supposedly equivalent versions of the scale to the same individuals and to correlate the results. Here there is less danger of the first questioning affecting answers on the subsequent occasion. However, there is the risk, which equally applies to repeat questions, that the characteristic itself has genuinely changed between the two occasions. Furthermore, differences between the two sets of answers will be a mixture of unreliability and differences between the items used, and there is no way of separating the two effects.

The most generally used way of testing reliability is the "split-half" technique. The assumption here is that all the items in the scale hang together—that the scale is unidimensional—so that any randomly selected part will fairly represent the whole. Respondents are asked to answer all the test items and these items are then split into two halves, by some random procedure, and the correlation between the total scores on the two "sub-scales" is taken as a measure of reliability. One difficulty of this method must be recognised. With most scaling techniques there is no direct test of unidimensionality, and the correlation between the scores on the two halves may be regarded as a relevant measure. But if it is, it cannot also be used as a test of reliability In other words, the measure of correlation is a mixture of two effects, which cannot be separated. Fortunately, the confounding of these particular effects is not as serious as might be thought, for with a low correlation—whether it is due to low reliability or to multi-dimensionality—one would in any case want to modify the scale, while a high correlation would give one confidence on both scores.

Fair reliability is one attribute desirable in any measuring instrument, validity is another. By validity is meant the success of the instrument in measuring what it sets out to measure, so that differences between individuals' scores can be taken as representing true differences in the characteristic under study. While it is easy to explain what is meant by validity, to measure it in practice is exceedingly hard.

One may avoid the problem by claiming that, since the common thread of, say, attitude to management runs through all the scale items, the resultant scale validly measures that attitude. But this is clearly not a test in any scientific sense of the word. Nor is it enough to compare the scale scores with the ratings of outside judges, taking the extent of agreement as a measure of validity, for this is an entirely subjective test.

I

The difficulty of applying rigorous and objective tests of validity in attitude measurement arises from the fact that such measurement is invariably indirect—in the sense that the attitude is *inferred* from the verbal responses. In consequence it is also generally impossible to assess validity directly. The next best thing is to chose as the yardstick of validity a criterion which is assumed or known to be closely linked with the attitude in question. If one were concerned with a scale measuring degree of "religiousness", although one could not conceivably test validity directly, one might judge it by the success of the scale in discriminating between church-goers and others. It is hardly necessary to point out the weakness of this sort of check, which begs the question as to how far attitudes and actual behaviour are related. The most one can say is that its results would give one increased (or decreased) confidence in the scale.

When the attitude being measured relates to future behaviour, its validity can, at least subsequently, be checked by its predictive power —a somewhat stringent test since many factors other than low scale validity may falsify predictions. Theoretically, the best validation procedure is to use some outside criterion—say, to test a social class scale by the correlation of its scores with income, occupation, car ownership or some such criterion. This again in a sense begs the question—for who is to say that the criterion is a good index of whatever it is the scale is supposed to measure? For, if the former were an entirely satisfactory gauge, there would have been no need for going to the trouble of constructing a scale.

In conclusion it should be noted that the reliability and validity of a scale—unlike those of a foot-rule—are always specific to a particular population, time and purpose, not invariant characteristics. In any given study, the researcher has to decide what degree of unreliability and invalidity he will regard as acceptable.

NOTES ON READING

1. One of the most readable discussions of question design will be found in the book by PAYNE [203] referred to in the text. Other valuable sources are the chapter by KORNHAUSER in JAHODA, DEUTSCH and COOK [129], and that by CANNELL and KAHN in FESTINGER and KATZ [78].

2. On opinion questions CANTRIL [28] and MOSTELLER [196] are worth consulting, as is the methodological paper by McNEMAR [183]. GALLUP [90] himself has published an account of Gallup Poll methods and aims. The journal literature on questionnaire design in general, and opinion questions in particular, is enormous; much of it is concentrated in the *Public Opinion Quarterly* and the *International Journal of Opinion and Attitude Research* (which has ceased publication).

3. On the scaling methods briefly mentioned in this chapter, the serious student should consult the original papers by THURSTONE and CHAVE [261],

LIKERT [160] and, on scalogram analysis and latent structure analysis, the volume entitled *Measurement and Prediction* [252] which is the fourth volume in the U.S. War Department Research Branch series on *The American Soldier*. This is written by STOUFFER and his colleagues and it shows the application of these last two methods in full detail and at their most sophisticated level. Good summaries of scaling methods appear in JAHODA, DEUTSCH and COOK [129], in GOODE and HATT [97] and in FESTINGER and KATZ [78]. See particularly the chapter by STOUFFER in the first of these, and that by PEAK in the last. A popular introduction to the ideas of attitude measurement is given by EYSENCK [74]. In the English survey literature, it is worth reading the report by WILKINS [286] on the prediction enquiry concerned with the demand for campaign medals; and the paper by FOTHERGILL and WILKINS [85] on analysis and interpretation.

CHAPTER 13

RESPONSE ERRORS

13.1. Response Bias and Response Variance

I HAVE AT many points in the previous three chapters referred to errors that may occur in the collection of survey data. This chapter discusses response errors systematically and with particular reference to interviewing; many of the points apply equally to mail questionnaires. The rather different types of error to which observational techniques are subject were discussed in Chapter 9.

What is meant by response errors? Let us assume that for each individual covered by a survey there is an individual true value (ITV).[1] This value is quite independent of the survey, of the way the question is asked and by whom. If we ask the respondent how old he is, there is one unique correct answer; if we ask him how much he spent on chocolate last week there is again a unique correct answer. It is true that many questions are not so simple and—for instance with opinion questions—it would often be difficult to define the ITV. However, this difficulty is beside the point here.

We assume, then, that there is for each individual an ITV; it is this the researcher is trying to ascertain. In only some cases will he succeed, and the number of "successes" in a survey will depend on the nature of the question, the way it is put and by whom, and how much precaution has been taken to minimise the chance of error. In any case, the difference between an ITV and the value recorded on the schedule[2] is the *individual response error* (IRE).

If the respondent says that he is 27 years old but the interviewer out of carelessness writes 25, then this is a response error. If the interviewer somehow makes her own political leanings felt and the re-

---

[1] I here follow the useful terminology of Hansen, Hurwitz and Madow [112].

[2] Errors of processing and analysis are left out of the present discussion, although most of it applies equally to them. "Measurement errors" would be an appropriate term to the aggregate of these and response errors.

spondent is thereby led to misrepresent his own views, we again have a response error. If the respondent went to the "pub" three times last week but tells the interviewer he went once—either because his memory is at fault or because he does not want to admit more frequent visits—we again have a response error.

The aggregate of the IRE's we term the *total response error* and it is clear at once that its seriousness in a particular survey will depend on the extent to which the IRE's cancel each other out.[1] The chances of this vary with the type of error. Let us pursue our three examples:

(a) If an interviewer through carelessness misrecords an answer, a response error results. Such errors are unlikely to be systematic. On one occasion the interviewer may under-record the age, on another she may over-record. The chances are that, for each interviewer and over the entire sample, there will be about as many errors in one direction as in the other and that the net error will be negligible.

(b) By contrast, in the second example, typical of what is usually meant by the term "interviewer bias", the interviewer may, by the way she asks the questions or interprets the answers, or through the effect of her personality upon the respondent, influence the answers that are given. One strongly pro-Labour interviewer may systematically "err" in that direction while her colleague with opposite views may produce a systematic error in the other. Such errors do not cancel out with each other but accumulate. The results for any interviewer doing this will be *biased*, in the sense that if she were to interview an infinite number of samples from this population, the average (expected value) of her results would differ from the true population value. The difference would constitute her net bias.

This does not mean that there will necessarily be a bias for the sample as a whole. If the net biases of the individual interviewers go equally in opposite directions, averaging to zero, there will not be any over-all net bias. Hence the suggestion, sometimes made, that an interviewing staff should be made up of two equal groups of interviewers, biased in opposite directions. In practice such cancellation of interviewer effects is probably rare. Investigators tend to come from a relatively narrow population stratum, in terms of social status, age and education, and it is more likely that their biases, if any, will be in the same direction.

---

[1] It should be realised that response errors apply not only to *sample* surveys; they are important whatever the coverage of the population.

(c) Finally, there is the "pub-going" example. If, for reasons best known to themselves, most people are reluctant to admit to a strong addiction to this habit, a systematic error will be produced. There is no likelihood of errors cancelling out.

We observe then that some response errors may be self-compensating for each interviewer, while others will be systematic but offset each other over the sample as a whole, while others still will leave an over-all net bias. Even this is a simplified picture, for errors that cancel out over the sample as a whole may not do so over any particular section of it. In case (c) we may suppose—somewhat fancifully—that it is the old people who are most concerned about appearing respectable and who under-state their frequency of "pub-going", while the young ones, if anything, exaggerate theirs. The effect might be that for the sample as a whole there would be little net bias, but that, for each age-group separately, the results would be distinctly biased in one direction or the other. Since the bulk of survey analysis deals with sub-groups and not with the sample in its entirety, it is never sufficient to know that there is no net bias for the whole sample.

The above analysis leads to an important distinction, stressed by Hansen, Hurwitz and Madow [112], between response bias and response variance. The "pub-going" example illustrates the former. Given a reluctance of most members of the population under survey to admit to the full frequency of their "pub-going", and assuming a certain set of procedures for collecting the data (other procedures might overcome the reluctance), repeated application of these methods under the same conditions would on average produce results below the true figures. The difference is the *response bias* and to get any idea of its size we would need external checks. What must be understood, however, is that this response bias is not, or is most unlikely to be, the total response error, since some errors will have cancelled out. The remaining response error—that is the difference between total response error and response bias—"may be thought of as the contribution due to response variation or *'response variance'*. . . . Response variance is a measure of the variability of these contributions to response errors that tend to be 'compensating' with large enough samples" (see Hansen, Hurwitz and Madow [112], Vol. I, p. 89).

The analogy with sampling variance and sampling bias (discussed in Chapter 5) will not have escaped the reader. The effect of response bias is similar to that of sampling bias. In both cases, the expected value of the estimate—let us say the average amount of pub-going—differs from the true value for the population. In the one case, this is because people systematically misreport their behaviour, in the other because the sampling procedure is biased, for instance if interviewing is done in the evenings and the "regulars" are missed.

Response variance, like sampling variance, can be estimated from the sample results themselves. Indeed, to the extent that individual response errors are completely independent of each other (as one would suppose to be the case, for instance, with errors due to pure carelessness) and compensating on average, they are actually allowed for in the ordinary formulae for estimating sampling variance.

Other parts of response variance can be allowed for in suitably modified versions of the sampling variance formulae, as long as the errors are compensating over the sample as a whole. This applies, for instance, to the second example above. The errors made by any interviewer are systematic and this produces a net bias for each interviewer. But, to the extent that these net biases offset each other, the effect is simply to increase the total variance. By suitably modifying the design and the formulae normally employed for estimating the sampling variance, account can be taken of this additional component. If the latter is ignored, one will in effect underestimate the true sampling variance.

This can be shown as follows. Suppose that r interviewers, drawn at random from a large population of R interviewers, interview n respondents, who constitute a simple random sample from a large population. Suppose also that these n are allocated randomly to the r interviewers. Let us further assume that the ith interviewer has a net bias b_i and that the variation between the biases in the whole population of interviewers is σ_b^2, defined as

$$\sigma_b{}^2 = \frac{1}{R-1} \sum_{i=1}^{R} (b_i - \bar{b})^2 ,$$

where $\bar{b}$ is the mean of the net biases.

It can then be shown that the true sampling variance of the sample mean ($\bar{x}$) is

$$V(\bar{x}) = \frac{\sigma_x{}^2}{n} + \sigma_b{}^2 \left(\frac{1}{r} - \frac{1}{n} \right) \qquad \ldots (13.1)[1]$$

This important formula shows the true sampling variance of the estimate to be composed of two parts: σ_x^2/n, which is the part estimated by the usual sampling variance formula, and an expression allowing for interviewer variability. This latter inflates the true sampling variance so that, if no account is taken of it, one will be under-

---

[1] See Cochran [36] or Sukhatme [256] for a proof of this formula, a statement of the various assumptions underlying it and a discussion of its implications for survey design. Observe that the assumptions noted above the formula—plus another, that there is no correlation between the errors committed by the different interviewers—are fairly restrictive.

estimating $V(\bar{x})$. In fact this component can be allowed for by suitable modification to the design and the formulae (see pp. 262–4 below).

The points made in the last few paragraphs are obscured by the distinction commonly made between sampling and non-sampling errors. Clerical errors, not being a sampling effect, belong to the latter category; but to the extent that they are independent of each other and compensating on average, they are automatically included in the usual sampling error estimates. Individual interviewer biases are literally non-sampling errors but they can be estimated, given the proper design and estimation formula. Thus, as regards *source*, the distinction between sampling and non-sampling (response, processing etc.) errors is valid; as regards *estimation*, it becomes confused and the really important difference is between variance (sampling + response), which can be estimated from the sample itself, and bias (sampling + response) which cannot.

13.2. Sources of Response Errors

To make the discussion more concrete, I shall now enumerate the various kinds of response errors. In this a clear distinction is needed between the sources from which such errors arise and the way in which they operate. An individual response error may be *due* to the interviewer possessing a strong opinion of her own; it may *result* in an error because of the way in which she asks the questions or interprets the answers. Equally, of course, her strong opinion may not result in an error at all. The distinction between sources and means is of practical importance. In order to decide on preventive action the surveyor needs to know what interviewer characteristics, if any, lead to substantial response errors and at what points of an interview there is scope for the introduction of errors. In this section I shall discuss sources of error; how they operate will be treated in the next.

In a sense it is unrealistic to discuss the various sources of error as separate entities. To say that the respondent's unwillingness to give a correct answer is a potential source of error clearly must not be taken to imply that this unwillingness is independent of the interviewer or of the way she asks the questions. An interview is an interaction between two people who may affect each other in various ways; this should be borne in mind throughout the discussion of errors.

Characteristics of interviewers

Until the NORC studies,[1] the only interviewer effects which had

[1] See p. 209 above. The NORC studies, the work of H. Hyman and his colleagues, represent by far the most important contribution to the subject of interview errors to date. They include case-studies of the interview situation, seen

received any attention were those arising from the personal characteristics of interviewers and from their opinions. Practitioners were
concerned that the personal characteristics of an interviewer, her sex,
age, education and social type, might influence the answers she obtained, either because of the impression she made on the respondent,
the way she asked the questions or perhaps because respondents
might give answers more willingly—and differently—to different
types of interviewers.[1] In addition, it is possible that some types of
temperament and personality are more prone to lead to error than
others.

Opinions of interviewers

The predominant interest of early research workers in this field was
in the biasing influence of interviewers' opinions. Would such
opinions, if strongly held, communicate themselves to the respondents and influence their answers? If the interviewers' opinions were
evident from the way they asked the questions, then some respondents would undoubtedly tend to agree—or disagree—with them, depending on their temperament. Or if their opinions influenced the
way interviewers interpreted—and coded—doubtful answers or para-
phrased the replies to open questions, bias would result. On the
whole, however, the NORC report showed interviewers' ideology to
be a less important source of error than had commonly been supposed.

Most studies on this topic have been concerned with opinions on
political and social issues. One is led to wonder to what extent response errors may arise, say, in market research through interviewers'
partiality for her employer's products.[2]

Interviewer expectations

One of the most interesting findings from the NORC studies was
that interviewer effects often arose, not so much from the interviewers'
social and personal characteristics or ideology as from their expectations of the respondent's views and behaviour. This may not surprise
the psychologist but survey experts had not, prior to the NORC
work, concerned themselves with such expectational biases. To make
clear what is involved, I will follow the NORC distinction between
three types of expectational errors:

from the angle of respondent and interviewer; a review of the literature on interviewer effects; an analysis of the various components of interviewer errors; and,
most important, many experimental studies of their operation.

[1] Wilkins in his enquiry into the demand for campaign medals found that "the
ex-Service men gave replies to elderly women interviewers which showed a greater
desire for medals than the replies they gave to young women" (see [286], pp. 22–3);
a clear instance of respondent-interviewer interaction.

[2] See discussion of, what they call, the "sympathy effect" in Yule and Kendall
[294], p. 550.

(a) The first are *attitude-structure* expectations. Answers to questions early in the interview give the interviewer an indication of the respondent's attitudes. If she—perhaps unconsciously—expects people to be consistent in their attitudes, she may interpret answers later in the interview in the light of these expectations. This is particularly likely—and was found to operate—where interviewers had to code vague or marginal answers. Smith and Hyman [238] report an experiment on this point. Two recorded interviews, each containing the same series of questions, were played to a group of interviewers. In the one interview the respondent answered all the questions preceding the test question as if she held isolationist views, in the other the respondent answered them as if an internationalist. The test question was the same on both interviews and so was the answer to it, a lukewarm and somewhat ambiguous one. The interviewers listening to the record were asked to code this answer. Some 75 per cent of them allocated it to the isolationist code for the first interview, but only 20 per cent did so for the second one.

(b) Secondly, and more important for factual enquiries, are *role expectations*. The interviewer gains early in the interview an impression of the kind of person she is interviewing—how old, what social type, what occupation and income, personality and so on. If she is later confronted with doubtful, ambiguous or marginal answers, she may interpret them in the light of the answers she expects from this type of person. The NORC studies produced evidence of this effect. In the extreme case, and especially when an interview is proving difficult, an interviewer may omit to ask certain questions altogether in the belief that she will be able to fill in the answers herself with fair accuracy. This applies equally to attitude-structure expectations. To the extent that expectations of types (a) and (b) operate in normal survey conditions, the effect would be to produce a more uniform set of responses than actually exist.

(c) Finally there are *probability expectations*. An interviewer may expect a certain distribution of opinions or characteristics among her respondents; for instance, she may think, rightly or wrongly, that about half of the total sample should be Labour supporters. If, as she works through her assignment, she has noticeably less than this proportion she may begin to interpret doubtful answers in the Labour direction (or, in the extreme case, distort them purposively). This seems the least plausible type of expectational error and we note that the NORC findings on it were largely negative.

Errors arising from the respondents

The respondent may give an answer other than the correct one because he lacks the knowledge to give the latter, because his memory plays him false, because he misunderstands the questions or because, consciously or unconsciously, he does not wish to give the correct answer. Although such errors are appropriately laid at the door of the respondent rather than the interviewer, the root cause is essentially the reaction of one to the other. A respondent may overstate his frequency of church-going in order to appear respectable in the eyes of the interviewer; he may give a false picture of his political opinion because the interviewer has put his back up; he may state what he feels would be the interviewer's opinion because he wants to get the interview over. This sort of thing is an ever-present risk; as in every-day life, what people say and how they say it varies with circumstances and according to the person they are talking to.

13.3. Operation of Response Errors

How do these potential sources of response errors translate themselves into actual errors? In the case of errors due to the respondent's unwillingness or inability to give the correct answers, this question does not arise. But in what way do the personal characteristics, views or expectations of interviewers result in errors? They may, in the first place, operate directly. A respondent may be put off by the very sight of an interviewer; he may react badly to her personality and manner, be put off by someone of her age or social type or be influenced by what he feels to be her standpoint on the subject of the survey.

But there are also many indirect causes of response errors. In spite of the standardisation of the modern survey interview, there still remains some scope for the investigator's individual judgement and discretion and hence for errors arising from her characteristics, opinions and expectations. In addition there is scope, as in every job, for errors due to forgetfulness, inefficiency, fatigue and so forth. Let us run through the main possibilities.

Asking the questions

Interviewers are usually instructed to keep to the wording and order on the schedule and to ask the questions in a stated manner. To what extent uniformity can be achieved is difficult to say, but there is clearly scope for interviewer effects to operate. Such effects may be accidental, in the sense that an interviewer by mistake alters the wording of a question, or they may be related to her characteristics, views or expectations. In the former case, the errors would probably cancel out; in the latter they would tend to produce a net interviewer bias.

Probing

In spite of instructions, interviewers may differ in the extent to which they probe in order to arrive at what they consider to be an accurate response. One interviewer might accept a "Don't know" answer, where another might have tried to find out whether it was genuine. One interviewer may accept a vague or ambiguous answer where another would, by further probing, have tried to ascertain exactly what was meant. Differential probing undoubtedly gives scope for the operation of response errors.

Recording the answer

Carelessness in recording is another potential source of error.[1] Interviewers may omit to record answers, or may record them incorrectly or ambiguously. With open questions, some will be more successful than others in getting down the complete response. If they in effect paraphrase the reply, there is again scope for the operation of interviewer effects, for instance those arising from attitude-expectations. If a respondent gives a long, rambling answer, the interviewer may, perhaps unconsciously, select for recording that part of it which tallies best with the other answers.

Coding

Interviewers are often required to code answers on the spot. If the answer is thought ambiguous or is marginal between two codes, the interviewer's judgement on the matter may cause a response error.

Cheating

An altogether different cause of response error is conscious distortion or cheating. It has been much discussed in the literature (see Notes on Reading).

Some experts regard cheating as a serious, others as a negligible, problem; some look on it as a matter of inherent dishonesty, others as a function of interviewer morale, connected with rates of pay, working hours, difficulty of questionnaires and general attitude to the job.

It is, of course, almost impossible, to obtain accurate information on the extent of cheating in a survey, but survey experts appear to be fairly confident that falsification of entire questionnaires, at any rate, is rare. If employed on piece-rates, field workers would indeed stand

---

[1] See Booker and David [12] for some findings on accuracy and completeness in recording answers.

to gain by filling in the forms themselves, but the chance of detection is considerable, particularly when a system of checking on a sample of the interviews is in operation. The known existence of this is a valuable safeguard.

Much less amenable to checks, and probably much more common than complete falsification, is partial cheating on isolated questions. The interviewer may—particularly in a difficult interview—leave the questionnaire incomplete and fill in some or all of the remaining questions in accordance with her experience.[1]

No view can be expressed here as to the extent of interviewer-cheating in everyday surveys. Most survey organisations have their methods for detecting it but the details are, understandably, not made public.

Relationship to the conditions of the survey

We have so far covered components of response error arising from interviewer, respondent and the interaction of the two. It will be clear to the reader that these errors are closely dependent on the other conditions of the survey. The chief factors will merely be summarised here; they are all discussed more fully elsewhere in the book.

(a) *The length of the questionnaire*. The nature and magnitude of response errors in a survey depend partly on the length of the questionnaire. Respondent and interviewer both tend to become less attentive and accurate after a certain time.

(b) *The order of questions*. This can affect response errors.

(c) *Question structure*. With questions involving a number of sub-questions (i.e. "If answer to Q. 3 is YES, . . ."), the interviewer may be tempted to avoid complications by filling in the answer *not* requiring further sub-questions, particularly if there is any room for doubt. The seriousness of response errors may vary according to whether open or pre-coded questions are asked; and, in the latter case, with the number and order of the alternative answers presented to the respondent.

(d) *Question content*. Questions involving prestige, social gain, personal circumstances and so on may lead respondents, consciously or otherwise, to give inaccurate answers. Questions involving memory have their own risks of error (see an interesting paper by Gray [100]).

(e) *Question wording*. The use of leading words, of technical or uncommon terms, of ambiguous or vague words and phrases may lead to error. Such errors may operate differentially with different interviewers.

[1] The possibilities for cheating in quota sampling (dishonest completing of quotas) are discussed in Moser [191].

(*f*) *Place of interview.* The physical location (and possibly time) of the interview may have an influence upon response errors, as also might the presence of a third person.

(*g*) *Interest in the survey.* The accuracy as well as the willingness of response probably depends partly on the respondent's interest in the subject-matter of the survey. The interviewer's accuracy also is affected by her own interest.

13.4. Detection of Response Errors

The potential sources of response error are thus plentiful and so are the points of the interview at which they can operate. What does this mean in terms of the average survey? Do the potential errors become actual errors; and, if so, how big are they and to what extent do they cancel out? Answers to these questions have to be very tentative. There is a substantial amount of *general* experience on the adequacy of different survey procedures and there are numerous findings on errors introduced in specific situations. But each survey is in some respect novel and what is lacking is a satisfactory methodology of measuring the size of response errors in the individual survey.

The simplest approach, on paper, is to check the accuracy of the final survey results against data from other sources, and certainly no such checks should ever be left untried. One may try to check individual answers, thus arriving at an assessment of *gross errors* (total response error) irrespective of whether they subsequently cancel out or not, or one may look only at the *net error* remaining after any cancellation has taken place; this can be justified by arguing that it is only the net errors which undermine the accuracy of the final results. However, from the methodological point of view, the surveyor's concern should certainly be with gross errors. Any hope of eliminating or reducing errors rests on knowing where and why they occur, which one cannot do by looking only at the final results. The study of gross errors is never easy and often—as with opinion questions—virtually impossible.

Gross errors

It goes almost without saying that the first step is to check the completed schedules. But editing (discussed in the next chapter), even at its most thorough, can only detect the more obvious mistakes and inconsistencies. Fothergill and Willcock [86] report a Government Social Survey experiment in which 56 interviewers interviewed dummy informants under observation. All errors of procedure were noted and it was subsequently found that only 12 per cent of these could be detected from the completed questionnaires. The main categories among the "invisible" errors were insufficient probing, altering the scope of the question through wording changes or biased probing, and wrong classification of answers.

The detection of procedural errors—failure to ask all the questions, to use all the appropriate prompts, to probe to the right extent, to record accurately and completely— is an important part of maintaining or raising the quality of fieldwork, irrespective of whether, in a particular case, they produce errors in the results (a failure to prompt correctly does not *necessarily* produce the wrong answer). In the present section we shall concern ourselves with "effective" errors only.

(*a*) *Record checks*. We come then to the individual validity checks— designed to ascertain how close the answer recorded on the schedule is to the individual true value. Sometimes it can be checked against records or documents of some kind. Birth certificates are an obvious example. If the information on the records can be regarded as reliable, this is an excellent way of checking survey answers. One's first reaction is that such checks are hardly ever possible. Yet Eckler and Pritzker [70] report the use of the following record checks in connection with the 1950 U.S. Population Census:

"(i) Birth certificates on file in our State Offices of Vital Statistics —to check age reporting.

(ii) Records of military service on file in our Veterans Administration—to check reporting on veteran status.

(iii) Tax returns on file in our Bureau of Internal Revenue offices— to check income reporting.

(iv) Reports by employers on file in our Social Security Administration—to check reporting on wages and salary income and reporting on industry.

(v) Naturalisation and alien records on file in our Immigration and Naturalisation Service—to check reporting on citizenship status.

(vi) Returns from the 1920 Census—to check age and birthplace reporting for persons who were thirty years old or over in 1950. This check is being made to supplement the birth-certificate check because it is known that our birth certificate records for many States are decidedly incomplete for 1920 and earlier years."

Of course, record checks, apart from being confined to a limited class of survey data, have their difficulties. The records may themselves be inaccurate, they may be incomplete—in which case one has to judge whether the people for whom records are not found are typical of the rest—and the matching and finding of records for survey individuals is often troublesome and expensive.[1] These are problems, certainly, but if response errors are to be taken seriously, they should at least be tackled.

(b) *Consistency checks.* Record checks are useful if one has reason to believe that the records are more accurate than the survey answers. Many checks used in surveys merely ascertain whether two sources produce the same or different answers, with little cause for believing one to be more accurate than the other. An interesting example was Kinsey's technique of asking both husband and wife questions relating to their sexual life within marriage, then comparing the answers [144]. This was useful but, like all consistency checks, negative. If the two answers agree, the surveyor is entitled to feel increased confidence. If they do not, and he has no reason to believe one more accurate than the other, he merely has a measure of variation. Still, this is useful knowledge since he can then go on to investigate reasons for the difference and try to find out which answer is right.

A common type of consistency check is to ask for the same information in two or more ways. As a crude example, one could ask the respondent, perhaps early in the interview, when he was born and casually ask him, at a later stage, how old he is. This is again a one-directional check and, even if the two answers agree, there is no proof that they are correct. To realise this, one has only to think of a woman consistently under-stating her age. It is indeed hard to invent consistency checks so disguised that the respondent who is determined to give a false answer will be caught out. If the questions are asked on separate occasions one reduces the chance that he will remember the answer he gave the first time, but then such checks only have point with factual data unlikely to change with time.

(c) *Re-interviewing.* In a sense, the most natural way of checking upon the accuracy of a measurement is to repeat it. True, if the two measurements are made in the same way, a difference in results is only an indication of variation, and does not tell one anything about the accuracy of either. But if the second measurement can be made by a more precise instrument than the first, one is in a good position to gauge the accuracy of the earlier measurement.

These principles apply to the present context. If an interviewer—either the original one or one similar in "quality"—is sent to re-interview a respondent, the difference in answers gives an indication of variability.[2] In order to check on the accuracy of the initial answer,

[1] Many potential records will, of course, not be accessible to non-official agencies.

[2] Strictly speaking, if the same interviewer is used on both occasions we get a measure of, what is generally called, *reliability*. If different interviewers are used—a more practicable proposition—we get a measure of *variability*.

One assumption must be noted, namely that the two measurements are inde-

we would have to ensure that the second interview was of a higher "quality".

There have been a number of re-interview experiments. Among the earliest were those reported by Mosteller in Cantril's well-known book [28]. A group of respondents were visited by interviewers and classified by economic status into four groups, the main criterion being income. After three weeks the same interviewers revisited them, and on a second classification 77 per cent retained their original grouping. In a parallel experiment, but with different interviewers doing the second interview, only 54 per cent of the cases retained their former classification. Mosteller reports similar findings on other variables.

Such researches give an indication of reliability, of how much variation is found in repeated measurement. To get at the accuracy of the measurement, we require that the quality of the second interview be raised above that of the first.

This is the basis of the re-interview checks—known as quality checks or Post-Enumeration Surveys—which have in recent years become a regular feature of census-taking in the United States. The scale of these censuses—whether of Population, Housing, Agriculture or Manufacture and Business—is so enormous that it is impossible to attain the quality feasible with smaller enquiries. The quality checks are intensive studies of relatively small samples[1] and every effort is made in them to attain the highest level of efficiency possible. We may give three examples of this. Whereas the 1950 Census (of Population and Housing) required some 140,000 enumerators, the quality check on it used only 250, who were carefully selected from the large group and intensively trained. Whereas in the census, information about members of the household could be given by several specified members of the household, in the quality check it had in each case to be obtained from the person directly concerned (apart from children or mentally incompetent persons). Again, whereas in the census a single question might be asked in order to secure a piece of information, in the quality check several questions were put, so as to make sure that the correct and relevant answer had been obtained. If the quality check had simply asked the original question again, the same response error—if due to a misunderstanding of the question—would probably have been repeated.

For these and other reasons the quality check answers were more

pendent of each other. With an opinion question, the first interview may affect the respondent's thinking and thus influence the second answer. This would undermine the value of the re-interview check.

[1] The quality check for the 1950 U.S. Population, Housing and Agriculture Census covered a sample of 25,000 households and 7,000 farms. The quality checks were designed to detect coverage errors—omissions, duplications and inclusions in wrong area—as well as response errors in our sense.

trustworthy than the initial ones, and the results published so far, relating both to completeness of coverage in the original censuses and to the quality of the information obtained, amply justify the expenditure and trouble taken. Though we cannot discuss the results here—references are given below—we note that *net* differences between the final quality check results and the census results were generally small, but that substantial *gross* errors were found. This strongly emphasises the importance of gross-error checks as a means of learning how to control and reduce errors. The case-by-case checking was reinforced by the record checks mentioned above, and this three-cornered check—census answer, quality check answer, record check answer—provided a sound way of discerning whether the quality check was in fact achieving a higher accuracy than the original census.

Quality checks can rarely establish with certainty the *correctness* of the original results, but they can and do often prove that the earlier result was wrong. If the first and second answer disagree, and the interviewer finds out that the original census question had been misunderstood, an error has been established. There are many such ways of locating errors in the original returns, but not even a quality check can help in the case of consistent errors, such as a woman consistently under-stating her age. Nothing short of her birth certificate or a psychoanalyst would uncover this error.

It must be admitted that, however much trouble is taken, even the quality checks will contain errors. But they probably bring us as close as we shall ever get to accuracy in real life, so we must be satisfied with them. One practical question is: should the interviewer on the second occasion know what answer was given on the first? There are strong arguments in favour of her knowing. One of the values of the quality check is that it tracks down reasons for a difference between first and second answer and so enables one to make sure that the second is the correct one. The interviewer must therefore know what the original answer was. The only danger is the possible tendency to confirm, rather than contradict, the original answer. Marks, Mauldin and Nisselson [177] report some evidence to this effect.[1] However, such a tendency should be responsive to careful training and instruction; and then it would seem on every count preferable for the second interviewer to be aware of the original answer.

It seems to me that these quality checks constitute a development of great importance, and one to be tried for large-scale enquiries in this country. What is more difficult to judge is whether such checks can

---

[1] They compare the errors disclosed when re-interviewers (*a*) knew the original answer, (*b*) did not know it and (*c*) were given the original answer but told not to look at it until they had obtained the second answer.

be useful in surveys where a few thousand rather than many millions of cases are involved, and where the interviewers are in any case at a higher level of quality than enumerators taken on for an occasional census. To my mind, quality checks are worth attempting even if they only consist of supervisors re-interviewing a small sample of respondents.[1] They keep the field staff up to scratch and are more likely than any other means to disclose sources of response error. I should note that the U.S. quality checks mentioned above are used largely for analytical purposes, not as a means of adjusting the original results.

Net errors

Apart from the U.S. quality checks, the literature on gross errors is rather limited; most research workers have concerned themselves with the net errors remaining in the final results. It is easy enough to understand this preoccupation. The practitioner in charge of a survey is mainly concerned about the extent to which errors have failed to cancel out; and, in any case, these net effects are easier to detect than gross errors. But even accuracy checks for aggregates are not at all plentiful. Demographic variables like sex, age, household composition and so forth can generally be checked. But for most of the questions which appear on survey questionnaires, external data suitable for checks are fairly hard to come by (and are not always more accurate than the survey results). Even where accuracy checks are at hand for the over-all results, sub-group figures—which may be quite as important—are generally difficult to validate.

Comparison of the results with data (on the same subject and population) secured in other surveys may strengthen, or weaken, confidence in their accuracy, but there are generally too many differences between the surveys to make this a firm check.

Many of the earlier studies of net errors were based on quota samples. Differences between the survey results and the check figures could then be due to a mixture of selection and response errors, with no hope of separating them. Mosteller [196] and his colleagues found this a handicap in trying to unravel why the forecasts of the 1948 U.S. Presidential Election had gone wrong. This illustrates a general "weakness" of checks upon net errors. Discrepancies between survey results and the check figures may be due to response errors, to bias in selection or to non-response, and are most likely to be due to a combination of all these factors. Checks on gross errors are not confused in this way.

---

[1] Kish and Lansing [148] report a study in which the accuracy of the original answers (on house values) was checked by sending along professional appraisers of house values.

Interviewer variability

One aspect of response errors that has always attracted attention is the fact that interviewers, working on equivalent samples and under similar conditions, tend to obtain different results. There are two reasons why this problem has received so much attention. One is that studies to estimate interviewer variability are easy to design. The other, and more important, is that the very difficulty of testing the validity of survey results leads surveyors to concentrate on their reliability. As Henry [118] put it in a recent address: "You are probably familiar with the story of the mother who watched her son's infantry regiment marching along the street and exclaimed: 'Look, my John is the only one in step!' It is always possible, I suppose, in our sort of work that the one investigator who differs from all the others *may* be the only one really in step, but as we have no criteria by which to judge this, all we can do is to insist that, right or wrong, he falls into line with the others." Consistency, that is low interviewer variability, becomes the aim, resulting in the ever increasing standardisation of interview procedures. By suitable selection and training, by strict instructions and by a rigid control of the interview, the risks of substantial interviewer variability are reduced.

Surveyors may be unwise to put so many eggs into this basket of consistency and not to make greater efforts with the—admittedly much more difficult—problem of validity. It is true, of course, that substantial interviewer variability inflates the total sampling variance and hence lowers precision, but at least it can, with suitable designs and formulae, be estimated from the sample itself; bias cannot.

The estimation of interviewer variability in essence requires the method of interpenetrating samples (see Section 6.8) which Mahalanobis [169] first used for this purpose. There have been numerous studies along these lines, one of the most recent being that of Durbin and Stuart [68].[1] In each area covered by their experiment, two interviewers (belonging to the same organisation) were allocated independent random samples, so that the variance between them could be compared with the random sampling variance. This comparison was made on 33 questions—all factual ones—asked in the survey and gave almost entirely negative results. Out of 99 ratios (33 questions on three types of sampling each—the type of sampling is not relevant here) seven were significant at the 5 per cent level. Two of these were on the same question and were, on closer investigation, found to be due to faulty questionnaire design or inadequate briefing. This question aside, there were five significant values out of 96 (roughly what would be expected by chance, on the 5 per cent level, if there

---

[1] See also Stock and Hochstim [249], Gales and Kendall [88] and Gray [101].

were no real interviewer differences). The authors concluded "that the variability between interviewers in replies obtained is so small compared with random sampling fluctuations that it can reasonably be ignored. . . . In other words the difference in the results obtained by two different interviewers working on separate sets of respondents seems to be no greater than the difference which would have been obtained if the same interviewers had worked on both sets" (see [68], pp. 409–10).

Many other studies on interviewer variability have shown equally negative results. This seems at first sight to contrast oddly with the evidence, produced from many sides, of substantial gross response errors. If this evidence is to be believed, why is there so little sign, in this and other recent studies, of interviewer variability?

Leaving aside the fact that much of the evidence both on gross errors and interviewer variability is tentative, it must be made clear that substantial gross errors are not necessarily inconsistent with small interviewer variability. An interviewer can make substantial gross errors without causing any net error; and, even if she does have a net error, other interviewers may produce net errors in the same direction, in which case interviewer variability may still be small. Let us look at these two arguments more closely.[1]

If an interviewer makes a great many errors, which are due to misunderstanding or carelessness rather than to biasing influences like strong views or expectations—and the NORC studies show evidence that this tends to be the case—these errors may cancel out on average, leaving little or no net error; this means that interviewer variability will be no larger than is normally to be expected. Variability becomes the larger and the more likely to be statistically significant, the more individual interviewers make systematic rather than compensating errors.

Now suppose that the errors made by an individual interviewer *are* non-compensating and thus result in a net error for that interviewer. If all the other interviewers have net errors in the same direction, gross errors will be substantial and there will be a net error for the sample as a whole; but interviewer variability will probably still be insignificant. Take a case where all the interviewers unconsciously exert a pro-Conservative influence. This will cause many gross errors because it tends to make people express, say, more Right-wing views than they really hold. There will be a net (pro-Conservative) error for each interviewer and a net error over the whole sample, the survey overestimating the pro-Conservative tendencies in the population. But a test of between-interviewer variance against random sampling

[1] For a rigorous demonstration, see Hansen, Hurwitz and Madow [112] or Sukhatme [256].

variance would probably yield negative results because the net errors are consistent. Thus low interviewer-variability is consistent with substantial gross errors.

In practice, net errors are unlikely to be as uniform as in the above example and, to the extent that interviewer variability is present, it will inflate the sampling variance. In the situation illustrated by formula (13.1), for instance, this variance decreases as the number of interviewers (r) increases. If there are as many interviewers as respondents ($r = n$), the second term in (13.1) disappears, leaving the standard formula for estimating the sampling variance of a mean.

Although many of the findings on interviewer variability have been reassuring, the subject is far from closed. More evidence is needed from everyday surveys and for a wider range of questions. The Durbin and Stuart experiment, for instance, dealt only with factual, pre-coded questions; one would expect greater variability with opinion, and with open questions. One would like to know how the cancellation of errors comes about and the extent to which it occurs. Is interviewer variability small because individual interviewers have little net bias associated with them or because their net biases all tend in the same direction? This requires a study of interviewer variability in conjunction with gross error checks on sub-group and over-all results. Finally, more needs to be known about the root causes of interviewer variability. Does it arise mainly in the asking of questions, interpreting of answers or their recording?

13.5. Control and Measurement of Response Errors

In the early sections of this chapter were listed the potential sources of response error and the ways in which interviews gave scope for their operation. The evidence on the actual operation of errors comes from many isolated researches and is often contradictory. At one time or another most types of error have been shown to exist and not to exist. Still, perplexing though it often is, there is enough evidence to suggest that response errors ought to engage the surveyor's serious attention. Indeed Hansen and his colleagues remark that "the paucity of dependable data on response errors is unquestionably the greatest present obstacle to sound survey design" (112, Vol. II, p. 280). Leaving aside experimental researches in this field, the question is, how can we control and reduce response errors?

One approach was dealt with in the preceding section. However much or little is done to prevent errors, their influence on results should be assessed, wherever possible, by validity checks on individual answers, sub-group results and over-all results.

But what should be done to keep response errors down to the

minimum? In considering this, we should recall the distinction between response variance and response bias. The former can, with suitable designs and formulae, be estimated from the sample results themselves; the latter cannot. Response variance causes concern because it inflates sampling variance; response bias because its magnitude is often unknown. If the surveyor had a genuine choice, he might devote himself mainly to controlling the bias-producing errors, since his ignorance of the extent of bias is a most serious weakness. At the same time he would so design the sample that response variance could be estimated from its results.

Theoretically this is sound advice; practically it is unhelpful. The difference between response variance and response bias lies in whether the errors are compensating or not and this one cannot tell in advance. Even if it seemed likely that recording errors would not be systematic, it would be hasty to decide to ignore them, quite apart from the fact that a large response variance arising from these errors would inflate the over-all sampling variance, thus reducing the survey's precision.

Some potential sources of error one associates essentially with bias. A leading question is to be avoided precisely because it will cause response error in a constant direction; the same applies to the use of a prestige name in a question and to other aspects of wording. For the same reason one might avoid employing interviewers with very strong views on the survey subject, which might cause systematic error. In short, many of the principles current in survey planning amount to an attempt to reduce response bias.

The most sensible course for the surveyor is to assume that none of the response errors are necessarily compensating in a survey and to take all steps, empirical and analytical, to keep them under control. We come now to specific possibilities.

Selection, training and supervision of interviewers

The selection, training and supervision of interviewers is closely bound up with response errors. If we knew what kinds of people made "error-free" interviewers, we could select accordingly. But survey life is not as simple as that. In the first place, there is probably no such thing as a good interviewer-type; some people are better for some surveys than for others, with some respondents than with others. Secondly, interviewing involves a number of different skills and a person who is satisfactory on one score may be hopeless on another. An accurate recorder is not necessarily a good interviewer. We need more knowledge, on the lines of the NORC findings, about the relationship between different interviewing skills, and what characteristics make for good interviewing. However, this subject has already been discussed in Chapter 11 and all we need stress is that response variance and bias must be to some degree responsive to careful selection, training, and supervision of the field staff.

Control of interview

We saw in Section 13.3 that there were various danger-spots in the interview at which scope for response errors was greatest. If field coding gives rise to substantial errors, perhaps office coding is preferable. If the recording of verbatim answers gives rise to many errors, it might be wise to forego their advantages and to use pre-coded questions. If differential probing is a source of trouble, perhaps probing should be strictly forbidden or allowed only along prescribed lines. It is easy to understand why the modern surveyor hankers after standardised methods. The more formal and standardised the technique, and the stricter the instructions, the less room will there be for the play of the interviewer's judgement. Standardisation finds its extreme form in mechanised methods. Portable tape recorders are used occasionally, and through them errors made in the asking of questions and recording of answers can be detected.[1]

Increasing the number of interviewers

While one way of reducing interviewer variability is to select, train and supervise the field staff so as to achieve maximum uniformity, an alternative, often suggested with a model such as represented in (13.1) in mind, is to increase the number of interviewers. Since the contribution of between-interviewer variance to the total sampling variance is a function of the number of interviews used, the greater this number, the smaller—*others things being equal*—this contribution will be. But other things are not generally equal. Using more interviewers may mean accepting a lower grade or spending less money on their training and supervision. Then the variation in the population of interviewers (σ_b^2 in the formula) might itself increase and offset the gain from increased numbers. If all potential interviewers were of the same quality, then, on the model implied in formula (13.1), it would be an advantage to have more rather than less of them. Indeed, it can be shown that it would then probably be best to have as many interviewers as respondents, each interviewing one randomly-assigned respondent.

---

[1] There is also on the market—but not, as far as I know, in operational use—a machine that asks the questions previously recorded into it in the office! Interviewer variability is thus eliminated, but with what effects upon validity one does not know. The aim of using this kind of machine may be understandable, but there is something distasteful and bizarre about some of these mechanical survey developments.

Matching of interviewers to respondents

We have seen that response errors may occur through the inter-action of interviewer and respondent. A working-class man, who per-haps had left school at 14, may resent being asked questions about his education by an obviously educated, well-spoken interviewer, but might be prepared to give the information to a person of his own type. On paper at least, some matching of respondents and interviewers seems attractive. But, apart from common sense cases such as not sending Jewish-looking persons to conduct interviews on anti-semitism, two points argue against matching. First, one is in practice limited to the interviewers who are available and this rules out matching on any scale. Secondly, and much more important, one would need to know much more than is known at present about the operation of such interaction-errors before one could confidently em-bark on any matching. For all one knows, the working-class man may be more, not less, willing to talk about education to a person of quite a different type than to someone like himself. Without secure evidence, there is no case for interviewer/respondent matching.

Analytical methods

Finally, I must refer briefly to the analytical approach to response errors. It has to be admitted that none of the above ways of de-tecting gross and net errors, or for controlling them, is very powerful; all encounter snags in application. So, whether or not they succeed in reducing errors, one must try in the analysis to estimate what re-sponse error remains. As should now be clear, this possibility is largely confined to response variance. In recent years progress has been made in setting up theoretical models according to which the re-sponse variance arising from different components, notably inter-viewers, can be estimated. These models are useful also in helping to clarify how response errors may affect the estimates one makes from a survey, both those of the population values and of sampling variances; and they are helpful in trying to determine the best sample design. Reinforced with cost data, they should make it possible to decide in advance what is the optimum number of inter-viewers to be used, how much it is worth spending on training and supervision and so forth. The theory involved in all this is beyond our present scope but references for further reading are given below.

I have in this chapter, as indeed throughout the book, concen-trated on general methods rather than practical details. Even given that response errors are important and may undermine survey accuracy, there must be a limit to what it is worth spending on their reduction. Money may be as difficult to obtain as accuracy, and in practice the surveyor, like anyone else, has to cut his cloth according to his purse. At any rate, I hope to have made clear that sampling errors are not everything. It is always worth asking whether some of the resources needed for keeping them down (e.g. by increasing sample size) might not be better spent in reducing response variance or in detecting response bias.

NOTES ON READING

1. The importance of the NORC studies has been emphasised at several points and readers are referred to the volume by HYMAN and others [124] for details. The following papers are worth consulting; many of them arose from the NORC programme: CAHALAN and others [27], CRUTCHFIELD and GORDON [45], FELDMAN, HYMAN and HART [75], FISHER [81], GUEST [107], GUEST and NUCHOLS [108], HART [115], HYMAN [122], KATZ [134], PARRY and CROSSLEY [201], SHAPIRO and EBERHARD [229], SMITH and HYMAN [238], SHEATSLEY [231], STEMBER [244], STEMBER and HYMAN ([245] and [246]).

2. Among the literature on cheating, readers might find useful CRESPI ([43] and [44]), DURANT [61] and BLANKENSHIP and others [10].

3. A well-known paper on errors was that by DEMING [49]. MOSER [191] discussed the literature on interview bias up to about 1950. The book by CANTRIL [28] contains some of the earliest findings in this field. MAHALANOBIS [169] is a good reference for work on interviewer variability. Other papers on the topic were noted in Section 13.4.

4. There have been a number of papers on the U.S. quality checks. Particularly useful are ECKLER [69], ECKLER and PRITZKER [70], HANSEN [109], HAUSER [117], MARKS and MAULDIN [176] and MARKS, MAULDIN and NISSELSON [177].

5. The most thorough theoretical treatment of response errors appears in Chapter 12 of the second volume of HANSEN, HURWITZ and MADOW [112]. The books by COCHRAN [36] and SUKHATME [256] are also useful on the theoretical level.

6. KISH and LANSING [148] report a study of response errors in the U.S Survey of Consumer Finances, which is particularly illuminating.

CHAPTER 14

PROCESSING OF THE DATA

14.1. Editing

WITH THE field part of the survey completed, the processing of the material and the highly skilled task of analysing it begins. First, the questionnaires have to be checked; secondly, the mass of detail has to be reduced to manageable proportions so that the wood can be seen for the trees; thirdly, where statistical analysis is to follow, the material has to be summarised in tabular form; fourthly, it has to be analysed, statistically or otherwise, so as to bring out its salient features; finally, the results have to be interpreted and presented in a report.

A characteristic feature of these final stages of a survey is the continual interplay between the research worker in charge, the coder, and the tabulator (in small-scale research surveys, they may all of course be one and the same person). Yet it is an obvious convenience to consider the operations separately, since they each have their specific purposes and problems. In this chapter I shall discuss editing, coding and tabulating, leaving the analysis and interpretation to Chapter 15.

The three operations now to be studied differ basically from each other. Editing is a routine task—though one which requires scrupulous care. Some types of coding are similarly reducible to repetitive operations, but others do allow a crucial role to judgement and skill. Tabulation, if done by hand, requires care, accuracy and patience rather than skill; if mechanised, it needs close acquaintance with the machines now in use. The planning of tabulation, as distinct from its actual execution, of course requires a good deal of skill.

Editing of the survey schedules is certainly the least exciting part of a survey. The work tends to be slow, repetitive and dull and gives cause for none of the enthusiasm associated with the initial planning, while also lacking the interest involved in collecting the data or the ingenuity required to analyse them.

Yet, anyone who has ever glanced through completed questionnaires returned from the field, will be aware of the absolute necessity for careful editing. Even the best interviewers are liable to make errors, omit to ask questions or to record answers and, when the field staff is inexperienced, editing assumes a crucial importance. Before the questionnaires can be regarded as ready for coding, tabulation and analysis, they should always be checked for completeness, accuracy and uniformity.

(a) *Completeness.* The first point to check is that there is an answer for every question. If an interviewer has forgotten to ask a question or to record the answer, it may be possible to deduce from other data on the questionnaire what the answer should have been and thus to fill the gap at the editing stage.

At other times the interviewer may be able to fill in the gap from memory. If she has omitted to record what type of house the respondent lived in, she may be able to recollect it later. At the worst, but only if the information is vital, one may return to the respondent for the missing information, most economically by a postal enquiry.

An omission is especially trying when neither the context of the question, nor answers to other questions, enable one to decide whether (i) the respondent refused to give an answer, (ii) the interviewer forgot to ask the question or record the answer, or (iii) the question was not applicable to the respondent. Non-applicability can most easily be deduced from other data, but as between the other explanations of an omission it is usually difficult to choose.

In most organisations, interviewers are instructed to record an answer for every question (there always being a "non-applicable" category) and good interviewers should not often be guilty of errors on this score. If many questions are unanswered (more likely because the respondent was unwilling than because the interviewer was inefficient) the whole questionnaire may have to be abandoned. But this is done only as a last resort. If the information that is on the questionnaire can be regarded as accurate, it is nefficient to throw it away even though it may cover only a small part of what was asked for.

Checking the completeness of the answers recorded for open questions is virtually impossible. Apart from seeing that the answer is legible enough for the coder (this applies to all types of answers, of course) and that it makes sense—i.e. that the interviewer has written down enough to make the meaning of the answer clear—there is little one can do; unless, of course, the interview has been recorded or respondents were re-interviewed.

(b) *Accuracy.* It is not enough to check that all questions are answered; one must try to check whether the answers are accurate. In the first place, inconsistencies should be looked for. Let us take the cigarette-smoking questions in the schedule on p. 215. If code (2)— "Doesn't smoke cigarettes"—has been ringed in answer to Q. 10 (*a*) and the answer "about 10" recorded for Q. 10 (*b*), clearly something is wrong. Here one could unhesitatingly alter the former code to (1), but often the matter is not so easily settled. If a questionnaire tells us that a clerk aged 29 is earning £30 per week, we may suspect that there is an error somewhere. His age may have been understated or his income overstated, or the interviewer may have failed to record that the gentleman is a Town Clerk. Every effort should be made to dissolve *clear* inconsistencies, but care should be taken to make corrections only where there has quite obviously been an error; inconsistencies *may* be genuine and to iron them out would result in a false picture.

Inaccuracy may be due to carelessness or to a conscious attempt to give misleading answers, and it may arise from either respondent or interviewer. In the stress and strain of an interview, the investigator may easily ring the wrong code or so place the ring that it is not clear which of two codes is intended. Answers needing arithmetic, even of the simplest kind, often cause trouble. If the interviewer is asked to summarise a household composition table (such as for Q. 17 on p. 217), she may give an inaccurate total; if she has to convert from one unit into another (say days into hours), she may similarly slip up. Thus it is generally better to have arithmetic done in the office rather than by the interviewer. Where answers have to be written (e.g. "five days") rather than codes ringed, mistakes also can occur. Some, though by no means all, of these errors will be caught by a careful edit.

(*c*) *Uniformity.* The editing stage gives an opportunity for checking that interviewers have interpreted questions and instructions uniformly. In a survey on the use of laundry facilities, recently conducted by a student group, one question asked how much per week the housewife spent on laundry. This was to be asked only of those who sent laundry out. It was discovered at the editing stage that some interviewers had mistakenly ringed the answer "under 1s. 6d." (the lowest category), instead of "not applicable", for housewives who did not send their laundry out.

In another survey, the instructions for the income question omitted to specify whether interviewers were to take account of Family Allowances in deciding upon the appropriate answer-code. Some did, others didn't. Since a woman with more than one child is entitled to Family Allowances, errors could sometimes be corrected during the editing. In brief, the editing staff should keep a keen look-out for any lack of uniformity in the way data have been collected or the replies recorded.

Once a questionnaire has been edited, it is ready for coding and further analysis. Any errors that have been missed are likely to go through to the final report undetected. If they *are* caught, say during the tabulation, their correction will hold up the proceedings. That is why scrupulous editing generally pays in the end.

One question that has always to be settled is whether a questionnaire should be edited as a whole or whether one section, even one question, should be edited at a time for all questionnaires. It is probably easier to avoid errors if one can concentrate on one or two questions at a time. On the other hand, editing a whole questionnaire facilitates viewing the individual case *as a whole*, noting the relationship between answers to the different questions and detecting inconsistencies. It also facilitates the judging of an interviewer's ability, and (a practical point) enables one to get on with the editing as the questionnaires come in, instead of having to wait until the fieldwork is complete.

There remains the question whether all, or only a sample of the questionnaires, should be edited. No general rule can be laid down, since the decision must depend on a balancing of the various error-risks. There is no point in spending the bulk of one's resources on a complete edit if the errors thus corrected are relatively minor and if it means ignoring other important sources of error. But experience of academic research surveys, in which inexperienced field-workers have been used, suggests that a thorough and complete edit pays handsomely.

Finally I should draw attention to the punched card equipment now being used for the detection of inconsistencies (see Yates [291], Chapter 10)—a way of editing mechanically.

14.2. Coding

Let us now suppose that the data are edited and ready to be prepared for analysis. In most surveys, certainly wherever results are to be put into quantitative form, the intermediate stage is the coding of the answers. Sometimes this and the editing are joined in a single operation.

The purpose of coding in surveys is to classify the answers to a question into meaningful categories, so as to bring out their essential pattern. Before discussing this operation I may mention in passing a rather specialised application of coding techniques. This is *content analysis*,[1] which is typically a systematic analysis and description of

---

[1] One could legitimately use the terms coding and content analysis inter changeably since both refer to the same process. In practice, the former term is generally used for research data, the latter for material existing naturally, like newspapers, books etc.

the content of communication media. Newspapers may be analysed to study the changing attention given to a certain political issue over several years; the content of different papers (or books) in a country may be studied to bring out their differing attitudes to an issue or their differing propaganda techniques and so forth. The reader interested in this field is recommended to the references at the end of this chapter; we will here confine ourselves to the use of coding in summarising survey answers.

The process involves two distinct steps. The first is to decide on the categories to be used, the second to allocate individual answers to them. Following Government Social Survey practice, I shall refer to the set of categories as the coding frame.

The coding frame

In cases where there are only a few possible answers to a question the preparation of a coding frame raises no problems. The question: "Have you smoked any cigarettes today?" admits only of the answers "Yes" and "No", together with "Don't remember", "Refuse to answer", "Not applicable", so that the frame decides itself. Most of the questions in the schedule on p. 215 are of this kind and could be given in pre-coded form for just this reason—that the set of possible answers could easily be decided upon ahead of the fieldwork. Where the frame does not determine itself automatically, it is a matter of deciding how detailed a grouping to allow for in the coding, which in turn will depend on how the answers are expected to be distributed and what analysis is being planned. As an example take Q. 16 (a) from the schedule on p. 215:

> *If (respondent lived) at home*
> What kind of house is it? . . .
>
> | | |
> |---|---|
> | Whole detached house | 5 |
> | Whole semi-detached house | 6 |
> | Whole terrace house | 7 |
> | Self-contained flat | 8 |
> | Other (give details) | 9 |
> | Not applicable | Y |

It was believed that these represented the main alternative answers[1] and that it was useful to keep them distinct. Codes (5, 6 and 7) might have been combined to constitute a "Whole house" code, but the difference between the three types was here of interest. One cannot lay down any hard-and-fast rules for this kind of decision. By and large, it is advisable to retain more rather than less detail in the coding, since it is easier to amalgamate groups in later analysis than to split

---

[1] Pre-coding for "type of house" questions actually causes a number of minor problems—e.g. how to allow for pre-fabs, flats over shops etc.

one group into several when these have been coded alike. On the other hand, a very detailed coding is extravagant as regards punched cards and makes the analysis unwieldy, and at the same time increases the difficulty of allocating answers accurately. The whole point of coding is to summarise the data and it is as unhelpful to retain too many categories as it is misleading to use too few.

Establishing a coding frame is, however, not generally so easy a task as the remarks so far suggest. One need only think of the general run of attitude questions to realise how hard it may be to set up, ahead of the actual interviews, a list of categories which will be exhaustive, mutually exclusive and suitable to the purpose of the survey. Answers to an open question like: "In what way are you affected by rising prices?" (see p. 277 below) may cover all sorts of points: about the cost of living in general as well as particular goods, about consequent changes in purchasing habits and leisure pursuits, about tax effects, about resultant changes in employment or wage claims, about effects on political attitudes and so forth. Any single answer may cover several of these aspects so that the researcher has to decide in terms of which factors (or dimensions, to use the technical word) the coding is to be done. He might wish to concentrate on the dimension of *general cost of living*, and to code according to how severely people feel themselves to be affected, or he might be chiefly interested in the individual price changes mentioned and categorise these; or he might take a number of dimensions, coding according to each in turn; he may even code all items mentioned. The point is that the coding frame has to be designed in accordance with the aim of the research, which will partly determine the dimensions chosen for coding and the number of categories distinguished for each. I say "partly" because the frame must also be influenced by the types of answers actually given. Respondents may, for one reason or another, answer in terms and at a level different from that in the researcher's mind and this must be allowed to influence the coding frame. In other words, the frame must suit the respondents' chosen terms of reference as well as the purpose of the survey. The researcher may begin by setting up the code categories according to his own ideas and aims, but he must be prepared to modify them in the light of an analysis of a sample of replies.

This is indeed the usual procedure. A representative sample of the completed schedules is examined and the answers to the particular question noted. (The Government Social Survey generally examines some 10 per cent of the schedules for this purpose.) Gradually a pattern emerges and on this the final coding frame is based. Groups containing very few cases can be combined into a "Miscellaneous" category—care being taken not to lose anything which may be of substantive interest later. A category with very few cases may be interesting just for this reason: if hardly any of the respondents mention a particular brand of chocolate, this negative finding can be of considerable interest but would have been lost if the few cases had been thrown into a residual group. This minor point emphasises that the construction of a coding frame is not a task to be delegated to routine clerks; it has to be done by somebody fully in touch with the purposes of the survey and of the way the results are to be used. Before the frame is finalised, every opportunity should be given to coders to test it further on samples of replies, so as to examine their differences and eliminate ambiguous or troublesome codes. This not only results in a better frame but also serves as good training for the coders. If insufficient trouble is taken at this preparatory stage, the final coding will repeatedly be held up because answers do not seem to fit properly into any code or, just as bad, could reasonably be assigned to more than one category. Furthermore, the more doubtful decisions there are to be taken, the greater the variability between coders will be.

Coding the answers

So much for the construction of the coding frame. The actual allocation of answers to individual categories can, as we saw earlier, be done by the respondent—as with questions offering a specific choice of answers; by the interviewer—as with questions answered freely but coded in the field; or by the office coder. The first two cases involve pre-coded questions and all the interviewer (or, in a mail questionnaire, the respondent) has to do is to ring, tick or underline the appropriate code or codes.

The third type of coding is used where an open question has been asked and the answer recorded as nearly verbatim as possible. It has now to be coded in the office. Sometimes a set of code numbers is printed on the schedule (e.g. Q. 1 (*b*) on p. 215) ready for use; sometimes the codes are written in on the schedule or on a special transfer sheet or card. The coder may be required simply to note whether the answer contains a reference to a particular item (e.g. to the cost of living in general) or he may have to allocate the answer to one of several categories, according to the strength of the reference or according to the various points made. Sometimes the coding is based on the answer to only this question; at others, the coder may have to look at the answers to several questions before coding this one. Coding instructions should be specific on such points.

What is clear is that the difficulty of the coding will depend to some extent on how well the editing has been done and on the soundness of the frame. If the latter has been constructed with care, difficult

K

decisions will be rare (particularly if the interviewer has provided adequate detail). If it is not well constructed, the coder will continually come up against answers which either do not fit anywhere or might fit into several categories. He then has to use his discretion or ask the supervisor or put the difficult answer into the residual category— none of these being an entirely satisfactory solution.

An experiment on coding variability

But even assuming the maximum help from the coding frame and the interviewer, coding is rarely a matter of automatically applying given rules. For all but the simplest questions, there will be doubtful answers on which the coder has to exercise judgement. In these cases there is inevitably scope for personal bias and for differences between coders (as well as errors due to carelessness). The variability of coding —that is the extent to which different coders would arrive at different codings—is a factor of importance in surveys, just as is the variability between interviewers, and it is worth referring to a recent experiment on the subject by Durbin and Stuart [67].[1]

Four professional coders and four students took part, each having to carry out ten different coding operations; these ranged from purely mechanical tasks to the coding of answers to open questions. The same 400 completed schedules were used throughout and each coding operation was completed before the next was begun. Thus, when the first coder had completed operation 1, the second carried out this operation, then the third and so on until the operation had been done by all eight coders; then followed operation 2 etc. Furthermore, having completed a particular operation for all the schedules, each coder had to code the first 50 of them again (his earlier codings not being available to him).

Note that each coder dealt with only one question at a time, coding it for all the schedules. This is the most common practice, but there is the alternative of coding an entire schedule before proceeding to the next. As with editing, this has the advantage that each schedule is treated as a unit, so that inconsistencies are more easily noticed. However, the system used in the experiment enabled the coder to concentrate on one question at a time and so saved him from errors he might have committed if he had had to bear in mind a large number of points. It also eliminated differences between coders on any one question.

I give first a few particulars of the coding operations, since they illustrate well the range of the coder's task in surveys.

[1] I have to thank the authors and the editor of the *Journal of Marketing* for allowing me to draw so extensively on the paper.

Operation 1

Coders had to classify each respondent according to his marital status and age; there was one code number for each of 12 combinations.

Operation 2

Coders had to classify each household according to its composition; the requisite data were given in the usual type of household composition table. This coding took account of the relationship to the respondent of the various household members and their ages. Nine categories were distinguished.

Operation 3

Coders had to work out each household's income by adding together the incomes of the household members (these incomes were themselves given on the schedule in code form).

Operation 4

Coders were given a table showing minimum household income in relation to size of household. Each of the 400 households had to be coded according to whether its income fell below the minimum for its size or not, or whether there was insufficient information.

All the above were routine operations, on which coders might make mistakes, but on which there was no scope for judgement. This was not so with the other six operations (5*a*, 5*b*, 6*a*, 6*b*, 7*a*, 7*b*). These were based on three open questions, the answers to each of which had to be coded in two distinct ways. I shall use one of the questions as an example: "In what way are you affected by rising prices?"

The following codes were to be used:

A. "Cost of living" rising; general rise in all prices; "in every way" lower standard of living.

B. General *household* expenses higher; difficult to make housekeeping money go round.

C. Had to cut down spending on pleasures, luxuries, non-essentials in general.

C_1. Had to cut down spending on drink, tobacco.

C_2. Had to cut down spending on entertainments, sports.

C_3. Had to cut down spending on non-essentials.

D. Specific item mentioned whose price has risen.

D_1. Food prices risen.

D_2. Clothes prices risen.

D_3. Other specific price rises.

E. Saves less; had to spend savings.

F. Increased taxation.

G. Had to take a job, or extra part-time work, to make ends meet.

H. Wages or income not rising to keep pace with prices.

I. Other answers (give details on separate sheet).

J. Recorded answer illegible.

Operation 5a

Here coders were to code every item mentioned in the reply. Thus, if the reply was "Clothes going up, food going up, everything going up", then they should have coded: D_2, D_1, A.

Operation 5b

Here coders were to use the single code appropriate to the most important part of the reply. In the example, the code would have been A.

Both systems (*a*) and (*b*) are common in surveys. There were two other open questions, each of which was tackled in both these ways, making a total of 10 operations.

The results were presented in two quite different ways. One was simply to compare the over-all frequencies produced by the different coders, e.g. what proportion of the 400 schedules were (on a particular question) given code 1, 2, . . . , and so on. This analysis shows the extent of *net* differences between coders. The second type of analysis was to look at each reply (to a question) and note how the different coders coded it. This leads to a measure of *gross* discrepancies between coders. Since some of these will cancel out, the first analysis gives little idea of the real extent of coding differences. Admittedly, it is the first kind of analysis which shows to what extent the survey results would be thrown out by using the different coders, but one could never *rely* on the cancellation of discrepancies. What is important from the point of view of assessing the reliability of the coding or of deciding on the amount of supervision and checking is the extent of gross discrepancies. I confine myself to this analysis here, only adding the remark that, for the coding of the open questions, even the *net* differences were sometimes substantial.

The most telling analysis was that showing, for each operation, on what percentage of the schedules there were a maximum of 8, 7, 6, . . . agreements on a code. Two coders were regarded as agreeing when "their codings of a particular question are identical in all respects. Thus, in operations 5*a*, 6*a* and 7*a*, which involve multiple coding of each reply, two coders were regarded as agreeing only if each gives the same set of codes for the reply. Thus there was a greater scope for disagreement on the A codings than on the B codings of operations 5, 6 and 7" (see [67], p. 62). The results are shown in Table 14.1 below.

On the routine operations 1–4, there was a good deal of agreement; on the others, however, and especially in the multiple codings of open-question answers, considerable discrepancies were found. As the authors say: "Even at stage (*b*), where coders were simply asked to code the most important element in each reply, complete agreement

TABLE 14.1

Percentage of replies in which 8, 7, 6, etc, coders agreed

Coding Operation	Maximum number of agreements							Total
	8	7	6	5	4	3	2	
1	84	15	*	*	—	—	—	100
2	91	8	1	—	—	—	—	100
3	88	8	2	1	1	—	—	100
4	91	8	—	*	1	—	—	100
5a	33	13	9	12	12	13	8	100
5b	38	12	14	13	14	7	2	100
6a	30	16	15	12	13	10	4	100
6b	44	15	13	11	12	4	—	100
7a	46	8	13	10	11	10	2	100
7b	66	11	6	9	6	1	—	100

— denotes zero ; * denotes less than 0·5 per cent.

Source: Durbin and Stuart [67], p. 62.

was only obtained on the average in about half of the 400 replies. Furthermore, the disagreements were not due to the oddities of one or two coders, as may be seen from the slow falling away of the frequencies as we move across the table to the right" (see [67], p. 63).

One other interesting analysis was that comparing each coder's re-coding of the first 50 schedules with his original coding. Table 14.2 shows the number of discrepancies (out of a possible 50) made by each coder on each operation:

TABLE 14.2

Discrepancies in re-coding 50 replies

Coding Operation	Students				Professionals			
	I	I	III	IV	V	VI	VII	VIII
1	2	1	3	1	—	3	—	—
2	—	—	7	2	—	2	2	—
3	3	8	1	1	2	1	1	—
4	2	5	2	1	1	1	1	1
5a	18	8	15	18	13	14	11	4
5b	10	6	12	23	8	11	12	6
6a	14	16	16	16	7	16	16	8
6b	5	12	13	10	7	12	12	7
7a	12	9	12	10	5	7	11	5
7b	5	6	11	4	1	4	3	5

Source: Durbin and Stuart [67], p. 65.

The number of discrepancies for operations 5–7 were considerable even for the professionals. The paper suggests, with substantiating evidence, that the discrepancies were due not to a "learning effect" brought about by coding the intervening 350 schedules, but to a "substantial inherent variability 'within' coders". In other words, their *reliability* appeared to be low.

In summary, the experiment revealed substantial discrepancies between coders, and for the same coder at different times. It was admittedly only a small-scale enquiry but its results suggest that the subject merits serious research.

14.3. Tabulation[1]

In the majority of surveys, the data, once edited and coded, are put together into some kinds of tables, either in preparation for the statistical analysis or straight for the final presentation. There is nothing statistically sophisticated about this. Tabulation amounts to no more, basically, than a counting of the number of cases falling into each of several classes. The editing and coding has sought to ensure that the information on the individual schedule is accurate and categorised in suitable form. It now remains to "add all the schedules together", to count how many of them have answer (X) for question A and how many answer (Y).

The process may be done manually or by machine. Hand tabulation is exceedingly simple, involving no technical knowledge or skill; and it need not, even for cross-analyses, be particularly laborious. If one wants an analysis showing the distribution of income by occupation, all that is required is a table skeleton showing one of the variables horizontally and the other vertically; tally marks are made in this as one goes through the schedules. If a number of tables have to be constructed, it may be inconvenient to go through the schedules afresh each time and an alternative is first to transfer the relevant schedule data on to sheets, from which counts can more easily be made.

Machine tabulation is an entirely different proposition. Before the coded answers can be tabulated by a machine, they must be transferred on to a punched card, such as the one reproduced—with some comments—on p. 281. (This is a Hollerith-dual-purpose card—see below.)[2]

The card contains 80 columns (there are other sizes), each of which has 12 punching positions—0, 1, . . . , 9, X, Y; the latter two are not

---

[1] This section discusses general principles, not how to make tables or to operate tabulating machines. For references on these matters, see p. 287.

[2] The Power-Samas system is similar in principle, the chief difference being that Hollerith machines "read" the cards electrically, Powers-Samas theirs mechanically.

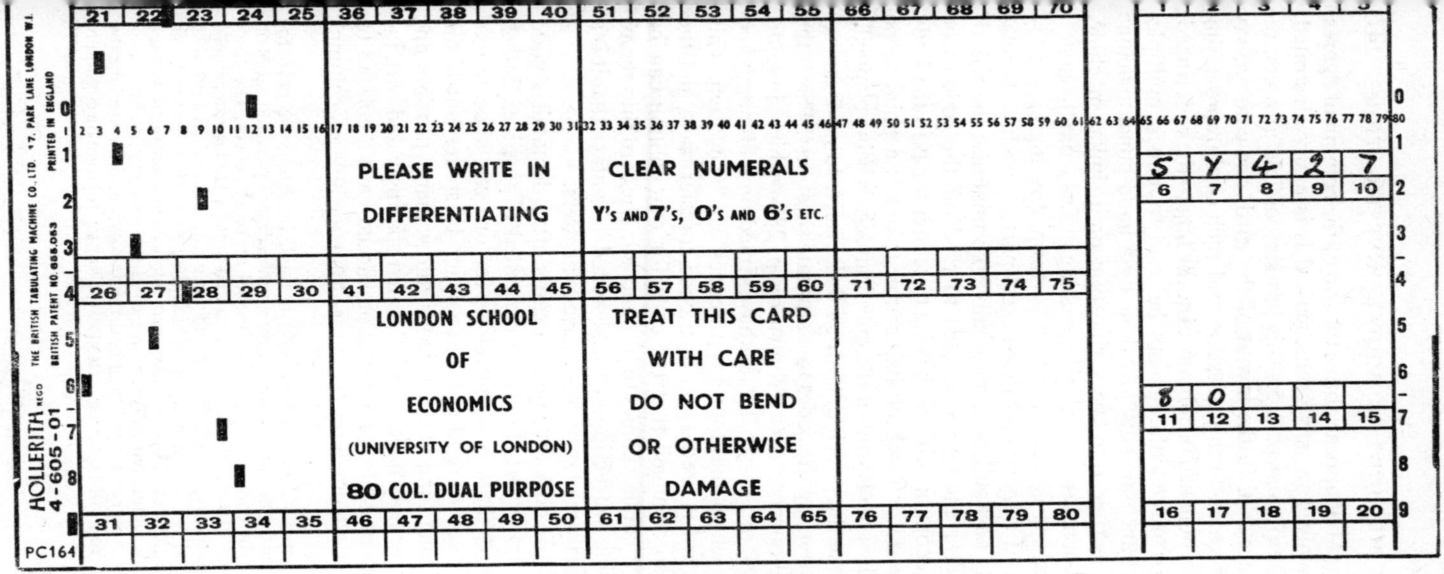

Fig. III. *A Hollerith Dual-Purpose Card*

The above card has all the features of the ordinary punched card, as well as the special code-box layout referred to on p. 282 below. There are 80 columns, the numbers of which can be seen running across the card about a quarter way down. Each column has 12 punching positions, 0, 1, 2, ... 9, X, Y. The first 10 are indicated by the digits down the margins, while the last two appear—but not in print—in two rows at the top.

The first task is, of course, to decide on the layout of the card in terms of the survey answers, i.e. to allocate columns to particular questions and positions within columns to particular answers. A set of columns may relate to a given "field" (e.g. age, household composition) and these titles can, if one so wishes, be printed on the card.

With ordinary cards, the code-numbers to be punched in the various columns are read off the questionnaire (or transfer sheet) by the punch-operator and punched. With the dual-purpose card they are first inserted into the respective boxes printed on the card. For illustration, this has been done for the first 12 columns above, and the respective positions in the columns have been punched. The advantages of this system are mentioned in the text.

printed on the card but appear above the top of the column of figures. The principle involved in using punched cards is easily illustrated. Let us take Q. 7 (*a*) from p. 215. This has six possible answers, represented by codes 1–6. In the layout of the card, one column, say column 15, is allocated to this question and each card (representing one respondent) is punched in column 15 according to the code ringed. Similarly, two or more columns can be used to punch multiple-digit codes. The punching is usually done by a hand-punch machine rather like a typewriter, and the verification on a similar machine, which will stop whenever the second punching differs from the first.

Although punching is a routine task performed at high speed by punch operators, it is inevitably the slowest part of machine tabulation, and the only part still done manually.[1] To minimise the risk of errors, the operator should be enabled to read off the code to be punched for each column without having to search for it in the body of the questionnaire or to check its accuracy; this is a point to be borne in mind when the layout of the questionnaire is being planned.

In order to make the punch operator's task easier, some organisations favour transferring the codes to a separate sheet first. This is the point of the dual-purpose card—shown on p. 281—which, in addition to the, say, 80 ordinary columns, has printed on it 80 numbered code boxes into which the appropriate codes can be written. This means that the card is used as its own code transfer sheet and the code boxes are so arranged that the code for any column can be clearly seen as that column comes to be punched. The card thus serves as its own punching instruction, with the added advantage that it is a permanent and easily read record of the code answers.

The laying out of codes for punched cards often demands a good deal of skill and an expert should be consulted if possible. With a short questionnaire, there is no problem, for one can allocate one column to each question and still have space to spare. But if the questionnaire is long, and the questions allow many possible answers, column space may have to be allocated sparingly and with ingenuity. Wherever possible, each question should have a column to itself, because multiple punching (i.e. more than one hole per column)

---

[1] Occasionally the method of mark sensing is used, obviating the need for punching. In its earlier forms, interviewers were given ordinary punched cards on which they recorded the code answers, using special graphite pencils. The cards were then fed into a machine which read the marks and punched holes accordingly. Alternatively a special recording card (bigger and more convenient than a punched card) can be used and fed into a machine which then punches holes on to an ordinary punched card. An even later development allows mark sensing to be used with an ordinary size schedule which is then micro-filmed; the micro-film is then mechanically translated into punched tape and the tabulation done straight (by electronic machines) from the tape. See Yates [291, Chapter 10] for a discussion of mark sensing.

causes difficulties in verifying the punching and in the tabulation. Where space is short, on the other hand, one would not devote an entire column to recording whether the respondent is Male (0) or Female (1), so wasting the other 10 positions. There are many ways, more or less intricate, of utilising card space to the full. One is simply to go on filling the rest of the column with new questions. In this example, positions 2–6 could be used to record to which of 5 age groups the respondent belonged, positions 7, 8 or 9 whether he was married, single or divorced (or widowed) and X or Y according to whether he lived in a house or a flat. Another approach towards column-economy is to use a composite code, combining several questions into one code. When there is a great deal of information, it may be best to have more than one card per case, rather than to use multiple punching or composite codes. The reader is referred to Yates [291, Chapter 5] for a discussion of the different possibilities.

Once punched and verified, the cards can go on to the machines and what is done now depends on the analysis required. A good deal can be achieved on the *sorter*, a machine which "looks" at one column at a time and distributes the cards into stacks according to the hole punched in that column. With a code occupying two columns, by sorting first on the one column and then on the other, the cards can be grouped into 144 cells. A *counter-sorter* at the same time counts the cards falling into each answer-group and shows the total in a counter above it. Such a machine can do most of the tabulations required in censuses and surveys and is reasonably convenient even for the many cross-tabulations that are generally required. Thus an income/occupation tabulation could be done by first sorting into income groups and then sorting the cards belonging to each of these by occupation. (There are elaborate types of counter-sorters which can deal with several columns simultaneously.)

The core of any sizeable punched-card installation, however, will be some kind of *tabulator*. These machines can add the numbers punched in a given column (or set of columns) on all the cards, arrive at any totals required and print both the numbers and the totals. They can also carry out complicated cross-tabulations. The use of the tabulator requires specialist skill or, at any rate, familiarity with the machine. Given this, the operator can carry out on the machines all the tabulations ever required in social surveys and some of the statistical calculations as well. Sorter and tabulator are thus the basis of any punched-card installation; other more specialised machines, such as the reproducing punch, multiplier and collator, are valuable for special tasks. The subject of machine tabulation is complex and for details the reader must be referred to the literature recommended at the end of the chapter.

Hand or machine tabulation

For a survey organisation equipped with a machine installation, and doing surveys involving thousands of cases at a time, the question of hand versus machine tabulation hardly arises. But with *ad hoc* social research surveys the choice is often a real one, and I shall suggest some of the factors on which it should be based.

(i) *Scale*. If the number of survey cases is small, say of the order of 200–300 or less, there is usually little point in tabulating by machine, since this necessitates punching and verifying and a certain amount of extra trouble.

(ii) *Analysis*. It most of the tables to be constructed are simple ones, involving only one variable at a time (say the numbers falling into different income groups), hand tabulation is quick and straightforward. Even for simple cross-tabulations it is not too difficult. But if there are complicated cross tabulations, involving more than two variables, or if there are a large number of even two-way tabulations, hand tabulation soon becomes slow and unwieldy. Furthermore, machines make fewer mistakes than human tabulators and those they do make are easier to find.

(iii) *Cost, speed and skill*. Machine tabulation tends to be costly and, for a fairly small survey, easily takes up a substantial proportion of the total budget. Therefore much depends on whether an installation is conveniently available for the survey and on what terms. Machine tabulation is generally—not necessarily—quicker, so that the researcher must make his choice on the basis of cost, time and resources. A machine expert should be able to make a fairly good estimate of the likely cost of a set of tabulations.

Machine tabulation, more likely than not, involves giving instructions to an operator; it *certainly* requires expert advice. Hand tabulation can be done directly under the researcher's eye, if he does not indeed do it himself. This has a certain advantage, if only because it brings to his notice the peculiarities of individual cases.

(iv) *Flexibility*. The flexibility of machine tabulation is one of its greatest advantages. When one is not certain what tabulations are going to be wanted, machine tabulation is preferable, for then the loss of time and work is not too great if some of them are not used. On the other hand, this convenience also spells one of the minor dangers of machine tabulations. It is all too tempting to run off any number of tabulations, worrying little as to whether they will really be needed. This is the "let us run off the tables and see what we can get out of them" attitude, reasonable up to a point, but a waste of resources if it gets out of hand. Many a research worker would have to admit to the possession of machine runs, which have barely been looked at. But, this minor danger apart, the flexibility of machine tabulation is a formidable advantage. However carefully the tabulation plans have been worked out, the surveyor is bound to think of new analyses as he goes along. He may have done tabulations of, say, the answers to the question "Do you smoke?" by the respondents' income and the respondents' sex, but not according to their sex *and* income, i.e. a three-way tabulation. With the answers on punched cards, the latter is easily done and at low cost; it involves no more trouble than the adjustment of a few switches. With hand tabulation, such "afterthoughts" can take a good deal of time.

There is no unequivocal summary to this discussion of the alternatives. For any survey which involves large numbers or for which a large number of cross-tabulations are required, machine methods have much to commend them. These cases apart, hand tabulation has much in its favour.

In conclusion, I should mention a method which aims to get some of the best of both worlds. This is based on a type of card (e.g. the Cope Chat card) in which answers are punched along the edges. Thus, the numbers 1–6 might be assigned to the answers 1, ..., 6 for Q. 7 (*a*) on p. 215 and the relevant code for a respondent (there being one card per respondent) is punched by a ticket-punch, so that the hole is opened up. This is done for all the cards. If a needle is then put through the stack of cards at, say, number 3, all the cards in which this hole has been opened to the edge can be made to fall out. They are then counted by hand.[1] The punching is fairly laborious but the method as a whole is quicker than ordinary hand tabulation. A useful feature is that the body of the card can be used for written material, so that the card represents a readable record of the data.

In concluding this chapter, I want once more to stress the sources of error inherent in all the steps and processes I have described. Coders make mistakes and errors of judgement, punching of cards leads to errors, and so does the tabulation, whether done by hand or machine. As with response errors, many of these errors may cancel out so that the net effect is small; but the surveyor is not entitled to *rely* on such cancellation.

I have already suggested that care taken in editing the schedules as they come into the office repays handsomely, and that the coding must equally be kept under check and supervision. Punching is invariably verified, so that the codes are punched twice (preferably by two different operators). Errors can, however, slip even through this mesh and it is always useful to check the punched data as they go through the machines.

[1] For a description of a mechanical device for counting, see a note in *Applied Statistics*, I, 2, 1952, p. 139.

The 1950 U.S. Census of Population provides a good example of a large-scale sample edit (see [112], Vol. I, Chapter 12), designed to check the coding and punching. There were questionnaires for 150 mn. persons, 40 mn. dwelling units and 6 mn. farms and a total of some 250 mn. punched cards. Errors were inevitable but editing by complete verification—as in some previous Censuses—would have been prohibitively expensive. Nor did there seem to be any point in aiming for perfection. The methods of industrial quality control were therefore adopted, the aim being to check on the quality of the *process* rather than of the final *product*. This is an important distinction, familiar in the industrial field. In survey terminology the aim was not to ensure that every questionnaire was 100 or 90 or 80 per cent accurate, but to detect those coders or punchers whose work consistently fell below a given level of accuracy, and then to dismiss or re-train them. Inaccurate questionnaires occasionally get through such a sieve but this process control ensures that, on average, the data will reach the desired level of accuracy.

Sampling in the analysis

This is the most convenient point for referring to the possibility of basing the analysis on only a sample of the results. If, for example, results are needed quickly, a sample of the schedules can be used to produce preliminary results. The 1951 Census of Population in Great Britain is an important example of this.

But quite apart from the pressure of time, it is sometimes sufficient, for the precision required, to analyse only a sample of the responses. It might seem that, in such a case, the information should have been *collected* only from a sample of the required size in the first place, but there are obstacles to this. One cannot always decide in advance how much accuracy is going to be required for each question; and even if this can be decided, it may be difficult to predict how big a sample will need to be analysed to produce that accuracy. Only when some of the data are available can this be seen and one may then still achieve some economy by only analysing a sample of returns. Apart from all this, a sample analysis can give very useful guidance for planning the final analysis and is often sufficient when the researcher decides on special studies of the survey material long after the main analyses are over.

Computations

This is not the place to discuss methods of computation, but the importance of computational checks may usefully be stressed. Some of the computations may be done on punched-card machines, but most will be entrusted to computors equipped with desk machines.

Their tasks will range from simple percentaging to computations involving a complicated series of steps. The calculation of standard errors, for instance, typically involves a long series of operations and, while nothing complicated is involved in any single step, the chain as a whole is complex. A good deal then depends on the analyst's skill in laying out the computations and instructions.

However, human computors inevitably make mistakes and it is therefore wise to check their work, the more so since errors made towards the end of the analysis are likely to have particularly serious effects. An odd recording or punching error made in the early stages is quite likely to cancel out with others and be swamped in the final results; but an error made in the analysis will tend to affect aggregates, not just the individual observations, and this is much more serious. All in all, every precaution to check the computations must be taken. Whether this is done by making computors do each job twice or by having it repeated by others (clearly a better check) is a matter of preference and resources. The best check of all is to use two different methods of arriving at a result. The analysis, too, can usefully be designed so as to give cross checks. If a large number of computors and operations have to be checked, quality control techniques similar to those already mentioned are applicable.

NOTES ON READING

1. Detailed practical instructions on the processes described in this chapter are given by PARTEN [202] and in a paper by BOYAJY, BARRY, KUENSTLER and PATON [17].

2. The literature on coding—apart from the general text-books—is small, but two useful papers can be mentioned. One, by MISS HARRIS [113], described the work of the Government Social Survey coding section which she directs; the other, by DOWNHAM [59], of the British Market Research Bureau, discusses coding problems in the light of commercial experience.

3. Qualitative coding is discussed by GOODE and HATT [97], by JAHODA, DEUTSCH and COOK [129] and by CARTWRIGHT in FESTINGER and KATZ [78]. All these deal with content analysis, and the last gives an excellent account of applications. Other references on content analysis are LASSWELL, LEITES and associates [152] and BERELSON and LAZARSFELD [7.]

4. On tabulation, both the references in (1) are useful. YATES [291], in Chapter 5, gives a thorough account of machine methods, punched card layout and so on. Useful papers are those by MANDEVILLE [170] and KEMPTHORNE [137]. BROWN, HOUTHAKKER and PRAIS [23] discuss the uses of electronic machines in relation to economic statistics.

5. A literature on checking and verification in the processing stages is gradually being built up. Most of it so far derives from the U.S. Bureau of the Census. Readers are referred to HANSEN, HURWITZ and MADOW [112], Vol. I, Chapter 12; HANSEN [109], VOIGHT and KRIESBERG [278], DEMING, TEPPING and GEOFFREY [53] and DEMING and GEOFFREY [52].

CHAPTER 15

ANALYSIS, INTERPRETATION AND PRESENTATION

15.1. Analysis and Interpretation

WE HAVE now reached the concluding stages of the survey. The data obtained from or about respondents have been edited and coded and the first steps of summarisation, usually a matter of constructing basic tables, have been taken. What follows is in many ways the most skilled task of all, the analysis and interpretation of the results.[1] Certainly it is a task calling for the researcher's own judgement and skill, not one to be delegated to assistants. The routine of analysis may not be difficult, but properly to guide it and the accompanying interpretation, requires a familiarity with the background of the survey and with all its stages, such as only the survey director himself is likely to possess.

These final stages of a survey are the least easy to discuss in general terms. No two surveys are alike in their problems of analysis and interpretation and the only rules one can lay down with any confidence are those of statistical methodology; these, however, are the province of statistical text-books[2] and I shall confine myself here to discussing the general approach to survey analysis.

To begin with, let me distinguish four different aspects of this approach:

(1) Analysis of survey material does not necessarily have to be statistical. To the extent that interest centres on the individual case rather than on the characteristics of the aggregate, non-quantitative methods of analysis and evaluation may be preferred; and even in surveys concerned chiefly with the latter,

[1] In fact analysis and tabulation proceed hand in hand but, as explained in Chapter 14, it is convenient to discuss them separately.
[2] See some suggestions at the end of Chapter 5.

288

such methods can play some part. However, I shall here confine myself to quantitative methods since, in large-scale surveys at least, they are the most important part of analysis.

(2) Much of what is usually called analysis is a matter of working out statistical distributions, constructing diagrams and calculating simple measures like averages, measures of dispersion, percentages, correlation coefficients and so forth. In a sense, analysis is too sophisticated a word for this activity: statistical description would be a better term, since all one is doing is to describe the features of the survey aggregate.

(3) Statistical description in this sense is, however, only one part of survey analysis. Inference—in the widest meaning of the word—is the other. One kind of inference is brought into play whenever the survey data are based upon a sample of the population about which conclusions are to be drawn. The researcher then has the problem of estimating the population characteristics from those of the sample and also of estimating sampling errors.

(4) Problems of inference arise also in a different context. It is one thing to work out a measure of correlation between two variables covered in a survey, it is quite another to seek an explanation by analytical methods of how this demonstrated relationship comes about. The use of complicated statistical techniques in surveys often stems from the desire to establish and interpret multi-variate relationships.

Statistical description

Here the term "analysis" will be taken to cover statistical description as well as inference in the above sense. The ordinary methods of describing survey data are quite straightforward. The schedule reproduced on p. 215, for instance, consists of 29 questions (including the sub-questions) and was answered by about 5,000 people. Each completed schedule can thus be looked upon as a series of 29 observations denoting the traits of that particular respondent: whether or not he has a paid job; whether he gets to work on foot, by bicycle, motor-car, . . . ; whether he lives at home, as a lodger . . . . . ; and so forth. Survey analysis begins typically by taking these traits one, two or possibly three at a time, and showing how the respondents are distributed on them. One might start by constructing a *frequency distribution* of the answers for each question (i.e. a table stating how frequently each answer was given). It might show, for instance, that 1,250 of the respondents get to work on foot, 500 on a bicycle, 50 by motor-cycle, 500 by car and 2,700 by public transport. The next step might be to convert these into proportions (e.g. 1250/5000 = 0·25) or percentages (e.g. 1250 × 100/5000 = 25 per cent) and this will virtually exhaust the information to be squeezed out of the answers to this question, at any rate if it is treated in isolation.

If the answers take a numerical form (in technical language, if one is dealing with a *variable* rather than an *attribute* question), one can go further. Q. 8 (*b*), on the same schedule, asked respondents, who said they had been to the pictures in the last seven days, how often they had gone during this period. The "Don't know" category apart, the answers would be in numerical form. The first step again would be to tabulate how many people said "once", "twice" and so forth, in fact to make a frequency distribution. The frequencies could then be converted to proportions or percentages as above, but one might also want some measure of *average*, of what is typical of this sample of respondents. Several kinds of average are available and the researcher must decide which is most suitable to his purpose. Once an average has been calculated, the question arises how representative a figure it is—that is, how closely the answers are bunched around it. Are most of them very close to it or is there a wide range of variation? This calls for one of the several *measures of dispersion*, and the choice between them again demands judgement.

These are the most elementary tools of statistical description, and a glance through a selection of survey reports will show that analysis often does not go beyond distributions, percentages, averages and measures of dispersion, supplemented by suitable diagrams.

This does not of course mean that such analysis proceeds necessarily by taking one variable or question at a time. Quite the contrary; usually it will be found to involve cross-classifications and consequently a study of relationships. The researcher wants to know whether the people who vote Labour are also those, on the whole, who think that the National Health Service is a good thing; whether those who go to the cinema a great deal spend less time watching television than those who go rarely; whether there is evidence of an association between a person's education and the newspapers he reads; whether the proportion of households owning a car increases with household size. In short, he is interested in whether the possession of one attribute is related to the possession of another, or several other attributes.

In its most elementary form the study of relationships may go no further than "breaking down" the sample by attribute *x* before analysing by attribute *y*. Lydall states that, in the *Oxford Institute of Statistics Savings Survey*, "Almost all the items were cross-tabulated with at least four of the classification attributes, such as region, size of town, age, sex and occupation of head, number of persons in the income unit and gross income group" [165, p. 230]. Breakdowns of this type are an invariable part of survey analysis and one barely thinks of them as studies of relationships.

Within such basic breakdowns there may be further cross-classification of variables, and measures like percentages, averages etc. can be computed as means of comparison. But, over and above these, one often wishes to have a measure of the *degree and direction* of the relationship between two (or more) variables. For this purpose again, several types of measure are available and the survey analyst intending to use one of the several coefficients must be familiar with its characteristics and sure of its suitability. Their computational simplicity easily misleads; and anyone who blindly applies the textbook formulae without understanding their limitations or the assumptions underlying them can quickly fall into error.

Although it is measures of statistical description like those mentioned above that predominate in survey reports, they far from exhaust the possibilities of analysis. Anyone who has glanced at the volumes on *The American Soldier* [251], the English studies on social mobility [92], the report on criminological prediction by Mannheim and Wilkins [173] or the monograph on methods of analysing family budget data by Prais and Houthakker [210], to name only four examples, will not need to be convinced that statistical techniques more intricate than percentages, averages and the like play their part in survey analysis. This is not the place to enumerate all such techniques or describe their mechanism, but it is worth looking at the two situations which most commonly cause complications in the analysis —the making of inferences from sample to population and the examination of multi-variate relationships. Problems of analysis and interpretation will be discussed in conjunction, since in practice the two are barely separable.

Population estimates and sampling errors

To the extent that the survey data are based on a sample of the population about which conclusions are to be drawn, one has to decide (*a*) how to make estimates from sample to population and (*b*) how to estimate the sampling errors. Both tasks are often a good deal more complicated than the introductory presentation of Chapters 5 and 6 might suggest.

In the first place, we should recall the many simplifying assumptions made in those chapters. I confined myself to large samples and discussed the theory in relation to only two or three—albeit the most important—statistics, like averages and proportions. Although the basic ideas apply equally outside these bounds, the techniques and computations soon become more complicated. Furthermore, when

comparisons between different sections of the population (technically called domains) are to be made, and especially when these
domains cut across the strata of the sample design, estimation and
sampling error procedures become complicated (see Yates [291],
Chapter 9 for a discussion of this class of problems).

Over and above all this, I simplified the explanations by the
assumption that *unbiased* estimation procedures were used throughout. This is a reasonable assumption for samples of simple design
such as are often used in social research surveys. If the over-all
sampling fraction is kept constant throughout, proportions and
averages calculated from the sample give unbiased estimates of the
corresponding population values. But, as soon as the designs become
more complex, estimation procedures become less obvious and supplementary data external to the survey can be increasingly useful for
improving the estimates. The estimation of sampling errors can
equally be very intricate when a complex design is used, i.e. when
there are several sampling stages, phases, stratifications and varying
probabilities of selection. The reader is referred to Chapters 6 and 7
in Yates' book [291] for a thorough technical presentation. Suffice it
here to stress once more that, with random samples, such errors can
be estimated from the sample itself, that their estimation can be
simplified if the sample is designed with this object in mind and that,
in any case, every report of a random sample survey should give an
indication of the sampling errors affecting the results.

Two more points about population inferences can usefully be referred to here: the generality claimed for the findings and the interpretation of significance test results. There is never any justification
for claiming more generality for survey-findings than is their due.
Often the population coverage actually achieved differs from that
initially intended: the sampling frame may have turned out to be incomplete or substantial population segments may have been lost
through non-response. Whatever the reason, the resultant loss in
coverage, as far as it is known to the researcher, must be acknowledged and the conclusions generalised only to the population
actually covered.

Similarly, when a survey has for reasons of convenience or lack of
resources been confined to, say, one town, the researcher must re-
sist the temptation of generalising to the whole country—even if the
town appears to be fairly typical on various relevant factors. The
localisation of a research project is often highly desirable but the researcher must be prepared to accept the consequent limitation in
his final conclusions.

Sometimes the research approach has altogether excluded the possibility of statistical sampling. This was so with Zweig [295], who

conducted several hundred interviews in public houses, parks and the like and who could hardly have used random selection. One could not deny that he managed to cover a wide range of workers, yet no strict rules of statistical generalisation were applicable. All one can ask in such a case is that the investigator should be aware of any major representativeness in his collection of cases, and that his claims of generality should err on the side of caution.

Many survey analyses entail the comparison of results for different parts of the sample—e.g. the proportion of men who smoke with the proportion of women who smoke — and if both results are based on samples, the comparison must take account of the sampling error affecting each of them. In statistical language, one has to test the significance of the difference between the proportions—how likely it is that the observed difference is due to sampling errors alone.

The mechanism of significance tests was explained in Section 5.5 and my purpose here is to comment on the interpretation of their results. To say that a difference (whether between two sample statistics or between one such statistic and a parameter fixed by hypothesis) is not statistically significant—at a given confidence level—is tantamount to saying that it can be accounted for by sampling errors alone; in terms of the example, that the difference between the proportions of the two sexes who smoke is no larger than would be expected as a result of chance sampling fluctuations alone. A statement about statistical significance is therefore a statement about sampling errors and, since sampling errors are a function of sample size, such a statement also is a function of the sample sizes involved. The larger the samples (and therefore, other things being equal, the smaller the sampling errors) the greater the chance that a difference of a given size will be found statistically significant.

This is one reason why the results of significance tests should be interpreted with caution and understanding. When a test produces a negative result—not statistically significant—this does *not* necessarily mean that the effect does not exist in the population, i.e. that between the populations of men and women from which the samples were selected there is no difference in smoking proportions. It means only that these particular samples have failed to demonstrate a difference. This is a comment on the size of these samples and their so-called "power" for showing up this difference as significant, as much as it is on the size of the difference actually observed. It is vital to the interpretation of significance tests to know what this power is. An example of how it can be estimated will be found in the paper by Moser and Stuart [194], describing the results of an experiment on sampling methods. When significance tests were carried out on the differences between the results obtained from various types of sample, most of them gave negative results. Did this mean that there *were* no differences between these methods or was it only that the experiment was insufficiently powerful to disclose them? The problem was attacked by asking: "How large must the difference (between methods) have been in order to have had a reasonable chance of detection by the experiment?" "Reasonable chance" was taken to be 50 per cent. The calculations showed that the differences would have had to be much larger than those observed to have had a "reasonable chance" of detection, which means that the experiment was insufficiently sensitive for this particular task.

There is another reason why caution is necessary in interpreting significance tests. An effect that has been shown to be statistically significant may yet be so small in magnitude that it is of no substantive interest to the researcher. Conversely, if the test has a negative result, he ought not to conclude that the effect has no importance or reality. In other words, statistical significance and substantive (e.g. sociological, political, medical, economic) significance are not the same thing. In practice the two are often confused: effects are written off as unimportant simply because they have not "come up" significant or are given great prominence because they have.[1] In order to keep a clear distinction between statistical and substantive significance, the former adjective should always accompany statements based on significance test results.

I hope by these few comments to have warned against too sweeping an interpretation of significance test results. Perhaps an even more general warning is not out of place. There is noticeable in the social science literature—possibly in other fields too—an altogether excessive emphasis on significance tests, to the detriment of the estimation of the magnitude of effects. When all is said and done, what is usually of importance is the magnitude of effects (e.g. the size of the difference between proportions in the population) rather than a test of whether the difference is statistically significant or not. Concentration on the latter question sometimes leads researchers to close their report when the tests have been made, not progressing to the generally more important task of estimation.

Multi-variate relationships

Many uses of relatively difficult statistical techniques in surveys stem from situations where a number of the variables (questions)

---

[1] Incidentally, it is well to remember that if one is making a large number of tests, some of them will always turn up statistically significant by chance. If one is testing at the 5 per cent level, about 1 in 20 would be expected to do so. If the proportion of significant results is found to be little or no more than this, one should not pay much attention to the few positive findings.

covered by the survey have to be considered in conjunction. One may wish to combine several of the observations for each individual into some kind of an index or scale value (see Section 12.6) or, on the basis of a number of his characteristics, to allocate him to one of several groups or to make a prediction about him. Perhaps most important, in order to interpret an established relationship between A and B, that is to get closer to a cause-effect explanation than is possible by merely measuring correlation, one would need to take into account simultaneously one or more other variables. These are some of the occasions for multi-variate methods, and a few general comments on them will be useful.

Let us imagine that we wish to combine several of the observations obtained for each survey unit into some kind of a score. A simple illustration of this occurred in Cauter and Downham's *The Communication of Ideas* [32]. Here the authors sought an index to measure a person's participation in ten "communication activities"—e.g. church-going, cinema-going, radio-listening, reading and so on. They decided on a system for scoring the frequency of a person's participation in any one activity and for combining these scores into a participation index.

The problems of constructing such indices are essentially similar to those encountered in attitude scaling (see Section 12.6). First, one has to decide what are the appropriate indicators of whatever it is one is trying to measure. What, for instance, is an appropriate indicator of a person's social class? Occupation? Income? Whether or not he possesses a car? Common sense will suggest many possible indicators and from them a limited number will have to be chosen. The choice can be governed by statistical techniques, resulting in a combination which is in some stated sense the "best" index of social class. This does not necessarily measure what the sociologist means by the term, but that may be, and is often claimed to be, strictly immeasurable. All one can do is to decide on a combination of measurable indicators that can be regarded as a reasonable approximation.[1] When this is done, the relevant data (each person's occupation, income and so forth) are collected and the various items combined into an index or scale value. In this combination it is the weights that are crucial, and methods for determining them range from arbitrary choices to the sophisticated statistical means used in multiple regression analysis

---

[1] See Downham [58] and Wilkins [287] for some discussions of indices of "social class". Mathematically-minded readers may also like to familiarise themselves with the technique of "discriminant analysis" described in most advanced textbooks. This is a method of so combining a number of observations for each individual that he can be allocated most appropriately to one of a number of groups. Its use for allocating sample members to social class categories is discussed by Gales [87].

or discriminant analysis. The standard text-books give technical accounts of these methods.

The important and obvious feature common to all these indices, scaling methods, multiple regression and discriminant analysis and so forth, is that they utilise simultaneously a number of the characteristics of each survey unit, thus getting away from "the one trait at a time" type of analysis. In looking through completed schedules one is sometimes struck by the distinct *pattern* of answers. The people who read certain papers also seem to tend to go to the cinema a good deal, to smoke a good deal, to be of a certain age, education, sex and so on. One then feels that it would be illuminating to treat the schedule, not as a series of traits but as a unit, to typify a certain kind of person. Such a pattern cannot be brought out by tabulation alone, for even these few questions would demand a six-way table. There are two possible solutions to this problem. One is to follow the "case-study approach". This is often—fallaciously—talked of as if it were a special way of collecting information, but its distinguishing feature is simply that each respondent (group or institution etc.) is looked upon as a unit and that the analysis aims to retain this unitary nature of the individual case and to emphasise the relationship between its various attributes. Generally this is achieved by "writing-up" the material in mainly non-quantified form.

The other solution, leading in the opposite direction, is to try to express the pattern by summarising a number of the observations into a scale value or index, the obvious advantage being that such an index reflects simultaneously several of the respondent's characteristics. Yet there is always some risk in this. In the example of the preceding paragraph, although there would be little technical difficulty in combining the six variables into some sort of index, the result would be sociologically meaningless. An index or scale must start out from a concise conception of what it is one is trying to measure and the most crucial step in its construction is the choice of relevant indicators.

One further point on the use of refined methods of analysis may be made. It sometimes seems that, where previously percentages or averages represented the height of statistical sophistication, the reader of a survey report must now be prepared to grapple with internal canonical analysis and discriminant functions. In their place refined techniques are invaluable, but their glamour—a glamour which percentages and averages altogether lack—may tempt researchers to use them too readily. The use of refined methods of analysis on crude data—as those of surveys often are—is to be deprecated, since it gives the results a quite misleading appearance of precision. Researchers must also avoid the danger of paying more attention to the mathematical requirements of a scaling or other analytical device, than to making sure that the end-product means what it is supposed to mean. Refined analytical methods can be an invaluable part of the survey process, but their application needs much care.

Interpreting relationships[1]

The study of relationships between two or more variables is straightforward so long as one is content merely to state the extent and direction of the association. But as soon as one tries to investigate its meaning, to make cause-effect inferences, difficulties arise. There is no problem in showing, by tables or diagrams, whether there is a correlation between, say, the incomes of respondents (I) and the extent (measured by a suitable index) of their Conservatism (C); or in expressing the degree of this correlation by a suitable measure. But what then? What does such a measure tell us? The statistician's answer is clear. It tells us to what extent the two variables move together—an increase or decrease in one being associated, on average, with an increase (or decrease) in the other; it tells us nothing about cause and effect.[2]

How, then, would a positive correlation between I and C be interpreted? Does it mean that people develop pro-Conservative leanings as their incomes rise, perhaps because they come increasingly into contact with Conservatively-minded persons or perhaps because they get more and more satisfied with the *status quo*. Or does it mean that being a Conservative helps people to get on in the world and thus leads to higher incomes? Which is cause and which effect? Perhaps neither explanation is the true one; perhaps the two variables are not causally related at all and only appear to be so because of the influence of a third variable? If, for instance, increasing age (A) leads people to be both more Conservative and to have a higher earning capacity, the real explanation would be that I and C are related because each is causally influenced by A.

Whatever the true explanation of this relationship may be, the statistical measure of correlation offers no clue to it. It merely states that I and C are (or are not) correlated and, while researchers are perfectly entitled to offer their own interpretation as to cause and effect, it is quite fallacious to suppose that the correlation coefficient itself is supporting evidence.

[1] There is much more to the interpretation of relationships, as disclosed by survey data, than can be covered in this brief presentation. The reader is referred to the book by Hyman [123], the major part of which is given up to the complexities of interpreting multi-variate relationships.

[2] Before any conclusion is reached even about degree of association, the sampling error of the correlation coefficient would have to be taken into account. The significance of observed correlations can be tested by well-established methods.

There are two difficulties in bridging the gap between a measure of correlation and a cause-effect interpretation. The first is the difficulty of establishing a valid time sequence as regards the variables; the second is to eliminate the effects of other variables which may produce an apparent causal relationship where none exists (see the discussion in Section 1.5).

Our example clearly illustrates the *time-sequence* difficulty. Which came first, the Conservative viewpoint or the high income? If one could answer this, translating a correlation finding into a cause-effect conclusion would be less risky. If, for example, it could be established that *I* (or a high value of *I*) necessarily preceded *C*, one could rule out the possibility that *C* was a cause of *I*. It would still not follow that *I* caused *C*, because there might be disturbing variables; but at least one possibility would have been excluded.

Situations where the time-sequence is self-evident are relatively rare, and when, as in this example, one of the variables is an opinion-attribute, it becomes virtually impossible to establish. Only if one had kept people under investigation over a long period, would there be a chance of determining when their opinions changed and of assessing how these changes were related to income rises. The panel method can clearly be helpful in this respect. Researchers sometimes try to achieve the same end by retrospective questions, asking respondents to recollect what their views (or other characteristics) were at given times in the past; but this is not a reliable basis for cause-effect deductions.

The time-sequence problem is perhaps the lesser of the complications in interpreting relationships. The main headache is to try to think of, and if possible to eliminate, the *disturbing influence of other variables*. I suggested that the relationship between *I* and *C* above might arise through the influence on each of a third variable, *A*. This would not make the statistical correlation between *I* and *C* less real, but any causative explanation of it which omitted to take account of *A* would be spurious and misleading.

If we assume that *A* is the only complicating variable and that correlations have been found between *A* and *I*, and between *A* and *C*, as well as between *I* and *C*, there are several ways in which *A* might be confusing the issue. To see what they are, let us note how the three variables might be linked causally. The arrow signifies the direction of a cause-effect relation.[1]

---

[1] I exclude cases of the type $C \searrow \atop I \nwarrow A$, in which the fact that *I* is also correlated with *A* in no way affects the causal relation between *C* and *I*. I also exclude cases like $A{\rightarrow}I{\rightarrow}C$ and $A{\rightarrow}I{\leftrightarrow}C$ which are more complex versions of the basic forms above.

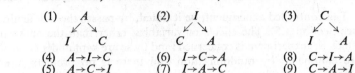

Since A (increasing age) can hardly be the effect of I or C, it is reasonable to exclude the schemes (2), (3), (6), (7), (8) and (9) (although with different "third" variables, some of these schemes might have been valid). This leaves us with the following possible explanations:

(1) The relationship between income and Conservatism is simply due to the fact that each is an effect of a third factor, age.

(4) Growing old enables people to earn more and this leads to Conservative views.

(5) Growing old leads to Conservatism and this to higher incomes.

Schemes (4) and (5) have this in common, that the third variable A precedes the other two, so that it, rather than either I or C, is the ultimate cause. More correctly, A is the cause of C (in case (4)) but the causation *operates via* I, while in case (5), A is the cause of I, the causation operating via C.

In scheme (1), A confuses the issue because it is related both to I and C, between which there is no causal connection. A *explains* why I and C are correlated. If one were to classify the respondents according to A into two groups—say people under 45, and 45 and over—one would find that, *within* each group, the relationship between C and I would tend to disappear.[1] A has served to explain the original relationship. If, on the other hand, the relationship persisted within the different A classes, then A would not be the explanation. This is a way, then, of testing whether an apparent causal relationship is real or spurious.[2] In practice, there are usually a number of potential explanatory variables and, ideally, they should all be tried, if possible in combination. But this quickly leads to very small numbers in the cells.[3]

The real life situation is immensely more complicated than the above because, generally, not one but a large number of potential disturbing variables ought rightly to be considered. To collect the necessary information is the least difficulty; the real problem is to re-construct the time sequence of the variables and their intricate inter-relationships.

[1] There are of course statistical methods—partial correlation and regression—to deal with this general situation.

[2] A still different situation is typified by scheme (7)—which, in this case, is meaningless. If A could be the effect of I, and the cause of C, it would in fact be an "intervening" variable, which helps to *interpret* how I manages to cause C.

[3] See Keyfitz [141] for an example of a rigorous investigation of the individual effects of several variables studied simultaneously.

The controlled experiment, be it noted, by-passes these difficulties (see Section 1.5). The effects of variables, other than the ones with which the experiment is concerned (and these are kept under control), are eliminated by randomisation and there is no problem about time-sequence. The troubles we have been concerned with here arise through trying to sort out these confusing factors *after the event*. Even if one has studied the disturbing effects of $n-1$ variables, it is always possible that the nth, which has not been thought of or for which one lacks data, is making a spurious effect appear real. Conclusions drawn from *ex post facto* analysis are necessarily more speculative, less confident, than those based on experiments.

Concluding remarks on interpretation

"Interpretation" of survey results is often no more than a common-sense reading of simple tables and explanation of simple descriptive measures. Where sample data are involved, this interpretation is set in the context of sampling errors and, where complicated relationships are concerned, it may be quite intricate. But whatever the nature of the data, the task of interpretation falls squarely on to the shoulders of the researcher himself. Some research workers take the view that it is their job merely to present their results in logical and convenient form, leaving it to the readers to draw their own conclusions. For an enquiry like a Population Census this may be the only practicable course, but for the general run of surveys it seems to me entirely mistaken. Most readers of a research report, fellow-scientists or laymen, lack the time and perhaps the will-power to go through the tables and pick out the crucial results. But even if they had both, it would be wrong to leave the interpretation entirely to them. There is after all more to a research than can be seen from the tables, and the researcher in interpreting his results is inevitably—and rightly—influenced by all that has gone before, by his acquaintance with the raw material behind the figures and by his own judgement. While every reader is entitled to draw his own conclusions, the writer of the survey report should not shirk the duty of giving his own.

Nor need he view his task too narrowly. The researcher who cautiously confines his conclusions to those strictly justified by the data may be safe from criticism, but he is not making his own full potential contribution. There is surely room in every research report for the research worker's own ideas and speculations, even if he cannot offer chapter and verse to substantiate them. In the course of his work he must inevitably develop theories and hunches, and so long as he makes clear that they are no more than this, it is a pity to omit publishing them with the results. As Cochran and his colleagues write in a methodological review of the first Kinsey report: "We are convinced that unsubstantiated assertions are not, in themselves, inappropriate in a scientific study. In any complex field, where many questions remain unresolved, the accumulated insight of an experienced worker frequently merits recording when no documentation can be given. However, the author who values his reputation for objectivity will take pains to warn the reader, frequently and repetitiously, whenever an unsubstantiated conclusion is being represented and will choose his words with the greatest care" [38, p. 707].

15.2. Presentation

The final step of a survey is to present its results, details of its methodology, any necessary background information and the conclusions drawn from the results, in some kind of report, the form of which will depend on the type of reader for whom it is intended. A report written as a private document for the department or firm which sponsored the survey will emphasise different things, perhaps give less space to methodology, than one written by a social scientist and intended to interest fellow-experts. Either will be more formal and technical than a report issued for the general public.

The researcher must keep constantly in view the kind of readers he is writing for, the extent of their knowledge, the type of problem and question that is likely to be of interest to them and the kind of language to which they are accustomed. Whatever the likely audience, he will do well to try to avoid the jargon and style that has become common in social science writing. Other sciences suffer from the same danger, but at least their technical jargon is often in Latin and Greek —truly an advantage, for then the reader is at least never in doubt whether he is, or is not, managing to understand. With social science writing it is otherwise, for although the words used are in the main everyday ones, they are used in complicated contexts and often with specialised meanings. As a result there is sometimes confusion and often an appearance of pretentiousness and pomposity.

Typical of this is a sentence taken from an unnamed sociological work and quoted by Goode and Hatt [97, p. 366].

"These concepts can hold only for ranges of variation of circumstances not too large to invalidate the assumption that for practical purposes the particular constant relations between the values of analytical elements which these type concepts in the concrete case represent, will not be so unreal as to exceed an acceptable margin of error."

It may be that some social scientists can understand this passage without difficulty; more probably most of them would find it unintelligible or confusing. What is more important, anyone unaccustomed to the social sciences and venturing to read in this field would soon be discouraged by such passages. To the report writer, clarity of exposition must be the first objective, taking priority over all else, including elegance of expression and style.

An allied duty which he must keep constantly in view is to translate technicalities into language which will be understood by the reader primarily interested in the substantive (e.g. sociological, economic, medical, . . .) results of the survey. The report writer has no right to confront the reader with numerous standard errors, significance-test results, correlation matrices and the like without telling him what these results mean in terms of the subject-matter of the survey. Whether these technicalities are put in the text or in an appendix is a matter of taste; what is crucial is that—except, of course, if the object of the research was primarily to study these techniques—they are entirely subsidiary to the presentation and interpretation of the results in economic, sociological, medical, . . . terms.

As regards the content of survey reports, I cannot do better than quote almost in their entirety the *Recommendations Concerning The Preparation Of Reports Of Sampling Surveys* issued by the United Nations Statistical Office in 1950 [272].[1] These authoritative recommendations arose from the discussions of the U.N. Sub-Commission on Statistical Sampling. Except for the sections on technical sampling matters, they apply broadly to all social surveys.

The United Nations Recommendations

1. General Description of the Survey

A general description of the survey should be given for those who are primarily interested in the results rather than in the technical statistical aspects of the sample design, execution, and analysis. These technical aspects should be described in fuller detail in separate sections or appendices; the ground to be covered has been indicated in the subsequent sections of this memorandum. The general description should include information on the following points:

  a. *Statement of Purposes of the Survey:* A general indication should be given of the purposes of the survey and the ways in which it had been expected that the results would be utilised.

  b. *Description of the Material Covered:* An exact description should be given of the geographical region and the categories of material covered by the survey. In a survey of a human population, for example, it is necessary to specify whether such categories as hotel residents, institutions (e.g. boarding houses,

---

[1] My thanks are due to the Statistical Office of the United Nations for permission to quote these extracts.

sanatoriums), vagrants, military personnel, were included. The reporter should guard against any possible misapprehension regarding the coverage of the survey.

c. *Nature of the Information Collected:* This should be reported in considerable detail, including a statement of items of information collected but not reported on. The inclusion of copies of the schedules and relevant parts of the instructions used in the survey (including special rules for coding and classifying) is often of value. If this is impracticable, it may be possible to make available a limited number of copies which may be obtained on request.

d. *Method of Collecting the Data:* Whether by interviewers, investigators, mail etc.

e. *Sampling Method:* An indication should be given in general terms of the type of sampling adopted, the size of the sample, the proportion it forms of the material covered, and arrangements for follow-ups, if any, in cases of non-response.

f. *Repetition:* State whether the survey is an isolated one undertaken without intention of repetition, or is one of a series of similar surveys.

g. *Date and Duration:* The date or period of time to which the data refer should be stated, and also the starting date and period taken for the field work.

h. *Accuracy:* A general indication of the accuracy attained should be given.

i. *Cost:* An indication should be given of the cost of the survey, under such headings as preliminary work, field investigations, analysis etc.

j. *Assessment:* The extent to which the purposes of the survey were fulfilled should be assessed.

k. *Responsibility:* The name of the organisation sponsoring the survey should be stated; also the name of the one responsible for conducting it.

l. *References:* References should be given to any published reports or papers relating to the survey.

2. Design of the Survey

The design of the survey should be carefully specified.[1]

---

[1] There follows a section defining the various terms connected with sample design—frame, elementary units, sample-units, sample, domain of study, block of domains, field of enquiry, stratification, uniform and variable sampling fractions, multiple stratification, multi-stage sampling, multi-phase sampling, interpenetrating samples, composite sampling schemes, successive surveys, pilot and exploratory surveys.

3. Method of Selecting Sample-Units

The reporter should describe the procedure used in selecting sample-units, and if it is not a random selection he should indicate the evidence on which he relies for adopting an alternative procedure. Purposive selection and quota sampling cannot be regarded as equivalent to random sampling.

A process is properly described as random if to each unit has been initially assigned a determinate probability of being selected. One expeditious way of effecting a random selection is by the use of random sampling numbers; equally, with more labour, this may be done by any of the apparatus used in games of chance. Systematic selection is often used when the person responsible for the planning of the survey is satisfied that it is in practice equivalent to a random selection in the respects required. In such cases he accepts personal responsibility for the judgement on which his plan is based.

Ordinarily all units within a given stratum are assigned an equal probability of selection, sampling being "without replacement", i.e. no unit is included more than once in a sample. In certain cases it may be advantageous, or convenient, to select the sample-units with probabilities proportional to some known quantitative characteristic of the units, such as size; if more than one unit is to be selected from the population (or from individual strata) exact probabilities proportional to size can only be simply attained if the sampling is "with replacement", units selected twice or more being counted twice or more.

The methods of calculating the population estimates appropriate to samples selected with probability proportional to size differ from those for samples selected with uniform probability.

4. Personnel and Equipment

It is desirable to give an account of the organisation of the personnel employed in collecting, processing and tabulating the primary data, together with information regarding their previous training and experience. Arrangements for training, inspection and supervision of the staff should be explained; as also should methods of checking the accuracy of the primary data at the point of collection. A brief mention may be made of the equipment used.

5. Statistical Analysis and Computational Procedure

The statistical methods followed in the compilation of the final summary tables from the primary data should be described. If any more elaborate processes of estimation than simple totals and means have been used, the methods followed should be explained, the relevant formulae being reproduced where necessary.

The steps taken to ensure the elimination of gross errors from the primary data (by scrutiny, sample checks etc.) and to ensure the accuracy of the subsequent calculations should be indicated in detail. Mention should be made of the methods of processing the data (punched cards, hand tabulation etc.) including methods used for the control of errors.

If a critical statistical analysis of the results embodied in the final summary tables has been made, it is important that the methods followed should be fully described. A numerical example is often of assistance in making the procedure clear.

It frequently happens that the quantities of which estimates are required do not correspond exactly to those observed; in a crop-cutting survey, for example, the yields of the sample plots give estimates of the amount of grain etc., in the standing crop, whereas the final yields will be affected by losses at harvest. In such cases adjustments may have to be made, the amount of which is estimated by subsidiary observations, or otherwise. Account should be given of the nature of these adjustments and the ways in which they were derived.

The amount of tabular matter included in the report, and the extent to which the results are discussed, will depend on the purposes of the report. Mention should be made of further tabulations which have been prepared but are not included in the report, and also of critical statistical analyses which failed to yield results of interest and which are therefore not considered to be worth reporting in detail.

The inclusion of ancillary information which is not of immediate relevance to the report but which will enable subsequent workers to carry out critical statistical analyses which appear to them to be of interest should be carefully considered. If, for example, in addition to the class means of each main classification of the data, the sub-class numbers (but not the means) of the various two-way classifications are reported, a study of the effects of each of the main classifications freed from the effects of all other classifications can be made (provided the effects are additive) without further reference to the original material.

6. Costing Analysis

An important reason for the use of sampling (instead of complete enumeration) is lower cost. Information on costs is therefore of great interest. Costs should be classified so far as possible under such heads as preparation (showing separately the cost of pilot studies), field work, supervision, processing, analysis, and overhead costs. In addition, labour costs in man-weeks of different grades of staff, and also time required for interview and journey time and transport costs between interviews, should be given. The compilation of such information, although often inconvenient, is usually worth undertaking as it may suggest substantive economies in the planning of future surveys. Efficient design demands a knowledge of the various components of cost, as well as of the components of variance.

7. Accuracy of the Survey

a. *Precision as Indicated by the Random Sampling Errors Deducible from the Survey:* Standard deviations of sample-units should be given in addition to such standard errors (of means, totals etc.) as are of interest. The process of deducing these estimates of error should be made entirely clear. This process will depend intimately on the design of the sample survey. An analysis of the variances of the sampling units into such components as appears to be of interest for the planning of future surveys, is also of great value.

The term "sampling error" has been used to denote both sampling standard error and limits of sampling error at some assigned level of probability, e.g. twice the standard error corresponding approximately to the 1 in 20 level of probability. The sampling standard errors and the limits of sampling error should be clearly differentiated and the multiples used in the latter should be specified.

b. *Degree of Agreement Observed Between Independent Investigators Covering the Same Material:* Such comparison will be possible only when interpenetrating samples have been used, or checks have been imposed on part of the survey. It is only by these means that the survey can provide an objective test of possible personal equations (differential bias among the investigators).

c. *Other Non-Sampling Errors:* Errors which are common to all investigators, and indeed any constant component of error (or "bias") in the recorded information, will not be included in the estimates of the random sampling errors deducible from the survey results. Another source of error is that due to incorrect determinations of the adjustments (referred to in Section 5) arising from observation of quantities which do not correspond exactly to the quantities of which estimates are required.

The existence and possible effects of such errors on the accuracy of the results, and of incompleteness in the recorded information (e.g., non-response, lack of records, whether covering the whole of the survey or particular areas or categories of the material), should therefore be fully discussed. Any special checks instituted to control and determine the magnitude of these errors should be described, and the results reported.

d. *Accuracy, Completeness and Adequacy of the Frame:* The accuracy of the frame can and should be checked and corrected automatically in the course of the enquiry, and such checks afford useful guidance for the future. Its completeness and adequacy cannot be judged by internal evidence alone. Thus, complete omission of a geographic region or the complete or partial omission of any particular class of the material intended to be covered cannot be discovered by the enquiry itself and auxiliary investigations have often to be made. These should be put on record, indicating the extent of inaccuracy which may be ascribable to such defects.

e. *Comparison with other Sources of Information:* Every reasonable effort should be made to provide outside comparisons with other sources of information. Such comparisons should be reported along with the other results, and the significant differences should be discussed. The object of this is not to throw light on the sampling error, since a well designed survey provides adequate internal estimates of such errors, but rather to gain knowledge of biases, and other non-random errors.

f. *Efficiency:* The results of a survey often provide information which enables investigations to be made on the efficiency of the sampling designs, in relation to other sampling designs which might have been used in the survey. The results of any such investigations should be reported. To be fully relevant the relative costs of the different sampling methods must be taken into account when assessing the relative efficiency of different designs and intensities of sampling.

Such an investigation can be extended to consideration of the relation between the cost of carrying out surveys of different levels of accuracy and the losses resulting from errors in the estimates provided. This provides a basis for determining whether the survey was fully adequate for its purpose, or whether future surveys should be planned to give results of higher or lower accuracy.

g. The critical observations of the technicians in regard to any part of the survey should be given. These observations will help others to improve their operations.

Concluding remarks

These are the U.N. recommendations and it remains only to emphasise one or two of their points. Special attention should be given to paragraph (1a) above. The researcher himself may have been interested in the subject of the survey for so long that nothing seems to him more natural than to have undertaken the enquiry; but for the reader it is otherwise. He may genuinely wonder why anybody should want the information the survey has provided or why the subject should have been approached as it was. It is up to the surveyor fully to explain his purpose and approach.

The detail and form in which the results are presented vary with each survey and the report writer inexperienced in these matters should acquaint himself with principles of presenting statistical information: how to arrange tables, what symbols to use, how much accuracy to give in the figures, what diagrams to employ for different purposes and so on. Enlarging on Section 5 of the Recommendations, I would emphasise that non-quantified material has a useful place in every survey report. To many readers, statistical tables are dull and difficult to comprehend, and a certain amount of verbatim quotation of answers, as well as verbal summary of the tables, enlivens the report and makes it easier to digest.

The presentation of sampling errors sometimes causes awkwardness. To accompany each figure by its corresponding standard error satisfies the most rigorous requirements but hardly makes for easy reading. On the other hand, simply to give details of sample size (and standard deviations, where variables are concerned) and leave it to the reader to estimate any sampling errors he may be interested in, is to shirk one's duty and to impose an undeserved burden on the reader. There are some useful compromises. If the figures in the report are all proportions, one can print a simple two-way table, in which the columns represent, say, different values of the sample proportion and the rows different sample sizes. In the body of the table, values of the standard error for a particular confidence level can then be given. Ideally, standard error figures should be quoted for two or three confidence levels, so that the reader can take his choice. Guidance on interpretation should also be given.[1]

A more fundamental point arises in regard to the presentation of inconclusive or negative results, which workers tend to be reluctant to publish. It is as important to make known negative results as positive ones. However sure a researcher feels that his hypothesis is right, if the research results point clearly against it, he must say so. If the results are inconclusive, not pointing decisively in one direction or the other, it may be useful to future workers to be told so, since often there is some lesson to be learnt regarding the scale or design of the research. I do not suggest that it should be made a rule to publish the results of every research, but inconclusiveness does not seem to me

---

[1] See the I.P.A. readership survey [126] and also the report on the 1 per cent Sample analysis of the 1951 Census of Population [91].

necessarily an argument against publication. As Durbin and Stuart put it, in replying to a discussion on their paper on "Callbacks and clustering in sample surveys": "We are also against the suggestion that one should always wait until one feels able to deliver some kind of 'judgement' before publishing one's results. It is possible that the belief that such an obligation exists might account for the small proportion of the survey experience gained in this country which has been made available to the public. If any statement of principles is called for, we would say simply that a worker has a right to publish his findings and his inferences from them without assuming any judicial capacity" [68, p. 427].

But, of course, one of the researcher's main duties must always be to point out any limitations of his results. That he should state the sampling errors is obvious and has been emphasised repeatedly. But this is not all. As the final section of the U.N. recommendations well brings out, there are many other relevant questions: how complete was the coverage, how far did the achieved sample differ from that intended initially, how efficient was the design, what evidence was there of the size of response errors and so forth. Nor is it enough to evaluate the methods of the survey in general terms. The results on each individual question must be qualified in terms of what is known about errors caused by its wording, definitions, interpretation and so forth. As social researchers become more conscious of the accuracy or otherwise of their observations so research reports will give increasing space to reporting errors. This will be all to the good.

Research workers writing for fellow scientists are generally careful to emphasise limitations; indeed they sometimes fall over backwards to argue that what they have been doing is worthless. Particularly when writing for a general audience is the temptation to soft-pedal limitations strong; the writer feels that the significance of technical shortcomings will not be appreciated, and shortage of space further encourages him to skip them. There is little need to stress how serious such omissions can be. One need only think of the harmful effects that can follow if the results of researches into, say, preventive measures for tuberculosis or polio are carelessly translated into popular literature. The original report may have paid due attention to the limitations attending the results, but these limitations are soon lost in its translation for the general reader. This sort of risk makes the hesitation to publish inconclusive results understandable.

As an illustration of how, in the heat of the moment, survey reports can deviate from desirable standards, I quote one of the conclusions offered in the authoritative Social Science Research Council study of the 1948 U.S. Election forecasts:

"In interpreting the results of the pre-election polls and presenting them to the public, the pollsters went far beyond the bounds of sound reporting of the results of pre-election polls. They attempted the spectacular feat of predicting the winner without qualification. The presentation of the results gave the impression of certainty as to the outcome. The final releases carried very little indication of the limitations of polling and the tendency in past election forecasts to underestimate the Democratic vote. Statements of conditions under which different outcomes of the election might occur were dropped almost completely before the end of the campaign.

"The polls also failed to provide the public with sufficient information about the methods of poll operation to permit assessment of the degree of confidence that could be placed in the predictions. The number of cases used, the type of sampling employed, the corrections introduced, the way returns from individuals who did not know how they would vote were tabulated, were not discussed adequately. It is recognised that there is pressure from newspaper editors and readers to omit qualifications and 'technicalities', but pollsters and social scientists have an important responsibility for educating readers of poll results to evaluate them and understand their limitations" [196, p. 302].

One final point. The survey report should aim to give leads to future researchers. It should explain the relationship of this research to previous work on the subject and suggest what part of the field would benefit from a further attack, perhaps on a bigger scale or from a different angle. This would help to avoid an appearance of finality in these conclusions when, in the researcher's more informed opinion, they are only speculative. At the same time it would lessen the risk of fruitless duplication.

NOTES ON READING

1. Most of the books recommended at the end of Chapter 2 deal with the subject-matter of the present chapter. The account by FESTINGER in the second volume of JAHODA, DEUTSCH and COOK [129] makes interesting reading and so does Chapter 9 in its first volume. PARTEN [202] goes into much of the practical detail which we have omitted. FOTHERGILL and WILKINS of the Government Social Survey have presented a paper on analysis and interpretation [85].

2. Some text-books on statistics were recommended at the end of Chapter 5. Some of the more intricate statistical methods used in survey analyses are explained by YATES [291, Chapters 5 and 9]. ACKOFF [2] has a useful account of significance tests.

3. On the investigation of relationships, thorough treatments are given by HYMAN [123] and by KENDALL and LAZARSFELD in the book edited by MERTON and LAZARSFELD [186]. A treatment from a more strictly Statistical

angle is given by YATES [291] in Sections 9.9 to 9.11. A recent paper on the examination of correlations is by SIMON [234].

4. On presentation, I need hardly add further references to the *U.N. Report* [272] from which I quoted at length. All the books on survey methods of course discuss the subject. The *Market Research Society* in Britain has published a short statement on survey reporting standards [175]. An amusing book on the pitfalls of statistical presentation is that by HUFF [121], and an excellent small volume on the psychological aspects of presenting technical information is by KAPP [133].

CHAPTER 16

CONCLUDING REMARKS

IT HAS been my aim throughout this book to give due prominence both to the strengths and the limitations of the social survey approach. One should not pretend that all the techniques used in the survey process have attained an equally advanced stage of efficiency and it may be appropriate to close with a discussion of the developments we may look to in the future.

In this it is helpful to recall the three phases into which survey methods conveniently divide: deciding on the population units to be studied; collecting from or about them whatever information is required; and subjecting this information to various stages of processing, analysis and interpretation. Perhaps the most striking feature of current survey methods is the lag—in terms of our knowledge and the efficiency attained—of the middle phase behind the other two, and particularly the first.

This is probably contrary to the view of the position held by the average researcher who is not wholly familiar with survey techniques. To him the main worry, certainly the one to which he most often gives expression, is sampling. He does not find it easy to accept that a public opinion survey to cover the entire country may, given sound sampling techniques, confidently be based on 2,000 or 3,000 interviews. To the practitioner, it is fair to say, sampling has ceased to be the major problem. By this I do not mean that the subject has been so well developed that there remains no room for progress or that sample design in practice causes no difficulties. Thus the sample designer is often handicapped by lack of knowledge about the population and about costs involved in the various survey stages; uncertainty about the uses to be made of the survey results often makes it difficult to decide on the precision required; lack of a suitable sampling frame can create problems, and situations where one is sampling for relatively rare events cause headaches. There are also a number of theoretical difficulties in the estimation of sampling errors yet to be overcome and, as noted in Chapter 6, a certain amount of complication in sample design is caused by the "multi-purpose" character of most surveys.

These are a few of the remaining problems in the sampling field and it would clearly be misleading to suggest that the sample designer's task is necessarily easy or a matter of automatically applying set principles. Yet, in spite of the technical problems that remain unsolved, the difficulties are no longer fundamental and the developed body of sampling theory is sufficient to enable the designer broadly to tailor his samples to the client's specifications and cost limitations. Future developments should be mainly in refinements, rather than on general principles.

These remarks relate to the design of samples and I am fully conscious of the major problem that still remains on the practical side: non-response. This problem is brought into special prominence with random sampling and it is right that survey experts should be giving it increasing attention. Nevertheless it is not true, as enthusiasts for quota sampling sometimes suggest, that non-response entirely undermines the soundness of random sampling, and that one might as well use non-random techniques. I suggested in Chapter 7 that in most surveys there are ways of reducing the magnitude of non-response to fairly reasonable proportions and of assessing broadly what bias may be introduced by the non-response that remains. As long as there is *any* non-response, the margin of uncertainty surrounding the survey results must be wider than one would choose, but with careful planning, analysis and interpretation, it need by no means undermine the value of the results. It would be well, however, if practitioners made a practice of thinking of non-response bias and sampling error in conjunction, rather than separately. It is wasteful to make strenuous efforts to ensure that the sampling error does not exceed 1 per cent, if the non-response bias is ten times as large. There is indeed evidence that non-response bias often swamps the sampling error, in which case it may pay to cut down on over-all sample size, thus tolerating a larger sampling error, and to spend more money on increasing response.

Turning now to the middle phase of surveys—the collection of the data—it seems to me that here we are faced by problems different in kind, not in degree, from those attending sample design and achievement. Our knowledge of data collection is, by comparison, primitive. The choice of a particular method or of a question form, is based mainly on experience, opinion and common sense and, although these are essential ingredients of any decision, they are not comparable to the theoretical basis of sample design.

The surveyor's most satisfactory guide in the data-collecting phases of a survey is direct experimentation. This can take the form of special experiments separate from the survey, or be incorporated into pre-tests and pilot surveys. Even the main survey can be designed on an experimental plan so that the answers obtained, say, to different forms of a question, can be compared. This is nothing more than the classical "split-ballot" method but, with modern methods of experimental design, it is an easy matter to arrange for a number of different question forms and other variations in data-collecting methods to be compared simultaneously. It is to be hoped that survey practitioners will try increasingly to base their choice of these methods, of questions, of interviewer selection and training and so forth, on experimental test; and to re-examine those parts of their methodology which are at present based largely on common sense and hunches.

I turn now to another, and in a way more serious, aspect of the non-sampling phases of surveys, namely the role of measurement, and particularly response, errors.[1] I tried to show in Chapter 13 how different types of response errors may operate in surveys and suggested that the possibility of such errors cancelling out was not very helpful to the survey designer, since it is equally possible that they will leave a net bias. Because of the difficulty of checking validity, bias is very hard to detect, whatever its cause; and the surveyor is therefore well advised to make some effort to check on gross errors (see Chapter 13).

There is incongruity in the present position. One part of the survey process (the sampling) is tackled by a tool of high precision that makes accurate estimates of errors possible, while in the other parts errors of generally unknown proportions subsist. This incongruity has a double implication. It means, first of all, that the survey designer is only partly able to plan towards his goal of getting the maximum precision for a given outlay of money, since the errors (and even costs) associated with the various non-sampling phases cannot be satisfactorily estimated in advance. And secondly, so long as these errors cannot be properly estimated from the results of the survey, the practitioner is in a position to give his client an estimate only of the sampling error, not of the total of *all* kinds of error. This is a weakness and there is here a fertile field of research for students of survey methodology. It may not be very exciting work, nor seem to offer the possibility of dramatic results, but it has vital importance for all engaged in surveys. The operation of memory errors, the kinds of errors introduced in informal as against formal interviewing, the effects of length of questionnaire on errors, the errors associated with

[1] See footnote on p. 246.

different kinds of question, the influence of interviewer selection, training and supervision, the errors introduced in coding and tabulation—these are but a few of the many fields in which, despite the work already done (notably by the National Opinion Research Center) there remains scope for research. Some of this can be done by special experiments but every single survey gives opportunity for some study of measurement errors. I should also like to voice the hope that, in the planning of the major censuses in Great Britain, the departments concerned will do what they can to study such errors. The U.S. quality checks (see Chapter 13) have set a good example.

In the final phase of surveys—processing, analysis and interpretation—methodology is likely to advance in a number of ways. The use of electronic machines is perhaps the major factor in the improvement of processing, whereas in analysis and interpretation developments are looked for especially in the field of multi-variate relationships. The interpretation of such relationships, in particular, causes much complexity, as is shown in the book by Hyman [123] which serves as a foundation for future research.

This discussion of methods has focused so much on the aspects that need strengthening that I must record the other side of the picture and point out how markedly survey methodology has advanced in recent years. Most striking has been the raising of standards on the sampling side, but in one way or another it characterises all survey activity. Far more surveys have resulted in published reports, and the standard of reporting, both of methods and results, has been much raised. In some universities, courses on survey methods are now given and research on techniques (as well as theory) carried out. Commercial users of survey methods, realising that they have few secrets from each other, are increasingly willing to do joint research, to discuss methods in public and to publish. As a result, those who commission surveys will demand increasingly high standards, and this can have nothing but a good effect on market research and all engaged in it.

The *value* of social surveys also has been established beyond all question and in widely different fields. I am not thinking primarily of the handful of surveys which have attracted attention because they are known to have saved their sponsors large sums of money; money-saving is not the most important criterion of usefulness. But it would be easy to quote, from many diverse fields, surveys which have provided their official, commercial or academic sponsors with knowledge interesting in itself or valuable as a basis for policy decisions. Whether, in the latter cases, use was always, or even often, made of the survey results is of course another question.

The use made of the results of different types of surveys would indeed be a fascinating subject for study. It might begin with the poverty surveys at the turn of the last century, which certainly caused a stir and probably helped to pave the way for the welfare legislation passed in succeeding years. Nearer our own day, one would like to know what influence the numerous town-planning surveys have had on the actual form of planning. Many people believe the influence to have been slight and, if this is so, one must ask whether the surveys themselves were insufficiently informative or whether those charged with the planning decisions were not prepared to give due weight to their results? Again, what use has been made of the many fact-finding surveys carried out for government departments since 1945? No sensible person necessarily looks for dramatic changes of plan being made in the light of survey results or the delaying of all decision until such results are available; indeed such devotion to surveys would be misguided. But it would be encouraging to know that the survey reports were at least seriously considered by the appropriate departments, as one part of the picture with which they were concerned. Or, in the field of market research, one would like to know what use is made of survey results once they reach the client. Not even the greatest enthusiast for market research surveys would wish the client's policy to be based entirely on survey results; but one would hope that these results, together with an intelligent appraisal of their implications, are considered by those who shape policy—again as merely one part of the total picture.

My impression is that, in government administration, commerce, broadcasting, public opinion research and the social sciences, surveys are now playing a role of solid usefulness, but that there remains room for further extensions in all these fields. In the official sphere, for instance, sample surveys are not nearly used to the full (or as much as in the United States). Not all the government departments are equally willing to avail themselves of surveys, although the situation is fast improving—as is shown, for example, by the recent decision to institute regular sample surveys of distribution and production, by the new capital expenditure enquiries and by those on hire-purchase.

The Government Social Survey, after a short period of uncertainty, is now well used by government departments and its high standard of work over the last few years should overcome in time any lingering distrust of survey methods. At present, it is still not hard to think of topics of national importance on which the Survey could usefully be asked to undertake enquiries (e.g. housing standards and needs; social services and standards of needs; internal migration and mobility; the functioning of the nationalised industries; earnings and wages).

One area of research falling somewhere between the official and the commercial field, and perhaps most suitably handled by an independent body, might here be mentioned. We have very little information in Great Britain concerning short-term economic movements and intentions, about business men's plans for capital expenditure, the state of their order books, and their assessment of, and plans for, the immediate economic future. Nor do we know much about what liquid assets consumers currently have at their disposal and what plans they have for spending them. In one or two countries, notably the United States and Germany, regular surveys on these topics prove to be highly informative and similar developments are to be hoped for here.

In market research, the bulk of present work is devoted to a relatively narrow range of mass-produced consumer goods, like chocolate, soap, detergents, drinks and the like; and to the readership of newspapers and to advertisement policy generally. As regards methods, market researchers—to whom, it is fair to add, much of the early stimulus to survey developments is due—are sometimes reluctant to venture outside the range of the straightforward, and there is scope for more use of experimental designs, of more advanced analytical techniques for prediction surveys and so on.

Most important, there is a considerable future for what has come to be known as "motivation research". Increasingly market researchers—and other users of surveys—aim to look beyond a mere description of behaviour towards a study of the motives underlying it. Since the respondents themselves may not be fully aware of their motives, or willing to formulate them, this means indirect questioning (e.g. projective tests) such as is common in personality research; and it also means psychological skill in interpreting the replies. In America this type of work has been going on for some years and its use in Britain, where it is very much in its infancy, deserves constructive research.

The value of radio and television research surveys was stressed earlier in the book and so was the interest of public opinion polls. Here I would only add my lack of sympathy for those who continue to see in opinion polls a positive danger to democracy. Surveys, like everything else, can be used dishonestly and irresponsibly. An unscrupulous business man, as much as an unscrupulous politician, may use them to his own ends, in which case they may be most harmful. But one would hardly be justified in arguing that it was the survey that is at fault. Used properly, and in accordance with present-day standards, public opinion polls can be valuable in telling the politician, as well as the general public, what people are thinking about current issues. It is up to the politician to pay what attention he likes to the results; he can ignore them or otherwise, but certainly they deserve more attention than the balance of opinions contained in his mail.

The case of election forecasts is more difficult. The *raison d'être* of these forecasts lies partly in the light they throw on the efficiency of survey methods and partly (*mainly*, as far as the general public is concerned) in showing how the election campaign is progressing. Recent elections have left no doubt that politicians and party officials, as well as the statistician and the man in the street, watch the forecasts with close interest. However, one cannot deny that forecasts *may* have an influence upon voting behaviour—adherents of the leading party may become apathetic about voting, supporters of their opponents may make a special effort to vote, some people may switch loyalties in order to be on the winning side (the so-called "bandwaggon" effect), others may do the opposite in order to prevent excessive majorities. For all we know, these influences will cancel out, but it would be dishonest to deny that they may not. It is a subject requiring serious thought and research, however difficult this may be.

So much for the role of surveys in the official sphere, in market research and in the study of public opinion. Least easy to summarise is their usefulness in the field of social and economic research. Where the purpose is straightforward fact-collecting, no doubts about usefulness need arise and many—perhaps most—of the social research surveys mentioned in this book are fact-collecting enquiries, just as much as are the bulk of Government Social Survey or market research enquiries. Nor is the preoccupation of social scientists with descriptive, fact-finding enquiry anything to be ashamed of. As Professor Sprott has put it: "Sociology is still to a large extent in the classifying, ordering, and descriptive stage, because we are still not sure what is relevant and what is not. The result is that a great deal of sociologising is more like a kind of random botanizing, a collecting of data, i.e. statistics, personal case histories and the like, uncontrolled by the purpose of verification. This is inevitable, and certainly provides material on which the theorist can build, but at the same time it must be admitted that, while unbased and unverified hypotheses are empty, a mere collection of data is blind" [242, p. 36].

The warning is salutary, for there is no denying that social researchers have on occasion been led into blind and scrappy fact-collecting of no benefit to anyone. A fourth leader from *The Times*[1] expresses, far better than I could, the futility of fact-collecting at its worst and I quote from it the first and last paragraphs:

"It has been ascertained—and not a moment too soon—that out of 1,200 Somersetshire children between the ages of three and four-

[1] *The Times*, 3rd August, 1955. Reproduced by permission of the Editor.

teen only two-thirds were present when their shoes were bought. This pregnant intelligence comes as a reminder that almost all over the world, almost all the time, research is going on into the habits and opinions of *homo sapiens*. Sometimes the results prove, or anyhow indicate, that in the political field the Independent Democratic Unionists are losing ground slightly to the Democratic Union of Independents; sometimes they show that 93 per cent of housewives between the ages of 40 and 50 would rather not swim the Channel than not own a television set; while from others it is possible, though not particularly rewarding, to trace a statistical connexion between porridge-eating and goldfish-owning. It is rather sad how seldom we are able to take very much interest in the results of these meticulous inquiries. There are, on the other hand, various foibles and idiosyncracies which do seem to offer profitable fields for research but which nobody ever looks into. Much, for instance, might be learnt about our national character if a survey were to be made of our practice in the matter of touching wood to ward off ill luck. . . .

". . . There are, of course—corresponding roughly to the staunch, impervious minority of don't knowers at the bottom of the public opinion polls—a certain number of people who never say 'touch wood'. Research would probably disclose that a high proportion of them also walk under ladders. Captains of their fate, they have no use for antiquated superstitions and make a point of writing their name against number thirteen when the list for a sweepstake on the Derby goes up in their club. It would be important to establish what proportion of this proportion used to say 'touch wood' when they were children but have since given it up: why they gave it up: and what (while we are about it) were their mothers' maiden names. But these and other matters into which the research team would have to delve pale into insignificance before the vital, the transcendent, the sixty-four dollar question: Are people who say 'touch wood' less unlucky than those who do not? It is to be feared that the difficulties of evolving a statistical yardstick with which to measure bad luck (and particularly bad luck which people have not had) might well prove too much for the research-team. Its devoted members—for in the unending battle for certainty there are bound to be casualties— might even have to be pulled out of the line and transferred, after a rest and refit, to comparatively light duties, such as computing the number of umbrellas lost in Monmouthshire during 1953."

Of course, the moral that not all facts are worth collecting applies as much to market, opinion, and government researchers as to social scientists, and is relevant to any empirical research, whether it uses survey methods or not. What is undeniable, though, is that the development of large-scale sampling methods has made fact-collecting along methodologically sound lines an easy and attractive way of doing research. It has accordingly stimulated a number of useless, as well as many valuable, survey projects. The sometimes excessive enthusiasm for surveys may still be excused by the relative youth of social research and it is reasonable to expect that, with the years, surveys will be used with increasing discrimination; also, that social researchers will become more discerning in the *type* of survey approach they apply to a given problem. As I have said earlier, not every empirical research project requires the formal apparatus of the large-scale survey. Sometimes it is more profitable to study intensively a handful of available cases rather than a representative sample; to use conversational rather than formal interviewing; not to aim at a set of statistics about a group so much as at a full description of each individual. There are many shades of survey approach and the researcher's art is to know which to use for his problem.

If survey methods have on occasion been used without sufficient discernment, it is still true that they have on balance made a very considerable contribution in advancing the social scientist's knowledge. Many outstanding researches in his field would have been impossible without modern survey methods; many others could not have been done so satisfactorily. It is proper to temper one's impatience with some surveys with a deep appreciation of the value of a great many others.

BIBLIOGRAPHY

(1) ABRAMS, M. (1951). *Social surveys and social action*. Heinemann, London.

(2) ACKOFF, R. L. (1953). *The design of social research*. University of Chicago Press, Chicago.

(3) ALLPORT, G. W. (1942). *The use of personal documents in psychological science*. Bulletin 49. Social Science Research Council, New York.

(4) BAKKE, E. W. (1933). *The unemployed man: a social study*. Nisbet, London.

(5) BAUR, E. J. (1947–8). Response bias in a mail survey. *Public Opinion Quarterly*, 11, 594–600.

(6) BENNEY, M., GRAY, A. P. and PEAR, R. H. (1956). *How people vote: a study of electoral behaviour in Greenwich*. Routledge and Kegan Paul, London.

(7) BERELSON, B. R. and LAZARSFELD, P. F. (1948). *The analysis of communication content . . . preliminary draft* (mimeographed). Universitetets Studentkontor, Oslo.

(8) BEVERIDGE, W. I. B. (1950). *The art of scientific investigation*. Heinemann, London.

(9) BIRCH, A. H. and CAMPBELL, P. (1950). Voting behaviour in a Lancashire constituency. *British Journal of Sociology*, 1, 197–208.

(10) BLANKENSHIP, A. P. and others (1947). Survey on problems of interviewer cheating. *International Journal of Opinion and Attitude Research*, 1, 3, 93–106.

(11) BONHAM, J. (1954). *The middle class vote*. Faber and Faber, London.

(12) BOOKER, H. S. and DAVID, S. T. (1952). Differences in results obtained by experienced and inexperienced interviewers. *Journal of the Royal Statistical Society*, A, 115, 232–57.

(13) BOOTH, C., ed. (1889–1902). *Labour and life of the people of London*. 17 volumes. Macmillan, London.

(14) BOURNVILLE VILLAGE TRUST (1941). *When we build again: a study based on research into conditions of living and working in Birmingham*. Allen and Unwin, London.

(15) BOWLEY, A. L. and BURNETT-HURST, A. R. (1915). *Livelihood and poverty: a study in the economic conditions of working-class households in Northampton, Warrington, Stanley and Reading*. Bell, London

(16) BOWLEY, A. L. and HOGG, M. H. (1925). *Has poverty diminished?: a sequel to "Livelihood and poverty"*. King, London.

(17) BOYAJY, J. S., BARRY, J. W., KUENSTLER, W. P. and PATON, M. R. (1949). Tabulation planning and tabulation techniques. *Journal of Marketing*, 13, 330–55.

(18) BRENNAN, T. (1948). *Midland city: Wolverhampton social and industrial survey*. Dennis Dobson, London.

(19) BRENNAN, T., COONEY, E. W. and POLLINS, H. (1954). *Study of social change in South-West Wales*. Watts, London.

(20) BRITISH MEDICAL ASSOCIATION (1953). Survey of General Practice, 1951–52. *British Medical Journal*, 26.9.1953.

(21) BRITISH TRANSPORT COMMISSION (1953). *Bristol on the move*. B.T.C., London.

(22) BROOKES, B. C. and DICK, W. F. L. (1951). *Introduction to statistical method*. Heinemann, London.

(23) BROWN, J. A. C., HOUTHAKKER, H. S. and PRAIS, S. J. (1953). Electronic computation in economic statistics. *Journal of the American Statistical Association*, 48, 414–28.

(24) BROWN, L. O. (1949). *Marketing and distribution research*. Ronald Press, New York.

(25) BURT, SIR CYRIL (1950). The trend of national intelligence. *British Journal of Sociology*, 1, 154–68.

(26) BUTLER, D. (1955). Voting behaviour and its study in Britain. *British Journal of Sociology*, 6, 93–103.

(27) CAHALAN, D., TAMULONIS, V. and VERNER, H. W. (1947). Interviewer bias involved in certain types of opinion survey questions. *International Journal of Opinion and Attitude Research*, 2, 341–8.

(28) CANTRIL, H. (1944). *Gauging public opinion*. Princeton University Press, Princeton.

(29) CARNEGIE UNITED KINGDOM TRUST (1955). *40th Annual report*. Edinburgh.

(30) CARR-SAUNDERS, A. M., RHODES, E. C. and MANNHEIM, H. (1942). *Young offenders: an enquiry into juvenile delinquency*. Cambridge University Press, Cambridge.

(31) CAUTER, T. (1952). Organisation of a statistical department: some details of a market research agency. *The Incorporated Statistician*, 3, 37–53.

(32) CAUTER, T. and DOWNHAM, J. S. (1954). *The communication of ideas: a study of contemporary influences on urban life*. Chatto and Windus, London.

(33) CENTRAL ADVISORY COUNCIL FOR EDUCATION, ENGLAND (1954). *Early leaving*. H.M.S.O., London.

(34) CHAPIN, F. S. (1947). *Experimental designs in sociological research*. Harper, New York.

(35) CLAUSEN, J. A. and FORD, R. N. (1947). Controlling bias in mail questionnaires. *Journal of the American Statistical Society*, 42, 497–511.

(36) COCHRAN, W. G. (1953). *Sampling techniques*. John Wiley and Sons New York.

(37) COCHRAN, W. G. and COX, M. (1950). *Experimental designs*. John Wiley and Sons, New York.

(38) COCHRAN, W. G., MOSTELLER, F. and TUKEY, J. W. (1953). Statistical problems of the Kinsey Report. *Journal of the American Statistical Association*, 48, 673–716.

(39) COCHRAN, W. G., MOSTELLER, F. and TUKEY, J. W. (1954). Principles of sampling. *Journal of the American Statistical Association*, 49, 1–12.

(40) COLE, D. (1956). Field work in sample surveys of household income and expenditure. *Applied Statistics*, 5, 49–61.

(41) COLE, D. and UTTING, J. E. G. (1956). Estimating expenditure, saving and income from household budgets. *Journal of the Royal Statistical Society*, A, 119, 371–92.

(42) CORNFIELD, J. (1954). Statistical relationships and proof in medicine. *The American Statistician*, 8, 5, 19–21.

(43) CRESPI, L. P. (1945–46). The cheater problem in polling. *Public Opinion Quarterly*, 9, 431–45.

(44) CRESPI, L. P. (1946). Further observations on the "cheater" problem. *Public Opinion Quarterly*, 10, 646–9.

(45) CRUTCHFIELD, R. S. and GORDON, D. A. (1947). Variations in respondents' interpretations of an opinion-poll question. *International Journal of Opinion and Attitude Research*, 1, 3, 1–12.

(46) CUTLER, S. J. (1955). A review of the statistical evidence on the association between smoking and lung cancer. *Journal of the American Statistical Association*, 50, 267–82.

(47) DAVID, F. N. (1953). *A statistical primer*. Griffin, London.

(48) DAVID, S. T. (1952). Public opinion concerning tuberculosis. *Tubercle*, 33, 78–90.

(49) DEMING, W. E. (1944). On errors in surveys. *American Sociological Review*, 9, 359–69.

(50) DEMING, W. E. (1950). *Some theory of sampling*. John Wiley and Sons, New York.

(51) DEMING, W. E. (1953). On a probability mechanism to attain an economic balance between the resultant error of response and the bias of nonresponse. *Journal of the American Statistical Association*, 48, 743–72.

(52) DEMING, W. E. and GEOFFREY, L. (1941). On sample inspection in the processing of census returns. *Journal of the American Statistical Association*, 36, 351–60.

(53) DEMING, W. E., TEPPING, B. J. and GEOFFREY, L. (1942). Errors in card punching. *Journal of the American Statistical Association*, 37, 525–36.

(54) DOLL, R. and HILL, A. B. (1950). Smoking and carcinoma of the lung. Preliminary report, *British Medical Journal*, 2, 739–65.

(55) DOLL, R. and HILL, A. B. (1952). A study of the aetiology of carcinoma of the lung. *British Medical Journal*, 2, 1271–86.

(56) DOLL, R. and HILL, A. B. (1954). The mortality of doctors in relation to their smoking habits; preliminary report. *British Medical Journal*, 1, 1451–5.

(57) DOLL, R. and HILL, A. B. (1956). Lung cancer and other causes of death in relation to smoking. *British Medical Journal*, 5001, 1071–86.

(58) DOWNHAM, J. S. (1954). Social class in sample surveys. *The Incorporated Statistician*, 5, 17–38.

(59) DOWNHAM, J. S. (1956). The function of coding. (In *Readings in Market Research*—see (73) below.)

(60) DUPEUX, G. (1954–55). *Electoral behaviour*. A trend report and bibliography. *Current Sociology* (U.N.E.S.C.O.), 3, 4.

(61) DURANT, H. (1946). The "cheater" problem. *Public Opinion Quarterly*, 10, 288–91.

(62) DURANT, H. (1954). The Gallup Poll and some of its problems. *The Incorporated Statistician*, 5, 101–10.

(63) DURANT, R. (1939). *Watling. A survey of social life on a new housing estate*. P. S. King, London.

(64) DURBIN, J. (1953). Some results in sampling theory when the units are selected with unequal probabilities. *Journal of the Royal Statistical Society*, B, 15, 262–9.

(65) DURBIN, J. (1954). Non-response and call-backs in surveys. *Bulletin of the International Statistical Institute*, 34, 2, 3–17.

(66) DURBIN, J. and STUART, A. (1951). Differences in response rates of experienced and inexperienced interviewers. *Journal of the Royal Statistical Society*, A, 114, 163–205.

(67) DURBIN, J. and STUART, A. (1954). An experimental comparison between coders. *Journal of Marketing*, 19, 54–66.

(68) DURBIN, J. and STUART, A. (1954). Callbacks and clustering in sample surveys: an experimental study. *Journal of the Royal Statistical Society*, A, 117, 387–428.

(69) ECKLER, A. R. (1953). Extent and character of errors in the 1950 Census. *The American Statistician*, 7, 5, 15–21.

(70) ECKLER, A. R. and PRITZKER, L. (1951). Measuring the accuracy of enumerative surveys. *Bulletin of the International Statistical Institute*, 33, 4, 7–24.

(71) EDGERTON, H. A., BRITT, S. H. and NORMAN, R. D. (1947). Objective differences among various types of respondents to a mailed questionnaire. *American Sociological Review*, 12, 435–44.

(72) EDWARDS, F. (1953). Aspects of random sampling for a commercial survey. *The Incorporated Statistician*, 4, 9–27.

(73) EDWARDS, F. ed. (1956). *Readings in market research*. The British Market Research Bureau, London.

(74) EYSENCK, H. J. (1953). *Uses and abuses of psychology*. Penguin Books, Middlesex.

(75) FELDMAN, J. J., HYMAN, H. and HART, C. W. (1951–52). A field study of interviewer effects on the quality of survey data. *Public Opinion Quarterly*, 15, 734–61.

(76) FERBER, R. (1948–49). The problem of bias in mail surveys: a solution *Public Opinion Quarterly*, 12, 669–76.

(77) FERGUSON, T. (1952). *The young delinquent in his social setting: a Glasgow study*. Oxford University Press, London.

(78) FESTINGER, L. and KATZ, D., ed. (1954). *Research methods in the behavioural sciences.* Staples Press, London.

(79) FINNEY, D. J. (1956). The statistician and the planning of field experiments. *Journal of the Royal Statistical Society*, A, 119, 1–27.

(80) FIRTH, R. (1939). An anthropologist's view of Mass Observation. *The Sociological Review*, 31, 166–93.

(81) FISHER, H. (1950). Interviewer bias in the recording operation. *International Journal of Opinion and Attitude Research*, 4, 391–411.

(82) FISHER, R. A. and YATES, F. (5th edn., 1957). *Statistical tables for use in biological, agricultural and medical research.* Oliver and Boyd, Edinburgh.

(83) FLOUD, J. E., HALSEY, A. H. and MARTIN, F. M. (1957). *Social class and educational opportunity.* Heinemann, London.

(84) FORD, P. (1934). *Work and wealth in a modern port: an economic survey of Southampton.* Allen and Unwin, London.

(85) FOTHERGILL, J. E. and WILKINS, L. T. (1953). Analysis and interpretation. Paper read to a conference of the *Association of Incorporated Statisticians.*

(86) FOTHERGILL, J. E. and WILLCOCK, H. D. (1956). Interviewers and interviewing. (In *Readings in Market Research*—see (73) above.)

(87) GALES, K. (1957). Discriminant functions and socio-economic class. *Applied Statistics.*

(88) GALES, K. and KENDALL, M. G. (1957). An enquiry concerning interviewer variability. *Journal of the Royal Statistical Society*, A.

(89) GALLUP, G. (1947). The quintadimensional plan of question design. *Public Opinion Quarterly*, 11, 385–93.

(90) GALLUP, G. (2nd edn. 1948). *A guide to public opinion polls.* Princeton University Press, Princeton.

(91) GENERAL REGISTER OFFICE of England and Wales; and of Scotland (1952). *Census 1951, Great Britain, one per cent sample tables*, Pts. I and II, H.M.S.O., London. (A number of volumes containing the full results have also appeared.)

(92) GLASS, D. V., ed. (1953). *Social mobility in Britain.* Routledge and Kegan Paul, London.

(93) GLASS, D. V. and GREBENIK, E. (1954). *The trend and pattern of fertility in Great Britain: a report on the family census of 1946.* Volume 6 of the Papers of the Royal Commission on Population. H.M.S.O., London.

(94) GLASS, R., ed. (1948). *The social background of a plan: a study of Middlesbrough.* Routledge and Kegan Paul, London.

(95) GLASS, R. (1955). Urban sociology in Great Britain. *Current Sociology* (U.N.E.S.C.O.), 4, 4, 4–76.

(96) GLASS, R. and D. V. (1950). Social survey. In *Chambers's encyclopaedia*, Vol. 12. Newnes, London.

(97) GOODE, W. J. and HATT, P. K. (1952). *Methods in social research.* McGraw-Hill, New York.

(98) GOTTSCHALK, L., KLUCKHOHN, C. and ANGELL, R. (1945). *The use of personal documents in history, anthropology and sociology.* Bulletin 53. Social Science Research Council, New York.

(99) GOWERS, SIR ERNEST (1948). *Plain words*. H.M.S.O., London.

(100) GRAY, P. G. (1955). The memory factor in social surveys. *Journal of the American Statistical Association*, 50, 344–63.

(101) GRAY, P. G. (1956). Examples of interviewer variability taken from two sample surveys. *Applied Statistics*, 5, 73–85.

(102) GRAY, P. G. and CORLETT, T. (1950). Sampling for the Social Survey. *Journal of the Royal Statistical Society*, A, 113, 150–206.

(103) GRAY, P. G., CORLETT, T. and FRANKLAND, P. (1950). *The register of electors as a sampling frame*. The Social Survey, London.

(104) GRAY, P. G., CORLETT, T. and JONES, P. (1951). *The proportion of jurors as an index of the economic status of a district*. The Social Survey, London.

(105) GREENWOOD, E. (1945). *Experimental sociology: a study in method*. King's Crown Press, New York.

(106) GRUNDY, F. and TITMUSS, R. M. (1945). *Report on Luton*. Gibbs, Bamforth, Luton.

(107) GUEST, L. (1947). A study of interviewer competence. *International Journal of Opinion and Attitude Research*, 1, 4, 17–30.

(108) GUEST, L. and NUCKOLS, R. (1950). A laboratory experiment in recording in public opinion interviewing. *International Journal of Opinion and Attitude Research*, 4, 336–52.

(109) HANSEN, M. H. (1952). Statistical standards and the census. *The American Statistician*, 6, 1, 7–10.

(110) HANSEN, M. H. and HAUSER, P. M. (1945). Area sampling—some principles of sampling design. *Public Opinion Quarterly*, 9, 183–93.

(111) HANSEN, M. H. and HURWITZ, W. N. (1946). The problem of non-response in sample surveys. *Journal of the American Statistical Association*, 41, 517–29.

(112) HANSEN, M. H., HURWITZ, W. N. and MADOW, W. G. (1953). *Sample survey methods and theory*. Vol. I.—Methods and applications; Vol. II—Theory. John Wiley and Sons, New York.

(113) HARRIS, A. I. (1956). The work of a coding section. (In *Readings in Market Research*—see (73) above.)

(114) HARRISSON, T. (1947). What is sociology? *Pilot Papers*, 2, 1, 10–25.

(115) HART, C. W. (1948). Bias in interviewing in studies of opinions, attitudes and consumer wants. *Proceedings of the American Philosophical Society*, 92, 399–404.

(116) HARTLEY, H. O. (1946) in discussion on YATES, F. A review of recent statistical developments in sampling and sampling surveys. *Journal of the Royal Statistical Society*, A, 109, 12–43.

(117) HAUSER, P. M. (1950). Some aspects of methodological research in the 1950 Census. *Public Opinion Quarterly*, 14, 5–13.

(118) HENRY, H. (1954). The importance of controlling investigators. Paper read to conference of the *European Society of Opinion and Market Research*.

(119) HILL, A. B. (6th edn. 1956). *Principles of medical statistics*. The Lancet, London.

(120) HILTON, J. (1924). Enquiry by sample: an experiment and its results. *Journal of the Royal Statistical Society*, 87, 544–70.

(121) HUFF, D. (1954). *How to lie with statistics.* Gollancz, London.

(122) HYMAN, H. H. (1950). Problems in the collection of opinion-research data. *American Journal of Sociology,* 55, 362–70.

(123) HYMAN, H. H. (1955). *Survey design and analysis: principles, cases and procedures.* Free Press, Illinois.

(124) HYMAN, H. H. and others (1955). *Interviewing in social research.* The University of Chicago Press, Chicago.

(125) INDIA—MINISTRY OF FINANCE (1952). *The national sample survey. General report No. 1 on the first round. Oct. 1950–March 1951.* The Dept. of Economic Affairs, Min. of Finance, Delhi.

(126) INSTITUTE OF PRACTITIONERS IN ADVERTISING (1954). *The National Readership Survey—1954 Edition.* I.P.A., London.

(127) INTERDEPARTMENTAL COMMITTEE OF SOCIAL AND ECONOMIC RE-SEARCH (1948–53). *Guides to official sources.* No. 1—Labour statistics; No. 2—Census reports of Great Britain, 1801–1931; No. 3.—Local government statistics. H.M.S.O., London.

(128) ISAACS, S. and others (1941). *The Cambridge evacuation survey: a wartime study in social welfare and education.* Methuen, London.

(129) JAHODA, M., DEUTSCH, M. and COOK, S. W. ed. (1951). *Research methods in social relations.* Vol. I—Basic processes; Vol. II—Selected techniques. The Dryden Press, New York.

(130) JOINT COMMITTEE OF THE ROYAL COLLEGE OF OBSTETRICIANS AND GYNAECOLOGISTS AND THE POPULATION INVESTIGATION COMMITTEE (1948). *Maternity in Great Britain: a survey of social and economic aspects of pregnancy and childbirth.* Geoffrey Cumberlege, London.

(131) JONES, D. C. (1934). *The social survey of Merseyside.* Hodder and Stoughton, London.

(132) JONES, D. C. (1949). *Social surveys.* Hutchinson, London.

(133) KAPP, R. O. (1948). *The presentation of technical information.* Constable, London.

(134) KATZ, D. (1942). Do interviewers bias poll results? *Public Opinion Quarterly,* 6, 248–68.

(135) KELLERER, H. (1953). *Theorie und Technik des Stichprobenverfahrens.* Deutsche Statistische Gessellschaft, München.

(136) KELSALL, R. K. (1955). *Higher civil servants in Britain from 1870 to the present day.* Routledge and Kegan Paul, London.

(137) KEMPTHORNE, O. (1952). *The design and analysis of experiments.* John Wiley and Sons, New York.

(138) KENDALL, M. G. (1950). The statistical approach. *Economica,* 17) 127–45. (Reprinted in *Readings in Market Research*—see (73) above.,

(139) KENDALL, M. G., ed. (1952). *The sources and nature of the statistics of the United Kingdom.* Oliver and Boyd, London.

(140) KENDALL, M. G. and BABINGTON SMITH, B. (1939). *Tables of random sampling numbers.* Tracts for Computers, No. 24, Cambridge University Press, Cambridge.

(141) KEYFITZ, N. (1953). A factorial arrangement of comparisons of family size. *American Journal of Sociology,* 58, 470–80.

(142) KEYFITZ, N. and ROBINSON, H. L. (1949). The Canadian sample for

labour force and other population data. *Population Studies*, 2, 427–43.

(143) KING, A. J. and JESSEN, R. J. (1945). The master sample of agriculture. *Journal of the American Statistical Association*, 40, 38–56.

(144) KINSEY, A. C., POMEROY, W. B. and MARTIN, C. E. (1948). *Sexual behaviour in the human male*. Saunders, Philadelphia.

(145) KINSEY, A. C., POMEROY, W. B. and MARTIN, C. E. (1953). *Sexual behaviour in the human female*. Saunders, Philadelphia.

(146) KISH, L. (1949). A procedure for objective respondent selection within the household. *Journal of the American Statistical Association*, 44, 380–7.

(147) KISH, L. (1957). Confidence intervals for clustered samples. *American Sociological Review*, 22.

(148) KISH, L. and LANSING, J. B. (1954). Response errors in estimating the value of homes. *Journal of the American Statistical Association*, 49, 520–38.

(149) KLUCKHOHN, F. (1940). The participant-observer technique in small communities. *American Journal of Sociology*, 46, 331–43.

(150) KORNHAUSER, A. (1946–47). Are public opinion polls fair to organised labour? *Public Opinion Quarterly*, 10, 484–500.

(151) KUPER, L. and others (1953). *Living in towns: selected research papers in urban sociology*. The Cresset Press, London.

(152) LASSWELL, H. D., LEITES, N. and others (1949). *Language of politics: studies in quantitative semantics*. G. W. Stewart, New York.

(153) LAWSON, F. (1949). Varying group responses to postal questionnaires. *Public Opinion Quarterly*, 13, 114–16.

(154) LAZARSFELD, P. F. (1935). The art of asking why. *National Marketing Review*, 1, 26–38.

(155) LAZARSFELD, P. F. (1944). The controversy over detailed interviews —an offer for negotiation. *Public Opinion Quarterly*, 8, 38–60.

(156) LAZARSFELD, P. F. (1948). The use of panels in social research. *Proceedings of the American Philosophical Society*, 92, 405–10.

(157) LE MESURIER, T. H. F. T. (1954). Problems in maintaining and continuing basis, *European Society for Market and Opinion Research Journal*, 1, 73–80.

(158) LEWIS-FANING, E. (1949). *Report on an enquiry into family limitation and its influence on human fertility during the past fifty years*. Papers of the Royal Commission on Population, Vol. I, H.M.S.O., London.

(159) LIEPMANN, K. K. (1944). *The journey to work: its significance for industrial and community life*. Kegan Paul, London.

(160) LIKERT, R. (1932). *A technique for the measurement of attitudes*. Archives of Psychology, Columbia University Press, No. 140.

(161) LITTLE, K. L. (1948). *Negroes in Britain: a study of racial relations in English society*. Kegan Paul, London.

(162) LIVERPOOL UNIVERSITY SOCIAL SCIENCE DEPARTMENT (1954). *The dock worker: an analysis of conditions of employment in the port of Manchester*. University Press of Liverpool, Liverpool.

(163) LOCK, C. M. and others (1947). *The County Borough of Middlesbrough survey and plan*. Middlesbrough Corporation, Middlesbrough.

(164) LONDON TRANSPORT EXECUTIVE (1956). *London travel survey, 1954.* L.T.E., London.

(165) LYDALL, H. F. (1955). *British incomes and savings.* Basil Blackwell, Oxford.

(166) LYND, R. S. and LYND, H. M. (1929). *Middletown: a study in contemporary American culture.* Constable, London.

(167) LYND, R. S. and LYND, H. M. (1937). *Middletown in transition: a study in cultural conflicts.* Harcourt, Brace, New York.

(168) MADGE, J. (1953). *The tools of social science.* Longmans, Green, London.

(169) MAHALANOBIS, P. C. (1946). Recent experiments in statistical sampling in the Indian Statistical Institute. *Journal of the Royal Statistical Society,* A, 109, 325–78.

(170) MANDEVILLE, J. P. (1946). Improvements in methods of census and survey analysis. *Journal of the Royal Statistical Society,* A, 109, 111–29.

(171) MANFIELD, M. N. (1948). A pattern of response to mail surveys. *Public Opinion Quarterly,* 12, 493–5.

(172) MANHEIMER, D. and HYMAN, H. (1949). Interviewer performance in area sampling. *Public Opinion Quarterly,* 13, 83–92.

(173) MANNHEIM, H. and WILKINS, L. T. (1955). *Prediction methods in relation to Borstal training.* H.M.S.O., London.

(174) MARKET RESEARCH SOCIETY (1954). *Readership surveys.* M.R.S., London.

(175) MARKET RESEARCH SOCIETY (1954). *Standards in market research.* M.R.S., London.

(176) MARKS, E. S. and MAULDIN, W. P. (1950). Response errors in census research. *Journal of the American Statistical Association,* 45, 424–38.

(177) MARKS, E. S., MAULDIN, W. P. and NISSELSON, H. (1953). The Post-Enumeration Survey of the 1950 Census: A case history in survey design. *Journal of the American Statistical Association,* 48, 220–43.

(178) MARRIOTT, R. (1953). Some problems in attitude survey methodology. *Occupational Psychology,* 27, 117–27.

(179) MARSHALL, T. H. (1947). *Sociology at the cross roads.* Longmans, Green, London.

(180) MASSEY, P. (1942). The expenditure of 1,360 British middle-class households in 1938–39. *Journal of the Royal Statistical Society,* 105, 159–96.

(181) MASS OBSERVATION (1943). *The pub and the people: a work-town study.* Gollancz, London.

(182) MAYHEW, H. (1861–62). *London labour and the London poor.* 4 volumes. Griffin, Bohn, London.

(183) McNEMAR, Q. (1946). Opinion-attitude methodology. *Psychological Bulletin,* 43, 289–374.

(184) MELHUISH, R. M. (1954). The use and operation of the Nielson Indices. *Journal of the European Society for Opinion and Market Research,* 1, 64–71.

(185) MERTON, R. K., FISKE, M. and KENDALL, P. L. (1956). *The focused interview: a manual of problems and procedures.* Free Press, Illinois.

(186) MERTON, R. K. and LAZARSFELD, P. F. ed., (1950). *Continuities in social research: studies in the scope and methods of "The American Soldier"*. The Free Press, Glencoe, Illinois.

(187) MILLER, J. M. (1952). Participant observer and over-rapport. *American Sociological Review*, 17, 97–9.

(188) MILNE, R. S. and MACKENZIE, H. C. (1954). *Straight fight: a study of voting behaviour in the constituency of Bristol north-east at the general election of 1951*. Hansard Society, London.

(189) MOSER, C. A. (1949). The use of sampling in Great Britain. *Journal of the American Statistical Association*, 44, 231–59.

(190) MOSER, C. A. (1950). Social research: the diary method. *Social Service*, 24, 2, 80–4.

(191) MOSER, C. A. (1951). Interview bias. *Review of the International Statistical Institute*, 19, 28–40.

(192) MOSER, C. A. (1952). Quota sampling. *Journal of the Royal Statistical Society*, A, 115, 411–23.

(193) MOSER, C. A. (1955). Recent developments in the sampling of human populations in Great Britain. *Journal of the American Statistical Association*, 50, 1195–1214.

(194) MOSER, C. A. and STUART, A. (1953). An experimental study of quota sampling. *Journal of the Royal Statistical Society*, A, 116, 349–405.

(195) MOSS, L. (1953). Sample surveys and the administrative process. *International Social Science Bulletin*, 5, 482–94.

(196) MOSTELLER, F. and others (1949). *The pre-election polls of 1948*. Bulletin 60, Social Science Research Council, New York.

(197) NATIONAL COUNCIL OF SOCIAL SERVICE (1954). *Over seventy*, N.C.S.S., London.

(198) NATIONAL INSTITUTE OF ECONOMIC AND SOCIAL RESEARCH (1957). *Register of research in the social sciences in progress and in plan and directory of research institutions*. No. 13. Cambridge University Press, Cambridge.

(199) NUFFIELD FOUNDATION (1947). *Old people*. Oxford University Press, London.

(200) ORR, J. BOYD (1936). *Food, health and income: report of a survey on adequacy of diet in relation to income*. Macmillan, London.

(201) PARRY, H. J. and CROSSLEY, H. M. (1950). Validity of responses to survey questions. *Public Opinion Quarterly*, 14, 61–80.

(202) PARTEN, M. B. (1950). *Surveys, polls and samples: practical procedures*. Harper and Brothers, New York.

(203) PAYNE, S. L. (1951). *The art of asking questions*. Princeton University Press, Princeton.

(204) PEAKER, G. F. (1953). A sampling design used by the Ministry of Education. *Journal of the Royal Statistical Society*, A, 116, 140–59.

(205) POLITICAL AND ECONOMIC PLANNING (1950). *Sample surveys*. Planning, Nos. 313 and 314, P.E.P., London.

(206) POLITICAL AND ECONOMIC PLANNING (1952). *Poverty: Ten years after Beveridge*, Planning, No. 344.

(207) POLITICAL AND ECONOMIC PLANNING (1954). *Graduate wives*, Planning, No. 361.

(208) POLITZ, A. and SIMMONS, W. (1949). An attempt to get the "not at homes" into the sample without call backs. *Journal of the American Statistical Association*, 44, 9–16.

(209) POPULATION INVESTIGATION COMMITTEE and SCOTTISH COUNCIL FOR RESEARCH IN EDUCATION (1949). *The trend of intelligence: a comparison of the 1947 and 1933 surveys of the intelligence of eleven-year-old pupils*. University of London Press, London.

(210) PRAIS, S. J. and HOUTHAKKER, H. S. (1955). *The analysis of family budgets*. Cambridge University Press, Cambridge.

(211) QUENOUILLE, M. H. (1952). *Associated Measurements*. Butterworth, London.

(212) REES, A. D. (1951). *Life in a Welsh countryside: a social study of Llanfihangel yug Ngwynfer*. University of Wales Press, Cardiff.

(213) REUSS, C. F. (1943). Differences between persons responding and not responding to a mailed questionnaire. *American Sociological Review*, 8, 433–8.

(214) ROBB, J. H. (1954). *Working-class anti-semite. A psychological study in a London borough*. Tavistock Publications, London.

(215) ROETHLISBERGER, F. J. and DICKSON, W. J. (1939). *Management and the worker: an account of a research programme conducted by the Western Electric Company, Hawthorne Works, Chicago*. Harvard University Press, Harvard.

(216) ROGERS, C. R. (1945). The non-directive method as a technique for social research. *American Journal of Sociology*, 50, 279–83.

(217) ROSE, A. M. (1945). A research note on experimentation in interviewing. *American Journal of Sociology*, 51, 143–4.

(218) ROWETT RESEARCH INSTITUTE (1955). *Family diet and health in pre-war Britain*. Carnegie United Kingdom Trust, Scotland.

(219) ROWNTREE, B. S. (2nd edn. 1902). *Poverty: a study of town life*. Macmillan, London.

(220) ROWNTREE, B. S. (1937). *The human needs of labour*. Longmans, Green, London.

(221) ROWNTREE, B. S. (1941). *Poverty and progress: a second social survey of York*. Longmans, Green, London.

(222) ROWNTREE, B. S. and LAVERS, G. R. (1951). *English life and leisure: a social study*. Longmans, Green, London.

(223) ROWNTREE, B. S. and LAVERS, G. R. (1951). *Poverty and the welfare state: a third social survey of York, dealing only with economic questions*. Longmans, Green, London.

(224) ROWNTREE, G. (1954). The finances of founding a family. *Scottish Journal of Political Economy*, 1, 201–32.

(225) RUSSELL, B. (1927). *An outline of philosophy*. Allen and Unwin, London.

(226) SCHULZ, T. (1952). Ten years of family surveys. *Bulletin of the Oxford University Institute of Statistics*, 14, 83–95.

(227) SCOTTISH COUNCIL FOR RESEARCH IN EDUCATION (1953). *Social implications of the 1947 Scottish mental survey*. University of London Press, London.

(228) SENG, Y. P. (1951). Historical survey of the development of sampling theories and practice. *Journal of the Royal Statistical Society*, A, 114, 214–31.

(229) SHAPIRO, S. and EBERHART, J. C. (1947). Interviewer differences in an intensive interview survey. *International Journal of Opinion and Attitude Research*, 1, 2, 1–17.

(230) SHEATSLEY, P. B. (1947). Some uses of interviewer-report forms. *Public Opinion Quarterly*, 11, 601–11.

(231) SHEATSLEY, P. B. (1949). The influence of sub-questions on interviewer performance. *Public Opinion Quarterly*, 13, 310–13.

(232) SHEFFIELD SOCIAL SURVEY COMMITTEE (1931–3). *Survey pamphlets* (on milk supply, housing, licensing, unemployment, adult education, juvenile employment and welfare, transport and standard of living). Sheffield.

(233) SHELDON, J. H. (1948). *The social medicine of old age: report of an enquiry in Wolverhampton*. Oxford University Press, London.

(234) SIMON, H. A. (1954). Spurious correlation: a causal interpretation. *Journal of the American Statistical Association*, 49, 467–79.

(235) SILVEY, R. S. (1956). B.B.C. Audience Research. (In *Readings in Market Research*—see (73) above.)

(236) SLETTO, R. F. (1940). Pre-testing of questionnaires. *American Sociological Review*, 5, 193–200.

(237) SMITH, H. L. ed. (1930–45). *The new survey of London life and labour*. 9 volumes. P. S. King, London.

(238) SMITH, H. L. and HYMAN, H. (1950). The biasing effect of interviewer expectations on survey results. *Public Opinion Quarterly*, 14, 491–506.

(239) SOCIAL SURVEY (1956). *A handbook for interviewers*. Central Office of Information, London.

(240) SOCIAL SURVEY (1956). *Some useful data when sampling the population of England and Wales*. The Social Survey, London.

(241) SPRING RICE, M. (1939). *Working-class wives*. Penguin Books, Middlesex.

(242) SPROTT, W. J. H. (1949). *Sociology*. Hutchinson, London.

(243) STANTON, F. (1939). Notes on the validity of mail questionnaire returns. *Journal of Applied Psychology*, 23, 95–104.

(244) STEMBER, H. (1951). Which respondents are reliable? *International Journal of Opinion and Attitude Research*, 5, 475.

(245) STEMBER, H. and HYMAN, H. (1949). Interviewer effects in the classification of responses. *Public Opinion Quarterly*, 15, 322–34.

(246) STEMBER, H. and HYMAN, H. (1949–50). How interviewer effects operate through question form. *International Journal of Opinion and Attitude Research*, 3, 493–512.

(247) STEPHAN, F. F. (1948). History of the uses of modern sampling procedures. *Journal of the American Statistical Association*, 43, 12–38.

(248) STEWART, C. (1948). *The village surveyed*. Edward Arnold, London.

(249) STOCK, J. S. and HOCHSTIM, J. R. (1951). A method of measuring interviewer variability. *Public Opinion Quarterly*, 15, 322–34.

(250) STOUFFER, S. A. (1950). Some observations on study design. *American Journal of Sociology*, 55, 355–61.

(251) STOUFFER, S. A. and others (1949). *The American Soldier*. Studies in social psychology in World War II, Vols. 1 and 2. Princeton University Press, Princeton.

(252) STOUFFER, S. A. and others (1950). *Measurement and prediction*. Studies in social psychology in World War II, Vol. 4, Princeton University Press, Princeton.

(253) STUART, A. (1952). Reading habits in three London boroughs. *Journal of Documentation*, 8, 33–49.

(254) SUCHMAN, E. A. and GUTTMAN, L. (1947). A solution to the problem of question bias. *Public Opinion Quarterly*, 11, 445–55.

(255) SUCHMAN, E. A. and McCANDLESS, B. (1940). Who answers questionnaires? *Journal of Applied Psychology*, 24, 758–69.

(256) SUKHATME, P. V. (1954). *Sampling theory of surveys with applications*. Iowa State College Press, Ames and Indian Society of Agricultural Statistics, New Delhi.

(257) SURVEY RESEARCH CENTER, UNIVERSITY OF MICHIGAN (1951). *Field methods in sample interview surveys*. S.R.C., Michigan.

(258) TAYLOR, S. J. L. (1954). *Good general practice: a report of a survey*. Oxford University Press, London.

(259) THIONET, P. (1946). *Méthodes statistiques modernes des Administrations Fédérales aux Etats-Unis*. Herman, Paris.

(260) THOMSON, SIR GODFREY and others (1950). *The relations between intelligence and fertility*. Papers of the Royal Commission on Population, Vol. V, H.M.S.O., London.

(261) THURSTONE, L. E. and CHAVE, E. J. (1929). *The measurement of attitudes*. University of Chicago Press, Chicago.

(262) TIPPETT, L. H. C. (1927). *Tables of random sampling numbers*. Tracts for Computers, No. 15. Cambridge University Press, Cambridge.

(263) TIPPETT, L. H. C. (4th edn., 1952). *The methods of statistics*. Williams and Norgate, London.

(264) TOWNSEND, P. (1954). Measuring poverty. *British Journal of Sociology*, 5, 130–6.

(265) TREASURE, J. A. P. (1953). Retail audit research. *The Incorporated Statistician*, 4, 148–59. (Reproduced in *Readings in Market Research*— see (73) above.)

(266) TULSE, R. (1957). Sampling for variables with a very skew distribution. *Applied Statistics*, 6, 40–4.

(267) U.K. MINISTRY OF AGRICULTURE, FISHERIES AND FOOD (1956). *Domestic Food Consumption and Expenditure: 1954*. H.M.S.O., London.

(268) U.K. MINISTRY OF FOOD (1951). *The urban working-class household diet 1940 to 1949*. First Report of the National Food Survey Committee, H.M.S.O., London.

(269) U.K. MINISTRY OF LABOUR AND NATIONAL SERVICE (1940–41). Weekly expenditure of working-class households in the U.K. in 1937–38. *Ministry of Labour Gazette*, December 1940, January 1941 and February 1941.

(270) U.K. MINISTRY OF PENSIONS AND NATIONAL INSURANCE (1954). *National insurance retirement pensions: reasons given for retiring or continuing at work*. H.M.S.O., London.

(271) UNITED NATIONS STATISTICAL OFFICE (1949 onwards). *Sample surveys of current interest*. Statistical Papers, Series C, Nos. 2, 3, 4, 5. United Nations, New York.

(272) UNITED NATIONS STATISTICAL OFFICE (1950). *The preparation of sampling survey reports*. Statistical Papers, Series C, No. 1., United Nations, New York.

(273) U.S. BUREAU OF THE BUDGET (1952). *Standards for statistical surveys*. Bureau of the Budget, Washington.

(274) U.S. DEPARTMENT OF AGRICULTURE (1952). *Problems of establishing a consumer panel*. Marketing Research Report No. 8, Bureau of Agricultural Economics, Dept. of Agriculture, Washington.

(275) UTTING, J. E. G. (1954). Sample surveys for household income and expenditure information. *Schweizerische Zeitschrift für Volkswirtschaft und Statistik*, 90, 329–36.

(276) UTTING, J. E. G. and COLE, D. (1953). Sample surveys for the social accounts of the household sector. *Bulletin of the Oxford Institute of Statistics*, 15, 1–24.

(277) UTTING, J. E. G. and COLE, D. (1954). Sampling for social accounts —some aspects of the Cambridgeshire Survey. *Bulletin of the International Statistical Institute*, 34, 301–28.

(278) VOIGHT, R. B. and KRIESBERG, M. (1952). Some principles of processing census and survey data. *Journal of the American Statistical Association*, 47, 222–31.

(279) WADSWORTH, R. N. (1952). The experience of a user of a consumer panel. *Applied Statistics*, 1, 169–78.

(280) WALLIS, A. W. and ROBERTS, H. V. (1956). *Statistics: A new approach*. The Free Press, Illinois.

(281) WEBB, B. (1926). *My apprenticeship*. Longmans, Green. London.

(282) WELLS, A. F. (1935). *The local social survey in Great Britain*. Allen and Unwin, London.

(283) WEST MIDLAND GROUP ON POST-WAR RECONSTRUCTION AND PLANNING (1946). *English county: a planning survey of Herefordshire*. Faber, London.

(284) WEST MIDLAND GROUP ON POST-WAR RECONSTRUCTION AND PLANNING (1948). *Conurbation: a planning survey of Birmingham and the Black Country*. Architectural Press, London.

(285) WHITFIELD, J. W. (1950). The imaginary questionnaire. *Quarterly Journal of Experimental Psychology*, 2, 76–88.

(286) WILKINS, L. T. (1949). *Prediction of the demand for campaign medals*. The Social Survey, London.

(287) WILKINS, L. T. (1952). Estimating the social class of towns. *Applied Statistics*, 1, 27–33.

(288) WILSON, E. C. (1954). New light on old problems through panel research. *European Society for Market and Opinion Research Journal*, 1, 87–92.

(289) WOMEN'S GROUP ON PUBLIC WELFARE. (1943). *Our towns: a close-up*. Oxford University Press, London.

(290) WOOTTON, B. (1950). *Testament for social science*. Allen and Unwin, London.

(291) YATES, F. (2nd edn. 1953). *Sampling methods for censuses and surveys*. Griffin, London.

(292) YOUNG, M. (1952). Distribution of income within the family. *British Journal of Sociology*, 3, 305–21.

(293) YOUNG, T. (1934). *Becontree and Dagenham. The story of the growth of a housing estate*. Samuel Sidders, London.

(294) YULE, G. U. and KENDALL, M. G. (14th edn. 1950). *An introduction to the theory of statistics*. Griffin, London.

(295) ZWEIG, F. (1948). *Labour, life and poverty*. Gollancz, London.

(296) ZWEIG, F. (1948). *Men in the pits*. Gollancz, London.

INDEX OF NAMES AND ORGANISATIONS

M

INDEX OF SUBJECTS